THE IRISH BROTHERHOOD

HELEN O'DONNELL
with KENNETH O'DONNELL SR.

The IRISH Brotherhood

John F. Kennedy, His Inner Circle, and
the Improbable Rise to the Presidency

COUNTERPOINT

BERKELEY

Library of Congress cataloging-in-publication data is available

ISBN 978-1-61902-705-3

Cover design by Faceout Studios
Interior design by Megan Jones Design

COUNTERPOINT
2560 Ninth Street, Suite 318
Berkeley, CA 94710
www.counterpointpress.com

Printed in the United States of America

To

Alice Justine O'Donnell

Clare Ann O'Flynn O'Donnell

For their grace, humor & many sacrifices.

They made it look easy.

CONTENTS

INTRODUCTION

*T*HE *IRISH BROTHERHOOD* is my attempt to capture the experience and spirit of the group of men who gathered around John Kennedy as he made his dramatic rise to the presidency—Bobby Kennedy, Kenny O'Donnell, Larry O'Brien, and Dave Powers—the friendships they formed, and the dreams they pursued and ultimately fulfilled. Although this book by its nature represents recollections of my father, Kenny, what cannot be disputed is that my father was often the only other person who was trusted and in the room during these critical moments in the lives of Jack and Bobby Kennedy. He was, as Chris Matthews once said to me, "one of the key apostles."

My father was always going to write this book. First, it was going to be my father, Bobby, Larry O'Brien, and Dave Powers. When Bobby left the White House in the wake of Jack's death, they were all supposed to leave. Larry stayed on with Lyndon Johnson, and things changed. Bobby, my father, and Dave soldiered on, but as we know, life and events they could never have foreseen got in the way. That book was never written. My father and Dave Powers wrote a book, but it was not this book.

Fortunately, at the urging of Bobby Kennedy, NBC White House correspondent Sander Vanocur had gotten my father on tape. Sandy was a friend to my father and Jack and was an exceptional journalist. He asked the thoughtful questions, the tough questions, and remained someone my father trusted. Sandy told me later, "It was as if your father was just waiting for someone to ask the right questions." That may have been, but the truth

1

was that Sandy was likely the only man my father would have trusted to ask those questions. The tapes Sandy recorded remained largely unused for more than forty years, and here I use these exceptionally personal and often intimate memories, along with stories I grew up with, to create the foundation of the book. While I cannot tell you everything my father might have included, this to some degree is his book, his recollections, his Jack and Bobby Kennedy, his Irish Brotherhood. But most importantly, what comes through, as my father tells his stories on these tapes, is Jack. You feel drawn in by him; you feel elated when he succeeds and frustrated when he is defeated.

While I grew up surrounded by the memories I never fully understood, John and Bobby Kennedy remained alive for me in the sometimes grainy photos that my Aunt Justine, my father's sister, would show me. My father, who died impossibly young himself in the wake of the murders of Jack and Bobby Kennedy, kept two photos of John Kennedy in the house. I grew up knowing he was someone we personally revered. He had changed many lives, and his tragic death was a loss not just for the Kennedy family. Because while Jack was indeed president, to us he was really a son, a brother, a father, and a friend. His sudden death had torn so many people's lives asunder, including many in my family.

My father died when I was young. He was my friend and remains my hero. While many people, including some family members, claim I view him through rose-colored glasses, what I discovered while working on these tapes was how smart, funny, savvy, cool, and sophisticated Jack, my father, and Bobby actually were.

They were surrounded by like-minded friends, Larry O'Brien, Dave Powers, and others, including someone I never thought I'd like, Joe Kennedy Sr. Contrary to what I had come to believe, and although he was tough and ruthless, he was unwaveringly devoted to his sons' dreams and futures.

Through my father's tapes, I learned that while Joe Kennedy and my father often battled, Joe never disrespected my father. They had come to respect one another, and Joe understood how valuable my father was to Jack's success. I liked that; I respected that, and in the end, as I completed this book, I really understood Joe Kennedy better than I ever had before.

Bobby Kennedy, whom I wrote about in my first book, was always my father's dear friend, but what I learned here was how critical he was to the relationship between Father and Jack. He was essential to the balance between my father and Jack and the tight circle as a whole. While Jack was the visionary and my father the political mechanic, Bobby was the heart of the relationship that existed between these three men. He was what kept Jack and my father, two war-weary veterans who had come to understand the risks in life, in balance. There are many gray areas in life, and to succeed we must live in those gray areas, and it was Bobby who always pulled them safely back to a fuller understanding of reality. The humor, repartee, and love for each other that existed between my father and Bobby is what makes their friendship a particular pleasure to hear retold.

My father and Bobby first met on the football fields of Harvard in the 1945–1946 season. My father had served in the Army Air Corps, having enlisted without telling his father. He fought in the war from 1942 to 1945, being shot down at least twice behind enemy lines. He received numerous medals for his heroism but never dwelled on it or discussed it. His war experience would be key to his relationship with fellow returned vet and politician Jack Kennedy, Bobby's older brother. Kenny returned to Massachusetts, and the GI Bill allowed him to attend Harvard University from 1945 to 1948, a feat that would have been impossible without the funding of the GI Bill. This removed him from Worcester and Holy Cross, putting him in Harvard Square, where a fateful meeting would change his life.

My father was already on the football team when he and Bobby Kennedy met. My father would in fact be captain in 1948; my Uncle Cleo captained the team the year before. My father was a gifted athlete who would leave several unbroken records in his wake at Harvard, but perhaps the most important thing that happened to him at Harvard was meeting Bobby, Joe

Kennedy Sr.'s son. Once again engineering fate, Joe—who had known Cleo O'Donnell Sr., my father's father, back at Boston Latin—had insisted that Bobby look up Kenny. While younger and not a natural athlete, Bobby was, as my father said, "one tough SOB on the field," which made up for any lack of athletic prowess and would serve the Irish Brotherhood well on the campaign fields to come.

Bobby and my father were roommates for a while. Then my Uncle Cleo and Bobby became roommates as well. But my father and Bobby shared two important things that cemented their brotherly bond, my Uncle Cleo noted: "politics and football" (or, as he also said, "football and politics"). My father and Bobby hit it off immediately. My father later confessed, "We would talk and argue for hours at the Harvard Varsity Club after practice, tossing the ball around, talking politics and what we thought we could do, were we ever given the opportunity." They were given that opportunity when Bobby insisted that after practice one day, Kenny should meet his idolized older brother Jack Kennedy, a war veteran running for Congress in Massachusetts's Eighth Congressional District.

With that fateful introduction, my father and Jack, unbeknownst to either of them at the time, would embark on a political journey that would change their lives and history. It was a journey that happened only because of Bobby.

The tapes also reintroduced me to the important women from that time. My memory of my mother had become so faint that in writing this book I rediscovered her as well. I found that she was devoted to my father. She loved him, but she willingly went on this journey with the Irish Brotherhood because she adored and admired Jack Kennedy.

The story includes my Aunt Justine, my father's younger sister, who had become his institutional memory. She was the keeper of the flame until the end. Smart, funny, and devoted, she could have done anything. She chose to give up her personal life to devote it to my father, because he was devoted to Jack. She pushed me relentlessly about the importance of my father's story and these memories. It is only now that I both understand and see just how critical his story is to understanding Jack Kennedy.

The other woman is, of course, "Madame La Femme," as my father dubbed her. Jacqueline Bouvier Kennedy Onassis comes through on the tapes as a real person, someone my father admired and, I believe, came to love. She was of course beautiful but also funny, smart, and completely unintimidated by either her husband, my father, or what she saw as the nonsense within politics.

She was also tough, like her husband and my father, but like an iron fist inside a velvet glove. I remember Jackie's constant presence in our house; my father was devoted to her in the wake of Jack's death. They were like two people who had returned from war. They shared memories, good and bad—a shared trauma that the world would constantly crave to know more about. But, by mutual agreement, they would never break their silence

Jackie was always his "Madame La Femme," and while she appreciated and loved my father, she also had his number and could not resist teasing him. She, like her husband, took the work, the dream, seriously, but she never took herself or those around her all that seriously.

This book is my father's story of *his* Jack and Bobby Kennedy. I tried to let him tell the story of the Jack Kennedy he personally knew and to whom he devoted his life, the political Jack Kennedy, because that is what drew my father and Jack together. Politics. They both loved it and saw it as a way to do good, not just for themselves but for others. My father talked often of writing this book, but in the end, I believe it was just too painful.

They were a new, post–World War II generation trying to shake up the drab, colorless political system and toss out the political hacks that they believed had moved the country off track. They were upstarts, outsiders, tough guys, and hard driving, and they had an unshakeable belief in themselves and in Jack's potential. They were young, arrogant, reckless, and smart as hell. They never lost track of their goal. They never faltered, they took no prisoners, and my father in particular was totally devoted to Jack.

This book is their journey. It's Kenny's story of Jack Kennedy and the Irish Brotherhood, who never gave up, never gave in, and always kept moving relentlessly forward.

Washington, DC
2014

CHAPTER 1

The Loss

THE BARTENDER POURED Ken's beer last. Kenny watched the foam, as carefully as if it were a list of poll numbers in Jack's election, as it licked the top of the glass. He'd earned this beer. Kenneth "Kenny" O'Donnell was John F. Kennedy's tough-talking, no-bullshit, political aide. His best friend was Robert F. Kennedy, whom everyone just called Bobby. Kenny and Bobby had known each other since the football days at Harvard, when Bobby had sought out Kenny, then captain of the team. Bobby had wanted to join the squad. He was then too small, a marginally talented athlete, but made up for it with sheer determination. That same tenacity echoed throughout everything Bobby undertook, but it hadn't been enough today. Not that day. Nothing was. The whole day—no, the entire week—had ended up with a loss. They got screwed. Thrown under the bus by the Democratic Party establishment, especially by the liberals, who had never liked Jack or his father. Former Illinois governor Adlai Stevenson, making his second run for the Democratic presidential nomination, along with Senator Carey Estes Kefauver, crime-fighting liberal from Tennessee, and the rest of the political establishment—"assholes," in Kenny's words—led the charge against the Kennedy brothers. They were men who saw Jack Kennedy and his Irish buddies as impossibly young, inexperienced, and arrogant. John F. Kennedy was, after all, the son of Ambassador Joseph P. Kennedy, a man who was loved by some but reviled by even more. John Fitzgerald Kennedy, or Jack, as his family called him, was the third child of Joe and Rose Fitzgerald Kennedy of Boston. When their firstborn son, Joseph P. Kennedy Jr., died tragically, a hero in the war, it supposedly fell to second son Jack to pick up the fallen standard. Or so the story had been told around Boston.

Kenny did not know whether he believed that story or not, especially based on what he had gotten to know about Jack; but what he did know for sure was that Jack Kennedy was his guy. He could, in Kenny's view, go all the way to the White House. Hell, he'd just proved it right here in Chicago at the Democratic Convention in '56. He should have been giving an acceptance speech this afternoon for the vice presidential slot to run in the 1956 presidential campaign with Adlai Stevenson at the top of the ticket.

But that had not happened. The boys from Boston would come to be called the Irish Brotherhood by some and, by others, the Irish Mafia, a term Kenny detested. Well, whatever they were called, Jack's close inner circle of political operatives didn't like to lose. And yet they had. Brutally. Still, the guys from Boston had come close. They had almost won the vice presidential nomination. When the Stevenson and Kefauver forces saw how close Jack was, they took action to make sure that was the end of it. The political establishment slammed on the brakes.

"Jobbed," Ken had told Jack. Ken was pissed off. Kenny lifted the beer, sipped it, and let the golden liquid try to quench his anger and disappointment. He hoped it might cool him down, maybe soothe some of his rage. It didn't. He brought the glass down hard on the table and stared straight ahead at the black-and-white etching of Chicago during the 1920s, just behind the bartender. He stared hard, as if he might find the answers there. He seemed oblivious to the noise of the convention crowd drinking and celebrating all over the pub. The room was thick with smoke and a lot of postgame bullshitting.

Kenny was accustomed to delivering victories for Jack Kennedy since he first came on board for real in the '52 campaign. Of course, nobody had expected John Kennedy to win the Senate race in 1952 either, but Kenny and Bobby believed he could. They let nothing stand in their way, and Kenny seemed perfectly suited to his role as Jack's political aide. With his tough, wiry build and intense gaze, he looked every part the IRA man that everyone joked he would have become were he back in the old country. He was a superb athlete, had been captain of the Harvard football team, and was a man's man whose college football records are yet to be matched or broken. He was also, like Jack, a World War II hero. He'd been awarded everything you can be awarded by the War Department and still be walking around. During the war, he'd been called a spook by some of his pals. Whether he had worked for the CIA then, nobody knew for sure.

One thing they did know was that Kenny was afraid of nothing. There was a legendary story of his climbing out onto a bomb stuck in the bomb bay of his plane. He jumped up and down on it to dislodge it, nearly plummeting to earth with that bomb. That deed had become mythological, better with each telling. But Kenny himself, like Jack, spoke little about the war, if at all. When others mentioned it, he'd shrug and walk away.

His job now and his focus since 1946, when his best pal, Jack's younger brother Bobby, had introduced them, was to deliver votes for Jack. He'd been doing it since the first campaign in 1946, when Kennedy first ran for Congress. At the time, Jack was a skinny, rich man's son with no chance to win, in the opinion of the professionals. Still, he'd won.

Then they'd beaten the odds in 1952 when they sent Henry Cabot Lodge Jr. packing. He was a son of famed United States senator Henry Cabot Lodge, who had famously hung around with Theodore Roosevelt. In fact, Henry Cabot Lodge Sr. had defeated Jack's grandfather for the same Senate seat in 1916. It was a devastating defeat for John F. "Honey Fitz" Fitzgerald, father of Jack's mother, Rose, a defeat from which he never fully recovered and that left him perpetually on the sidelines from then on.

Jack and Kenny had chuckled the next morning in 1952 as the press descended on Kennedy headquarters after Jack's surprise victory over Lodge.

During that campaign, against all expectations, Kenny and Lawrence "Larry" O'Brien, his Irish buddy and fellow political numbers genius from Springfield, Massachusetts, had again beaten the odds and snatched victory from the Massachusetts Democratic Party machine and the political hacks in Boston. Only a few years later, that duo handed that vaunted machine on a silver platter to Jack Kennedy.

At the time, Kennedy was pissed. He had told them to leave the party hacks alone. Still, it was an opportunity Kenny and Larry simply couldn't resist. Most of the time, Kenny did what he wanted anyway. Jack would tell him no, but most of the time they both knew he meant yes.

So when they arrived in Chicago in 1956 for the Democratic Convention, Jack had checked in with "the Old Man," as Kenny liked to refer to Jack's father. Most people called him "the Ambassador." Kenny didn't. At this point, Kenny couldn't stand the guy.

Kenny was not alone in that view. Many people could not stand Joseph P. Kennedy Sr.; liking him was, frankly, a challenge. But Kenny knew more than most about the Old Man. Kenny's dad, Cleo, had gone to Boston Latin School with Joe Sr. Cleo, for his part, had gone on to break records and stack up wins on the football field as the coach at Everett High School, Holy Cross College, and other schools almost as fast as Joe began raking in the millions. Joe chose business and banking as his path through life and went on to make a fortune in bootlegging and Hollywood. Like so many men of that era, often looking the other way when a deal had to be done and the right hand needed shaking, Joe connected with people whom for any number of reasons he would later pretend not to know. Joe was a brilliant businessman, a tough son of a bitch, but not, Cleo had warned Kenny, "a likable fellow."

Along the way Joe also captured the heart of Rose Fitzgerald, Honey Fitz Fitzgerald's daughter. She was classy, black-haired, and blue-eyed, with a sharp mind and a deep devotion to Catholicism that would serve her well through the challenges that lay ahead in her turbulent life with Joe Kennedy.

Despite his difficult personality, Joe Sr. knew a thing or two about politics, maybe more than Kenny gave him credit for. The Old Man was about to teach Kenny and Jack a few things about paying attention to his advice. Neither for the first time nor the last, Joe would be right.

When Jack instructed Bobby to call their dad from the suite at the Biltmore Hotel on the Miracle Mile in Chicago to say, "Yeah, Dad, we understand. We are not planning a run at the VP slot," Jack gave Kenny and Bobby "the look." Nothing more needed to be said. Bobby, whose prep-school looks with his thick, wavy, reddish-brown hair and mischievous blue eyes belied a tough and shrewd political organizer, knew what that look meant. Kenny did too. It meant, *Yeah, you two SOBs better deliver that VP slot to me.*

So, with that, Kenny and Bobby set out to win Jack the VP slot, even though the Old Man and anyone with a minimum of political common sense knew it was the dumbest political move Jack could have made. Still, once Jack was in the race, he liked the taste. He liked the idea of it. He liked the power of it, and, well, Kennedys don't like to lose.

But they had lost. In the end, they came damn close. Despite having no experience, no organization, and maybe no sense, Kenny and Bobby had nearly pulled it off. At the time, as they were racing from meeting to meeting across the convention center, Kenny told Bobby it kind of felt like '52 all over again. Bobby had agreed, even though he shuddered as Kenny said it.

Kenny had patted him on the back. "Remember, Bobby," Kenny told him, "a win is a win." Bobby had just nodded.

It wasn't the win in '52 that bothered Bobby; it was what happened once they had won: All the fakers and the hacks who had written Jack off appeared out of nowhere to take credit for their hard work.

"Grow up, Bobby," Kenny said. "It's just fucking politics; don't take it so personally."

But Bobby, unlike Kenny and Jack, always took it personally. He never was able to achieve their cool detachment, though he envied it. Bobby had decided then and there that he hated politics. He told Jack and Kenny that it wasn't for him. He was done. Jack and Kenny had smiled, exchanging knowing glances. Whether Bobby realized it or not, his future had already been decided. The only one who seemed unaware of that was Bobby.

The night of the '52 election, it had been just them in the campaign headquarters on Tremont Street: the Irish Brotherhood and Jack's best pal and resident jester, Dave Powers. Everybody else had jumped ship. As the hours slipped past midnight into one o'clock in the morning, the polls showed Lodge clobbering Kennedy. Still, the Irish Brotherhood had stayed put. Their numbers and their new counting and polling system had shown them winning. They were sure Jack had it. Positive.

Jack was not so sure. His dad had told him to forget it. Save your career, admit defeat gracefully, the Old Man had said. Kenny and Bobby told Jack to stay the course. "We'll get there." Jack, as was often the case, more than would suit the political legend, listened to his gut and to Kenny and Bobby over his father.

But then CBS called the race for Lodge. The head of the Massachusetts Democratic Party called and begged Kennedy to throw in the towel for the good of the party. They'd live to fight another day. Jack sucked on his cigar, listened, and looked at Kenny, who shook his head. "They're wrong," Kenny said. "We've got Worcester."

Worcester. It had all come down to Kenny's hometown of Worcester. The working-class, blue-as-blue-could-get town of Worcester, Massachusetts, with its mills and hardworking, everyday blue-collar Irishmen. Kenny was sure they'd turn out; there were more Irish than Yanks in Worcester, and Kenny's brother Cleo and younger brother Warren, whose best pal happened to be Jack and Bobby's younger brother, Ted, had worked their asses off. They were sure that Worcester would put Jack Kennedy over the top. They waited.

It took an impossibly long time. Everyone left. Lodge's headquarters across Tremont Street in downtown Boston filled up, his supporters anticipating a victory party. Why the hell wouldn't Kennedy concede? Arrogance, Lodge had supposed, but he was too classy a man to make such a charge publicly. Youth and arrogance. Jack simply could not face it, Lodge figured. Dwight D. Eisenhower, the Republican stalwart, the hero of World War II, had swept the entire country in a massive landslide. Who the hell was Jack Kennedy in the face of that? He was a pampered rich Irish kid from Boston who thought he had the grit to withstand an inexorable force. It was laughable.

The pressure had built. Irish thugs had even gathered outside the windows of Kennedy headquarters yelling insults at Jack, calling him names, and spitting at the glass. Bobby had to restrain Kenny twice from going out and kicking some ass. Kenny, like Jack, as with most former war veterans, could take a punch. More important, he could give one.

"Come on, Kenny," Bobby had said. "Control that Irish temper. We don't need that right now." Bobby had been right, of course, but Kenny had wanted to beat the shit out of some of those guys.

Then, at about 4:00 a.m., the results turned. Amazingly, Kenny and Larry had been right. Larry's unorthodox and unique new numbers system, based on the numbers from 1948, had been right. All the professional polls had been wrong. The Massachusetts political establishment was wrong. Kennedy had won.

When the political hacks found out, they couldn't believe it. The son of a bitch had won! But how? He had won Worcester. He'd beat Lodge. By six in the morning even CBS had officially changed its mind. Young Jack Kennedy, the handsome, wealthy son of Ambassador Joe Kennedy, had sent the prestigious and powerful Republican senator Henry Cabot Lodge back to the Lodge farm in Beverly. In an Eisenhower sweep, Jack Kennedy was the only Democratic boat still afloat. It was just amazing!

"A thing of political beauty," Powers had exclaimed as he pulled out the one beer they could all share. Nobody had brought anything stronger. They were not really all that confident in their system going into that night.

It had all turned on Worcester. As the friends stood around the card table that cold November morning, shirt sleeves rolled up, shirttails hanging out of their pants, hair askew, and all smelling a bit ripe, the room itself was replete with the aroma of stale, overcooked coffee and day-old donuts.

Bobby had turned to Kenny and said, "Worcester. I'll be damned. Kenny, you are either the most brilliant political strategist in the business or just one lucky of son of a bitch."

They had laughed. Kenny had smiled his characteristically tight-lipped, just-at-the-edges kind of smile. Later, he'd find out the answer. Luck. He was just damned lucky, but he never saw a need to explain that to Jack or Bobby.

As his father, the legendary football coach Cleo O'Donnell, had said to him, "Son, politics is like football. A win is a win. Even an ugly one is still a win. Take it and be happy." And now Kenny was.

In 1956 in Chicago, however, there was no miracle. No luck. Nothing. Jack was exhausted and disappointed. The Kefauver forces had outsmarted them, outmaneuvered them, outworked them, and, just to be sure when Jack was getting too close, had called in favors from the convention's counting board. The board mysteriously shut down. That move meant the vice presidential nomination would be decided by a voice vote only. Kefauver's people wisely flooded the convention floor with Kefauver loyalists, thus ensuring a voice vote victory.

The Kennedy forces were so meager that they were simply drowned out. Kenny's dad said to his son, matter-of-factly, "You lost. Pick yourself up and figure out where you go from here."

Bobby and Kenny had been furious. Bobby had called Jack and told him what happened. "Protest it!" Bobby had uncharacteristically yelled, challenging his brother.

"Fight it," the Old Man had said. Unhappy at first with his son's decision to run, once Jack was in the fight, Joe Kennedy, in his own characteristic fashion, had wanted Jack to win.

Kenny had said nothing. He waited. He had learned to read Jack's mood. And Jack, with that "computer of a mind of his," as Kenny described it, had already moved on.

"No," he had said, "let it go." He then went on to give the speech of his life at that convention. In losing, Jack had blown poor Estes Kefauver off the stage with his own powerful presence. He had all the delegates wondering why the hell they hadn't voted for this guy. For his part, Jack was already sizing up 1960.

So, as they sat later in the pub across the street from the International Amphitheater on the South Side of Chicago, where the Democrats had just held their convention, Kenny and Bobby nursed their wounds. Jack was already thinking about the next step, though admittedly Kenny and Bobby found it harder to let it go. Kenny had a beer. He figured that might help. It usually did. Jack had a cocktail and Bobby had a glass of milk. Kenny shook his head. Typical.

"Bobby," Kenny had told his wife, Helen, "was a Boy Scout."

"Be careful, Bobby," Kenny warned, leaning forward and looking past Jack to him. "Remember, you are driving." Jack and Kenny laughed.

Bobby shot Kenny a dirty look and huffed indignantly. "One of us should at least be sober." Then, as soon as he said it, he wished he hadn't.

"Why, exactly?" Kenny asked sarcastically, completely nonplussed. Bobby could kiss his ass. Jack laughed. The moment passed.

Just then the bartender, a thick, heavyset Irishman with a haggard face, realized who Jack was. "You Jack Kennedy?" he growled.

Jack nodded. "Yes. At least that's what my mother calls me," Jack said, anticipating a smile. He assumed the fellow was a fan. He put out his hand, but the man looked angry, disgusted.

"Your old man is a coward and a bootlegger! You got some nerve comin' into my fuckin' place!" he snarled.

Before Jack could respond, the man leaned forward. Jack moved back in his seat, not sure what to expect. That's when the guy spit in Jack's drink. Just spit in it. Jack stared. He almost laughed, he was so relieved. Given his health, if the guy had hit him, Jack figured he'd be in the hospital for two weeks.

Bobby leapt to his brother's defense.

Kenny said nothing, but he vaulted quick as a cat over the bar and grabbed the poor fellow by the collar before pushing him against the wall and belting him. The room fell into stunned silence. Jack leaned forward and picked up his newly poured drink, nervously poured by a second bartender. Brushing off his hands, Kenny returned to his seat and picked up his beer. Bobby shook his head and smiled, picking up his milk.

"To 1960," was all Jack said.

That was all that needed saying.

◆◆◆

ALTHOUGH JACK LOST that day, in losing he ended up victorious. He may have fallen, but he damn well would make the best of it.

"You're the luckiest man in America," Bobby exclaimed to his brother. "Stevenson's going to lose," Bobby said, at the time with a dose of more wishful thinking than fact, though Bobby would ultimately turn out to be correct. Bobby would study the Stevenson campaign in 1956 and all Stevenson's wrong moves, everything that Jack would avoid in 1960.

Jack sent Kenny and Bobby to sort out the unhappy labor union people and soothe the injured feelings of the disappointed, ragtag Kennedy forces. An exhausted Jack and Jackie joined his sister Eunice and brother-in-law Sargent Shriver for dinner. Was he disappointed? Of course he was, he had told them. Mostly, he was just tired. But his sister and brother-in-law could tell Jack had already set his sights on '60. He was not a man who spent a hell of a lot of time focused on the past.

Kenny and Bobby took the train back to Boston. Upon arrival, Bobby happily bid Kenny adieu after pushing back hard on Kenny's suggestions that he run for mayor or governor in Massachusetts.

"Politics," Bobby told Kenny icily, "is not for me. There are lots of ways to serve the public good besides public office."

Kenny shrugged and sipped his beer. *Damn*, he thought, *even taunting Bobby didn't help.*

"Don't do anything stupid," Kenny snarled at Bobby as they headed to the connecting train to DC. "Remember, your brother is in the Senate; whatever you do reflects on him."

Bobby laughed and squeezed Kenny's shoulder. "You're just mad because I wouldn't run for governor. Don't worry. You'll find someone to run. Just not me."

With that Bobby was gone, back home to Washington to meet up with his new boss, Arkansas senator John McClellan, to see what the future held.

Kenny returned to what was left of the Kennedy headquarters, pulling his suit coat around him to protect himself from a cold gust of wind off Boston Harbor. Maybe there was some truth to what Bobby said. Right now 1958 seemed a long way off, and Kenny had to keep busy until Jack gave him the signal to jump. *Shit*, Kenny thought to himself, *I can't wait till '58, when Jack will be up for reelection.*

As it turned out, Kenny would have to wait longer than he had planned, and Bobby dealt him a bit of a detour. That detour was called the United States Senate Select Committee on Improper Activities in Labor and Management or the McClellan Committee or, as it was later simply dubbed, the Rackets Committee, where Bobby planned to take on the labor unions as chief counsel to the committee. The unions were soon to be infamous, thanks in no small part to Bobby, teamsters boss Jimmy Hoffa, and a fellow from Chicago named Sam Giancana, who would loom uncomfortably large in the Kennedy story.

The next step was for Kenny, with his wife and kids in tow, to join Bobby in Washington.

When Kenny stopped by upon his arrival, Jack was as surprised as anyone to see Kenny in DC. "What the hell are you doing here?" Jack had wanted to know. "I thought you were in Boston working for me!" Jack had snarled at Kenny when they met in Jack's DC office.

Kenny was surprised. "Don't you two talk to each other?" Kenny had asked, puzzled. He had assumed that when Bobby pulled him out of Massachusetts and down to Washington it had been cleared with Jack. He had even asked Bobby when they spoke on the telephone, point-blank, if Jack knew about him coming to Washington. Now that Jack had snapped at him, Kenny realized that Bobby had been a bit evasive in his answer.

"No," Jack growled. "That's your job."

It was the first time that Kenny understood his role was to be the middleman, the guy between Bobby and Jack when they either couldn't or wouldn't deal with something political directly. The truth was that Jack hated confrontations, and he hated telling Bobby no. Therefore that role would fall to Kenny. Of course, telling Bobby no didn't actually mean he'd listen to Kenny or anyone else for that matter, and therein lay a major problem.

So Jack's Irish Brotherhood ended up playing politics with each other in Washington. Bobby would relentlessly grill the union officials and the mob during the day, with Kenny sitting right outside Bobby's office. Then, promptly at five o'clock, according to the chief clerk, Ruth Young Watt, the door would be closed. At that time, Kenny would sit and make calls on Jack's behalf well into the night, soothing ruffled feathers and beginning to build some political bridges beyond Massachusetts borders. Kenny would make appointments for dinner and drinks, generally trying to convince the union leadership that Jack was not a bad guy.

"Don't worry too much about Bobby. He was only after the bad guys," Kenny tried to explain to people like labor and civil rights attorney Joseph "Joe" Rauh, or Walter Reuther, head of the United Automobile Workers. Both men were liberals whom Kenny knew Jack would eventually need if he were ever to secure the presidential nomination, never mind the White House itself.

"Look," Kenny pleaded, "Bobby is after Hoffa and those guys, not you. You guys are Jack's kind of fellows; he will be with you all the way." While many of the labor guys liked Kenny and even liked what he had to say, they remained unconvinced about Jack. After all, he was on the United States Select Committee on Improper Activities in Labor and Management, perhaps better known simply as the McClellan Committee, named for its chairman, Arkansas Democrat John L. McClellan—the very committee that the unions saw as impeding and threatening their independence. Jack was a member of the committee, among Senators Barry Goldwater, Karl Mundt, and many others. Bobby had convinced Jack to serve on the committee. He felt it was an opportunity to showcase the Kennedy brothers doing good work in politics. Kenny and the Old Man both felt it was a stupid idea, a rare moment of agreement between them. "Don't get me wrong," Kenny told Bobby, "I think your role with the committee is one thing, but why put your brother in that position? He does not have to serve on the committee, and a million political things can go wrong."

Joe Kennedy was much more direct when during a Christmas holiday, Joe and Bobby had it out. Joe thought the whole thing could come back and bite Jack on his political ass. "Who the hell goes after the labor unions when you want to run for the White House and you can't win without them?" Joe had bellowed.

Bobby, perhaps a little intimidated, had held firm. As Kenny had said a million times before, "once Bobby made up his mind, just get the hell out of the way."

In the end, Jack agreed to reluctantly serve on the committee, and while his father was still pissed about the entire issue, he was pleased Kenny would be there to watch Bobby and, more important, Jack's backside.

"It was clear," said Rauh, "that from the moment Kenny O'Donnell arrived, he may have been on the committee, keeping an eye on Bobby. But it was also clear that Jack Kennedy was running for president," and that was a key factor in Kenny's presence.

From five o'clock in the evening onward, Bobby's office at the old Senate Office Building was the headquarters of the Jack Kennedy for President operation. In 1957, while Bobby may have been focused on the labor union and the mob, Jack and Kenny were eyeing 1960. They'd let Bobby chase Hoffa and the mobsters for now, but soon Bobby would also be looking toward 1600 Pennsylvania Avenue.

CHAPTER 2

Early Days

THE DAY WAS unremarkable. It was an early spring morning with a deep chill in the air, courtesy of one of those stiff New England breezes off the cold Atlantic Ocean that refuse to give winter up for good.

Kenny sipped his coffee in Harvard Square, which he'd called home since escaping Worcester, Pleasant Street, and Holy Cross. He was standing just beyond the brick walls that surrounded Harvard College, walls convenient before the end of the war for keeping the moneyed Yankees safe from those pesky immigrants—the Irish, Italians, and Greeks, whose wish to have their kids attend Harvard was until very recently just a pipe dream. Some of them, however, like Joseph P. Kennedy Sr., a friend of Kenny's father, Cleo, another up-from-the-bottom Irishman, had somehow broken through and gotten into Harvard. Cleo was smart enough to go to Harvard. He just did not have the dough. Somehow, Joe Kennedy had pulled that off.

This didn't surprise Cleo. "Darn smart fellow," Cleo always said. "Darn smart. Not my cup of tea, but darn smart."

For Kenny, Cleo's rebellious second son, that always translated into *I don't like the guy, but I admire any Irishman who can kick down some Yankee doors and succeed.*

Just then, Kenny's eyes glanced across the headlines of the morning paper. He moved quickly from the national news to the local Boston political front. Like his father, Kenny was a political junkie. He was at a newsstand that served up lousy but hot coffee and a few slightly stale donuts. It was not far from the small apartment that he shared with his young, blue-eyed bride, Helen.

She was also from Worcester, the Turkey Hill neighborhood to be exact. Her maiden name was Sullivan. Like the O'Donnell clan, the Sullivans were blue-collar, struggling, hardworking Irish. Helen's father, Bart, was a tradesman, first generation not long off the boat from county Cork. Like so many of the Irish, he had come here seeking the American dream. But it had all ended in despair. Bart's beloved mother and sister had died on the journey over, of some dread disease that seemed to plague especially the poor. Bart landed in Boston alone, embittered, and already homesick. He eventually made his way to Worcester with the help of some friends and set himself up as a tradesman, half electrician, half jack-of-all-trades. There he met a blue-eyed Swedish beauty by the name of Hilda.

They married. The Sullivans were what you might call working-class poor. Hilda had cleaned the homes of the upper middle class and the wealthy, who could afford such extravagances.

Bart and Hilda had two children: a daughter, Helen Mary, and a son, Robert. But this new family could never compete with the one Bart had lost, and in the end their ghosts (and the liquor that suppressed their memory) won out.

Helen spent much of her young life retrieving her father after hours from some bar or tracking him down after days on a bender. Her first date with Kenny had been interrupted by such an excursion. Cleo and Alice, Kenny's parents, liked Helen but saw trouble and suggested they were too young. Kenny told them to go to hell, just as he had when he enlisted and lied about his age, telling his father the day he left. Cleo had been furious in an Irish way that suggested more pride than anger.

After Kenny married Helen, they soon had their first son, Kenny Jr. Their marriage had occurred rapidly despite the fact that Kenny's financial situation would seem to have ruled it out. Apparently, Kenny Jr. was coming, wedding license or not.

Once married, Helen was as eager as Kenny had been to escape Worcester. They moved to a lousy, small, postwar apartment in Cambridge. It was so cheap in fact that one night after a few too many beers, Kenny and his older brother, Cleo Jr., managed, while wrestling, to go right through the wall and land in the living room of the next apartment!

No matter. The apartment was the Ritz-Carlton as far as Helen was concerned. Never had Kenny seen someone so happy with so little. She was also an athlete, a sports nut, and competitive as hell, so she fit right in with Kenny's boys, the "Harvard Irregulars" as Kenny jokingly called them. And she got along splendidly with Kenny's chum, sort of an adopted kid brother, Bobby Kennedy.

Robert Francis Kennedy was Ambassador Joseph P. Kennedy's sixth child. He had become Kenny's and the Harvard football team's best pal. Bobby was not the best athlete and he made the Harvard football team by sheer determination and toughness. It was a trait Kenny would come to admire and later find himself unsuccessfully trying to rein in.

It was the spring of 1946 when Bobby, as he was known to the gridiron gang at Harvard, wanted Kenny to meet his older brother Jack. On the appointed day, Kenny was waiting for Bobby, who was late—nothing new.

Kenny was bored. He didn't know why he was here, and he didn't much care about meeting Bobby's older brother. Bobby had been pestering the hell out of Kenny about it, though. So Ken figured, *Well, okay*, after some prodding from Helen. *What the hell, I might as well meet the guy. Get it over with, for Christ's sake.*

In the end, it would be a meeting that was remarkable for what did not happen. Lightning did not strike. Ken did not shake Jack's hand and know right away he was meeting a future president and the man who would change his life. Instead, Kenny found him to be a nice guy, clearly a young man of wealth and means, handsome, but otherwise totally unremarkable.

"He seemed too boyish and shy to be running against experienced politicians like Mike Neville and John Cotter in that tough congressional district," Kenny later reported to his pals. Kenny was unimpressed, but Jack was running for Congress, so he agreed to help. "Yeah, sure," he had said to Bobby, "I'll do it, but as a favor to you. He'll never make it."

Bobby, who clearly idolized his older brother, saw only success for Jack. And rightly so: Jack was a war hero, author, journalist, bon vivant, and generally nice guy. "He's going all the way," Bobby had announced to Kenny with his adoring (though politically naive and uninformed) enthusiasm.

"Whatever you say, Bobby," Kenny had laughingly replied.

Of course, Jack would go all the way that year, going on to win the 1946 open congressional seat, in large measure due to a remarkably funny, perceptive little Irishman from the town of Charlestown, which lay just across the Charles River from Boston. His name was David Francis Powers. Dave would later become a good pal of Kenny's, almost as close to Kenny as he was to Jack. But that was yet to come.

Later, Kenny would laugh at himself when people asked him about his first meeting with Jack. *Shit,* he thought, *I wish I had been that perceptive. Honestly, though, he just seemed like another returned vet. Nice guy, rich kid, playboy, good looking, and Joe Kennedy's son. Nothing more.*

But Bobby pressed. Bobby always pressed when he wanted something. He could be a pain that way. What Bobby wanted now was for Kenny to see in his brother what he saw—a hero and a future president. Mostly, what Bobby wanted Kenny to see and understand was that his brother was, above all else, a natural politician.

As a young returning vet in Massachusetts in 1946, Kenny did not pay a hell of a lot of attention to Congressman Jack Kennedy. Jack was Ambassador Joe Kennedy's boy, after all, and the ambassador was not very popular among those working-class Massachusetts men who had risked life and limb fighting in the Pacific during the war. Joe Kennedy had been recalled from his ambassadorship in England around the time of American intervention in the war for comments that were construed as sympathetic toward the Axis powers.

Furthermore, most people in the state, war vets or not, had no clue who Jack Kennedy was. It wasn't personal. He was just an obscure congressman; just another son of a famous family, a rich kid with connections. Most Massachusetts voters did not give a damn about their congressman or senator anyway. Hell, most could not even name them.

It was the governor who controlled the power, the jobs, and, most important, the patronage. At the time, that power was held by Robert F. Bradford, Massachusetts's fifty-seventh governor, who would serve only one term, from his election in 1947 to 1949, because in those days Massachusetts's governors were elected to two-year terms. Bob Bradford, who had replaced Maurice Tobin as governor, was a pipe-smoking Harvard fellow. He was highly thought of and came from a respected family. He was the scion of "an old traditional Yankee, Brahmin family," as Kenny would describe them. In a manner of speaking, he embodied everything Jack and Kenny were not. Bradford was a socially aware Republican governing at a time when the men returning from the war were reshaping the political climate in Massachusetts, as well as across the nation. The overall political atmosphere in 1946 into which young war vet Jack Kennedy stepped is critical to understanding what happened next.

Immediately after the war, Maurice Tobin had been governor. Tobin had been mayor of the city of Boston from 1938 to 1944. In 1944, he was elected governor with a largely liberal agenda. Unfortunately, he was opposed at every turn by the Republican-dominated legislature and eventually was defeated by Bradford in 1947. For Kenny, the political atmosphere in the state was stained by "those terrible Boston politicians" whose "ethics" left Kenny and many voters like him looking for a political alternative.

This is the way most vets and voters of his age demographic looked at it, too, especially those in the western part of the state, which included the industrial area of Worcester. They were outsiders who did not have much use for Boston pols.

In 1946, in addition to Bradford winning the governorship, a rich, well-respected Yankee by the name of Henry Cabot Lodge had beaten David Ignatius Walsh for Senate. Walsh had been lieutenant governor, had already served in the Massachusetts Senate, returning in 1926, and had served until Lodge soundly defeated him.

In fact, Lodge had even carried Boston, the first time in recent history that a Republican had won the city. It was an impressive display of political power as far as Kenny was concerned. There was, in fact, a tremendous revulsion toward the Democrats growing among the voters.

The Republican slogan was "Had enough?!" And apparently the voters had. So they sent the Democrats packing. The Democrats were also victims of the economy. There were still breadlines everywhere. You could not buy the things you needed. It was tough to find jobs. Even returning vets looking for work to feed their families could not get jobs.

Walsh had also been in part a victim of a campaign involving *The Boston Post*, which did not like him, and in fact most of the working-class press felt the same way. Still, Walsh was one of the few state politicians at the time who was, or appeared to be, honest.

Walsh was an isolationist and very conservative. He was out of step with the change in the pulse of the voters and especially with the returning vets. Times were changing, and he had failed to take the temperature of the public as Lodge had.

Into this time of great political change in Massachusetts stepped young Jack Kennedy, a new breed of politician in the right place, at the right moment. He won with the help of a few working-class Irish vets, who early on sensed that Jack was the real deal.

Jack began by recruiting some of his old war vet buddies as well as personal school chums to help on the campaign. The political machinations would, in this campaign at least, be left to his father, Joe, to handle. Among those who jumped into the campaign were young war veterans, such as Thomas Broderick. Broderick was a small, wiry fellow and had first met Jack in 1943 in the Pacific Theater. "I was attached to the LST-353," Broderick recalled later. "It was during a bombing attack. We had to race to go rescue some officers on another LST, turned out to be his. They had been hit, so we took them aboard; and then when we got to the safety of the beach, the War Department had someone there taking pictures because we had rescued so many officers. One thing led to another. He overheard me telling the photographer I was from Boston; and then he turned around to introduce himself. 'Hi, I am Jack Kennedy,' he said. 'I am from Boston.' It was," Broderick would laugh later, "a hell of a situation under which to meet."

When Jack decided to run in '46, Tom Broderick was one of the fellows Jack called. "Can you help?" "You bet," Tom had answered. Kenny noted, "As inexperienced as Jack was in organizing a campaign, Kennedy seemed to know by intuition how to select committed people and recruit staff with no previous political background or connections who would turn out to be conscientious and able, and usually tireless, Kennedy crusaders." Many of them would stay with Jack through this campaign and the many campaigns to come.

Jack explained to Dave Powers, who had joined the crusade, that he wanted young, new people, preferably veterans, not experienced politicians. "Get me some people who have not been involved in politics," he told Dave, "fellows like yourself, with no experience, preferably just out of the service. I don't want experienced politicians, who bring their own agenda, their own baggage and ideas. I want fellows like yourself." Billy Sutton, another Boston Irishman, who like Powers, Broderick, and others was drawn to Jack by his youth, his war record, and the fact that he was of his generation, felt and agreed with Dave Powers that even early, during the '46 campaign, "Jack Kennedy was a breath of fresh air." From the start of the first campaign in 1946, Jack demonstrated an evident disdain for the overblown rhetoric and corny style of the older generation of politicians. As Kenny described it, Kennedy was "well suited to the changing times; his air of quiet refinement and his unaffected and sincere platform manner were a welcome contrast to the hard-boiled pols of the previous [James Michael] Curley era."

Writer Francis Russell wrote, "When Jack Kennedy appeared without forewarning on the Boston political scene in 1946, the middle-class suburban Irish hailed him with joy and relief. After a half a century of oafishness— Honey Fitz [singing] 'Sweet Adeline,' Southie's annual St. Patrick's Day parade enlivened by japers like 300-pound Knocko McCormack mounted on a dray horse, of deft operators and blackmailers, of silvercrossed younger pols—this attractive, well-spoken, graceful, witty, Celtic, Harvard-bred and very rich young man was what every suburban matron would like their son to be. In fact, many of them came to see Jack *as* their son." That, Kenny explained later, is how Jack won in 1946, by being someone genuine and new to the political scene. Truly that breath of fresh air. He could afford this of course, because in this race and the subsequent one, he left the business of politics to his father and a few of his father's well-chosen loyal staff, including Joe Kennedy Sr.'s right-hand man, Joe Kane. This would remain true until 1952, when Jack shocked them all by bringing together the Irish Brotherhood. At that point, the political futures of Jack Kennedy and Kenny O'Donnell would change forever.

It became quickly apparent that there was something different and new about Jack Kennedy from the moment he arrived for duty as a congressman in Washington on January 3, 1947. He had just gotten off a private plane from Palm Beach, where the Kennedy family spent the holidays. Ted Reardon and William "Billy" Sutton, Kennedy's two young political lieutenants from Boston, nervously checked their watches and stared helplessly at the revolving doors of the famed Statler Hotel Washington while they waited for Jack. This was his first day in Congress, and he was already late.

When he finally arrived at the Statler, Jack announced that he was starving and wanted to go the drugstore across the street to have some breakfast. Reardon and Sutton were horrified. They had just driven all night in a snowstorm down from Boston in Jack's sister Eunice's Chrysler. They were tired, cold, and hungry themselves, but breakfast would have to wait.

"Speaker John McCormack's been calling every ten minutes looking for you!" Billy Sutton announced, agitated, the blood rushing to fill his face. Despite his small frame, Sutton looked as though he might just take a poke at the newly arrived and very tardy congressman from the Eighth District in Massachusetts. "John McCormack wants you on the Hill right now for a party caucus, and he means now."

Kennedy smiled and waved Sutton off. With that, he turned on his heel and began sauntering toward the front door, his hands stuffed into his pockets in what would become a very familiar pose. Despite his back pain, he walked with the grace of an athlete as he headed toward the drugstore across the street.

Jack knew almost as soon as he arrived that he was uninterested in minority whip and dean of the Massachusetts delegation John McCormack's offer of tutelage in the ways of the House of Representatives. Jack Kennedy was determined to steer his own course, which was evident to McCormack.

"Mr. McCormack has been getting along fine without me here in Washington for twenty-eight years," Kennedy said as Reardon and Sutton rushed to catch up with him. "He can get along without me for another fifteen minutes. Let's go into the drugstore and get some eggs."

The other thing Jack knew almost immediately after arriving in Congress was that he needed to begin planning his exit. But he would need to assemble the right team to help him calculate his next move. What he wanted was a group of tough, like-minded, blue-collar, no-bullshit vets who thought the way he did. He wanted outsiders who were tired of looking in from the outside at all Washington's political game playing and its outdated, traditional decorum.

Still, nobody paid a hell of lot of attention to Jack until he refused to sign a petition for a presidential pardon for James M. Curley. Curley, the longtime mayor of Boston and former congressman from Jack's own district, had held the seat that Jack Kennedy now held. Mayor Curley had gone to jail and deserved to be there. Jack Kennedy, who it would seem was fostering larger political ambitions of his own, should have been first in line to sign Curley's pardon petition. But he didn't. He said no. He didn't even show up.

Consequently, Boston's political insiders were pissed at both Jack and his father.

After all, this pardon was for James Michael Curley, the mayor of Boston, who was still mayor even while doing time at the federal correctional institution in Danbury, Connecticut.

Curley had been convicted of wartime construction fraud but remained a popular figure in Boston and was, as Kenny put it, "a martyred hero in young Jack Kennedy's political district." He was not the kind of guy you voted against. Curley had even shown up in the courtroom in a wheelchair, though he had never needed one before he was convicted. He was also wearing a neck brace too big for his neck and complaining of at least nine ailments, including, he was certain, an "impending cerebral hemorrhage." How he could foresee a brain hemorrhage was anyone's guess.

As it turned out, Kennedy was the only one among the Massachusetts congressional delegation to withhold his signature from the petition. People were stunned but reasoned it must be a fluke. Somebody needed to bring him up to speed on the way politics worked in Boston.

The stories began to circulate quickly among the returned vets. Kennedy had been handed the petition to pardon James Michael Curley on the floor of the House, right in front of the assembled House members and a full press gallery. Then Jack Kennedy shocked everyone and refused to sign.

The war vets who made up the Harvard gridiron gang and the Harvard varsity football team—Kenny, Nick Rodis, Paul Lazzaro, and others—took notice. Kenny was not pissed but quietly surprised, maybe even slightly impressed.

The second thing Jack did really made Kenny think twice. Jack attacked the American Legion for its strong opposition to low-cost public housing projects. Boston pols were really pissed this time. Jack had done either the boldest or the dumbest thing possible as a returning vet.

The American Legion was stunned at first, then livid. Who the hell did Joe Kennedy's kid think he was? And Joe was right there with them. Everyone wanted to know, What the hell was Jack thinking?!

Jack Kennedy's attack on the American Legion in 1949 was remarkable. This time everyone could see very clearly that Jack understood exactly what he was about. Oh, he got it all right. He understood politics, their politics, but what he was telling them, loud and clear, was that their politics were not his politics. A new day and a new era were dawning, and Jack Kennedy meant to be the guy who would shape that future.

Is he nuts? Kenny asked himself as he read about it first in the Boston papers while sipping that lousy newsstand coffee. He tried to evade Bobby's toothy, told-you-so grin.

Jack's attack on the American Legion was, as Kenny recalled, "like attacking or opposing J. Edgar Hoover, the Boy Scouts, and Billy Graham." You just didn't do it, especially if you had political ambitions beyond the Eighth Congressional District in Massachusetts.

Kenny said, "In those days nobody, and I mean nobody, challenged the conservative brass and powerful American Legion. Nobody who wanted to stay in politics, that is. But Jack was frustrated, didn't give a damn, and unlike so many others, his political gut told him of changing times. He could smell it in the wind. In that computer-like mind of his, he knew the risk would be worth it. He wasn't worried about the boys in the smoke-filled back rooms. No. Jack was focused on an entirely different audience.

"As a returning vet and a young congressman, he had been working his tail off to organize veterans' groups into a united, cohesive group to support a low-cost housing bill. The bill was urgently and desperately needed in postwar America. So urgent was the need that even a right-wing conservative like Senator Robert Taft stood up and sponsored the damn bill. However, the American Legion, which was supporting the private real estate and construction interests, had fought the bill every step of the way. They fought and fought hard."

Ultimately, the debate, which moved to the floor of the House, was over a so-called Bonus Bill that the American Legion was sponsoring as political cover for their opposition to federal funds for low-cost public housing projects. Jack sat and listened to the debate and the evasion and the lies. Finally, Jack had had enough. His Irish temper got the best of him during a heated debate on the House floor. Not heeding an aide's warning to keep his cool, Jack rose to speak. In what would eventually become a familiar gesture to Kenny and the nation, he ran his hand nervously through his tousled, thick red hair before beginning. Was he nervous or just so angry that he had to take a minute to control himself?

It was hard to tell. Tapping his finger rapidly on the desk, Jack began a tirade that escalated with each deadly, well-directed word. Finally, he ended his outburst with his conclusion that "the leadership of the American Legion has not had a constructive thought for the benefit of this country since 1918!"

There was an audible gasp from the gathered House members. After the shock wore off, one after the other scrambled to the microphone to make sure they were on record condemning young Congressman Jack Kennedy's inappropriate, unwise, and simply unpatriotic remarks. Was he even an American?

Everyone condemned him. Congressman John Rankin of Mississippi declared the American Legion "to be the most patriotic organization in the United States," indicating without saying so that Jack didn't know a hell of a lot about patriotism. Echoes of Joe Kennedy's shady past underlay dog whistles like these.

Even Edith Nourse Rogers, a longtime Kennedy supporter, felt compelled to make a public apology for her fellow representative from

Massachusetts, gently reminding House members that the Kennedy family had suffered a loss in the war. Jack had been terribly injured as well. Perhaps, just perhaps, he had been affected in "some way we are not currently aware of," she had said, giving Jack's father a chance to save his son's career.

What the House members didn't know was that Joe was even madder than they were about what Jack had said. Joe had his own unfulfilled, unfinished ambitions, and Jack was screwing them up. "He's going to become a one-termer," Joe had bellowed at anyone who would listen.

Jack Kennedy's father angrily counseled him to retract his statement. Even Jack's war-vet pals called his small, closet-like office, urging Jack to make an immediate apology retracting the statement before he faced certain "political ruin."

Jack held his ground. He was dismayed by how many people ran for the door, but he also noticed who did not run. In those people he saw the political future. So he asked for the floor, looking for more time to speak.

Relieved, the Speaker of the House granted him the time right away. Everyone assumed Jack had come to his senses or that his father had persuaded him to apologize. Everyone assumed he was going to use the time to fall on his sword for his foolishness and retract his statement.

They were wrong. Instead, he took the opportunity to denounce the Legion one more time, just in case somebody had missed the point the first time. With his unrepentance reiterated, Jack made his way slowly, painfully back to his office, which felt somehow even smaller on this particular day. His back was hurting like hell. The glacial silence on the House floor and the ice-cold stares from many members—not to mention how quickly they moved to get away from him lest he speak to them or lest their photos be taken together—told Jack Kennedy, as he walked down that long aisle, that once again his idealism had cost him friends. When he finally arrived back at his office, he slid painfully into his chair, nodding his head in thanks for the coffee from his loyal aide Ted Reardon.

"Well, Ted," he said with a wry smile, "I guess we are gone." Reardon, a young Irish guy from Worcester and a friend of Kenny's, looked up and smiled.

"Not so fast," Ted explained. "Attacking the leadership of the American Legion is not the same as attacking the membership. You might be okay."

Jack's ears perked up. Another political lesson. But they would have to wait and see what kind of mail they got in order to judge who was right: Jack and Ted or the Old Guard led by Jack's father.

It would turn out that Ted Reardon had been dead-on. The mail ran ten to one in support of Jack's position. The remark would make headlines, raise eyebrows, and transform Jack into a hero among returning veterans—men who knew a bit about heroics and knew the difference between the talkers and the doers. They were ready to fight the political war, but they needed a leader. In young Jack Kennedy they might well have found one.

It would turn out to be one of the most remarkable moves Jack Kennedy made during his six years in the House of Representatives. Jack Kennedy's decisions on these two points were a startling display of political courage and independence. They were not the sorts of the things you would do if you wanted a long political career in Massachusetts or anywhere else. They were definitely not the kinds of things you would do if you wanted to be president of the United States someday.

On the other hand, these two "bold acts of political independence," as Kenny later called them, also made returning war vets take notice. Suddenly, this boyish, skinny, shy kid with the year-round suntan was becoming a hope, a beacon of light for those who had risked their lives to save the country; hell, they had helped save the world only to return home and find politics as usual. As Kenny put it: "We were finding that politicians wanted to keep things the way they were before the war. We felt cut out of the process by the establishment and ignored by older politicians who thought we had nothing to offer."

Maybe, just maybe, they saw in young Jack Kennedy some hope. "Here was a guy," Kenny argued quietly with some friends over a beer on the front steps of the Harvard Varsity Club, "who is one of us. And maybe Jack Kennedy will be able to take on these politicians and the establishment."

"You sound like Bobby!" one of his pals teased Kenny.

Kenny paused, smiling his slight, reserved smile. Yeah, maybe he was sounding a bit like Bobby. But maybe Bobby was right.

Kenny was impressed enough to ask Bobby to set up a second meeting in Kennedy's suite at the Bellevue Hotel—the grand dame of Boston hotels, situated at the corner of Beacon and Bowdoin streets, a stone's throw from the historic Massachusetts State House.

Yes, Kenny was impressed, and this time when he and Jack shook hands, Kenny was firmly on Jack's team.

The American Legion fracas, like the Curley incident, would end up doing Jack Kennedy more good than harm. It proved to vets that he was their man, the guy they could turn to, and somebody who, most importantly, was his own man. It showed that Jack Kennedy was not a guy afraid to take political risks. That should not have been a total surprise to anyone who understood his war record.

If they had only known about Jack's health and the risk it posed for his entire political career, they might have had second thoughts. Still, nobody knew about that then. Nobody but his father knew or understood how many times Jack had faced death. Anyway, Jack was all about taking a risk if the reasons made some political sense.

The results of the American Legion struggle were especially a surprise for the old party brass in Massachusetts, who had expected Jack to be a team player. They wanted him to be a seat warmer while they taught him the ropes and made sure the Kennedys' fortune was as indebted to them as possible.

Jack understood their type more than they knew. He had gotten into politics to satisfy his own ambitions and not to follow in his dead brother's footsteps or to realize his father's dreams. He was no seat warmer, and the party establishment would have to learn that he made his own decisions. Jack wanted it understood that he had gotten into politics to be his own man. Jack Kennedy was a self-possessed striver. Kenny, for his part, very much liked what he saw.

"More often than not," Jack later told Kenny, "the morally right thing to do turns out to be the politically right thing to do as well." At the time of his stand against the Legion, however, very few people would have agreed that Jack was pursuing the moral high ground. The vets did, though, and Jack understood this better than anybody, except maybe the American Legion, whose brass watched in horror as their membership sided with Kennedy. Politically astute, they moved quickly to invite this vibrant young politician to speak at their next state convention, where he received an overwhelmingly warm welcome.

Later, when the American Legion incident was far in his rearview mirror, Jack laughed about it with Kenny, his brother Bobby, and his dad at their Hyannis Port compound as they tried to decide what the next move in his career would be. The one thing Jack knew for sure was that the House of Representatives was not for him.

"Had I retracted the statement, I would have done myself more harm than I could have suffered by sticking to my political guns. But my friends didn't realize it at the time; and, frankly, neither did I," he said in a rare moment of self-reflection.

The voters of Massachusetts were about to see for themselves whether this new breed of politician was what they wanted in the United States Senate, and Kenny O'Donnell was about to make a decision that would seal his fate. His life would soon be forever intertwined with those of Jack and Bobby Kennedy.

CHAPTER 3

Building the Team

B Y HIS SECOND term in Congress, Jack knew he was headed for the U.S. Senate. While it was obvious to him, it was not so clear to the political pundits or the political establishment. Even his father had doubts, suggesting that perhaps Jack needed more time and experience in the House. But Jack had a vision for his future. He was not by nature a man who would settle for second place. He gave orders and didn't take them, hadn't taken them since he was in the war. Even then he didn't take them well. Hell, if he had followed orders, he wouldn't have risked nearly killing himself while rescuing endangered crewmembers. Yet it never occurred to him not to do it. Later on, struggling with the effects of a broken back, among other serious illnesses, Jack knew he had done the right thing. For Jack, politics was no different.

He had spent a good part of 1948 campaigning across his state on behalf of Harry Truman, then the Democratic presidential candidate. It was someplace between Springfield and on the way to Westfield that he made the decision. He had two choices: run for the Senate against the legendary Republican stalwart Henry Cabot Lodge Jr. or go for the governorship. Either way, Jack knew he was finished with the House.

The Irish, like so many recently immigrated groups before and after them, had historically been dismissed as lower class or inherently inferior when compared to their WASP fellow citizens. While Jack was lucky to have grown up amid great wealth, all the same, he represented the ambitions of a larger Irish political class that had struggled for years against the ethnic bigotry and anti-Catholic paranoia of traditional American society. He was a symbol of a new generation that represented the potential for a new and bright political future. "You have to understand," Kenny told journalist Sander Vanocur years later, "he came to represent the hopes of this entire class of people, the working class Irish, who were kind of proud to see one of their own do well."

Kenny had a point, and it was one both men understood in their political guts. "This is a period of time," Kenny explained, "when the average person does not relate much to their congressman or senator for that matter. Political power and patronage are held locally by the governor, who controls the state."

As Kenny got to know Jack Kennedy and experience his charisma and presence with the voting public firsthand, he came to believe that any specific elected office was irrelevant to what actually made people pay attention to Jack Kennedy. It was, in fact, the man himself who captured their imagination, just as he had done with Kenny.

Despite that first meeting, Kenny had been watching Jack grow politically. He had also, courtesy of Bobby, had a chance to spend more time with Jack. While that did not mean they had become friends by any means, he was beginning to realize that there was more to Jack Kennedy than he had initially believed. He also had gotten to know the Kennedy family better, and this would all serve him well in the future.

Whether Kenny realized it or not, he was being drawn deeper into the midst of their family, which provided him a unique perspective on family relations and especially the relationship between older brother Jack and younger brother Bobby. It had actually started, Kenny recalled, at one party at Hyannis Port for Bobby's birthday. "Ten or twelve of us lived in the Harvard Varsity Club. This is where Bobby spent most of his time from then on. We ate there, the training table was there, and most of the squad would hang around there, but only ten or twelve of us lived there. Bobby spent most of his waking moments there. At the end of the season, November 20, 1946, Bobby turned twenty-one and his father had this big birthday party for him."

Kenny and Helen both went; it would be fun, and they were both always up for a trip to the Cape.

The party was at Hyannis Port and Kenny said, "It was at the big house. It was the only house they had at that time. This is the first time I really met Mr. Kennedy, the Old Man. I had met him after a football game just to say hello, but this is the first time I had really met him. This is the first time I had any particular conversation with him. I remember it clearly, because Helen was very self-conscious about meeting the rest of the Kennedys. What I remember was how charming Joe Kennedy was to Helen. He put her at ease very quickly and they spent a great deal of the party chatting, which surprised me since I was no fan of his. My brother Cleo Jr. was also back from the war. He had been in the Pacific. Also came back a war hero like Jack and had been elected captain of the Harvard football team that year. They all came down to the party. Quite bluntly they were not the type of fellows Joseph P. Kennedy was used to his son associating with or any of his children associating with. I think he was a bit taken back."

The crowd was entirely different from the kind Jack usually associated with. Kenny noted, "You know Jack's friends that were there, elite, educated types, most of whom had not fought in the war.

"Bobby's crowd, myself included, were rough, tough-type fellows, returned war vets, hardened by what we had seen. We were all very cynical about people and especially about politics and politicians. We were all twenty-two years old and, experience-wise, years beyond that. All different nationalities and races, which I know bothered Joe Kennedy a lot. He kept mentioning it and not in a pleasant manner. Honestly, it was evident that the father was not really pleased or impressed with Bobby's choice of friends, and he made it quite plain. Bobby seemed to enjoy his father's reaction.

"I think there were ten or fifteen guys. Nick Rodis, who Bobby later brought to work for the State Department, a big Greek god, and Charlie Glynn from New York, who brought two or three of his girlfriends with him. These fellows were all about 225 pounds each, real athletes. Nobody was impressed or liked Joe Kennedy. Helping themselves to his alcohol, testing his cigars, and pulling out books, all without being asked or invited to, just helping themselves.

"None of us liked Joe Kennedy, because of what he had done in the war, and he had to know that by the way he was treated. I do not think he was used to being treated that way anymore, certainly not in his own home, by friends of his son. They criticized his liquor, didn't like his cigars, thought the house was old and drafty.

"Everyone was there. Jack was there with his friend Lem Billings. Billings was completely intimidated by this crowd, which they sensed and picked on him. Jack seemed quite astonished that this rough, tough crowd were not only Bobby's friends but that Bobby fit in with us so well. I think it really astonished him. Teddy was a very young, little boy at the time. He was hanging around as kids at that age do, and the girls were there, but they took one look at us and were not pleased. They were not terribly friendly and seemed very appalled that we were even allowed in the house, never mind by the front door. Jean was much younger than the other girls. She was quite friendly and one who seemed to not have that attitude problem. Mrs. Kennedy was there and was quite appalled. I mean she didn't know what had happened to her beloved, young boy Bobby that he had become friends with all these tough, rather cynical returned vets.

"Jack was astonished, but being a vet himself he fit right in. It was rather extraordinary. He quickly became the center of the party and we thought of him as one of us. He had that something that we now know was part of who he was. He just walked in the room and he was it. Bobby enjoyed the reaction of his family to us, and the reaction of us to Jack.

"Honey Fitz was there. We arrived earlier than the others, because Bobby wanted me to meet Jack apart from the crowd. I remember Mrs. Kennedy went and mixed drinks for us; I think she just couldn't figure this out. This is when Honey Fitz begins his dirty joke performance. I remember it clearly because he was in a bathrobe of all things, and it had a coat of arms on it. We just thought it was odd to wear a bathrobe to a party, never mind with a coat of arms of the Fitzgeralds on it. I remember it because Nick Rodis and the others began to tease Bobby, and asked Bobby if he wore underwear with the Fitzgerald coat of arms.

"Charlie Glynn, who was a great comedian, started re-creating a scene from a movie with Clifton Webb. In the scene, Webb begins to take all his clothes off one piece at a time, and everything right down to his underwear has a monogram on them. Glynn begins mimicking this scene and mimicking Honey Fitz and really giving Bobby the business. Glynn went through this great performance. Very funny."

For his part, Kenny thought, "Jack just seemed to take it all in. He seemed to almost glide above everyone. He seemed quite taken and amused with the entire scene, but in a distant sort of manner. He laughed like hell at Glynn; so did Bobby. Nobody else in the family did; I don't think Mrs. Kennedy or Mr. Kennedy were particularly amused. We talked about football and so forth with Jack. He had a girl with him and they headed out afterward. Jack spent more time talking to my brother Cleo Jr. than me, because they were both in the Pacific and had horrendous experiences, so they had more in common. My war experience had been in Germany. This is the first time Jack had met all of Bobby's friends, and I think he was quite surprised by Bobby's choice of friends. Jack was then a congressman, and yet again, there was no discussion of local politics or the House."

Kenny left again convinced that if Jack had a plan, it did not involve staying in the House or the local political scene for very long. "There was something about him that evening," Kenny said. "You got the sense this was a guy on the move."

As Kenny remembered, "At the party his father presented Bobby with a check for two thousand dollars for keeping the pledge not to drink before his twenty-first birthday. That was it; he just handed him the check. I thought it was fairly disgusting, if that is the best your father can do, to write you a check as opposed to spending time with you. Once again, I realized Bobby had a fairly tough relationship with the Old Man. It was not a pleasant scene in front of all the team. The check was found three years later rolled up in a ball in a football locker when they cleaned out his locker after he went to UVA. They gave it to me to give to him. He told me to toss it."

Kenny thought the entire incident revealed much about the complicated relationships in the Kennedy family and perhaps gave him a better insight into why two brothers, Jack and Bobby, could be so different. Kenny never forgot the incident and moved ahead determined to be the friend to Bobby that Kenny's dad, Cleo, was to him, since it was a relationship Bobby seemed to need.

Kenny and Helen were now married and remained close to Bobby. Kenny briefly flirted with law school before taking a job at a paper company to support his family. This was not what Kenny wanted or planned to do, but as it turned out, he, like Jack, was waiting for the next shoe to drop. A door to open.

By 1950, while Kenny bided his time, Jack began to seriously eye his next step, which would be either the governorship or the U.S. Senate. Jack waited for Paul Dever to make his decision about which of those positions he would run for next. Paul Andrew Dever was the fifty-eighth governor of Massachusetts and was, as Kenny described him, "a rather remarkable figure in his own right."

At the age of thirty-one, Dever was the youngest attorney general ever elected in Massachusetts. He had challenged political legend Leverett Saltonstall for the governorship in 1940 in what appeared to all political observers as a quixotic run. Yet Dever had again shocked pundits in Massachusetts and scored a small but significant upset.

His own family had a significant political pedigree. Dever's cousin William E. Dever, originally from Woburn, Massachusetts, had moved to Chicago, run for mayor, and won, gaining a national reputation as "the man who cleaned up Chicago."

Back in Massachusetts, the Republicans had control of local government for two years and then lost that power totally. Since then, however, the Korean War had begun, and the Democrats were increasingly unpopular. It nonetheless appeared that Governor Dever would be there forever if he wanted to be: He was still leader of the Democratic Party in Massachusetts and controlled all the patronage.

Kenny believed Dever was running the state while toying with the idea of a run for Senate. He had been elected by 387,000 votes, a huge majority. "Christ," Kenny commented as he watched election returns at the bar with his Harvard buddies, "this was the largest majority anyone had received at that point. Dever was the accepted leader, whether we liked it or not, and there was no challenger to him when, in 1950, Dever again cruised to victory."

As the political calendar hurtled toward the 1952 elections, John F. Kennedy was for all practical purposes just another quiet congressman. However, the political drumbeat around the insiders began to get louder now that the young congressman was looking to move up and out of the House.

Kenny had more than just Bobby to confirm this. Over in Cambridge, usually after the Harvard football game, he and his pals would drop into the local bar to have a couple of drinks. They had a relationship with the bartenders and tavern owners in Cambridge that could be described only as peculiar.

The bartenders did not lump in the football players, both current and former, with the elite of Harvard. These boys may have gone to Harvard and played at Harvard, but the townies knew that they were blue-collar guys who got over the Harvard walls only because of the GI Bill. Most could never have afforded it otherwise.

Moreover, all the bartenders were Irish, and most knew Cleo O'Donnell, Kenny's dad, as the football coach at Holy Cross. The O'Donnells didn't have Kennedy money, but they were athletes, and Cleo had won many championships on the Jesuits' behalf. So the Irish bartenders of Cambridge liked the O'Donnells just fine.

These working-class bartenders loved talking politics, and they were all great Dever people. Their first conversations were about whether Dever would run against Lodge for Senate. The general view was that they hoped he didn't, because the office of senator was of no use to them.

"You know whoever the senator is, he doesn't care about us. He can't really help us, but the governor can," they'd point out to Kenny. They didn't think Dever had it in him to run for Senate. He was too parochial, too Irish, and too partisan to run against a polished, moneyed, shoe-shined guy like Lodge from the tony suburbs of Beverly, Massachusetts.

Jack's plans were helped when Dever began to slip a bit here and there, making "unforced political errors," as Kenny called them. Dever was getting older, his health wasn't good, and he didn't look forward to a risky run for the Senate. Risk was a young man's game. Many were concerned that Dever could not beat Lodge. They hoped for his sake and their own—and for the sake of all the political patronage that was the bread and butter of the Boston Irish—that Dever didn't make the run for Senate and stayed in the governor's office.

Henry Cabot Lodge Jr. was a formidable politician. He had already shown that he had the political muscle to carry the city of Boston once. He was getting great publicity. Why tempt fate? Leave the risk of losing to a younger man, said the Irish bartenders to Kenny. Jack Kennedy, for instance. He can live to fight another day. Besides, he's rich, he can afford the run, and anyway, it's not as if he really needs the job.

Those in the know, those like Kenny, knew Jack was going to run for something else someday. But when? With his money, looks, and skills, it was evident to everyone he was not going to hang around in the Congress.

Kenny had the advantage of access through Bobby, and from what he gathered, Jack was restless.

Jack was making a lot of speeches across the state of Massachusetts and was becoming known statewide. His speeches had nothing to do with his congressional district. He was an attractive candidate who had risen far above the other Massachusetts congressmen in the restive public mind. What made Jack different from others was his unwillingness to wait his turn, work the system, follow the rules. Many returned veterans who had fought in the war and survived were no longer willing to accept the political system as it was or had been; they wanted change, and they came to view Jack Kennedy as the agent that would bring it.

Wanting to run for an office, yearning to move up the political ladder, and wanting change was all fine and good, but you still needed the political organization to get you there. Kennedy, however, had not done any organizational work to further his ambitions. There was no indication in terms of organization or groundwork that would give the general public the impression that he was going to be a candidate in 1952. Yet the public at large still sensed that there was almost no question that he was going to be a candidate for statewide office at some point.

Kenny, like so many others, had thought that Jack would run for governor. As he explained it to his brother Cleo Jr. one evening over a beer at one of their favorite taverns in Harvard Square, "I would rather see the governor clean up the state and have Kennedy bring in his people to do it."

Why? Well, Kenny wasn't stupid. He felt sure Jack would bring him into play. It was not as if they had a close relationship or anything. In truth, Bobby was their connection. But Kenny was a political junkie from way back. Kenny realized that a U.S. senator does not in fact have any organization. To Kenny and many others of his generation, the Senate was a very high office that people did not care too much about. A senator had no real power to affect the average person's life. As Kenny told Helen one night, the

Senate had nothing to offer guys like Kenny. Jack couldn't help anyone if he lost, and Lodge would be tough to beat.

Kenny, like many others of this growing band of brothers, was hopeful that Dever would run against Lodge (they doubted he could win, but he could make a race of it) and that Kennedy would run for governor. That was the expectation, the logical, safe political move for Jack. Kenny felt sure Jack could win, which would mean to do so, he'd have to build a statewide political organization. Kenny felt that was a sure bet for himself and others like him to get involved in politics and influence. Let Dever take the risk of taking on Lodge; Jack should take the "safe political bet."

Unbeknownst to Kenny at the time, and as he would have repeated occasions to learn in the future, Jack Kennedy was not a man who wished for safe harbor. Jack lived for the stiff breeze and the unpredictable swell. The more outrageous and unlikely his chances of success, the better, as far as Jack was concerned. As Kenny would come to know, Jack, on many levels of his life, was a man who simply courted risk.

And it wasn't just Kenny and his band of Irish brothers who were pushing Jack to run for governor; Jack's own guys were, too. Well, they were not really his guys: They belonged to Joe Kennedy. The Old Man and his lieutenants, such as they were, pushed for the safe harbor of the Massachusetts State House. They were even going so far as to slant the internal reports to convince Jack he had no chance in hell against Lodge.

Jack didn't know that yet. It would take Kenny to figure that out. Still, these were the Kennedy men. Jack's nonexistent organization was a void filled by the Old Man's people, who were now running around the state, making connections for Jack and whispering to anyone who would listen that Joe's son was headed for the State House. For his part, Jack was too busy making speeches across Massachusetts with his pal Dave Powers to notice or even care about what his father was up to. Up until now, as with '46 and '48, he had left the organizational side to his father. Everyone was pushing him now, pressing him, talking to him about running for governor. Nobody cared about the Senate.

There were two problems, however, that nobody had counted on: One was Paul Dever, who, as Joe and his men had failed to notice, was not yet ready to leave the State House. The other problem was Jack Kennedy. Kennedy wanted the Senate, so he quietly hoped (and his political gut told him) that Paul Dever wasn't going anywhere.

Jack, who never said a word to anyone about his thoughts or plans for 1952, turned out to be right again. The decision was made for him when the still-popular Democratic governor decided not to risk his political neck in a heavy battle against the entrenched and powerful Henry Cabot Lodge Jr. This left the door open for Jack to run for Senate.

Jack was thrilled. Joe Kennedy was concerned but on board. Kenny O'Donnell, among other men who would later become part of Jack's new team, was surprised but excited by these developments. Even though the Senate was not what they had expected, they were ready to go just the same when Jack called.

"Okay," Kenny said to Helen. "If anyone could make that position relevant, it would be Jack Kennedy."

Jack had few illusions about the difficulty of the coming race. While he had the money to run the race (Joe had seen to that), what he didn't have were the credentials or the necessary name recognition. What he lacked in those two categories he made up for with sheer hard work and audacity.

He began by using his Charlestown pal, Dave Powers, to get the word out that he was available to speak at any place and at any time. He charged no fee, not even expenses. That suddenly made the young congressman very popular. He was a Kennedy: rich, handsome, and a war hero to boot. Powers had no trouble booking him.

Jack set a routine that would vary little as the days and months drew nearer to the announcement of his run for the Senate. Kenny knew the pattern well: Jack would fly into Boston from Washington on Friday afternoons in time to attend various meetings with veterans' groups, fraternal organizations, civic clubs, and school organizations.

On Saturdays, Jack attended every meeting, cut every ribbon that needed cutting, and spoke everywhere he could until his voice began to crack from exhaustion. Sunday mornings, he made sure to hit every Catholic community breakfast. He ate more damn pancakes and drank more bad coffee than anyone could imagine. He would go anywhere: Catholic meetings, Protestant socials, and everything in between.

By Sunday night, Powers would take him to Boston's Back Bay Station, where Jack would board the Amtrak "Federal" and make the long trek down to Washington, DC. His back killing him, Jack would then literally drag himself into a sleeping berth, falling exhausted onto his pillow.

This was not glamorous travel for Jack. For a man used to private planes, New York City hotels, Hyannis Port, and Palm Beach, these stumping tours through Massachusetts marked a good, long step down. The drives were tedious and painful. The motels were small, grimy, and far-flung.

They were often dives with rooms situated down dark, slightly dank corridors. A typical room had only one lousy light bulb affixed over the bed and a questionable bathroom — in the sense that whether one used it or not hinged on tolerance for a certain degree of filth.

With his spine in tatters, his health generally shot, such travel was difficult, but Jack, as he had most of his life, learned to cope. He always had crutches in the car, which he would use when his back really bothered the hell out of him and when nobody was looking. But the minute the door of the VFW hall or church parish opened and the greeting committee arrived, Jack was all smiles. The crutches safely tucked away in the backseat of the car, Jack, with that ever-present Palm Beach tan, would walk with the grace of an athlete, shaking hands firmly even if doing so sent a bolt of pain through his body, right down to his toes. Jack would smile, wave, shake hands, and tell jokes as if he had not a care in the world. Once back in the car and away from prying eyes, he would rest his head back against the seat. Dave, Ted Reardon, or Bob Morey, another Irishman who had been pressed into service as a driver, would watch helplessly while the color drained from

Jack's face and Jack gritted his teeth in agony, the pain coursing through his body violently, shaking him to the core. Then he would open his eyes and begin to discuss the event that just happened, who was who, who had done a good job, who should be deep-sixed. After this debriefing, they would move quickly on to the next event.

When a hellish day was finally over, they would arrive at that night's two-bit flea-ridden motel. Jack would get his crutches out of the back of the car and limp painfully into the room. He would sit in anguish as Dave drew Jack a steaming-hot bath. Then, with Dave's help, Jack would limp to the bathroom and painfully lower himself into the water, allowing it to envelop his body and momentarily ease his torment. He would close his eyes and sit for a moment in silence as the water loosened his tightened muscles and provided a much-needed but only temporary relief.

"He'd be up again the next day at the crack of dawn," Dave recalled to Kenny over a beer, "ready to go make more speeches, shake hands at some factory gate or whatever."

Dave Powers, Bob Morey, and John Galvin, who for the moment any-way represented Jack's team, were awed at his stamina and persistence. This was the beginning of a long pattern. Jack's ambition would drive him and enable him to withstand endless pain, both mental and physical, in pursuit of his goal. The goal right now was to send Senator Lodge into retirement.

In the meantime, Kenny, still unhappily working away at the paper company, now a married man with a son and twins on the way, continued to wait and hope for a political opening. In the meantime, he had bills to pay. Like it or not, he had a job, even if it was a lousy one with a paper company in Somerville.

Bobby had gone on to law school at the University of Virginia and then later took a government job in Washington, DC, that required his full-time attention. Bobby was determined to have his own life, away from his fam-ily and his older brother. But Kenny and Bobby kept in touch by phone, and whenever possible, they would get together to talk politics and Harvard football and would often toss the football around in front of the Kennedy home in Hyannis Port. "What do you two talk about?" Helen would ask with a chuckle. "Politics and football," Kenny answered.

When Jack finally let everyone in on his decision, that he had decided to go for the Senate seat, he needed a staff. It worked well, because Kenny needed a job that he actually cared about. As fate would have it, the timing could not have been better. Bobby knew well that Kenny had been hungering to get into politics, and while Kenny had been initially skeptical of Jack, by now he had been won over.

Bobby had been pushing to get Kenny involved, even arranging what would turn out to be a disaster of a meeting between Kenny and Joe at his apartment at the famed Waldorf Astoria in New York. Kenny went because Helen and Bobby pushed him to meet with The Old Man. Their hope was that Joe could help Kenny get a proper job and perhaps a well-paying one within Joe's own operation. At least that was Helen's hope. Bobby had other motives. Helen had asked him, and Kenny was his pal, so he wanted to help, but Bobby had another agenda as well. Much had changed since the winter of '46, when he wanted Kenny to see Jack's potential and presumably Jack to see that he needed a tough, local political guy like Kenny. Bobby's hope in connecting Kenny and Joe was to get Kenny onto the Kennedy team until Jack knew what he wanted to do next.

Whether Kenny guessed all this, we don't know, but we do know that Kenny agreed to the meeting to keep the peace and took the train down to New York, but he wisely made no promises to either Helen or Bobby.

The trip was a very expensive one for Kenny at that time. A trip to New York might well mean they'd have to miss some meals. This was not a small thing for the O'Donnells.

"But Helen and I talked, and she felt I should go. I went down to New York and I had my only white interview shirt. I went down on the sleeper, 'The Federal,' at night, to New York. I had one clean shirt in a paper bag, and I was going to change when I got to New York, so I would look my best when I went to see Mr. Kennedy. This would really be my first official meeting with him seeking employment. I will tell you, I told Helen, I will hear what he has to say, see if he has some advice, some connection, but I made clear, I made one vow before I left Boston: I would not go to work for the Kennedy family or for Joe Kennedy under any circumstances, because I just knew it was a bad idea. It would not work. I was and remain a very independent fellow."

Kenny arrived at the Waldorf Astoria on time. "The Old Man was in the towers," he recalled, chuckling about it later. "I remember thinking, as I walked through the lobby, about General MacArthur and all of that. I remember I had the shirt in a paper bag and I walked up to the desk and said, 'I want to see Ambassador Kennedy.' The man was snotty, as they always are, and he gave me a dirty look. He said, 'Well, I doubt he wants to see you. After all, who are you anyway?' Then he looked me up and down. I wanted to punch him. So he finally calls Joe Kennedy, who says yes, send him right in. Well, he was astonished. I was mad. I handed him my paper bag and said, 'Jeeves, hold this till I get back. Don't lose it.' He took it like it was a piece of dirty linen. It was funny.

"I went to see the father, and I was reasonably uncomfortable, ill at ease, and knew instinctively this was not my cup of tea, but it was too late, so I went ahead. Joe Kennedy came out and asked me, 'What are you going to do?' Now remember, he sent for me. I said, 'I don't know; I might go to law school next year. I have a couple of offers.' Now remember, he sent for me. Then he said, 'No, you are going to work for Jack.' I told him I had no interest in going to work for his son's congressional office. The Old Man shook his head and sat down. 'Jack,' he said, 'has bigger plans.'"

Overall, the meeting was testy and uncomfortable. Kenny walked away, by his own choice, empty-handed and empty-stomached, taking the long train ride back to Boston to tell Helen he'd told the Old Man to go to hell in so many words. But he had come away knowing one thing: His political gut had been right; Jack had bigger plans. Now all Kenny could do was wait and hope to be included. With his stomach growling and a wife and children at home, he'd have to find a way to make a living while waiting for Jack to make his decision.

While Bobby was not terribly surprised at Kenny's refusal to take a job with Joe Kennedy, he remained determined to get him involved in Jack's campaign. Whatever that was. Only Jack knew for sure at the moment. Kenny had come away from the meeting with Joe convinced that even Joe did not know for sure what Jack would do. It was clear what Joe wanted him to do, but Kenny was increasingly seeing that Jack was, like himself, a rather independent fellow. But Bobby was determined. He felt it was the perfect opportunity for both men. Jack needed a tough, reliable political antenna, a right-hand guy who would always play it straight with him and someone he could completely trust. Kenny wanted to see a candidate for Massachusetts senator in whom he could place his full confidence. He wanted a candidate with a future, who represented their generation, the returning war veterans who believed that they would have to get involved in order to change the direction of this country. They would need and indeed wanted a stake in the direction of the future of the country they had fought for and seen so many friends give their very lives to protect. This new generation of Americans—Jack, Kenny, and Bobby's generation—was ready for somebody new to represent their views and, as Kenny said, "be their voice."

Kenny said that Jack Kennedy came to represent the opportunity for change. "We were unhappy with the status quo and John Kennedy became a symbol to our generation. He was certainly more so for me, because I knew the family. I would say that the Irish in general were fascinated by the wealthy Kennedys, and that helped. Frankly, had he run for dogcatcher, people would have wanted to know more. What made people pay attention to Jack Kennedy as a congressman was not the job. It was the man."

While Jack had made the decision to run for something, nobody informed Joe Kennedy that he wasn't the one managing the campaign. Jack had envisioned this as his own campaign and a new beginning. While he respected all that his grandfather Honey Fitz and his father had accomplished, they were as much a part of the past in Jack's mind as the hangers-on who constituted the Boston political machine run by Paul Dever. He had been content to let his father run the show in '46 and '48. Jack had yet to completely invest himself in the House. Now, whether it was running for Senate or for the governorship, he was ready to make that personal investment.

When he was in the House, everyone had told Jack to politically "marry" Speaker John McCormack: Have dinner with him every night; be his new best friend. Jack had been horrified. While Jack respected McCormack, to his mind McCormack represented a dead end and the past. From Jack's perspective, it was time for these older guys to step off the stage.

"Don't get me wrong here," Jack explained to one longtime pal. "I love my dad. I respect him. But I don't need his help. I just need him to write the checks." And write the checks he did.

Jack would even occasionally ask Joe for advice. He rarely took it, but he always asked.

When the invitation came to join Jack's campaign, Kenny was ready. He was bored out of his mind and still working for the paper company and chomping at the bit to get out. It came in the form of a call from Bobby. Kenny was headed to New York for a paper convention. Bobby would be in Brooklyn working with old football pal Jimmy Noonan on a case and wanted to talk to Kenny. At the time, 1951–1952, Bobby was happily working away for Jimmy McNerney at the Department of Justice. These were happy years for Bobby. Kenny and Bobby agreed to meet in Brooklyn at Bobby's temporary office there.

"Now," Kenny said later, "there is no question in my mind that Bobby's offer was because he wanted to help me. He knew of my great interest in politics, but no question in my mind this came from Bobby. Not Jack. Bobby and I had been talking about politics all our lives. He knew Jack was going to need someone. I met Bobby over at his office in Brooklyn. We chatted about politics and went out dinner, had some drinks."

It was January 1952. "Bobby asked me if I would do it, work for Jack. I said I would be delighted to. I would go see Jack when [Jack] came up to Boston. Sure. Why not, I said to Bobby. Bobby laughed. I then asked Bobby, 'Do I have a task?'"

Bobby shrugged and said, "I have no idea. You have to ask my brother."

"So," Kenny said, "it is clear they have no idea what I am supposed to be doing, since Jack has not chosen which office to run for yet, because he still had to wait for Paul Dever to decide whether to run for Senate or governor. Then Jack would run for whichever seat he did not. But frankly there was no question in my mind or Helen's: Bobby's interest was strictly personal in helping me. The truth was, in my view, Jack Kennedy would not remember me and would not consider that I would know anything about politics. I just simply could not conceive of this coming from him."

The next call was from Jack four or five days later. "He called me and asked to see me. I went to see him at the Federal Building in Boston. He was very vague. I asked him what he was going to run for. He said he had not made up his mind but was clearly very irritated that I would be asking questions of this variety of the candidate. He was operating a two-office setup. He had been working the field; he now had these reports as they came in. I was to go to work then with a fellow named Mark Dalton, who had his office right across from the Federal Building at 10 Post Office Square."

"When can you start?" Jack asked.

"Tomorrow," was Kenny's terse reply.

"Good," was all Jack said.

The next day, Kenny headed out from his Winthrop home (they had moved to the shore to accommodate their growing family) to the Kennedy headquarters in Boston to work on the campaign for an office Jack had not yet chosen. Kenny's life was about to change forever. For that matter, so was Bobby's.

What Bobby could not have known was just how much getting Kenny to say yes would change his own trajectory so completely. Years later, when Sandy Vanocur asked Kenny if he had known, if he had thought this through, Kenny could only smile, that tight-lipped, just-around-the-edges kind of smile, almost as if he had known all along.

CHAPTER 4

The Upset

WHEN KENNY ARRIVED at the newly minted Kennedy headquarters at 10 Post Office Square, he found two things that scared the crap out of him. The first was Mark Dalton, a slightly built, sensitive young man with the best of intentions but the wrong temperament for a rough-and-tumble political campaign.

Kenny recalled, "Dalton was an Irish fellow from a very lovely family. His brother wrote for the *Herald Traveler*. The family was a Boston College, Irish, and well-known family. He has a good practice. He was the lawyer at this time for the Boston Teachers Union. I think he probably still is. He also ran cram courses for the law school. But an extreme intellectual. Smoked a pipe, tall, thin, very nervous fellow. Nervous all the time. Just talking to him about the time of day, he'd get nervous." Kenny feared, correctly, that Joe Kennedy and his political lieutenants would eat him for breakfast.

Among those lieutenants was Frank Morrissey, the Old Man's chief "coat holder," who was running Jack's office in the Federal Building. Kenny had been there only about twenty-four hours and realized there was a real conflict.

"Immediately, I saw we had a real problem. It is evident that Morrissey was attempting to torpedo Dalton and wants him out. Morrissey was working for the Old Man. So the father is out to torpedo Dalton. He could not control Dalton, so they are out to torpedo him. Just a mess. Not the kind of atmosphere that wins campaigns."

The second thing he found was utter and complete chaos. Because Dalton was spending so much time fighting for his political life at the campaign, the campaign itself was in chaos.

Kenny said, "There was no structure, no assignments, no strategy, no plans."

Jack had worked his butt off to raise his profile across the state, but he had not done a damn thing about building a statewide organization. Of course, not knowing which office he was running for, governor or senator, might have had something to do with it. Years later, Kenny would come to realize that while Joe, Bobby, Kenny, and others were wondering which office Jack would go for, Jack made clear he never had a doubt. He had always planned on the Senate.

The truth was, in Kenny's view, "I think Jack very definitely had a preference for the Senate, but he could not move until Dever made up his mind. He was going to go talk to Dever and then whatever Dever picked to run for, governor or Senate, Jack would pick the other. Now, Jack had already talked to Dever once and Dever had blown him off as a joke. He would not give him an answer.

"There was no question Jack wanted to run for the Senate, but he realized that the governorship would be much easier. Lodge will be a very tough candidate. At this time Lodge is in the midst of the presidential nomination, waiting to see if Eisenhower would be the nominee, but as I recall, Ike was very strong. One could not imagine him not getting the nod."

Kenny was well aware that once the conversation between Jack and Dever took place, Jack's decision would be made. Governor Dever did not unfairly prolong that conversation and make Jack wait too long. Dever made clear he would stay and run once more for governor.

Kenny recalled, "Dever and I became close and he told me that he had made the decision just based on the cold hard political reality that he would not be able to defeat Lodge. Dever believed that if anyone could possibly beat Lodge, it would be Kennedy."

However, Dever later confided to Kenny that even then he did not really believe Jack could win.

Jack later told Kenny that Dever had told him he "ought to run for Senate, that he would be well financed, obviously, since he had his own money and he could take on Lodge; that he was quite pleased to have him on the ticket as the candidate for the Senate. He also told him that . . . [he] ought to build his own organization. What he meant by that was, you are not going to get any of mine and we won't help you, because they could not care less who was running for Senate and the truth was, as [Jack] told me, 'I realized at that moment he did not believe I could win, well financed or not, so politically he was not going to extend himself.'"

There was no antagonism to it all, as Kenny later reflected, "hell, I think largely because of the Old Man. Joe Kennedy had a strong influence on the relationship not getting hostile. Dever liked [Joe Kennedy], but the truth was, Dever, like much of the political establishment, was not thrilled with the son. They thought [Jack] was not serious, not willing to pay his dues, wait his turn, that he was too young and arrogant. But the Old Man understood this, and he and Dever and politicians like Dever sort of talked the same language. I am sure that Joe Kennedy had been helpful to Dever in his campaigns. Dever's contact generally was with the father. But very little with Jack. After the original conversation where the decision was made, I think Jack maybe talked to Dever six times after that. He had no use for Dever and I think Dever felt the same. He liked the father but not the son very much."

It was still early in terms of campaign cycles, but until Dever decided in those early months, nobody knew what the campaign was for. As far as Kenny could see, "the only thing they did was work on speeches. Mark Dalton was basically a speechwriter and helped Jack with his speeches. Bill Gavin was a public relations man. When [Jack] would come up in the state, they would do some work; when he did not, none of them did. They didn't work unless he was there. Morrissey did nothing but snoop. It was chaos. It was not a long period of time from the time I came to the office when he made his decision and announced. Maybe a couple of weeks or a month. Dever and Jack had their meeting. The decision was made."

Still the chaos remained. The internal office politics, which included slanted political reports from a team sent by Joe Kennedy to influence Jack's decision, was Kenny's first assignment. He read the reports and knew immediately they were, as he put it, "a lot of crap."

As Kenny read the political reports, which were clearly designed to push Jack to the governorship, Kenny was disgusted. "I was not well versed enough in state politics to make an accurate judgment of the reports, but my instinct told me they were wrong. I was versed enough to make a judgment on their ability to write the reports and it told me something was wrong. These made no sense to me, just on the local areas; they called the wrong people, and my follow-up calls proved they were wrong. My own judgment at this point was that if this was his organization, Jack was in real trouble. None of these people were up to the job. Dalton was an intellectual. Nice guy. Pipe-smoking academic, but he didn't have instinct for the political jugular required to get Jack Kennedy elected to the Senate. They pushed him around, lied to him and laughed at him. I knew the Dever guys; they were not nice fellows and they saw Dalton as a joke."

The one good thing that came out of this period was a follow-up call Kenny made to a well-respected Irishman who worked for Foster Furcolo, one of the most prominent Italian politicians in the state. Furcolo, who was then in the House of Representatives, was eyeing the treasurer's office and, rumor had it, wanted the governorship.

Kenny wanted to suss things out for Jack, so he put a call in to one of Furcolo's top political guys, a fellow named Larry O'Brien. Based on their political conversation, Kenny sensed that he had met what he later called "a Kennedy man."

Kenny arranged to meet O'Brien as soon as possible. But the truth remained that, back at 10 Post Office Square in Boston, nobody knew what to do next. Jack was never there and Mark Dalton was out of the office at the Boston Athenæum. He was there reading and trying desperately to avoid Joe Kennedy and Jack Morrissey as much as possible.

"It is utter chaos," Kenny griped over the phone to Bobby, who was still in Washington enjoying the hell out of his government job and his freedom. "Now we know what he is running for, but he still does not have an organization."

"So fix it. Isn't that your job?" Bobby snapped in return.

No, technically that was not his job, Kenny complained to his wife, Helen. He still did not know Jack Kennedy that well and wasn't comfortable telling Mark Dalton he was incompetent or even just mentioning Dalton's incompetence to Jack.

Jack seemed as wary of Kenny as Kenny had been initially skeptical of him. Jack didn't give Kenny any authority to make decisions. Not wanting to step in and kick Mark Dalton around, Kenny waited for a sign from Jack. It never came. Kenny waited a few more weeks, biding his time to see if the situation improved. It didn't. Instead it got worse, courtesy of Jack's well-intentioned father.

Sensing the confusion and leadership vacuum that he had helped create, seeing an opening, and needing a mission, the Old Man moved in with full force and began to take over the campaign. He brought with him a cadre of his old-time political cronies. The cronies included Tammany Hall–type politicians such as Jim Farley and Ed Flynn, both former Franklin Roosevelt presidential campaign men from 1932.

Kenny was both appalled and pissed. Because Kenny felt he was not yet in a position to intervene directly, all he could do was wait and hope things improved. They didn't. Joe's guys sniped relentlessly at Dalton. They were on his butt about everything, from the lack of pencils to his decision to buy more pencils. Their complaints ranged from the petty to the significant, and Kenny watched the griping and backbiting with increasing dismay. What was worse, Jack was never there. He was on the road with Powers, Morey, and Galvin, introducing himself to the public.

Jack had no clue that his campaign was in disarray. "I am telling you," complained Kenny to fellow football pal Nick "the Greek" Rodis, "there is a serious chance this fucking campaign will never get off the ground."

"Call Bobby," Nick countered; the answer seemed obvious to him. Kenny decided Nick might be right.

"Viewing the chaos around me," Kenny explained to Bobby over dinner and drinks, having caught up with him in New York, where Bobby was still working on his first big-time federal case, "I decided nobody can talk to the Old Man or Jack but another Kennedy family member. It is not my place. You have to come. Only a Kennedy can tell another Kennedy to go to hell."

Bobby was not pleased and balked immediately. "Don't drag me into it," he groaned at Kenny. "I don't want to get involved."

Frustrated, Kenny realized he would have to be patient and keep pushing Bobby to change his mind. He was going to have to bide his time and find just the right moment. Over the course of the coming days, Kenny called Bobby twice. Bobby was increasingly dismayed by what he was hearing from Kenny. During the second call, Bobby told Kenny there was nothing he could do. Kenny sensed he was losing the argument.

"Dammit, Bobby!" Kenny growled through the phone, his voice dropping low, barely above a whisper. "More than the campaign organization is in a mess! Dalton can't handle your father. There is nobody to run the campaign the way Jack wants it, and Jack is doing nothing to straighten it out. If he doesn't make an effort to straighten it out, I am telling you right now there will not be any damn campaign."

The friends sat in angry silence.

Bobby finally heard him. Kenny waited patiently. He knew Bobby well enough to know that he would make the right decision. He only had to give him the time to make it on his own.

Finally, Bobby said quietly and firmly, "I will talk to my father."

Kenny and Helen were happy in their small house in Winthrop, a tiny community right on the ocean, not far from downtown Boston and Kennedy's chaotic headquarters. It was Saturday and Kenny was on the local golf course. Kenny, not really a golfer, was having the best round of golf in his life when he heard his name being called out by one of the pages at the club. Bobby was on the phone for him. Kenny headed toward the clubhouse. "Now what?" he wondered aloud.

"There you are, playing golf," Bobby snapped, "and here I am with Jack, my mother, and my sisters at a big tea party in the heart of Quincy. I hope you are satisfied!"

Kenny chuckled. "Mildly," Kenny said.

"Not funny," Bobby snapped. "Get down here right away! I want you to tell Jack some of the stuff you've been telling me."

Kenny hung up. He stood for a minute by the phone, letting a smile begin at the corners of his mouth. This was good. This was very good. Kenny turned on his heel, tipped the boy who had brought the message, and headed for Quincy. Now Jack's campaign could really begin.

Kenny strode through the doors of the Quincy Armory, pushing his way past rows of well-coiffed women bathed in perfume who had just had tea with Jack and his family, their faces still flushed with excitement.

Kenny could tell immediately that Jack was pissed. Jack's handsome face was drawn tightly, bringing even more emphasis to his green eyes, which were now ice-cold. *He looked*, Kenny thought to himself, *like he was going to pop me right here.*

Jack waited till the tea ended, then ordered Kenny to ride back to Boston with him and his brother Bobby. Frank Morrissey, Joe Kennedy's right-hand guy, whose principal job in the campaign was to snoop and report back to the Old Man, was told to get a ride with someone else. Morrissey stood at the curb, disappointment etched on his face, as Jack, Kenny, and Bobby pulled away.

Jack, sitting in the front passenger seat, turned around to face Kenny and Bobby in the backseat. He seemed to gather himself as if trying to control his temper. When he spoke, his voice was low, cold, and measured.

"What the hell is wrong with you?" Jack growled. "What the hell have you been telling Bobby?"

Kenny shot a look at Bobby. Bobby shrugged. He had not wanted to come, but he had because Kenny had called. Kenny had said that Jack was in trouble, and based on Kenny's call alone, Bobby had dropped everything and come back to Massachusetts. Bobby was clearly not planning to help Kenny on this one.

Now it was up to Kenny to confront Jack. Kenny was not easily intimidated. He had jumped out of planes behind enemy lines three times in his military career, gotten shot in the leg, and flown over enemy territory, taking fire the whole time. Kenny was the kind of guy who would look you straight in the eye and tell you he was coming right at you. The problem was, Jack Kennedy was the same kind of guy. This was new to Kenny. He was used to giving someone "the look," as it became known, and watching him back down. At that moment, though, it was Kenny who was receiving "the look." Bobby said nothing.

"I told him," Kenny began, his voice equally low, focused, and intense, his black eyes just as cold, meeting Jack's stare without flinching, "that I've been waiting for two months for us to get a statewide Kennedy organization, and we haven't got one yet. You know we're not supposed to use Dever's people—you don't want them, and he doesn't want you to use them. You announced that you were running for the Senate the first Monday in April. Here it is the end of May, and we haven't appointed a single Kennedy chairman or organizer in any city in Massachusetts."

As Kenny finished, it dawned on him that this was indeed the first time he was actually speaking to Jack about politics or, for that matter, the campaign. For the past two months Jack had been on the road across Massachusetts almost constantly, and Kenny had been left at 10 Post Office

Square, watching helplessly as the Old Man and his pals stomped the hapless but well-meaning Dalton into the ground. Already, Kenny reasoned, Bobby's presence had made a difference.

"You're supposed to be doing those things!" Jack snapped. "As far as I am concerned, you can go ahead and start naming anybody you want. That's what we hired you for. It's not my job, for Christ's sake."

Jack's sharp response brought Kenny back to reality. Both Kenny and Jack were getting heated. This was not how Kenny had figured their working relationship would begin. Still, despite being used to intimidating other people, Kenny liked that Jack had no intention of taking crap from anyone, including Kenny.

"All right," Kenny replied tersely. "As of tomorrow morning, we start naming chairmen of local 'Kennedy for Senate' committees all over the state."

"Jesus," Jack fumed, "I thought you were doing that all along. I don't know what the hell else you've been doing over there."

Kenny grimaced but said nothing. Bobby smirked and stared straight ahead. Bobby knew Kenny had gotten the two things he wanted. The first was the authority to name the chairmen and begin building a state organization. The second thing he had gotten was Bobby. And Bobby knew the faith Kenny had placed in him, that his presence would mean the difference between success and failure.

"Why?" Nick the Greek had asked Kenny later that evening at their usual spot.

"Because Bobby is Bobby," Kenny said. He is just that damned good." To Jack's later surprise, Kenny had been right on target. It would be Bobby's first political campaign, but certainly not his last, and it would be the beginning of a bond of ambition and brotherly ties between Jack, Bobby, and Kenny.

Bobby was indeed a damned good organizer, and what the campaign needed right now was a tough-minded, top-notch organizer. The campaign also needed someone who could stand in for the candidate, stand up to the entrenched political bureaucracy, and perhaps most important stand up to Joe Kennedy and his cadre of political hangers-on. The only person who could do all those things and do it well was Bobby. Despite his anger, even Jack could see this was true.

From Kenny's point of view, Bobby's presence on the campaign allowed Kenny the freedom and authority to put together the statewide organization that he knew Jack wanted and needed in order to win. The race for Senate had finally begun.

Kenny, or "Black" as he was known to the gridiron gang, now had the job of a lifetime. Of course, two things made a big difference: Jack finally knew what office he was running for, and Bobby was campaign manager.

"Sure," Kenny said to Nick, "Bobby was a kid, could be a pain in the ass, but his organizational skills were unmatched."

Anyone who had played football with Bobby knew that was true enough. He had no manners, but that was not a problem for Kenny. Mark Dalton, whom Bobby sent packing as the first order of business, was the nicest fellow you would ever want to meet but definitely out of his depth.

Kenny told Bobby point-blank, "Look, Dalton is a saint and ought to be in Rome, but he sure is not the guy to deal with the Dever guys. They push him around, lie to him, and laugh at him." Egged on by Morrissey, they treated Dalton as the punch line to every joke.

The truth was, Frank Morrissey, the Old Man's coat-holding snitch and backstabber, and the other political pros working for Joe Kennedy had eaten Dalton for breakfast and spit him out.

"No," Kenny stated flat-out, "Bobby would never be accused of being smooth, but that was hardly what was needed right now."

What they needed was someone who could make decisions while Jack and Dave were on the road, give Kenny the direction he needed, and finally stand up to Joe Kennedy.

Morrissey was furious. He'd been mad as hell when Jack had hired Kenny without his permission or foreknowledge. If he had been consulted, which he wasn't, Morrissey would have alerted the Old Man, who would have taken one look at O'Donnell, his tough-talking, rough-around-the-edges background, and said no.

Morrissey was hysterical when Kenny strode through the door that first day. He was on the phone right away to the Old Man.

Kenny had chuckled to himself as he watched Morrissey's frantic, whispered conversation over the telephone to the Old Man. He had gotten to know Morrissey during school breaks at Harvard when Jack had first been elected to Congress. Jack had been great, stellar really, about getting Bobby's football buddies jobs and favors at the Post Office. Kenny and Bobby would always refer their friends to Jack's Massachusetts office. Morrissey was always hovering around, sniffing out gossip, and reporting back to the Old Man.

Everyone knew him. Kenny and Bobby knew exactly what he was and what he was about. They had no use for him. Kenny had made that plain to Morrissey then and would do so again now, if necessary. Kenny knew Morrissey's general reputation around Boston: He never came through for anybody on anything. In the end, Kenny made it clear to Morrissey that he would not be pushed around the way Morrissey had played Dalton. The games were over now.

When Bobby came in the door, Morrissey was really done. Bringing Bobby on board was a beautiful power play on Kenny's part. Kenny watched with amusement as Morrissey tried to undo the inevitable. But he could not. Frank Morrissey's days were numbered and he knew it.

Jack had not asked Morrissey or his father for permission to build his own campaign; he had just gone and done it, hiring Kenny first. Unexpectedly calling Kenny one day, Jack had asked him to come on board. Kenny immediately agreed, knowing that Bobby would be delighted to hear that his friend was now working for Jack. At the time Bobby probably hadn't expected that Kenny would walk into a mess, only to turn around and convince him to work for Jack, too, in a desperate effort to straighten out the campaign.

Morrissey didn't want Bobby in the way. He could not play his games with both Kenny and Bobby floating around, sticking their noses where they didn't belong. It was Joe Kennedy's money and his call. Who needed Bobby? He was a nice kid and all, but he was just that, a kid. What did he know about politics, and Boston politics at that? Morrissey knew that he and the Old Man had Jack's future in their hands; they didn't need O'Donnell or his pals around, and they sure as hell didn't need Bobby.

The first thing Kenny and Bobby had to do was send Morrissey packing, along with the rest of Joe's old-fashioned cronies.

"If you are not going to work, get out!" Bobby had ordered, rather rudely and unceremoniously. Kenny just shook his head and chuckled. You had to love Bobby. Statesmanship was not his strength, that's for sure. But then Kenny knew that already. That's why he wanted Bobby here. What Jack needed was action, not a bunch of talkers and old-timers.

The political hangers-on, encouraged by Morrissey, were not amused. They complained to Joe Kennedy, who was caught between his sons and his friends. Any observer could guess how that went. As Kenny suspected, the Old Man took his sons' side and retreated quietly, albeit temporarily, to develop a different strategy. In the meantime, Kenny, now accompanied by the newly acquired Larry O'Brien, began to name Kennedy secretaries all across the state. All this should have been good news to Joe Kennedy (and, for that matter, Paul Dever), but it wasn't.

O'Donnell and O'Brien were picking new people, mostly untested, untried young vets, political newbies like themselves who had no experience and, more important, owed, as Morrissey groused, "nothing to nobody." Of course, that was the brilliance in Bobby, Kenny, and Larry's plan.

Very deliberately, the three of them reached out for people who had no predetermined political ties and fresh faces representing their generation of returned war vets who had had enough of the status quo in both political parties. These were guys in search of a politician they could relate to.

In addition, the Kennedy for Senate campaign received no help from the Dever organization. They knew Paul Dever did not really want Jack to succeed. Dever truly did not believe that Lodge was beatable; if he had, hell, he would have run against him. Dever thought that Jack Kennedy would make a decent run and make a name for himself in losing. He was young, he would lose, but he could live to fight another day. So why would he, as governor and head of the Democratic Party in Massachusetts, waste the talents of his own well-established, time-tested organization by loaning it out to Jack Kennedy?

No matter; Bobby, Kenny, and Larry had another plan. They knew what Dever's strategy was. It was politics. They could hardly blame the guy. Nevertheless, if Dever wasn't going to allow them to use his guys (and the truth was that Kenny and Bobby did not want to use his guys anyway), then Jack would have to build his own organization outside the establishment. They had in mind a network of upstart Kennedy supporters who would fan out across the state, working to get local men in each district who reflected Kennedy's own audacity and desire for change.

Worcester was as good an example as any of the newly minted Kennedy strategy in action. It was Kenny's hometown, and he had a personal stake in Jack's success there. Worcester would be the first time he really understood that Jack had "something," a special charisma that Kenny had never quite seen before. While it was still early, Kenny was now convinced that, if they made no mistakes, they could beat Henry Cabot Lodge.

To make things work in Worcester, they first had to get past a lovely, affable, but determined Kennedy cousin by the name of Polly Fitzgerald, who, as Kenny explained, "seemed to be the main wheel on this thing." It almost didn't happen.

Kenny had never met Polly before, but she was formidable. She'd been working with Jack's well-heeled Harvard classmate Torbert "Torby" Macdonald, and events had become more of a social affair than a political one. Torby was the friend of Jack's who had staffed the local Kennedy campaign in Worcester. This meant he had simply called up another old Harvard classmate, a fellow lawyer from Worcester, and asked him to be secretary. Unfortunately, everyone in Worcester hated the guy, and he was, oddly enough, a Republican to boot. It was a disaster in the making.

Polly and Torby meant well but had no clue what the demographics for the Worcester event were. Polly's idea was to put on a lovely high-society tea for Jack and his family.

"It would play right into the Dever crowd's hands," Kenny explained to Bobby. "They were looking for this kind of stumble so they could attack Jack Kennedy as a faker, a rich man's son, and worst of all 'lace curtain Irish.'"

Dave Powers later said that this first event in Worcester was critical, because it started things off, set the tone. He for one, as a blue-collar, three-decker Irishman who had been with Jack since '46, felt these receptions were a success "because the only thing these poor working folks ever got in the mail was a bill."

Powers went on to explain, "When some of these people got an invitation to have tea with the Kennedys, they were amazed. It was great, because these are all very poor people, and it gave them a sense of importance they might never have had otherwise. There was nothing the working-poor Irish liked more than a rich Irishman who had done well, someone they could look up to, brag about, and be proud of."

Jack Kennedy fit the bill. While the teas were a genius political move, Dave and Kenny understood that the teas were not meant for the people whom Polly and Torby were inviting.

Jack did not need to impress a bunch of rich Republicans who would not vote for him anyway. He needed to impress, as Kenny said, "Mary Gromoli," as an example, "the working-class Italian lady who has five kids, her husband works in the factory, and she gets to buy her first new dress in a year in order to go have tea with the Kennedy family."

But Polly Fitzgerald was strong-willed and had a vision for how she wanted the teas done. She consulted with a well-known social climber in Worcester, and they came up with a list of rich Irish locals. If you were rich and Irish in Worcester at that time, it meant you were a Republican.

Kenny told Bobby, "This isn't going to work."

"Fine," Bobby agreed. "Then you fix it."

Bobby convinced his father that it should be Kenny who went up there to Worcester to, as Bobby put, "turn the thing around."

Kenny, thrilled, headed to Worcester, bunked at his family home, and spent some time with his dad, who gave him the inside story on the guy running the Kennedy campaign in the area. His name was William Maher. He was rich, disliked by the working-class Worcester Irish, and, just as Kenny had suspected, a Republican.

The list Maher had come up with was completely wrong—not the regular, working-poor Irishmen and -women. There wasn't an Italian or a Polish name in sight. Even Helen's Swedish mother had been excluded.

Kenny called Maher and met him at the local drugstore in Tatnuck Square, just down the street from the O'Donnell homestead at 1301 Pleasant Street. Maher had suggested the country club, and Kenny had quietly decided, for this suggestion alone, the guy had to go.

"No," Kenny made clear, "the drugstore down the street." Kenny sat, arms folded, and listened to Maher's explanation. Then, with what would become known as Kenny's trademark curtness, he told the poor sap in no uncertain terms, "This is a list of the biggest fakers and climbers in Worcester. Your list is out. So are you."

"I'm not going to have some friend of Bobby's interfering in my event! You are not telling me what to do!" Maher hollered at Kenny.

Kenny stood, finished his coffee, and put on his suit coat. "Tough. Your list is out, and so are you."

Maher raised hell. He called Torby, Polly, and Morrissey, who called the Old Man. But it didn't matter. The chief of Jack Kennedy's Irish Brotherhood had found his voice and would never look back.

As for Worcester, the weather that day was as flawless as the event itself turned out to be. "It was a beautiful day," Kenny recalled. "The congressman was on crutches. You just stood there and looked at him, and even on crutches he had to be in pain. He walked in, and the room came to a halt. Everyone stared. The electricity was as if he'd hit a switch. I stood there, watching Mary Gromoli and these Worcester ladies. [Mary] takes one look, heads right over, almost running, to shake hands with that young congressman. They all did. He walked in and took over."

Kenny knew his audience. Here was this poor Italian lady wearing a new dress, hat, and gloves that she had paid $100 for, a steep sum in those days. She could not get to Jack fast enough. These were the hardworking poor of Worcester, all dressed up to shake the hands of Jack Kennedy and his family. The place was packed, lines out the door. You could not move. Even Kenny and Helen's parents arrived dressed to the nines, all dolled up like everybody else. And they never came to political events.

Kenny could feel the significance of the moment in his gut. "I knew then, we've got something going here. This guy, he's got it. We could go all the way."

The tea was a huge success. Jack spoke and shook the hand of every single person in that room. It was clear to Kenny that Jack's hand had become swollen from both the crutches and all the grip-and-grin greetings he had made that day. But he pressed on. He stayed the entire time, shook every hand, and listened to every story.

As Kenny watched the congressman get back in his car after the event, his face etched with agony, Kenny grew concerned.

As Kenny recounted the event later to his wife, "This was the first time I realized not only that he had something, but there were some substantial health issues. He was in real pain."

The candidate's health had not been anything he'd considered previously. After all, he'd had only brief glimpses of Jack up until then. Bobby never mentioned any health issues. But Kenny had seen it himself. And it was a heck of lot more than just a bad back. He was worried, not only personally but strategically and politically as well.

Can you elect a candidate that has to be on crutches all the time? Kenny wondered.

His wife had no answers for him. She told him maybe he was overreacting. Kenny did not know the answer either and for the moment at least decided to savor the victory of the day and the success of his political power play.

"Let's not dwell on what might be just a passing issue," Helen had urged him.

At least Kenny hoped that this was all it was.

Now it was time to build an organization. This required a second telephone call to Springfield and once again to that savvy political operator by the name of Lawrence "Larry" O'Brien.

LARRY O'BRIEN ARGUABLY had more political experience than Jack, Kenny, or Bobby put together. O'Brien had grown up in Democratic politics in Springfield and had worked for three years as an administrative assistant for Foster Furcolo. John Foster Furcolo was an Italian American who hailed from the vital western town of Springfield, Massachusetts. A formidable fellow, Furcolo was one of the first Italian American freshman congressmen to be invited, by President Truman, to the White House. Furcolo would go on to be appointed Massachusetts state treasurer by Paul Dever in 1952, and he later became the first Italian American governor of Massachusetts.

O'Brien and Furcolo had recently parted ways under less than amicable circumstances. Kenny thought they had had a falling out so serious that taking on O'Brien would cost him Furcolo's support. Indeed, a rift between Kennedy and Furcolo over O'Brien would simmer for years, eventually becoming a consistent political headache for Jack and Kenny. Still, Kenny explained to Jack, "O'Brien would be worth it."

Kenny had turned out to be correct. Furcolo was livid with Jack for, in his view, choosing O'Brien's side over his, though neither Kenny nor Jack knew what the dispute was about. Furcolo quickly turned on Jack and refused to support him in Western Massachusetts, simply because Jack had hired O'Brien. But, as Kenny argued to Jack, "If you could lose Furcolo that easily, you never had him in the first place." Jack was not pleased, but he was learning, especially after the Worcester incident, to reluctantly trust Kenny's judgment.

"Great," Jack griped at Kenny. "In return for one Irishman, I lose all the Italians. I need another damned Irishman around like I need a fur hat."

Kenny told Jack he'd made the right call. O'Brien's sharp mind, organizational talent, and formidable political skills would prove Kenny correct.

"He was well worth losing Foster Furcolo's support," Kenny said to Jack later. O'Brien was, in Kenny's view, "just that damned talented."

Despite the fact that this decision had cost them the entire Italian vote of Springfield, even Jack could see that O'Brien was worth the sacrifice. Larry was a numbers aficionado, and he and Kenny immediately worked together like hand in glove. It was extraordinary.

Kenny had found his political partner, and a key piece of Jack's Irish Brotherhood had fallen into place. If Kenny was a tough, go-by-the-gut, take-no-prisoners political operator, O'Brien was a numbers genius. He shared with Jack, Kenny, and Bobby a love of political history and an abiding respect for the power of the electorate. An accomplished political strategist, he had a solid knowledge of Massachusetts politics, who the players were, and where they should start, and he had a ready list to call. Dave Powers's role would continue to be what it was from that first meeting in Charlestown: to travel with Jack, stay with Jack always. His role was always personal, not political, but always, Kenny would chuckle, "entertaining."

With Kennedy secretaries now chosen and in place across the state that Jack had, by November, crisscrossed more times than he could remember, the Kennedy team was ready.

As Election Day, November 4, 1952, arrived, they divided the state into two distinct communities. One was Boston proper. The other was composed of the western and midwestern parts of the state, which were worlds apart from Boston politically.

Anyone who knew the western part of the state understood how different it was from Boston. The main problem in Boston was to make sure the workers were all there, that the headquarters and the phones were manned throughout the state, and that the coffee and donuts were plentiful at every voting place.

They were not concerned that they would suffer drastic losses in the outlying areas, as rumors had predicted, but Boston had them worried. General Eisenhower was going to be a very formidable candidate. Making things worse, Governor Dever had been weakened considerably by mistakes and missteps, some of which were not really his doing, but for which as governor he would take the blame. That being the case, and no surprise to Kenny or Larry or Bobby, Jack would not get assistance from the Dever organization.

In other words, as Election Day dawned, Jack's team found themselves isolated and on their own, and not for the last time. There would be no lifeline from the political establishment.

The polls closed, and the Kennedy forces felt that they were in the same position in which they had begun the campaign.

They needed to hold their own in the Democratic areas and hope that, by the extra effort that the candidate had put in over the past six years and the extra emphasis that O'Brien in particular had placed on Boston and the towns where they thought there were Democrats or independents who would be inclined to vote for Jack Kennedy, they might be able to garner more support from the people.

It was an important lesson for the boys. From here on, the Irish Brotherhood would never again place Jack in a situation in which his political success rested on the success of the establishment or anyone else's political fortunes. After this election, the Kennedy team would make their own way, create their own success, and, as Kenny liked to tease Jack, "make their own friends and enemies."

"You two are certainly good at that," Jack said to Kenny and Larry, only half-jokingly, as he stared across the breakfast table in his Boston home base, a one-bedroom apartment at 122 Bowdoin Street.

As the first reports started coming in to headquarters, they were consistent: There was a large voter turnout, and it was about what the guys had anticipated. At the time, this meant nothing to Kenny, Larry, and Bobby.

In Boston and the smaller towns immediately outside it, they were getting some fragmentary returns. They had installed friendly clerks where possible and where both parties would open ballots at a specific time, but this did not mean much except that Jack was getting about what they expected. They were running reasonably even in some districts, getting in others what the normal Democrat might get. And that was okay by them.

The numbers were telling O'Donnell and O'Brien that they were being hurt by President Eisenhower's growing tidal wave and somewhat hurt by Dever. "Hell," O'Brien noted glumly to Kenny, "Dever is not only not helping us, he is actually hurting us at this stage. I am not even sure that we can hold our own in Boston."

Concern among Jack's political team was quietly growing. Jack had bet everything on playing an outsider's game. So when the numbers began to drop or didn't appear at all, Jack had few if any friends or favors he could call in for help. If Jack failed now, it would not only strike a political death-blow to his career, but Kenny, Larry, and a few others would be finished as well.

After all, they had convinced Jack to go it alone. Dump the Old Man, the political henchmen, and the hangers-on. Build a new team, largely of inexperienced but devoted supporters who shared Jack's wartime background and generational sensibility. If Jack failed tonight, it meant more than the loss of just one candidate.

As the polls closed, Bobby, Larry, and Kenny headed to dinner that night in Club 99, a well-known pub: dark, heavy wood fixtures and private booths with nice, well-worn, red leather seats. The 99 was a place where they would go once in a while to have a few drinks and eat a solid, much-needed meal, a welcome break from the stale sandwiches and burnt coffee at Kennedy headquarters. A good place for good food, a few stiff drinks, and, if needed, private talk that would remain within its walls. It was a political hangout owned by John Fox, the publisher of *The Boston Post*. As they chatted with Fox and ate, the first returns began to come in.

It was not the size of the vote that mattered to the Irish Brotherhood—it was that they were staying in range of Dever, and that was important. It meant that Dever and all the Democrats were polling normally in Boston and that Jack was not being cut by Democrats within the city.

Lodge had carried Boston in 1946; however, first reports were the sena-torial campaign, the governor's campaign, and the state ticket, and from these returns it appeared Jack was indeed, contrary to predictions, holding his own with Dever.

The Brotherhood was now convinced: If they could emerge from Boston with approximately the same numbers that Dever did, Jack would be home free, and they'd have a win.

Having gotten a good meal, some breathing room, and a newfound burst of confidence, they went back to the headquarters with those early numbers in hand. "They were all feeling rather pleased at this point," Kenny joked later.

Once back at headquarters, they began to receive the first phone calls. These came from the city of Lynn, from a handpicked Kennedy secretary named Dan Day. Day, whom Kennedy would later appoint assistant direc-tor of the postal region in New England, was like most of the newly picked Kennedy secretaries: new to politics but a reliable Kennedy man.

Dan told Kenny point-blank, "It appears on the basis of the vote that Eisenhower will carry the city of Lynn by a considerable majority." Lynn normally went about 30 percent Democratic, the rest Republican, but not this time. Kenny and Larry began to worry again about just how close they could stay to Eisenhower if he were going to run that big. Eisenhower had already shown big numbers in the fragmentary returns they had from Charlestown, East Boston, and South Boston precincts, all working-class areas, so this news from Lynn was more unsettling than it normally would be. The early excitement they had shared at Club 99 with John Fox began to give way to growing concern.

By this time, the polls had closed, and the television news reports began. The second city that concerned Kenny was Brockton. Brockton at the time had a population of eighty to one hundred thousand, and the vote split would run about fifty-fifty.

Kenny learned that Eisenhower was carrying Brockton by about twenty thousand and the Republican voter turnout was heavy. This was not good.

On the basis of returns from these two cities, the media began to report or predict a heavy Eisenhower victory in Massachusetts. Sitting in their headquarters, running the numbers with their new system, the Brotherhood could not help but become increasingly concerned. Whatever initial opti-mism had existed disappeared almost immediately.

Just then, Jack called. He had seen the same report and was up in his apartment at 122 Bowdoin Street, just up the hill from the headquarters and across from the State House. He spoke with Bobby and confirmed that he was getting some pretty grim reports as well. Reports were coming in from their father's friends, men whom Jack's guys had pushed aside, and the news was not good.

Bobby, Kenny, and Larry had set up a chart to calculate the returns based on how Massachusetts had been carried by President Truman in 1948. They had gone down other traditional avenues of electoral prediction but had thrown them all out after deciding that the 1948 race was indeed the best measure of the kind of upset Democratic victory they hoped to pull off in their state. It didn't make sense for them to model their predictions on the '46 Senate race when Lodge had beaten Walsh. Everyone had expected those results. But in '48 Truman had come from behind, shocking the hell out of most people. If Jack could be shown to run as well as President Truman, they would win. It was that simple. Any serious fall from this standard and they were in deep trouble.

They had recruited a numbers guru, Ned Dewey, who had been a classmate of Kenny's at Harvard.

Dewey knew next to nothing about politics but could run a slide rule like nobody's business. The Kennedy team's transition into the "smooth, highly technical, real first-class Kennedy operation" that the rest of America would value in coming years was, as Kenny joked, due to this fellow who owned a computer. But it was due to something else as well: Larry and Kenny's decision to use as a guide the numbers from Harry Truman's unexpected presidential win in 1948. In addition, Larry and Kenny were on the telephones. They would get a return from, for instance, Lynnfield, and Dewey would compute just the percentages. Every call they got, they ignored the totals and placed the percentages on a chart.

While television was reporting returns, these really didn't mean anything unless you looked at the overall percentages. The projection by ten o'clock was that Eisenhower had carried the state by a quarter million. It was a substantial and stunning majority.

The television networks were making broad predictions, based on Eisenhower's strong run in the state, that the entire Democratic ticket was in jeopardy.

Jack was watching these same TV reports in his apartment. The news was increasingly pessimistic. Alarmed, he would call Bobby. And Bobby would become more and more upset after talking to his brother each time. In his worry and near panic, Bobby would then demand answers from Kenny and Larry.

Despite the increasingly dour reports, Kenny and Larry would chart the numbers from the calls, including the congressman's. Based on the chart, it was clear that Jack was consistently running as well as Truman in '48, if not a little better. And this was in the small, more Republican-leaning communities where Dever was running below Jack and where Democratic presidential candidate Adlai Stevenson was running far below him.

Despite the official reports, therefore, Kenny and Larry remained cautious but optimistic. Listening to the divergent information, Jack kept calling Bobby, confused by the difference between the numbers in the news reports and the percentages he was getting from his campaign headquarters. "Where the hell are you getting these numbers?" Jack demanded.

It was not that he didn't find some solace in the numbers; sure, they showed him winning, but Jack did not want to be set up as a fool. He was worried that his guys, tough and eager though they were, might be too inexperienced to know what they were doing. Jack was concerned that they were telling him what they thought he wanted to hear rather than what was real. Maybe they were kidding him; maybe they were kidding themselves.

Jack was getting his numbers from the media and from his father, and they all had him losing. Could the pros really be wrong? Bobby tried to explain, but he would not or could not understand O'Donnell and O'Brien's system, so his explanation only left Jack more confused and suspicious.

Jack kept saying to Bobby, "Look, these are reporters, newspaper men, Dad and his contacts. These are professionals." Still, Bobby insisted that Kenny and Larry were right. Jack was going to win.

Frustrated, Jack talked to Kenny. "Come on!" he argued. "Where are you getting this stuff?"

"I don't know whom you are talking to," Kenny countered, "but they are wrong." Jack slammed the phone down in frustration.

As the evening wore on they were picking up a steady stream of positive numbers, not huge, but they did not need huge numbers to win. In Brookline, 5 percent. The same in Newton. And on the numbers went, small but steady, running just as the Truman '48 model had suggested. The big cities had still not come in yet. By twelve o'clock that night, the media concluded that Eisenhower had carried the state by at least two hundred thousand votes.

John Barry at *The Boston Globe*: "On the basis of the returns now received by the Boston Globe, it is definite that Governor Dever has been defeated for Governor of Massachusetts and that Congressman John F. Kennedy has been defeated and Senator Lodge has been re-elected to the United States Senate."

Well, all hell broke loose. Jack called Bobby, furious. Bobby cut him off and said, "Look, on the basis of our numbers and our chart and the basis of our computations, we are winning the race, and if this trend continues with little drop-off, we will defeat Lodge. The television and newspaper predictions are wrong, Jack. They are just wrong!"

Jack had had enough. You can imagine that by this point he was thinking his boys at HQ had gone nuts. But they insisted. Their figures continued to show steady progress. Later, it would turn out that they had run almost even with Dever in Boston, with only a small drop-off, which they were able to trace directly to the Jewish vote.

These Jewish voters did not vote against Congressman Kennedy, but in the Jewish wards they "blanked" him—that is, they turned in empty ballots.

When he found out, Kenny was pissed, but Jack didn't want to publicly attack those voters, a disagreement that would lead to a heated dustup between Jack and Kenny. But that was all in the cool light of day, a few days later.

For now they were still battling the numbers, and after getting calls from CBS, *The Boston Globe*, the head of the Democratic Committee, and his father, Jack was incredulous. He angrily put on his suit coat and called out to Powers, and the two of them walked down the hill, with Jack in the lead.

"What are you going to do?" Powers asked cautiously.

"I'm going to find out if my brother, O'Donnell, and O'Brien are nuts!"

When he stormed into the office in a well-tailored, French-cut navy suit, Jack was a stark contrast to the pale and puffy faces he greeted there, their eyes lined from too many hours counting numbers, too much coffee, and not enough sleep.

"There we stood," Kenny said, "resplendent in our shirts: smelly, sweaty, ties pulled down or off, sleeves rolled up; the air replete with stale coffee, even staler donuts; cigarette and cigar smoke. But that air was thick with hope."

Jack stood in silence for a moment, surveying the scene. By now, all the volunteers had left, despondent. Bobby had sent all the women home. It was just the men: Bobby, O'Donnell, O'Brien, and some numbers genius Jack had never met: Dewey, whose sweaty, pencil-stained hand Jack shook in greeting.

"If this is what victory looks like," Jack quipped, "I'd hate to see defeat."

The comment broke the tension. They needed a laugh. Bobby pulled out one of the metal chairs by Dewey's computer, and his brother eased himself into it, pain etched on his face. *There it was again*, Kenny remembered thinking briefly. Jack began to run the numbers quietly, determinedly. It didn't take him long.

Jesus, Jack thought to himself. *They were right. I'm winning.*

But there was no shouting, no back slaps or whooping. It was still too early to call the election, and Jack was not the kind of guy who easily lost his composure. Instead he motioned for everyone to sit. It wasn't official until it was official. So the count continued. Jack would, however, remain at his campaign headquarters for the night.

As the night wore on, Jack and his team sat around the card table. They watched as the Lodge forces, headquartered just across the street, began to set up for a victory party.

The numbers were still unclear. Lodge had not yet won, and Jack had not yet lost. So the count continued. But occasionally Jack caught a glimpse of Henry Cabot Lodge and his staff, political pros to a man and woman, all dressed impeccably, waiting for Jack to do the right thing and admit defeat.

Jack did no such thing. He did look around his bedraggled crew and chuckle to himself. What a sorry group they must look to Lodge's forces. Still, Jack had seen Larry and Kenny's system in action for himself. While the numbers were small, they were steady, and they were climbing. Patience.

There was only one brief interlude in the tension, when a group of rough Irish locals, who had had one drink too many, came by after the bars closed. Having heard the predictions announced in most bars that Jack Kennedy had gone down to defeat, they began drunkenly yelling through the window and giving Jack and his brother the "Irish salute" (the middle finger).

Kenny was tired, and he'd had enough. Quick as a cat, he was up and heading toward the door.

"Bobby," Jack said.

Bobby put himself between Kenny and the door. "Come on, Kenny, we don't need this; ignore them."

Cooler heads prevailed, and the crowd eventually dispersed, their jeering echoing along the empty street.

It would be the first of many long nights like this for Jack and the Brotherhood. In fact, it would take the officials all night to catch up, and it would be almost five in the morning when they called the election for Jack. The establishment had been wrong. John F. Kennedy of 122 Bowdoin Street, Boston, had won!

Once victory was assured the next day, Kenny would say in retrospect that his initial predictions were "close to correct, by 95 percent, no less." Jack had won, the only Democrat to stay afloat against the Eisenhower onslaught, making them all look pretty damned smart.

THE NEXT MORNING the Brotherhood prepared to open the door of their small office and face the growing crowd outside. Reporters and members of the public were eager to meet the newly elected upstart John F. Kennedy, the guy who had stood against the Eisenhower tide and won.

Jack eyed Kenny, who stood, arms folded, leaning against the desk, too tired even to celebrate.

"Worcester," Jack said. "It all came down to Worcester. You are either a political genius or the luckiest SOB on the planet, O'Donnell."

Kenny opened his eyes slowly and smiled but said nothing. Luck or genius: It didn't really matter. They'd won.

Jack cast a sideways glance at Bobby. "Jesus, Bobby. Brush your hair, for Christ's sake. You look like a slob."

The brothers prepared to go out and give a brief speech. But in a move that would make Honey Fitz proud, the Kennedy brothers climbed up on a table and sang a little Irish victory song. As they climbed down, Kenny was plugging his ears and grinning.

Jack had just one more question before he stepped outside, though. He almost didn't want to ask. Still, he could not help himself. He turned and stared evenly at Kenny. "Worcester?" he repeated. "How did you know?"

Kenny shrugged. "I just guessed and turned out to be right."

Jack turned fast enough to feel a tight twinge in his back and winced. "You SOB! I knew you guessed! I just knew it!"

Bobby stared at Kenny and then Jack. "Oh my God! You weren't sure?"

"Pretty sure," Kenny replied.

Maybe it was the sudden realization of how fragile their victory was, how close it had come to not happening at all. Or maybe it was just the airless room. But Bobby threw up, right there in the wastebasket. Kenny laughed as he handed him some paper towels.

"Jesus, Bobby, it's just politics."

That was easy to say now that they had racked up their first substantial political victory, rising from the dead after the powers that be had deluded themselves into thinking there were no signs of life left in the campaign.

CHAPTER 5

Taking Over the State

E VERYONE WHO WAS there that victorious morning in 1952, anyone with a relative who had been there, or anyone who just wished they had been there would claim to remember Jack's speech. They would say it set the tone for events to come.

Kenny, however, claimed not to remember what Jack said. "Frankly," he explained later, slightly embarrassed, "I just remember being so relieved and still so tired. I just recall it was a very humble speech. It was a real thanks to the campaign workers, and he thanked all of us by name. He made clear that if he had not had this organization across the state, he would not have been elected. He was gracious and passed this victory off to the people who had worked for him. It was appreciated."

With that, Kenny and Helen returned home to their small house in Winthrop where her mother, Hilda, had been watching the children. They sat and watched the returns come in for the governor's race, and Kenny fell asleep on the couch until the phone woke him up.

The call was from an equally exhausted Bobby Kennedy, inviting Helen and Kenny to spend four or five days at Hyannis Port to recover, recoup, and discuss the next steps for Jack. As exhausted as he was, Kenny was delighted.

The next day, after leaving the kids with Hilda, they headed to the Cape with Bobby. Jack and Bobby's wife, Ethel, joined them there. Kirk "Lem" Billings, whom Jack had known since their days at Choate prep school, was also there. Kenny took an instant dislike to Billings, and as it turned out the feeling was mutual.

"How can you dislike him?" Helen had asked. "You just met him."

Kenny shrugged. "He's too eager to please," Kenny said by way of explanation.

"That's a problem you'll never have," Helen whispered, as Joe approached to invite them over for a drink. Of course she was right; she usually was about Kenny's tough personality.

That Jack could maintain relationships with men as different as Kenny and Billings was a testament to Jack's ability to compartmentalize his life. He was able to see what each person could contribute. He was clear about what each person brought to the campaign and how he could make the best use of those qualities. Jack had a unique ability to bring together people from a variety of backgrounds yet was able to relate to all of them on a personal level. It was a skill, Helen teased Kenny, that "he would never suffer from."

Kenny and Helen stayed for a few days, taking a much-needed break from all things political, enjoying walks on the beach, nice meals, and some touch football on the Kennedy lawn in front of Joe's house. From the relative safety of the front porch, Helen, Joe, and Rose would watch the boys and Ethel play football on the lawn. For Kenny the trip also provided fascinating insight into the relationship between Bobby and Jack. Jack was the older, more sophisticated, and more worldly brother. Like Kenny, Jack saw the gray areas of politics and life, in large measure due to the war. Bobby did not. He was and would remain for many years to come a man of very few in-betweens and doubts. It would take the eventual murder of his brother, then president, for Bobby to begin to fully understand that in politics and life one often has to comprise. Kenny used to say, "Don't let the perfect be the enemy of the good."

In these early days, Bobby believed in the white hats, the good guys, versus the bad guys, the black hats. This would lead him to an ill-advised job with communist hunter Senator Joe McCarthy and an obsessive pursuit of teamster boss Jimmy Hoffa and the mob, which would have consequences far beyond anything Bobby or Kenny could have imagined at the time.

The first night was a family dinner that included Jack, Lem, and some of Jack's other friends. Then Jack and Lem took off to visit old school friends. This was not the first time Jack would need time away from politics and the pressures of his family to recharge and renew his spirit, Kenny would learn.

What surprised Kenny the most was not only that Joe Kennedy himself was there the entire time but that he was, as Kenny quipped to Bobby, "well behaved and actually seemed to want to hear what they had to say." Kenny later joked, "It's amazing what a victory can do for you." Kenny, Larry, and Bobby had just delivered the impossible. Jack was more than just senator-elect: He had shown to a national audience that he could overcome steep odds. He alone had overcome the Eisenhower onslaught. Joe Kennedy may have been a difficult man—certainly he had that reputation—but he rewarded results.

The men sat up late into the night in the huge Kennedy living room that overlooked Nantucket Sound. As the cold wind whipped across the sound and the waves crashed on the beach, they sat drinking, smoking cigars by the roaring fireplace, and going over the campaign in great detail.

This time the Old Man listened and listened closely. He had come to realize that Kenny and Larry knew their business. They understood politics. He was surprised, because at some level they still seemed to him young kids who were wet behind the ears politically. They had, like Joe himself, cut-throat political instincts. At first Joe had thought putting Bobby in charge was a terrible mistake, but the entire experience of watching Bobby, whom he had spent little time with up to that point, work with these blue-collar Irish "ruffians," as Rose called them, and bring Jack across the finish line had impressed him. Joe wanted not only to hear them out but also to understand the strategy behind their success. Moreover, he wanted them to know that they were all on the same team: Team Kennedy. And the plan was for Jack to end up in the White House.

Nobody dared say it out loud, though. Not yet anyway. After the drinks were poured and the men were huddled together in the living room, they discussed in great detail where the mistakes had been made in the campaign, who had made them and would not make the cut, as well as which mistakes Lodge had made and why. Joe thought in some ways that Eisenhower's actions, or lack of them on behalf of Henry Cabot Lodge's campaign, had helped Lodge go down to defeat.

Kenny was surprised and maybe a bit disconcerted to find himself in agreement with Joe. If Eisenhower had flexed any campaign muscle in opposition to them, even with all their effort, Jack's win would have been that much more unlikely. But Eisenhower stayed on the sidelines of their senate race. The Kennedy team was grateful then and would be again later as they sat in Bobby's house across the lawn, anxiously watching election results some eight years later in November 1960.

With the Senate race analyzed, the discussion moved to the presidential race: what Stevenson had done right, but mostly what he had done incorrectly. In many ways, as Kenny noted later to Helen, the sound of the ocean crashing off in the distance, it was the first time Kenny realized that Joe Kennedy, for all his bluster, knew his stuff when it came to presidential politics.

Kenny listened closely, out of interest and good manners, but also because Kenny, like Joe, was thinking of the next step. Even though it went unsaid, they both knew Jack Kennedy was not going to stay in the Senate forever. That is what they both believed, though neither gave voice to that opinion yet. It would take time before they would feel that comfortable with one another. So Kenny listened as Joe went through the Stevenson campaign, dissecting it.

Kenny quickly learned that Joe and Stevenson did not like each other at all. Joe's criticism was harsh but not inaccurate, Kenny felt. While Joe had been a substantial contributor to the Stevenson campaign, he remained unimpressed with the candidate. Joe related detailed conversations with Stevenson that had left him politically cold. "You cannot be above the voter," Joe had said. Stevenson, he felt, was too aloof, was too distant, and saw himself as smarter than the average voter. Perhaps a lot of politicians saw themselves in that light, Joe had said, but Stevenson let the voters know he felt that way. It was not a strategy to win elections.

"Was [Joe] trying to impress you?" Helen later asked as they lay in the guest bedroom of Joe's house.

"No," Kenny replied after some thought. "He wasn't trying to impress us. He was trying to educate us."

To Kenny's surprise, Joe had been strongly for Stevenson even before Stevenson had received the nomination in 1952. Joe had offered Stevenson more than just money; he had wanted to help him.

But Stevenson was no fan of Joe Kennedy, which did not entirely surprise Kenny. Still, one would have thought that the desire to beat Eisenhower would have trumped Stevenson's personal feelings. It had not. Instead, Stevenson and his people had rebuffed Joe, embarrassing him personally and publicly.

Stupid, Kenny thought to himself. No matter what you thought of a man like Kennedy, if you wanted to win the White House, you had to kiss the asses of a lot of people you'd much rather tell to go to hell. Politics are politics. The goal is always to win, but Stevenson was a man who, as it turned out, cared more about his moral position than a Democratic victory. This was a mistake that Joe Kennedy and the Irish Brotherhood would never make.

Stevenson made it clear that he did not want Joe's help for a number of reasons, both political and personal. Kenny got a sense, listening to Joe talk with bitterness around the edge of his voice, that the rejection had hurt him deeply. For all Joe's money and power, Kenny sensed, still an Irish kid trying to make good and did not take to being told no or "we don't want your help" very well. He had a chip on his shoulder, as so many immigrants do, brought about by the very struggle he had endured for success.

Joe really wanted to see Stevenson elected and was surprised to be so harshly rebuffed. But there was never any wavering of Mr. Kennedy's support of Stevenson, even though his efforts to help were not received with great enthusiasm.

Joe explained that he "took a very dim view of Stevenson's declining to work with the regular Democratic organizations and going his own way with the left-wing extremists in the Democratic Party." He felt sure that was a critical mistake if one wanted to win on a national scale and that it was essential to understand that the middle of the country and the all-important South would never stomach the political left. If you wanted to win the White House, you had to find a middle ground.

As he spoke, Kenny sensed an honest and underlying anger. His gut told him Joe was revealing his true views to Jack's young team, not out of hubris but out of a shared bond with these young vets who had just gotten his son elected to the Senate.

Kenny's gut also told him something else had happened between Stevenson and Kennedy, though Joe never said what it was. The next day, as Bobby and Kenny walked on the beach, tossing a football back and forth, Kenny pressed Bobby for more information while Joe stood off in the distance on the porch of the main house and watched.

Bobby didn't know of anything more between Joe and Stevenson. "Why are you asking?" Bobby wondered.

Kenny demurred. But it mattered to Kenny because he was thinking nationally even as he basked in the glow of their recent victory and Jack's new fortunes. He wanted to know what landmines might lie out there for them to find as they mapped Jack's national strategy.

Of course, he admitted this to no one but Helen. It would have sounded arrogant, foolish in those early days. But as Kenny shook Joe's hand before returning to Winthrop, refreshed and renewed, Joe said a funny thing.

"Remember what I said about Stevenson's national strategy?"

Kenny nodded. Yeah, he got it. It turned out Kenny was not the only one with the White House on his mind.

Kenny and Joe had begun to find some common ground in the future success of Jack Kennedy. The two men would never really like each other, but perhaps, just perhaps, they could learn to respect what each brought to the table. They could put up with each other as long as the discussion focused on Jack.

With the election over, Bobby's plan was to get to Washington and back to his job. Kenny was asked by Jack to take over the office and take care of loose ends, which included tending to Jack's desire to solidify his newly created constituency. This meant a thank-you to everyone who had voted for him. He wanted to get the files together in a proper fashion, instructing Kenny to stay until January 1.

Jack never directly asked Kenny if he wanted to go to Washington, but he opened the door should Kenny want to walk through it. He was not at all sure that Kenny had the temperament for the legislative grind of the Senate, but he wanted to be sure both Kenny and Larry were given the chance.

Both men declined. Kenny had two reasons: First of all, he knew that was not his strength. Organization and politics were his strengths. The second reason was particularly hard to explain to Helen with three small children at home: He did not want to be on Jack's office payroll.

"It would change the relationship," Kenny explained. "I cannot be on his payroll. I need to be able to look him straight in the eye and tell him the unvarnished truth without fearing for my job. He needs to know what I am saying is not bullshit. I need to speak to him as an equal, man to man. He will respect that and understand. I cannot do it if I am his paid underling."

Helen sat stunned for a moment, taking a long draft of her cigarette to cover her dismay. She knew Kenny was right, of course. She had excellent political instincts herself, and she had seen the Kennedys up close now and well understood Kenny's need for independence. She might have felt better about it if they could have afforded Kenny's independence.

He kissed her on the forehead. "I will make it up to you, I promise." She smiled. He would make that promise a lot in the years to come, but Jack's political ambitions and agenda meant that many of Kenny's promises to Helen were substantially delayed or went unfulfilled altogether.

Kenny told Jack thanks, but no thanks, and Larry did the same. Jack was relieved. His real hope had been that they would stay in Massachusetts and build his organization. He never asked them to do that, nor did they offer, but they did it anyway. Again, they had read his mood without ever being asked.

They would build the organization unofficially in Jack's name. If they succeeded, Jack would be the recipient of the goodwill they had spread; if they screwed it up, they did not work for him and he could deny any connection. This would be the pattern. Jack's chieftains seemed to know the long-term game plan, even if they had never actually discussed it. They had come up with the strategy that had won him Massachusetts, a strategy they were sure would translate in time to the national arena.

WITH THE NEW year dawning, Kenny and Larry's first course of action was to reestablish the Kennedy headquarters, moving it to Tremont Street. A few secretaries, whom Kenny had decided to keep on, staffed the headquarters with O'Brien, who still lived in Springfield but drove in every day. Two crack secretaries had been sent down to Washington with the senator.

Kenny, Helen, and Bobby took three or four of the young women who had worked the hardest for the congressman out to a Christmas dinner. They headed over to John Fox's 99. With the cocktails flowing, the group got into an excited political discussion about the future and Jack's potential.

"We are dealing with a fellow who could be president of the United States. This may well be December 19, 1952, but mark my words, if it is not 1956, it will be no later than 1960. That could be our year," Kenny said suddenly. Helen was startled. She knew Kenny had thought this since the first tea in Worcester, but that he would say it out loud and in mixed company surprised her.

"Look," Kenny said, "I am not saying anything that is not something we all—by that I mean Bobby, the senator, Larry, and I—knew from the start and had confirmed with this victory."

Bobby laughed. "I hate to say it, Kenny, but more and more you sound like my dad." That brought a general round of amused laughter, but the discussion quickly moved into the political possibilities, with Kenny, Bobby, and Larry discussing at great length the opportunities now before them and how it might unfold.

A few days later, the conversation resumed, this time over drinks at the Kennedy apartment in Boston, with Joe Kennedy present. Both Bobby and Kenny agreed that the senator had the potential to run successfully for president.

"There is no question," Kenny concluded, "that his victory here was simply a step in that direction." The others agreed.

This was the first step. Absent from the discussion, however, were next steps for the Kennedy organization in Massachusetts.

Bobby was planning a return to Washington for a job arranged with the help of his father. It was a job with another ambitious Irish politician, a grandstanding "dangerous fellow," as Kenny called him, by the name of Joseph McCarthy. It would lead to some of the most difficult moments between Bobby and Kenny and to some of Bobby's most unhappy days. It was a decision that would test their friendship more than anything else.

It would also lead Kenny to rethink his then thawing feelings toward Joe Kennedy. "What the hell was he thinking letting Bobby take that job?" Kenny snarled at Helen.

Helen had suggested that perhaps Joe did not control Bobby, either, and that Bobby had made his own decision to go to Washington. It would turn out that Helen was right. Joe Kennedy had as little control over Bobby as Kenny did, and in the end Joe explained to Kenny that he "only facilitated what Bobby planned to do anyway." At the time, Joe still thought Kenny was overreacting about McCarthy, only later agreeing that Kenny had been right all along.

With Bobby in DC and Senator Kennedy now focused on national and international issues, Kenny and Larry were left to build on their victory and expand their power base.

While Joe's dislike for Kenny was also beginning to thaw, he was not thrilled about the Kennedy organization being in the hands of these young upstarts. He simply could not see where it would lead. What did they need the organization for? A second Senate campaign for reelection in 1958 was a long way off. Joe feared it would simply lead to trouble for his newly elected son. Furthermore, he felt that there was no point in focusing on the day-to-day operations of the state Democratic Party in Massachusetts. Having lost the governor's race, the Democrats were out of power. There was nothing to be gained.

Kenny and Larry saw things quite differently, and not for the first time in his political life, Jack had two different political horses within his organization competing for the same finish line. Kenny and Larry were sure that consolidating the Kennedy organization was the correct move. They saw that a powerful, well-built political organization that eventually took over the State Democratic Party might be very useful to them in the future. Joe Kennedy could not have disagreed more. He firmly believed Jack should stay out of the internal political squabbles in Massachusetts, believing Jack should stay above the political fray instead.

They all knew Joe objected. But Jack did not intervene. He said nothing one way or the other. Kenny and Larry sensed this as Jack's signal to them to keep going.

With both Jack and Bobby gone to Washington, however, Joe was not about to let the Brotherhood make their own decisions about his son's future. He pointed out rather coldly that one election did not make them experts.

Kenny and Larry shrugged him off, as much as anyone could shrug off a man as powerful as Joe Kennedy. But with Jack absent, the Old Man could meddle all he wanted. He told Kenny that Jack was simply no longer interested in state politics.

The truth was that Kenny, in Joe's view, came across as too blue-collar and rough around the edges to have a leading role in Kennedy family politics. On the other hand, Joe thought of Larry as an excellent tactician, but only in the very localized terms of what Larry had accomplished in Springfield and Western Massachusetts. He was not known around the state. Besides, as Joe reminded Morrissey, Larry's split from Furcolo had been the source of the Kennedy organization's as-yet-unresolved problem with the Italians. So Joe felt the best thing Kenny and Larry could do for Jack was go home.

"We will call you close to the next election. Maybe see you in '57."

Why did Joe Kennedy need a bunch of outsiders, known only to his sons, hanging around?

Joe and Morrissey agreed that this was their chance to get control again, and Joe wanted Morrissey back in place as the Kennedys' source of influence in the state. Morrissey and the Old Man figured that with Bobby in Washington, Jack in the Senate, and Kenny and Larry sent home, there was an opening in the organization again. Joe's stooge would once more assume a position of influence.

Kenny and Larry had other plans, though. They intended to stay in place and build that organization. And they had their eye on the governorship—not for themselves, of course, but for a Democrat who would owe his success to the Kennedy organization.

They just had to find the right candidate. Joe listened. He agreed to make some calls. Then Joe came to them, saying he had just the right man for the job.

"Who?" Kenny had asked.

"Bobby," Joe had replied. It took a few moments for the information to sink in.

"Bobby?" Larry replied, stunned but at the same time seeing the brilliance in the thing. This was all the more remarkable considering that Larry was not disposed to agree with Joe Kennedy about anything.

"You discussed this with Bobby? He likes the idea?" Kenny asked cautiously. Kenny was thrilled with the prospect. Still, it surprised Kenny that Bobby had not told him this privately.

Kenny remembered the brutally tough conversations required just to get Bobby to come up and save his brother's campaign. In fact, until the campaign, Bobby had never exhibited any personal interest in politics.

Kenny and Larry exchanged glances, remembering how disgusted Bobby had been the morning of the '52 victory. Hell, one of the reasons he'd gotten physically sick was seeing all the fakers and phonies who had written Jack off suddenly arrive just in time for photo ops with the candidate and their chance to claim credit.

Joe confirmed to Kenny that this had been discussed with members of the family, who felt that this was the time for Bobby to run for the governorship.

"The family," Joe explained, "all agreed it is Bobby's turn."

"But you never mentioned whether you talked to Bobby," Kenny ventured.

Joe scoffed. Bobby would do what he was told. He was no Jack, who was too independent for Joe to even consider trying to control. Bobby would be happy to go along. Kenny suddenly realized why this was the first he was hearing of this. Bobby probably didn't know a thing about it. It wasn't that it was not a good idea, it was just that if Kenny knew Bobby, and he did, Bobby was not leaving Washington, DC, certainly not for the State House in Boston.

Of course, in this political battle Kenny was squarely siding with Joe Kennedy in terms of strategy, but it was something he could hardly say to Bobby. Still, Kenny knew something about Bobby that his father did not: Bobby, like Jack, was his own operator. He made his own decisions. Kenny feared his decision would not be the one he and Joe would want to hear.

A few days later, as Kenny walked Bobby to South Station to catch his train to Washington, Kenny's hands shoved deep in his pockets to protect against the biting spring wind off the harbor, Bobby tried to explain his decision not to run.

When they finally got to the station, they stopped for a coffee to warm up their frozen hands before Bobby jumped on the train. Bobby pushed the paper cup of half-consumed coffee around in a circle on the counter. Kenny thought he looked torn, conflicted, almost as if he felt guilty. "In fairness, I have worked twenty-two hours a day in the campaign for Jack. You know that. I have had enough. I hate dealing with these Boston politicians, who are nothing but trouble. Everything is a power game."

Kenny shrugged and laughed. "That's politics, Bobby. I rather enjoyed it. In fact, I am going to miss them all."

Bobby scoffed. "It is just . . . the compromise, the baloney . . . it is all extremely distasteful to me. You get into these arguments and political fights that could get quite tough and brutal. I just realized I simply don't enjoy it. I'm not cut out for politics. I'm just tired of it, tired of all the infighting and the lying. I'm much happier in Washington, quite honestly, just doing my own thing. On my own."

Kenny nodded. He could have tried to explain how it would be different this time: Bobby would be the candidate, not the campaign manager. He would not have to take all the crap, kick all the tires, do all the dirty work. He could rely on the Irish Brotherhood for that.

But Kenny said nothing. He understood. He may not have understood a lot about the Kennedy family yet, but he understood Bobby. He felt that Bobby, without daring to say it publicly, even to Kenny, wanted to build a life away from his brother and his family. Bobby wanted to be independent, his own man. He did not want to be in his father's shadow, his family's shadow, or Jack's, either.

As they walked to the train and waited for it to pull up, Bobby was silent, still straining to explain, as if he had let them down. Bobby knew Kenny would understand, but Bobby was clearly struggling with his own sense of guilt over letting his father down.

As the train pulled up, Bobby's face contorted with both concern and determination as he turned to say good-bye. "Look, Kenny, I think Dad is more than a bit—" he paused and struggled with the word before settling on "frustrated," repeating it twice to make clear Kenny understood. "I think Dad is very frustrated with me at the moment. But I am glad to get out of Massachusetts and go to Washington. I don't like politics."

"Don't let it bother you, Bobby. We've all been frustrated with you for years."

"Thanks," Bobby said, shaking this head and laughing. "I think." He seemed satisfied that if his father did not, Kenny had at least understood his decision.

With Bobby gone and out of the race he had never really been in, Kenny and Larry had the problem of both building the organization and finding a candidate, a Kennedy loyalist. Keeping all the regional Kennedy secretaries in place was easy. Finding a suitable candidate for governor was a different matter. In the end, they needed to find a candidate who would appeal across ethnic lines, as Jack had, to a new generation of voters. More than that, they needed someone who was malleable, independent but not too independent, and willing to represent the Kennedy organization as much as the Kennedys were willing to throw their weight behind him.

◆◆◆

LATER THAT EVENING, sitting in his living room as Helen put the kids to bed, Kenny stared glumly out the front window.

Helen joined him and tried to gauge his mood.

"What's wrong?" she asked.

"Bobby," he replied, still staring into the black emptiness of night. I don't understand. What else is he going to do?"

"Go back to Washington," Helen replied. "The Justice Department perhaps. He seems to enjoy that kind of work."

Kenny shrugged. "I don't get it. I can't see him going back to Washington. He and I were awfully close. He's like a younger brother to me. I thought I knew what was best for him, and I wanted him to stay here in Massachusetts. I wanted to keep him close, where he could be pulled in quickly for the senator's next move."

"Why?" Helen asked, truly puzzled. "I don't understand."

"I wanted to keep the presence of the Kennedy flag in the state," he explained. "You see, I realized once they all left, whatever political potential we had dissipated rather rapidly. To have Bobby in Massachusetts on a day-to-day basis within the state, well, that is political power. The race for governor is two years away, and I can't believe I am saying this, but I agree with Joe. He'd be good. He has the same type of attraction to the voter. He has gone around the state and is extremely well-known. He's a natural executive. I was hopeful that he would stay. I just think Bobby should have given it more thought, more time before deciding one way or the other. But it was my feeling from our conversation today that it got to be too much pressure, or else he feared it would be too much pressure from his father. So he returned to Washington, and that could mark the end of an era."

Kenny finished his drink.

Helen laughed. Getting up, she put her arms around him. "You're a true friend. I can see your concern, just as his father's concern, was all about Bobby's well-being and happiness."

Kenny turned and shook his head. Okay, he had to laugh. Maybe he deserved that.

But only Helen, who knew his motives better than anyone, could have gotten away with that line.

KENNY AND LARRY, both men with growing families, had to return to what Helen, only half-jokingly, called the "real world," while also heading up the so-called Kennedy organization in their free time. Joe saw no reason for either Kenny or Larry to stay on full-time, and there were no funds for offices or salaries. Larry returned to his full-time legal practice in Springfield, and Kenny went back to the dreaded paper company.

Almost immediately, Kenny was faced with a choice. Hollingsworth and Whitney Company Paper Mill, then owned by Scott Paper, was moving the entire operation to Pennsylvania and made clear that it wanted Kenny to head up the new office. Kenny downed several cold ones at the pub in the Bellevue Hotel over that offer, complaining to Larry that he could not possibly move to Pennsylvania. Kenny needed to find a way to convince Helen that they had to stay in Massachusetts, job or no job with the paper company.

As it turned out, Kenny needn't have worried. That evening, as they had their after-dinner cocktails, he broached the subject. Kenny had hardly finished when Helen made clear that she had no intention of uprooting her children and moving so far away from her parents to, of all places, Pennsylvania. Besides, she had teased him, "We both know you have no intention of leaving here. Nor would the senator allow you to if you wanted to leave."

Kenny was a bit surprised but mostly relieved. Helen may have harbored wishes that Kenny, like Bobby, would tire of electoral politics and move to Washington for a reliably secure government job. As Helen later lamented to Bobby, it was all just "an intellectual exercise" at this point as long as Jack remained aloof from Kenny and Larry's efforts, making it unclear what the future would hold for them as campaign strategists. But Kenny at least had the assurance for now that Helen supported his political ambitions.

While Bobby no doubt understood Helen's worry, he said little to convince Kenny to come to Washington. Not yet anyway. Not because Bobby did not want him there. He certainly did. But he knew Jack would have been furious, so Bobby, being Bobby, was determined to find a way to help. Until something was in place, Kenny needed to support his family. Jack's ambitions at this stage could not pay his bills.

Kenny was without work for only a few weeks. Jack helped secure Kenny a job in a public relations that would pay him a decent salary but that also allowed him to dabble in politics on the side. The job's true duties remained fairly vague and Kenny would spend most of his time working on building the Kennedy organization.

Once again, Jack never articulated or gave any direction per se to Kenny, but he did not say no, either. Kenny was pleased. He could support his family and still continue to work with Larry to build the organization.

WHILE THE BROTHERHOOD struggled with life-changing decisions, Jack had been dealing with his own life-changing struggle. He had been trying to convince New York socialite beauty Jacqueline Bouvier that she should be his wife. Jack, whose wandering eye had already become a thing of much discussion, had not been eager to tie the knot, but his father had begun to push him hard by 1950. He needed a wife and a family. When he met Jacqueline "Jackie" Bouvier, he was smitten. She was beautiful, savvy, well educated, smart, and funny; she was his equal in ways that he never expected to find in a woman. She was also independent-minded and very much her own person, something Jack would both treasure and find maddening during the later White House years. For her part, Jackie would find her independence vital in surviving the competitive, raucous, highly ambitious Kennedy family. Jack and Jackie often ran across each other at the same events and social functions, but as legend goes, it was Jack's newspaper pal Charlie Bartlett who made the formal introduction at a dinner party in Georgetown in 1952. Jack and Jackie's on-and-off-again romance finally came to a head, after Jack had won the Senate race, when Jack finally popped the question and she said a well-planned yes.

With the help of a swift, timely kick in the pants from his father to take the plunge, "Washington Gay Bachelor circa 1953" was off the market. Almost as soon as Jack proposed, *Life* magazine published a piece on the engagement. Joe had convinced an unhappy Jackie to hold off on any official announcement until after publication. It would be the first of many such sacrifices Jackie would endure for her husband's ambition.

With Jack happily engaged to Jacqueline Bouvier, Helen announced that they were going to have an engagement party for Jackie at the Parker House in Boston, right at Tremont and School streets. Due to the frequent presence there of Jack and his political chieftains, the Parker House was fast eclipsing the Bellevue Hotel as Boston's most famed political hangout.

Kenny and Larry, while at first reluctant, decided they would use the opportunity to bring together the Kennedy organization, thanking the secretaries for all their hard work and making sure to keep everyone in touch. Larry later explained, "We figured if our wives were going to drag us into this thing, we'd seize upon it to bring people together around the Kennedy flag."

Helen was less than delighted, but when she learned that turning the party into a political event meant that Joe Kennedy was willing to pick up the tab, she decided she could live with it.

The purpose of the party was completely political by the time Larry and Kenny were through with it. Nobody was invited who was not a Kennedy secretary. The party, as Kenny and Larry explained to Jack, would give the Kennedy team an excuse to communicate with their secretaries, strengthen the political organization, and indicate to them that this was a continuing operation with more activity to come.

"How do Helen and Jackie feel about your taking over their party?" Jack asked.

Kenny shrugged. "They're mad, but it will be fine."

Jack said, "Better they be mad at you than me."

Larry agreed.

Kenny laughed. "I don't really care if they are mad or not. It's good politics."

As would become the pattern, Kenny and Larry did what they wanted, and Jack pretended from a safe distance that it was news to him.

Kenny and Larry, despite not yet having settled on a slate of candidates, were determined to the keep the organization in place and active.

There was no election, no reason for them to be there, yet when called, all the secretaries came. After being presented with a wedding present from the Kennedy organization, Jack, who at first had been reluctant to come to his own party or even to give the official green light to building and sustaining the organization, stood on the stage of the Parker House ballroom, surveying the crowded scene before him. Jack reasoned, "Kenny might be a pain in the ass, but he and Larry were on the right track."

Kenny and Larry had achieved their goal: The Kennedy organization was intact, they had strengthened political ties, and maybe, just maybe, they had impressed Jack. As for their wives, well, they could not complain too much. After all, it had been a hell of a party, for which they got all the credit and did not have to spend a dime. Maybe this political nonsense had some side benefits.

Jack and Jackie were finally married at Saint Mary's Church in Newport, Rhode Island, on September 12, 1953, in a smashing affair that both Kenny and Helen were invited to attend. The reception, held at Hammersmith Farm in Newport, Rhode Island, the Bouvier family's grand estate on the ocean, featured some twelve hundred guests, which meant anyone and everyone Joe Kennedy thought might be helpful to Jack's political future was in attendance. As they stood at the edge of the lawn, overlooking the ocean with the rambling Hammersmith house behind them, Kenny remarked casually to his wife, "It was okay, if you like this sort of thing."

Helen looked at him and shook her head. "My Prince Charming," she teased.

CHAPTER 6

The Kennedy Operation

KENNY WOULD LATER say that there were, in fact, three Kennedy operations under way in the period following Jack's election to the Senate: "the Kennedy Washington operation," "the Kennedy organization in Massachusetts," headed by O'Donnell and O'Brien, and finally the "Kennedy family operation," headed by Joe Kennedy.

It would eventually require the national campaign in 1960 and Bobby's force of personality to bring all these operations together. But that was yet to come. Right now, there were three distinct operations with different mandates, and Jack seemed, for the moment at least, to like it that way.

By the close of the 1952 Senate campaign, both Kenny and Larry had become political figures in Massachusetts. People knew Kenny was close to both Jack and Bobby. As Jack's political right hand, Kenny had Jack's ear and now wielded the considerable influence that went with Jack's new office. It became a position of power that Kenny both enjoyed and wisely used to Jack's advantage. He had little, if any, interest in his own personal gain.

As journalist Sandy Vanocur said years later, "Kenny had no ego. It was all for Jack Kennedy. He was in it totally and completely to enhance the career of Jack Kennedy."

While that may have been true, Kenny was no fool. He liked politics, liked power, and knew if Jack succeeded that his position would most certainly be enhanced. If he did a good job for Jack, Kenny rightly assumed, Jack would reward him.

Unlike Kenny, Larry O'Brien had held a prior political position. While this was certainly a smaller state-level gig, he was very well-known and respected in Springfield and Western Massachusetts. Larry's father had been involved in politics on a minor, local level in Massachusetts as well.

But now no other Democratic operatives in the state had reputations that could compare to those of O'Donnell and O'Brien. Frank Morrissey was no competition in an organizational sense. He never paid any attention to the Kennedy organization. His relationship, or what was left of it, to the Kennedy organization at this time was strictly through the Old Man or through Ted Reardon to Jack's office in DC.

Both O'Donnell and O'Brien admitted that they realized "selfishly," as Kenny said, that "what would be politically good for Senator Kennedy would be good for them."

They had to take every step possible to preserve the Kennedy organization as an entity, especially in light of Jack's absence from the state and his new national and international priorities as a legislator. Kenny and Larry felt they almost had to propagandize this newly minted Kennedy organization and give the appearance to other politicians and the public that this was a cohesive, well-functioning group that was directly responsive to Senator Kennedy.

"We needed people to understand and accept that when we spoke," Kenny made clear, "we spoke for him, acted for him, and we were in fact Senator John Kennedy's agents in Massachusetts." They had no titles, no office, and no direct authority, making this a very difficult task. Moreover, they received no financial support from Joe Kennedy and the Kennedy family organization and almost no support, or even encouragement, from Washington, DC.

It was in some ways an extraordinary act of political courage and audacity on their part, or, as Joe Kennedy might call it, "political hubris." The most they would get was an occasional call from Jack in Washington. The chat would often be general in nature. Kenny and Larry were left to draw from what was unsaid, to read between the lines in order to understand what he wanted from them. This would be a pattern and approach that would continue well into the White House years. Kenny, in particular, learned to read Jack's wishes and act on them. The strategy always left Jack free to accept or deny the results of Kenny's actions. This approach required a tough-guy personality, someone who could take the political hit, if necessary, a role that perfectly suited Kenny.

At this point, despite Kenny's and Larry's positions as heads of the Kennedy state political organization, if Jack wanted something done publicly, it was now communicated by Joe Kennedy and carried out by Frank Morrissey. Whether this was done by Jack to keep peace with his father and Morrissey, or whether it reflected a strategy or lack of interest on Jack's part, Kenny and Larry never knew for sure. But the fact that Jack never acted to stop their efforts was enough of a green light to ensure their position and continued behind-the-scenes influence.

The truth was that Joe Kennedy did not want his son embroiled in what he considered the older, nastier political fights. He thought getting into those contests would only weaken his son, and Joe himself had nothing to gain by them. Joe also did not share Kenny's or Larry's interest in the state party apparatus.

From Joe's point of view, as he said to Jack, "control or hold of a state organization, which was essentially defunct, would do him no good and, worse still, might cause him unnecessary political problems."

Joe well knew that the Democratic Party in Massachusetts had historically been largely devoted to individual politicians and their personalities, such as James Michael Curley, Paul Dever, and now Jack Kennedy. In the state organization as such, the party exercised power only secondhand. The state chairman had been used under Dever as a patronage dispenser, but only when Dever did not want to be involved in saying no.

Joe recognized all this and had his own agenda; therefore he felt it essential to sideline Kenny and Larry, who seemed bent on embroiling Jack in state politics. Joe was determined to keep Jack out of what he called "these silly political fights." Furthermore, Joe was convinced that O'Donnell and O'Brien had a vested interest in being associated with the Kennedys. Joe believed that some of the Brotherhood's actions in Massachusetts would be in their own selfish interests. Joe, by nature, was cynical about people's motives, and while Kenny and his guys may have done a great job for Jack in '52, Joe was still a bit sore over being pushed aside. He was also suspicious, correctly as it turned out, that they had their own political agenda for Jack. Joe was also not at all convinced that Kenny and Larry were needed again before the '58 election. With Jack successfully in the Senate, the Kennedy operation run by Kenny and Larry had ceased to be necessary from Joe's point of view.

While Jack did not share his father's views, he was careful to pick his battles. He agreed with his father, all the while knowing that Kenny and Larry could handle themselves. When Bobby asked him about their role, Jack shrugged. "Kenny can handle himself," was all Jack replied. Kenny would have to determine exactly how much power or room that provided for him to operate. Not shy by nature, Kenny sensed the opening and, with Larry at his side, moved quickly to fill the vacuum.

"Essentially, Jack Kennedy wanted us to take actions," Kenny explained, "but he wanted at the same time to be in a position to disavow them if they became injurious to him. That would be in 1953, 1954, and then in 1955."

The division among the Kennedy organizations was further deepened when Ted Sorensen appeared on the scene. Theodore Chaikin Sorensen hailed from Nebraska, the son of a Danish-American father and a mother descended from Russian Jewish immigrants. After earning his law degree at the University of Nebraska–Lincoln, he eventually headed to Washington, DC. Jack spotted him in January 1953, bringing him on board as his legislative aide. Sorensen was then twenty-four years old.

Jack had done himself an enormous favor by hiring Sorensen. Ted would prove to be more than just a brilliant writer; he was, in Kenny's view, "damn near mythological" in his use of the English language. Ted was, Jack agreed, a "brilliant wordsmith," and Ted would go on to write some of the most memorable words uttered by Jack Kennedy.

Kenny and Ted would make a powerful albeit reluctant team. Sorensen's brilliant turns of phrase gave literary expression to Jack's ambitions, while Kenny's political genius and take-no-prisoners attitude won elections. While Kenny more than agreed that Sorensen was a critical asset, he and Sorensen were destined to battle over political turf and power for years to come. They would never be friends, they would never perhaps go on vacation together, but as with Kenny's relationship with Joe Kennedy, they eventually arrived at a mutual respect for each other's skills and a shared dedication to Jack's success. Still, the start was rocky. Sorensen, in order to take control of Jack's Washington operation, had a clear interest in agreeing with Joe Kennedy's suspicions of Jack's "Boston Irish Brotherhood."

Sorensen, like Joe, saw little need to worry about Massachusetts politics and questioned the need for a Massachusetts political operation.

"Ted," Kenny later said, "had a vested interest in hoping that any future Kennedy organizational power and political operation would focus more in the Washington office and in his hands. His competition in the Washington office was Ted Reardon, which was not significant to someone as bright and aggressive as Sorensen."

With these divisions, the organizations naturally began to develop distinct agendas and personalities. Jack would come to believe that these divisions served him well, and he would keep them in play even in the White House. The Kennedy Washington organization was really Ted Sorensen, while Joe Kennedy and Morrissey, as Soreson's eyes and ears in Massachusetts, were determined to oppose whatever actions Kenny and Larry might take in the state, assuming they got wind of it in time to stop them.

Fully aware of this, O'Donnell and O'Brien became increasingly adept at saying one thing and then doing exactly what they wanted anyway, which was, as it turned out, exactly what Jack wanted them to do.

Although Joe Kennedy and Ted Sorensen argued repeatedly with Jack over the actions Kenny and Larry were taking in Massachusetts, Jack was confident in the Brotherhood. They understood politics, both external and internal, and they could damn well handle any opposition from his father and Ted Sorensen. Jack would listen to his father and Sorensen's complaints and concerns but repeatedly take no action to stop Kenny or Larry. That alone was a green light as far as Kenny was concerned. Helen urged Kenny to be more of a team player, but he refused, instead saying clearly, "I don't work for Joe Kennedy or Ted Sorensen. I work for the senator. If he wanted Larry and me to stop, he'd tell me. Silence is permission. We move ahead." Helen knew her husband well enough to let it go.

Kenny explained the same strategy later to Sandy Vanocur: "We felt we had our relationship with Jack Kennedy. Our positions with him were clear. We knew what we had to do, we planned to do it, and we did not give a damn what Joe Kennedy, Frank Morrissey, or Ted Sorensen thought."

What did become clear was that the senator was less than willing to put his own political prestige on the line, much less so than his father. In truth, Jack felt he had no choice but to refrain from these internal power struggles. Kenny, not for the first time, felt John Kennedy was a much better judge of political horseflesh than his father. The senator was much less sanguine than his father about the candidates that O'Donnell and O'Brien eventually settled on to head the Kennedy slate in Massachusetts.

In 1954, they chose Robert Murphy, a well-respected, fairly smart, good-looking lawyer of the same generation as Jack and the Brotherhood. He had, Kenny and Larry hoped, the chance to be governor without being a superstar who would end up outshining Jack. The senator was rather reluctant about placing all his chips on Murphy. He made it clear to Kenny to hold back his best resources. At the same time, Jack wanted to get full credit for being a good Democrat and placing Larry and Kenny in the service of the Murphy campaign.

Jack did not care whether Joe Kennedy could be convinced to bankroll the campaign. In his view, that was his father's decision to make. But Jack was clear to Kenny: He did not want to tie himself and his image too closely to Murphy.

Dick Maguire, a close friend of Kenny's who would later become a member of the extended Irish Brotherhood, was a key aide to Murphy in those early days. Dick had become quite close with Kenny and Larry by then, and Dick deputized Kenny to approach Jack for help.

When they got into negotiations regarding the senator's willingness to throw his support behind Murphy, Jack made clear he was not willing to make television endorsements for the candidate. Jack was not feeling well: He was in incredible pain and had been, unbeknownst to Kenny at that time, in and out of hospitals.

Kenny suggested to Jack, "Why don't we go down to the Cape? Let them tape the ads down there." As Kenny would recall later, "I was thinking about his health emotionally and physically. I recognized there was a health issue, suspected it was more than his back, but was very naive about the extent of the issues at that time."

Jack immediately said no. Absolutely not.

"Why?" Kenny asked, probing a bit.

"Well, I don't think that makes much sense," Jack said, frustrated and annoyed at Kenny's persistence. "You tape it, and then they have control of it. They may use it forty or fifty times. I only want it used once. And it makes me look like a chowderhead to be all over the television forty or fifty times for Murphy, a fellow who is probably not going to win."

Jack was wary of the harm that association with a losing candidate would cause to his reputation. In what would become a Kennedy precedent and a source of much frustration to other candidates seeking an endorsement from Jack Kennedy, he would never support a candidate until he had won the nomination. He was politically savvy enough to recognize that if that candidate failed in the primary, he might get hit by some of the backwash. It was a chance he was not willing to take. It became an ingrained part of the Kennedy approach.

"Aren't you supposed to think of these things first?" Jack had asked Kenny. Jack was no doubt frustrated and in much more pain than Kenny understood at the time.

For his part, Kenny admitted that he had not thought about it that way; it was very wise on the senator's part.

Jack shook his head. "This is what we will do. I will come up there. We will do a television show live, do it once, then it will be over and done. That's all they get."

Dick Maguire was disappointed but trusted Kenny enough to know that he had gone to bat for him, for Murphy. For his part, Kenny was impressed with Maguire and had bigger plans for him in the future Kennedy organization. Kenny was careful to make clear to Maguire he had done all he could for Murphy, but that to kick the door open a bit, perhaps Maguire should start thinking beyond Robert Murphy and focus on the future, a future that would involve Jack Kennedy.

For his part, Maguire understood Kenny's strategy, while he was unhappy with Jack's decision. If this was all they were going to get, then they'd take it.

Jack made the trip up from Washington to the Ritz-Carlton, where the taping was to be conducted. Larry and Kenny met him that morning. Kenny was stunned when he laid eyes on the senator. He immediately knew there was something much more serious going on here.

Jack was in terrible pain and once again on crutches, his left foot dangling above the floor. He then explained quickly to Kenny and Larry that his back was in some contraction, and this was the only way he could keep the pain from overwhelming him. They sat down and discussed the television show, the mechanics of it.

Jack said then, "Look, I've been thinking. I can't do a television show with Murphy without doing one with Furcolo. You know how I feel about Furcolo." He directed this at Larry rather than Kenny.

"Furcolo is the candidate for United States Senate. He has been nominated by the party. I cannot place myself in a position where I am endorsing one and not the other. If I endorse Murphy, they are going to ask me to endorse Furcolo. I am neither willing nor physically up to doing several shows, so I feel very strongly, unless either of you have any objections, that I should do the show with Furcolo also. I could do both of them at the same time."

Kenny was shocked, largely because he believed that they were trying to evade Furcolo. "Obviously, Jack had thought this out himself and made his decision," Kenny remembered. "In retrospect, it turned out to be a very wise decision, though I did not feel that way at the time."

Kenny recognized that Larry was now in a tough spot due to his old grudge with Furcolo. Kenny also understood that such an endorsement would weaken Larry and upset his position in local Springfield politics. Larry was unhappy about all this, but he did not object. He was tough and understood politics. He knew he had no choice, and he took the hit for Jack. There was no question that Jack had made up his mind. He was not asking their opinion, really.

In fact, Kenny noted, "He was just telling us what he was going to do and wanted to let us know ahead of time so we wouldn't screw it up. I did not agree, nor did Larry, but it was clear he would not brook any disagreement. I was not yet at the stage where I felt comfortable taking him on when I felt he was completely wrong. After this, it was a mistake I would not make again."

In the end, it was a political decision on Jack Kennedy's part, one that he would come to regret.

"The decision to do the show," Kenny said, "came directly from him. He had made this decision after thinking it through, because it made total sense in a cold, political manner. We did not argue about it or discuss it. A position I would not take in the future. He then proceeded to the format of the show."

Jack explained that his script would be written by Sorensen, "who we did not know well but had heard about and we knew he was not on our side," Kenny recalled. But the senator made clear he would have Sorensen write his script.

"The other fellows," Jack said, meaning Murphy and Furcolo, "can have their people write theirs, and then they can sit down and argue about the script. Once they've agreed, we will go with a one-time television show."

They pretaped the show. Kenny later watched the television show in a barroom with Dave and Larry. Kenny recalled later, "As far as I was concerned, it went off perfectly. If one did not know what was in the background, you would say it was a perfect show. Everybody in there assumed it was a perfect show. He was most friendly to Murphy, though the show was a one-time event with both Murphy and Furcolo. All you saw on television is that Jack is sitting with the two of them."

In the studio Jack was still on crutches; on television, however, he was already seated with the two of them and made a speech. He thanked and endorsed them both.

"As I say," Kenny recalled, "it was a typical fifteen-minute political show. The senior senator endorsed the two candidates and nobody in the general public interpreted otherwise."

At the end of the show he said, "Good luck to both of you." But, Kenny noticed at the time, Jack was very distant and cold. Not warm. "There was no question," Kenny thought later, "as I looked at the screen and as did others who knew Jack Kennedy, it was not a warm endorsement of either man, and it was evident in his manner that he did not like Foster Furcolo. It was clear Foster Furcolo did not like him, either. It was clear to the general public that he had simply endorsed the ticket, Bob Murphy and Foster Furcolo, but it was not overt."

Jack's final statement was simply, "I endorse the entire Democratic ticket." He did not say or at any time mention Foster Furcolo's name. He said, "Bob Murphy is the leader of the ticket as the candidate for governor. I therefore endorse the entire Democratic ticket." That's all he said, which was an endorsement of sorts of Foster Furcolo.

Kenny and Larry headed back to the headquarters that night, and for half an hour or an hour all seemed fine. Then, by word of mouth, it began to filter through that there had been a terrific fight at the studio about the content of the speech. This was news to Kenny (he had apparently left by then), but Bob Morey, Jack's driver, was there. Dave had gotten the story from Bob Morey. Furcolo told Jack he would not go on the show unless he received a more forthright and direct endorsement from the senator.

Jack said to him that famous line, "You've got a hell of a nerve, Foster. You're lucky you are here." Senator Kennedy then quite coldly went on to remind him of the time Furcolo had refused to endorse Kennedy. The exchange was quite heated. The television show itself emerged unscathed. The next day the papers did not mention the problem. The papers went along with the show, "Kennedy endorses Murphy/Furcolo."

However, as Kenny was riding into town that next morning, he heard on the radio that Senator Kennedy not naming Foster Furcolo had been a direct affront, causing an argument during the show. The report went on: that Senator Kennedy had deliberately attacked Furcolo, that Senator Kennedy had done it on purpose, and that the senator, in fact, was not endorsing Foster Furcolo and had staged the entire thing to embarrass Furcolo politically. The report quoted Frank Morrissey.

Kenny was livid. All their hard work had been undone by Morrissey! It was one thing, behind the scenes, to attack Mark Dalton, to challenge them, but this was spilling into the public. It made Jack look like an amateur and mean-spirited, almost childish. It also had the potential to create long-term political enemies that could only do them more harm than good. Furious, Kenny stormed into the Bellevue Hotel and ran into Bob Morey.

His voice low and dripping with anger, Kenny asked Morey, "Did you hear that report?"

Morey said, "Yup, evidently that fellow Connie Hurley [the radio reporter] had called Morrissey and asked him, you know, 'You don't think it was done on purpose by Senator Kennedy, do you?' Morrissey confirmed that it was done on purpose."

"Why?" Kenny turned white with anger. "It was not done on purpose; it just happened. Morrissey putting the dispute into the public blows the whole thing." Kenny later recalled, "I was furious. I went up to the senator's apartment at 122 Bowdoin Street. He is not there; he has gone back to the Cape. What I don't yet know is he is very sick and is preparing to go into the hospital, which is why Morrissey figured he had free rein to act. I called Frank Morrissey and asked him to come over immediately. He got there. He could see I was angry and sort of backed away.

"'Hey, Kenny,' he said, in a sort of defensive posture.

"I put it to him straightaway and asked, 'What happened here?'

"He told me Hurley had called him, and he thought they were old friends. He thought it was off the record. I just stared at him. Couldn't believe it. All the preparation and work out the window. I was so angry, I recall I advanced toward him; he backed up to the window. I stood there trying to control my temper. I remember my exact words. I walked over and opened the window and said, 'Frank, jump, because this time you went too far. You're 'done brothers.' You never embarrass Jack Kennedy publicly. You're gone.'

"He looked around for help. There was no help. He looked as though he would cry."

Kenny picked up the phone and called the Cape. He was not able to get through to the senator, but he did talk to the father, who defended Morrissey and told Kenny just about to go to hell. He asked who cared about Furcolo.

"I told him, 'I don't give a damn about Foster Furcolo, but I do give a damn about your son.' I slammed the phone down. I was in the apartment still. Then I called Bobby at the Cape and then, finally, reached him in Washington. Bobby was livid."

As it turned out, to Kenny's startled surprise, Bobby told him Jack was in an ambulance and literally en route to the hospital and could not be reached, that the family was trying to keep it quiet. "While I was startled, I did not have time to react at the moment. I had a political problem to solve. The personal stuff would have to wait. I told Bobby the story. I said to him, 'It seems to me it is a terrible thing to leave this on the record. The fact is this statement by Morrissey has now destroyed any credibility of the show, which will hit Murphy as well as Furcolo. What are we going to do now? As an organization we have to work for the ticket and this looks bad. We either are going to be for Furcolo or not be for Furcolo, but the senator cannot be out there seemingly to say one thing if he means something else. Whatever we do we are in an untenable position from my viewpoint. We cannot possibly go to work today at the Murphy headquarters until this is resolved. It will raise credibility questions in their minds as well. I just think that Jack ought to disavow Morrissey completely. He does not have to say anything about Furcolo, but he can simply say he stands on the record and his statement from the show, that he endorsed the entire Democratic ticket and let the tape speak for itself.'

"Bobby agreed. He was very upset and could see the long-term permanent political damage to his brother's political credibility. He said he would call me back. He did. In the end, we had four or five conversations. I had a few more very difficult and unpleasant conversations with Mr. Joe Kennedy. Mr. Kennedy said to me, 'He's headed to the hospital. This is a hell of a time for this!' I pointed out the damage could be permanent; hospital or not, if the senator was to have a future, this would have to be fixed. Period. Finally, I ended up with getting to the senator directly; by now he was in his room at the hospital. He was so unhappy with himself for making the mistake, and frankly, I realized as he talked, he was so unhappy with his personal life at the moment that he said to me, 'Look, Kenny, at the moment I do not care if Foster Furcolo dropped dead tomorrow. If Furcolo likes me or not I don't care. Hell, I don't even know if I have a future.' Even over the telephone it was clear the old fire and dash in his voice wasn't there at all. His political acumen was not firing on all twelve cylinders.

"I told him that was a stupid thing to say, that we could not let this stand. Once he got out of the hospital, his first question to me would be, did you fix this?

"He answered with, 'If I get out the hospital.'

"It was clear he was not himself. I turned to Bobby."

Hanging up from Jack, Kenny called Bobby back.

"'He's not thinking clearly,' I said to Bobby. 'We need to fix it ourselves. Your father is no help.' I kept pushing, and through some process of negotiations and with Bobby's help we finally extracted a statement from Jack. It was unsatisfactory but covered the problem. We did disavow Morrissey.

"Now the father was the problem here; he kept calling me and saying 'the hell with them' and 'my son might die' and describing Furcolo in less than pleasant genealogical terms two or three times. He was very upset about the whole thing. He was screaming at me, 'Jack is going into the hospital; he is very sick. It is a hell of a time to be worrying about these things.' He was rather angry, but I knew he was angry as much at his son being sick as anything, and quite frankly I did not care if it upset him or not. Morrissey had to be disavowed. It was quite clear that Morrissey was trying to save himself and was calling him on the other line saying, 'O'Donnell is overreacting. Nobody is talking about this. Forget it.' Of course, he was pretending it was about him in order to save himself. But it could not be left the way it was; Morrissey had finally gone too far."

In the end, Kenny said, "We finally issued a statement that Bobby worked out. Bobby actually wrote it and put it out under his name without talking to the father or Senator Kennedy. Bobby put it out under his name saying that they stand on the record of the television show script.

"The father was not happy with either Bobby or me at this point. Senator Kennedy was too depressed and told me he didn't really care. He has his own problems right now and he even said, 'Maybe I don't have a future to save.' I told him that was, well, let's say I said something a bit stronger than 'nonsense.'

"The end result was it was very clear that Senator Kennedy did not endorse and does not like Foster Furcolo. That could not be undone. This incident cost us much of our effectiveness in the campaign. The Murphy people are standing back at arm's length now and no longer trust us. They are not sure that Senator Kennedy's words mean anything. In politics you're dead if that happens. Bobby has done what he could. Jack has gone under the knife at this time, so we have no way to produce him to fix the problem with Murphy. We were in an untenable position, as now Larry and I had no political credibility."

Kenny said, "I remember we got, well, Larry and I began to get flooded by calls from Kennedy people asking, 'What is the line? Are we for the ticket or just Murphy and not Furcolo? Or not both of them? What do we do? Are we openly for them or against them?' Well, you know, we try to be as clear as possible, we are for them, he endorsed the whole Democratic ticket, but of course this does not help us with the Murphy people. We just felt and realized there was nothing we could do anymore. The situation was lost. There was no cutting and running here; what could we do? If we go after Foster Furcolo, we would have to produce Senator Jack Kennedy to openly say, 'I am not for him,' so it does not mean anything if Ken O'Donnell is for him or not."

But the question was damaging to Murphy. If Senator Kennedy was really not for Furcolo, then was he really for Murphy? In one move Morrissey had undercut both candidates, damaged Kenny and Larry's political credibility, and perhaps destroyed Jack's in the process.

The next two weeks, the Dever people, the regulars, were distraught and furious with Jack Kennedy. This, they told Kenny angrily, confirmed their original view of Jack Kennedy as being out for only Jack Kennedy. Frank Morrissey's reputation was as such a peasant among the politicians that they could not believe he would have acted without direction from Senator Kennedy.

Kenny recalled, "To this day many people will not be convinced that Frank Morrissey on his own initiative put that statement out. But that is a fact. Frank Morrissey claimed later that [Joe Kennedy] told him to put it out, but that is a load of crap. I talked to the father, and he was shocked when I told him what happened. Sure he was distracted by his son's illness, but he was not a faker; I could tell that he was shocked when I told him. I met Frank Morrissey twenty minutes after my first conversation with the father. I will tell you, I have never seen a so frightened, distraught, almost terrified little man than Frank Morrissey. He should have been. I might throw him out a window, but when Joe Kennedy and his son began to focus on what he'd done, heaven help him."

In the end, Kenny came to the view that it was a totally careless, arrogant, and stupid error on Morrissey's part. Kenny was clear: He had talked to Jack Kennedy. At that moment, Jack couldn't have cared less if Foster Furcolo lived or died. But again this would affect Senator Kennedy's career later on, and that was Kenny and Bobby's concern. "We were building up a solid residue of party regulars who now pointed to this and said, 'We were right about [Jack Kennedy] in '52. He and his people are a bunch of Harvard bastards who take care of themselves. They don't care about the party. Kennedy does not want Furcolo in there, because he will compete with him. Kennedy does not want two Democratic senators.'

"In this period, there is a little anecdote that interests me a great deal and adds some information here," Kenny recalled. "John Fox and I worked in offices side by side at 10 State Street. Bobby and I had breakfast with Fox every morning in '52, and now in '54 we were working in offices side by side, at 10 State Street. It was just such a political office that Paul Dever had used as his headquarters. John Fox is a lawyer and now a federal probate judge. He had been Paul Dever's private personal secretary. He spoke for Dever, totally.

"John Fox was now working for Murphy at Dever's request. That afternoon we went in. Now Fox is a fast-talking, very smart, able operator and a character.

"John said, 'It's awful what has happened. I don't know what we can do.' I said I was in the process, at this stage, of trying to call Mr. Kennedy to see if we can at least get the record clean.

"John said, 'Can I see you for a minute?'

"Now John is probably the most responsible man in the state of Massachusetts for Foster Furcolo. He was Dever's principal advisor, later became Furcolo's principal advisor when he was governor. Furcolo appointed John as a judge. John calls me in. Closed the door. He is a very secretive fellow. He said, 'I don't blame you guys. Furcolo is a real proper son of bitch. You know what he did to us in 1952?'

"I said, 'No, no idea.'

"He said to me, 'In 1952, Dever appointed Furcolo treasurer. Now understand, Dever spent more time campaigning for him than he did for himself to get him the nomination in the primary. Dever went down and had a fight with Jack Kennedy to get him to come out for Furcolo. Had a real fight with him. Kennedy said he would not do it. Dever really put himself on the line for Furcolo and it damaged the relationship. God, to this day [Dever] said he would never forgive himself for having that disagreement with Jack Kennedy. But he got Jack Kennedy to endorse [Furcolo]. Jack Kennedy went on television and endorsed him. Then [Furcolo] won the nomination. Then you know what he did then?'

"I said, 'No idea.'

"'The only reason we had him there,' Fox explained, 'was because he was an Italian and we thought he could help us with the election. You know what he did, after the convention he went to the Cape for the summer. He had no opponent save some pushover who was no contest. We could never get him to make a speech on Dever's behalf. I would call him every day and ask him to make a speech on Dever's behalf to Italian audiences. He would refuse. Be indignant. He would say, "I am not just an Italian candidate." He wouldn't help us one damn bit; that is the kind of fellow he is.'

"Now, what is funny here is later Fox ends up as Furcolo's personal secretary and gets a judgeship through him. Now that's Massachusetts politics!"

But, in this moment, John Fox was in total agreement with Kenny and Bobby that Furcolo was a son of a bitch, but that was a sideline of the complicated political atmosphere in Massachusetts.

"By now, they were getting to the tail end here of the race," as Kenny recalled. "We continue to work for the ticket, but the damage was done. The slings and arrows of outrageous fortune in Massachusetts politics get redirected mainly at me, which was lovely. Every day is another argument and fight. Nobody trusted my word, so everything I said was questioned. To this day, I regret not tossing that little man out the window at 122 Bowdoin Street.

"Fortunately, Furcolo stayed true to form and managed to get himself to a point where the Murphy people don't like him very much, any more than they liked me. He was giving them the leg at every point and every turn," Kenny said. "The Murphy people had liked the Kennedy people. They suddenly see Furcolo up close and began to say, 'Well, you know they are probably right about [Furcolo].' You see Foster thought he was winning, which he wasn't, but he was convinced he was, so he begins to duck events with Murphy. [Furcolo] refuses to go on television with [Murphy]. [Furcolo] went on one show with [Murphy]. Furcolo talked twelve minutes out of the fifteen and took the entire program; Murphy's being kind of slow and deliberate and never quite got into the act. So, as they see him up front, they began to see that there is perhaps some merit in Kennedy not being too in love with Furcolo!"

By this time, Election Day was upon them. Murphy was not too far behind, but not considered a favorite, and they were having difficulty getting money. Dick Maguire, Kenny's friend, was the chief fund-raiser and personally went in the hole pretty substantially for Murphy. It was a close bet. The Republicans played the whole Furcolo/Murphy contest.

The Italians were saying they would not vote for an Irishman. Speaker John McCormack was on the Armed Services Committee. This was a recession year of note, 1954, and there was considerable unemployment in the Bethlehem Shipyard. All of sudden, a week before the election, the Armed Services Committee was awarded a contract for a great big carrier. "Completely by accident, of course," Kenny laughed. "There was a great big play on the front page of all the papers about what Republican Saltonstall could do for the state because of his relationship with Eisenhower. This picked up his numbers and campaign considerably. The campaign went on, and other than this damaging fight with Furcolo, it would have been one of the most boring campaigns in the history of the state. Herter was a bore as a campaigner, Furcolo was not much as a candidate, and Murphy was a just a total bore." In the end, Kenny and Larry just wanted it over.

Underlying all the political drama, Jack remained in the hospital. "It was clear," Kenny had confided to Helen, "things were much worse than just a bad back, but the Kennedys remained secretive." It was not Kenny's manner to pry. "I talked to him quite a bit, but there was not too much to tell him. None of it was good and I did not want to add to his deepening depression. At the end of the campaign, I gave an interview in which I announced that all the Kennedy workers were going to be working for the Murphy/Furcolo ticket. This I did purely to reemphasize the senator's statement and was done purely for the record. It was an extensive newspaper interview. I still have it. I rarely did that. I went on to explain that they all had worked very hard and extensively for the entire ticket from Furcolo on down, so it at least clarified the record. It was of some use later, but nobody really believed it. The senator was pleased. It was the moment he seemed to actually take some interest," Kenny recalled.

By the time election night arrived, Kenny was exhausted. Jack was still in the hospital. He had not yet had the operation on his back, because his immune system remained dangerously vulnerable. While Kenny suspected it was bad, he did not know how bad it really was; nor did he realize that Jack was actually near death. The Kennedy family kept a tight lid on Jack's illness and closed ranks even on Kenny about how serious things had gotten for Jack as he fought for his life.

"I spoke to him often about the campaign from the hospital and got no indication from him of the seriousness," Kenny noted. "Again, we are building the relationship; he has no reason in his view to tell me this, nor felt any obligation to do so. Maybe he thought I knew? Maybe he thought Bobby had told me, but Bobby had not. He continued to give me the impression that this was just a slight corrective thing, like that, he would snap his fingers.

"I knew he was in terrible pain. Frankly, the tenor of his voice was tinged with pain. You could detect pain even over the telephone. It was the first time in my experience with him, and I would say in his life, when he was in fact disinterested completely in politics. He would call regularly. He wanted the facts, but he did not really appear to care very much one way or the other. I almost got the feeling sometimes he just wanted to talk. So he would. I would listen. These conversations never went any further.

"He talked about life, his thoughts, views, and what he wanted to do. I just listened. I never asked any questions, never had an opinion. Most out of character for him. He did not know me well, but he knew or was learning I had his best interest at heart; and he was also learning anything he said to me stayed with me, so he could freely express himself. Sometimes it is easier to do with someone like me than your family. I got the feeling he did not want his parents or brothers and sisters to see this side of him. Normally, anything you said to him, he would grill you and check it with you fifteen different ways, always, even as president. Fifteen different questions always. But during this period, anything I said he would just accept and never question, and then go back to his own thought process."

On the night of the election, Kenny recalled, "I went to the headquarters that night, but my heart was not in it. My mind was quite firmly on the senator and his personal struggles. Election night, not knowing if he would make it or not left me cold. He needed to be there. He wasn't. Instead, he was in the hospital fighting for his life."

He left it to Kenny and Larry to keep his political life viable.

Despite his worry about Jack's health, Kenny joined the Kennedy political group and monitored the returns. As Kenny described it, "We started in his apartment at 122 Bowdoin Street. Then we moved to an apartment above his, which had a bigger television. Dave was there, Larry O'Brien, Helen, some other girls, and myself.

"My own personal opinion was that it was a fifty-fifty fight. I thought it had been a boring contest, Murphy a boring candidate, but with the Democrats even under normal circumstances before Kennedy, that Murphy had a chance and it was a fifty-fifty contest.

As the night dragged on, Kenny recalled, "Furcolo had won up until three o'clock in the morning; they had conceded that Furcolo had been elected. He was ahead by the usual Democratic majority; it was dwindling, but on the basis of their projections Furcolo had been elected by about ten thousand votes. It was very interesting as we left that night, on the basis of their projections there were three contests being decided on the basis of the same amount: Abe Ribicoff in Connecticut by two or three thousand. He was being defeated at the time by five thousand, though he eventually won. Ives was being elected in New York by twenty thousand. Of the seven million cast in New York, Harriman finally won by eleven thousand votes. So here we are sitting in the Kennedy apartment and poor Larry O'Brien sees Furcolo is winning. One has never seen such a picture of sadness and despair as O'Brien believes that Furcolo had won. He is so disgusted, he gets up and leaves without a word and drove to Springfield at three a.m."

Kenny figured they might as well go home as well. "Helen and I drove Dave home," Kenny said. "I remember it so well, because Dave was, even at that moment, with that sunny Irish disposition, explaining away what had happened. That the candidate we were for just got beat; the candidate we were against won. I was sick to my stomach. Dave was saying, 'You know the worst Democrat is just that much better than the best Republican!'

"He then went on to say what was wrong with Saltonstall, and he knew a couple of fellows whose sisters had met Furcolo, and he was not such a bad fellow, and he knew Furcolo's wife, and she is a good egg. He went on and on and on trying to cheer me up. I thought Helen was going to hit him with her shoe!

"We took him home. He got out and I think that is probably the only moment when Helen did not like Dave in her life! We arrive home and we are sick. Helen is sick. Just awful night. When I arrived home, we turn on the television and to our astonishment Saltonstall had won by twenty-seven thousand votes; the earlier projections had been off. It was all over and Furcolo was done. Politics is great. You just never know; the result changed our whole evening. We cheered, had a drink, and called Dave to tease him!

"Anyway, that was the end of the 1954 campaign, but over the course of the next several weeks, Kennedy takes a brutal beating. Each Republican columnist and many Democrats stuck the knife into Kennedy, blaming him for the losses. Everyone who could blamed Kennedy over the Furcolo loss. They all said Kennedy did it deliberately. Larry remembered it as a 'terrible time. The fact is Murphy got a substantial knifing from the Italians.'

"Unfortunately, we did not hurt Furcolo one darn bit. Murphy lost by seventy thousand votes; Furcolo lost by twenty-seven thousand. This was a tough time for Jack Kennedy. This is kind of a low point politically for Kennedy. This combined with the Saint Lawrence Seaway political disaster that Jack is blamed for.

"Jack remained in the hospital, under the knife, and the odds were against his survival, and the view among political people was that he would not live. That if he did live, he would be a cripple. Now, as I say, we did not realize how sick he was until after the election; then it became clear he might not make it.

"The political wise guys and the word on the street was that John Kennedy, if he lived, was through in politics. Period."

Kenny remembered one particular incident, which was an example of just how difficult Jack's illness had become for the Kennedy team. "Now a fellow named Frank Tracey, who is one of the closest advisors to Mayor Hynes," Kenny recollected, "and still a power in Boston politics, bet me $5 in a restaurant that Jack Kennedy would be dead by the end of the month. That was the rumor. Judge Jim Mellon, who was with me at the time, tried to hit him, but I stepped in just in time. Frank said John Kennedy would be dead by end of the month and, if he lived, would never win another Democratic nomination and would never walk again. Ever. I will never forget it. He said all this while laughing. Maybe I should have let Mellon poke him."

Kenny remembered this as a particularly "ugly time." John Kennedy, if he lived, seemed to be through in politics. "At the end of that election, 1954 to 1955, John Kennedy was at the lowest point of any time I have known him in his career . . . physically, mentally, and politically. He was at the bottom. It seemed over."

CHAPTER 7

Jack's "Valley of Depression"

Throughout 1954, Jack struggled through two failed back surgeries, having a metal plate put in his back, and countless hospital visits. While the details remained largely mysterious to them, Kenny and Larry knew it was not going well but forged ahead and nevertheless kept developing the Kennedy organization, assuming its leader would return to take charge soon. Privately, though, Kenny told Helen that Jack's health problems really cast doubt on the Kennedy organization's future.

For Jack, the next three or four months were periods of convalescence and recovery. Things were so tentative with regard to his medical situation that neither Kenny nor Larry were thinking beyond this year.

If they had any doubts, Bobby's call confirmed their fears. The minute Kenny took the call, he could tell by Bobby's tone the news was bad. Jack had once again been given last rites. The family gathered. A political career looked increasingly unlikely. "If he survives," Bobby said quietly, his voice just above a whisper, "it is unlikely his quality of life would allow him to continue in elected office."

Jack's surgery was in New York, ostensibly for back problems that had plagued him since the war. The truth was much more complicated, and though Kenny never addressed it publicly or with anyone save Helen, it was evident that he knew much and said almost nothing. This would be proven by documents and records that Kenny had kept hidden for years in his basement, but when he felt his own death approaching, with Jackie's guidance, everything had been destroyed. What we do know now is that in 1954 neither Kenny nor Larry yet had the full picture. Besides the bad back, in 1954 Jack began treatment for Addison's disease. That was only part of what Kenny would learn.

Much of this information was revealed years later, long after Kenny had died, in a book by historian Robert Dallek, *An Unfinished Life*. Dalleck enlisted the help of Dr. Jeffrey Kelman to comb through John Kennedy's medical records, then stored at the Kennedy Library. Kelman described Jack's condition in stark terms: "Addison's disease is adrenal insufficiency. The adrenal gland makes corticosteroids and other hormones that are used for salt metabolism, response to stress, response to inflammation. In '47 he was officially diagnosed in England as being adrenally insufficient, and from that point on, at least that point on, he was being treated with daily corticosteroids of some form or another. There is some evidence he was actually being treated earlier. . . . But from '47 he had to receive daily steroids to survive." Kleman said later, "It's always dangerous; without being supported, patients die. And the steroids themselves have side effects, including susceptibility to infection. Kennedy needed multiple courses of antibiotics, he had urinary infections, skin infections, he had respiratory infections. By the time he was president, he was on ten, 12 medications a day. He was on antispasmodics for his bowel, paregoric, lamodal transatine [ph], he was on muscle relaxants, Phenobarbital, Librium, Meprobomate, he was on pain medications, Codeine, Demerol, Methadone, he was on oral cortisone; he was on injected cortisone, he was on testosterone, he was on Nembutal for sleep. And on top of that he was getting injected sometimes six times a day, six places on his back, by the White House physician, with Novocain, Procaine, just to enable him to face the day."

Whether Kenny or Larry knew or grasped the full picture of Jack's illness in 1954 remains unclear. We know that Kenny became familiar with it later but kept it to himself. But in 1954 Bobby was a conduit. Jack and Kenny had not yet reached that level of trust in their relationship. Bobby called Kenny again around this time and said he had to come up and see him. "I talked to Bobby before and especially after the senator became ill and this thing had broken, and it was clear the damage had been done. Bobby came up to see me to discuss the senator's position politically. By this time the dies had been cast; there wasn't much any of us could do. Bobby's involvement in that campaign was not at all, until Jack went into the hospital and the political damage was clear. Then he came up to see me to determine what if anything we could do to salvage the situation."

In fairness, at this time, Kenny did not take a position, because when Bobby came up to see him and told him the entire background and completely explained Jack's situation, he suddenly realized how very sick Jack Kennedy was.

"Clearly, I knew it was bad," Kenny said, "but I never fully grasped the gravity until that moment. I realized when Bobby called and told me that they had just given him the last rites of the church.

"Suddenly," Kenny said, "I was not particularly interested in his political situation, but rather his survival. This was January or February 1955. I talked to Bobby, who was in Rhode Island, Newport. I was so shocked, I could not believe it. I don't even remember who called me, someone else in the family, who said Bobby was having a tough time and prompted me to call Bobby again. Then I was upset, having just got Bobby calmed down; I got a call from a newspaperman, who had called and said he had contacts at the hospital and that Senator Kennedy had been given the last rites. I was not happy with that call and told him where to go."

Remember, at this time Kenny believed, as did many, that this was an adjustment, a minor injury, which had gone a bit awry, which is what Jack had told Kenny and Larry at the Ritz months before. That night, Kenny sat down with Helen and asked her what to do. How he should handle it.

"She told me that I must call Bobby again and say, in essence, what the hell is going on?

"I finally got through to him, but Bobby said he really didn't know much more than we did. That it was true. He was given the last rites. But he is better now. He had a temperature of 104 or 105 degrees, and he almost died. I said, "My God, Bobby, I just did not realize it. I am so sorry. I did not realize it.

"Bobby said, 'Yeah, it is okay now, none of us did, but it was a close thing, but he is okay now. He is over it now. They gave him the last rites, the entire family was called in, but amazingly he pulled through. He is a tough guy. It looks like he is going to pull through, but he is still a very sick guy. You could call him and talk to him about the political situation to cheer him up.

"I remember thinking, *what?* I doubt he wants to hear from me again just now. That is the first time I ever realized the extent of his sickness. I had no political thoughts at the moment. I was shocked. We had to try to be optimistic and hoped he would live; then, if he lived, that he could make a comeback into politics, but it did not look good."

The political wise guys were saying, and Kenny and Larry now realized it was probably true, that, if he lived, he would not be walking again at a minimum. Kenny said, "If he had the temperatures of 104 and then 105, the back had been that bad, they had operated on it twice, and Bobby [said] that they had put a steel plate in, then it had caused another infection. They were hopeful they could get [Jack] out, but [Bobby] did not know for sure."

"While the words were optimistic, the tone in his voice was not," Kenny remembered. "I read between the lines . . . [that] whatever political future Jack Kennedy had was tentative at best; as far as getting into the maelstrom and brawls and the fights that were necessary to control the party, that Jack Kennedy was not capable of that. That quite frankly this might be the end of it right here; and possibly, if Jack Kennedy recovered, Bobby said they were hopeful he could be at least on crutches for the rest of his life, rather than a wheelchair. Bobby said that if that happened and he could use crutches that [we] might possibly be able to think about him running for Senate again, but even that was a long shot. He said simply he was not sure Jack would be physically up to it again.

"I am not sure I even raised the party issue or went through it; I had no thoughts up until the astonishing spring of that year that there would be any interest [in] Jack Kennedy in any future control of the Democratic Party or even his own political future. There was a total drumbeat that if he lived, he was not going to return to the Senate. There were stories almost every day that he was going to be a cripple for life, if he lived, and never run again. The politicians made sure the 'He's going to be a cripple for life' stories were in the press at least ten times a day."

If Kenny had hoped Jack's illness would make other politicians sympathetic, he was wrong. Did his plight not make them at least a little sympathetic? For Jack's enemies, it did not. His enemies almost exulted, because they saw Jack's condition as a way in which he would be removed from the political scene without them having to defeat him.

Kenny recalled, "They wrote Jack off as finished and they were looking forward to the next fight and planning who would replace him in the Senate. Furcolo had already looked forward; he had made up his mind, and he had made a good run, and was going to run for governor. The stories were being planted—he was a great public relations guy—that an Italian could not be denied twice and this proved to be right. Kennedy could not be against him again since Kennedy was removed from the political scene now and in the future. There were no other candidates around. Murphy could not run again, and so from that moment on Furcolo was then a candidate and was the political force in politics for the governorship."

Kenny felt sick. He'd known during that first event in Worcester, when he saw Jack in one unguarded moment, that the situation was graver than anyone in the Kennedy family would admit. He did not know any details at the time; he just knew the situation was bad. Based on his conversations with Jack, he had gotten a deepening sense of the problem but still did not have the full picture. Neither Bobby nor the father had filled him in completely. In the end, he felt it was up to Jack to decide what was and wasn't his business.

He had his fears all along, but he brushed them aside. Jack seemed to recover each time his back pain flared up, so Kenny convinced himself, as no doubt did Joe Kennedy, Bobby, and other Kennedy family members, that Jack would rally. Kenny had begun to spend a lot of time with Dave Powers, in whom he found a kindred spirit.

For Dave, Kenny was a welcome friend, someone in whom he could confide about Jack's health without fearing that it would not be kept confidential. Dave confirmed what Bobby had already said. It didn't look good. Still, Kenny and Larry hoped for the best. Neither the Kennedy secretaries nor Jack's constituents back home in Massachusetts knew anything about his health situation. And for political reasons, Kenny and Larry had no intention of enlightening them.

"We really do realize that we would be fortunate if Senator Kennedy ever came back," Kenny confirmed to Helen. "And if he does, he would be at the bottom of his political power. The jockeying for the 1956 governorship had commenced and our vaunted Kennedy organization has neither a candidate for governor nor our political leader."

Without Jack's even tacit involvement in the state races, Kenny and Larry could go only so far.

As Kenny remembered it, "We did not appear to have a candidate, and if we did, it would probably have been very difficult for us to put him across, because we would have had to take on Foster Furcolo. That would have meant that any Irish candidate, and it would have to be an Irish candidate, would have split the Irish vote wide open and therefore could not be elected in 1956."

The political elite in Massachusetts, ready to move in at a moment's notice, had begun to smell a bit of blood in the water. Maybe they had been right the first time: This Kennedy kid did not have staying power. He was physically fragile, which made him and his organization vulnerable.

Kenny and Larry were good, but neither of them were Jack Kennedy, and until Jack was on his feet, assuming that ever happened, the Kennedy organization was headed nowhere. The one thing that worried Kenny and Larry the most, beyond Jack's simple survival, was that they knew power abhorred a vacuum. If they could not move soon, all they had built since 1952 would be lost.

It was a low point, no question, and things only got worse when Dave confirmed another suspicion of Bobby's. "There are real problems with his mental situation at this time," Bobby had said. "He is deeply depressed. I am very worried."

If Bobby and Dave were worried, that worried Kenny. It was Dave, not Kenny, who had spent the most time with Jack at this point. Kenny, a man of action rarely given to inward reflection, felt helpless before the rumors of Jack's slipping mental health.

Kenny would upon occasion chat with Jack, mostly at Bobby's or Dave's request, trying to get some spark of interest out of him about the political situation in Massachusetts. "I had no idea what to say to him," Kenny said, "except to say, look, we need you up here. We need you now. Often, he would then go off into other areas, and again, all I could do was listen, then try, mostly unsuccessfully, to bring him back to politics and the present."

Helen suggested that just listening to him might be enough. Kenny wasn't sure. He feared for Jack's future, for their political future, if Jack didn't make it. For the first time since jumping in full throttle behind Jack Kennedy's political ambitions, things were beginning to slip out of Kenny's control, a feeling he was both unfamiliar with and did not at all enjoy. All his political skill and toughness could not save Jack's life or get Jack back on his feet or shake him out of this depression, if he did not want to be. So while receiving regular updates from Bobby and Dave, Kenny, like the rest of the Kennedy family, had to wait and hope for the best.

Jack Kennedy's recovery had been miserably slow. But he seemed to find strength and even some solace in updates on his foundering political organization in Massachusetts. Kenny would talk to him more often about the political situation, but up until the spring of 1955, it remained a general concern whether or not Jack would be back. Rumors that he was up and walking would begin, then the next day there would be a setback and he would be bedridden once more.

"Here we were," Kenny said later, "from the end of '54 in this 'valley of depressions.' We had begun to create a pretty good Democratic organization of our own, but we recognized we had nowhere to go politically without the senator. The Kennedy organization was treading water."

As Kenny said later, "We'd brought on some very good people. They found with us they could get to Jack Kennedy through Ken O'Donnell and Larry O'Brien, whom they felt some common bond with. Therefore, they strongly wanted to be with us, in case our candidate were to return to his full physical powers. We all certainly believed he had the potential to recoup his political fortunes should he return."

The problem was, the longer he was out of the picture, the harder it would be for Kenny and Larry to hold on to this group of people and move forward. Eventually people would want to speak to the candidate directly. There would come a time when only Jack Kennedy himself, his presence, could hold the organization together.

The wait was longer than planned or anticipated, but in late spring 1955, as Kenny was headed out the door, the phone rang. His political fortunes were again about to turn. He stopped long enough to hear Helen laughing and joking with someone on the telephone before he dropped his briefcase and took the call. He had assumed by her teasing tone that it was Bobby. He was stunned but relieved when he picked up the receiver to hear Jack's voice on the line.

"Thanks for keeping things moving," was all he said. That was all that needed to be said; he was back and he had an agenda.

It took Kenny a moment to cover his surprise as Jack quickly asked for an update since their last conversation. "Pretty much where you left it, Senator," Kenny explained. "We could not do much without you, frankly."

Kenny gave Jack the latest overview. He could tell Jack was sharp, on his game.

"I am ready," Jack said.

"Good," was all Kenny said. He would have to ask Bobby later what had happened.

Later, when Kenny asked him, Bobby had been quiet and then said, "He lived. He made it. Then he realized, maybe he had made it for a reason. You'd have to ask him what changed."

Kenny, not a man to pry, felt when the senator was ready, he'd tell him directly. On one level, the Kennedy family were very private people. Kenny felt maybe he owed them some semblance of privacy. There was time enough to hear what had happened, but what Kenny wanted Jack to focus on now was what could happen in the future with Jack at the helm. Jack seemed ready, albeit frustrated that more hadn't been done in his absence. Somehow, perhaps because of the extra time on his hands, he had suddenly decided to build that Kennedy organization after all; that Kenny and Larry might just have been right. His political juices were again flowing.

Jack understood the delay, but now he wanted action. On a conference call later that same day, Jack told them of his plans. When he returned to Massachusetts, the first thing he wanted to do was have a political reunion of the Kennedy secretaries. This was good news.

Jack had recognized during his down period that he had a problem, and he made a couple of key decisions. He was going to take several strong steps. Proving he was healthy was the main step, but he also needed to find a candidate for '56. Because of the advent of a convention system, which had not existed in '52, Jack realized that unless he had a candidate to back in '56, he would not have much influence at the convention. Also, he was already looking ahead toward '58, and he knew he had to move fast. He had to solidify his forces, reintroducing himself to his most powerful constituents. To further this goal, he decided to have a clambake at his father's house on the Cape in mid-June 1955.

The clambake, Jack explained, was going to be a political first. He wanted to use it as an opportunity to bring everyone together, all the political players in Massachusetts, for an afternoon at the Kennedy compound. "I want this to be a huge success."

THE CLAMBAKE WAS billed as a reunion for the Kennedy secretaries, and the entire Massachusetts legislature was invited. It was the first of what remains to this day a Kennedy political tradition. From Kenny's perspective, this event allowed the Kennedy organization to show that Jack was back in full form and ready to take charge of his organization. This was essential as they looked toward both the 1956 Democratic Convention the following summer and the 1958 Senate race.

Kenny had nodded, his political instinct kicking in. With a quick glance to the father, Kenny recognized the brilliance of Jack's plan. "The event would consolidate the work that he and Larry had been doing in a vacuum for the last couple of years in the wilderness. With Jack, Jackie, and the compound center stage, it would immediately give the impression that Jack was the returning political hero. It would be by design to set the stage for the takeover of the Massachusetts Democratic Party and to sideline Furcolo all at once.

"I mean, come on," Kenny had said to Helen, "after this event, if Jack was firing on all cylinders, Furcolo would go back to being second string."

Helen had laughed. Personally, she had wondered aloud whether one event could do all that.

"But," Kenny had explained, "the event and really not just the event, Jack's presence and appearance of health and strength would convince the political doubters that Jack was back and ready for action. Jack personally would just tie the strings together of all the hard work and pieces we had put in place."

In truth, Helen didn't care that much how it was accomplished. She was just happy to see Kenny back in action. "Back on the field," as she told Bobby with a laugh.

What struck Kenny the most about Jack's appearance at the reception was that he no longer needed crutches. He was even able to play a little softball. In the end, Jack demonstrated without a doubt that he was back and able to take charge politically.

The event was a successful all-day affair. There were games, sailing, plenty of food, and plenty to drink. As much as Jack's presence, his ability to shake hands and move without crutches or obvious pain relieved everybody who had been so concerned for him. What Kenny remembered the most from that day was that Jack still had the same vivid attraction for people. All the Kennedy people naturally loved him.

Kenny and Larry were also watching the professionals and the decision makers. Those were the people about whom Kenny and Larry were concerned now. Their reactions to Jack's health and competence were what mattered the most.

"The state politicians loved him despite themselves," Kenny recalled. "There he was after all these rumors about his health, walking around tanned and in his brightest form, and the professional politicians [who had written him off] were now chasing him around with their cameramen and trying to get a picture with Jack Kennedy. It was very clear to me at that moment that Jack Kennedy was a breath of fresh air and a shining light in politics to these people."

With great relief, the Irish Brotherhood began to move the organization forward, knowing they once again had a leader at the helm. Kenny and Larry realized another critical point about the Kennedy organization that breezy afternoon in mid-June. They realized they had perhaps inadvertently kept some of these high-profile decision makers in the Democratic Party, Kennedy fans all, away from the senator and that it was now time to bring them in closer. It was evident that many of these people were thrilled to be at the Kennedy compound, excited to be in Jack's presence.

"They in fact did want to be associated with him," Kenny noted, "and some of them were excellent political fellows, though some of them were rogues, as they have in any party. But it was important for our political future and for the senator's that if we were going to take the next step and get involved in the party, we should know them on an intimate, personal basis. We realized then that it was important that they should feel we were not snobs, that we did not look down at the 'regulars' in the political organization and in the legislature. We would like to work with them." These regular political types had never been to the Kennedy compound as such, had never touched such glamour. Jack's arrival electrified the event. They were delighted to be included along with their wives and their families.

With Jack's successful return, the future of the Kennedy organization in Massachusetts was assured. No matter what Joe or Frank Morrissey did, no matter what Ted Sorensen did in Washington, Jack's Irish Brotherhood now had a role to play.

"It was time to get to work," as Kenny explained. "We felt what we had felt from the beginning. In the proper hands, this Kennedy organization, properly used, side by side with an office holder, and a powerful office holder such as Jack Kennedy, would place us in a commanding position within the state power structure."

Jack, Kenny, Larry, Dave, and a reluctant Bobby Kennedy were now squarely looking toward Chicago and the Democratic Convention of 1956.

Kenny summed it up: "Jack Kennedy's magic was as solid as it ever had been. He was on his feet. He was healthy again, physically and mentally. The great attraction of the candidate was on display, and the fear that he might not return, that siding with Jack Kennedy was a risk, was finally put to rest. Too many of these regular politicians who had eyed Jack with suspicion as an outsider, a rich kid, and a lightweight now saw something else. They saw their political future and the future of the party in Massachusetts. They knew now it was better to be on the winning side, and for the regulars that meant siding with Jack Kennedy. For the Brotherhood's part, we accepted that Senator Kennedy may have hit bottom, but he had gotten back up. He had now a solid foundation from which to build forward, and that was our plan." Given what Kenny learned later, and what we now truly know of Jack Kennedy's illness and his literal fight to live, that he survived and decided to return to politics and pursue the presidency makes this story even more remarkable.

It was a dramatic, theatrical, unusual, and critical comeback. With Jack simply struggling to survive and Bob Murphy defeated, the political power structure had begun to seriously look to Foster Furcolo as the "up-and-coming politician," Kenny noted. "Look," he told Vanocur, "nobody was overly thrilled by him, but with Murphy's defeat, Jack seemingly on the ropes, everyone was looking for somebody to lead the delegation. Seemed Furcolo was the man. He was an Italian; though he had been defeated once for governor, he figured, correctly as it turned out, he could not be defeated a second time."

With Jack Kennedy's return to the political arena, the Kennedy organization, such as it existed at the time, was back in action. "We realized both selfishly and in what we thought would be politically good for him [that] we had to take every step possible to maintain our contacts with the Kennedy organization. To preserve it as an entity in his absence and to in fact keep him viable in his absence and until he could or would reemerge. We had to, in fact, propagandize this organization and give the appearance to other politicians and the public that this was a cohesive, solid group and that we were responsive to Senator John Kennedy. That we spoke for him, acted for him, and as a matter of fact we were Senator John Kennedy's agents in Massachusetts. We had no titles. We had no office. We had no direct authority and it was a very difficult task to perform. We received no help or encouragement from Washington. Occasionally, Jack would call me and it would be a general chat. If he wanted something done on a political basis, it was now done again through Frank Morrissey and communicated by the father."

Kenny learned only later from Jack himself that he had during his illness made a mental decision to survive. He had reached a point where during illness you have to decide, am I going to fight this or am I going to give in. Once he decided to fight it, to make that comeback, then that meant committing completely to succeeding in politics. That meant a call to Kenny and Larry, because any politician worth a damn must have a successful team around him and a top-notch organization. Jack perhaps discussed this with his father or Jackie, but Kenny and Jack were still learning to trust each other. Kenny could say to Larry only that it certainly appeared to him that Jack had overcome some mental obstacle. Made some decision. Not an introspective man, Kenny was again hesitant to pry. Bobby had no real answers but did say, "I think he figured if he made it through this, he can make it through anything."

In the fall of 1955, the success of the event was in the proverbial rearview mirror and the boys were looking to consolidate their power and get Jack control of the Massachusetts Democratic Party as they eyed the upcoming convention in Chicago in 1956. They intended to arrive in Chicago with Jack as the party leader.

"At the time," Kenny laughed later, "none of us were even thinking of his running for the VP slot with Stevenson." And years later, when Kenny would read about the "vaunted Kennedy organization," he would laugh. "Organization?" He joked, "if that had existed we'd have been ready for the vice presidential race in '56, we'd have run with Stevenson, lost, and Jack's whole career would have been over. Larry and I would have been the biggest political bums in the world!"

By early fall, "the senator understood what we were doing. The national situation had begun to emerge and he had made his decision in that regard.

He knew he was looking nationally and now was looking for an opportunity. The state committee has now begun to have fights. John McCormack and Paul Dever had discovered it was a paper tiger. Kennedy was not interested, because he was looking toward national office. Whatever he'd come through, he had made the decision, he was going national," Kenny said.

Quite apart from Jack Kennedy's political aspirations, Speaker McCormack made the decision to take over the state committee. McCormack's people had sensed that there was an area of power that was vacant here. It was evident that again the senator had taken a pass, and so McCormack decided that he would have his guys move in.

Dick Maguire had come over to the Kennedy organization from Bob Murphy's campaign. Kenny later teased, "Well, Murphy may have lost, but we won, because we got Dick Maguire." With each new acquisition, Kenny and Larry saw themselves building toward a national run, though they did not say that directly to Jack Kennedy. They felt it was unnecessary, since they knew instinctively they were acting at his behest and carrying out his wishes.

Speaker McCormack and allies' reasons for moving in were slightly different than ours—that is OBrien, O'Donnell, and Maguire. "The reason was that the speaker's son Eddie McCormack was now making his move into politics and they want to nominate him for Massachusetts attorney general," Kenny explained. "As I have said, those who are interested in becoming attorney general are rather peculiar people. They are all lawyers. There are other forces of politics and the fringe groups are very interested in who becomes attorney general. On the face of it, [Eddie McCormack] had a pretty good background. Graduated from Annapolis, Boston University Law School, lawyer. He had run for the city council of Boston, he was one of nine, but he always ran near the top or at the top, as anyone named McCormack would.

"Looking back," Kenny said, "in fact, our position before Jack's return at this time was at best a tenuous one and, as I say, a propaganda one, to maintain our position and the appearance of a political organization to the politicians. Now, I'm talking about those generally interested in the next gubernatorial or Senate fight. We were selfish to some degree to maintain this position. We also felt it would be good for him in the long run, even if at the moment he was largely removed."

Kenny and Larry agreed. "There were two parts to this," Kenny said. "My feeling was that Mr. Kennedy did not want his son embroiled in what he considered the old Irish fights and had other concerns about his son at the moment. He thought getting into those contests would only further weaken him politically and he had nothing to gain by them. He also felt that his control or hold of a state organization which was essentially defunct did him no good." In truth, Joe believed even when it acted, the state organization had little effect. The Democratic Party in Massachusetts had historically been a party of individuals: the Curley organization, the Dever organization, the Tobin organization, and now the Kennedy organization.

The truth was—and Kenny guessed as much—that Joe Kennedy was also intelligent enough to realize that "O'Donnell and O'Brien have a vested interest in being associated with the Kennedys; perhaps they want something for themselves. So they probably will be taking some actions in Massachusetts, which will be in their own selfish interests but might not be in the interests of Jack Kennedy. [Jack] should be very careful in what actions they did take. Make sure those actions were known to [Jack] and were not taken without [Jack's] knowledge."

Jack had dismissed his father's advice. He was well aware of what O'Donnell and O'Brien were doing. Jack just needed to be able to disavow anything should it go wrong. Should it work, then Jack would walk into the convention as political leader.

Kenny noted, "I always had the feeling that Mr. Kennedy was against Jack's further involvement and always felt that [Joe Kennedy] believed O'Donnell and O'Brien were pushing themselves and thinking of only themselves."

"Don't be used," Joe warned his son.

"Mr. Kennedy," Kenny said, "encouraged by those like Morrissey, felt we were thinking of our own personal ambitions, problems, and through this organization and the Kennedy association were trying to advance our own goals, our own political careers, or become the conduit for Kennedy to the candidate for governor, who would then reward us in some fashion with a job, etc. It was his firm belief by this time that our views and judgments did not coincide with the interests of his son Senator Kennedy. I think the senator assumed we were thinking of ourselves, and, in fairness, the Kennedys always think of themselves and take care of themselves first. And they don't expect anyone else to be much different. That would not be totally untrue."

With that in mind, Joe watched their actions with some care, though at the same time, as Kenny noted, "Whatever actions we took to maintain the Kennedy organization and to maintain our positions in the hierarchy of the party, without hurting him, were to his advantage."

This was all going on in the background when, with '56 and the Chicago Democratic Convention looming, Kenny and Larry decided to make the move to take over the Massachusetts Democratic Party with a shrewd, savvy political operator by the name of John "Pat" Lynch.

JACK'S FATHER HAD wanted Jack to stay out of the fight for control of the Massachusetts Democratic Party, but pushed by circumstances and hard sells by Kenny and Larry, Jack had jumped in with the same competitive spirit he would demonstrate in Chicago. He ended up in control of the Massachusetts Democratic Party, putting Lynch in charge. He had not really wanted Lynch, but his choices had been limited.

Lynch was the longtime mayor of Somerville. He seemed exactly the type of old-school politician that Jack was determined to defeat. When Kenny brought Lynch in to meet Jack, it was priceless when Jack looked at Kenny as if Kenny had lost his mind. Lynch was a small, bald-headed Irishman who wore a wide-brimmed felt hat and a velvet collar typical of Boston Irish politicians. He looked, Kenny later joked, like a "fifty-five-year-old leprechaun" smoking a cigar.

Kenny chuckled to himself as he saw the "look of shock on Jack's face."

"You've got to be kidding," Jack whispered to Kenny.

No. Kenny was not kidding. Lynch may have been old-school, but he was a political realist and he would play ball Jack's way, and that was exactly what they needed. Jack had reluctantly agreed. In the end, Lynch was elected and Jack uneasily and perhaps somewhat unhappily took the reins of the Massachusetts Democratic Party.

"I felt," Jack later told Bobby, "like I needed to take a shower when the battle was over."

Nevertheless, it had put Jack front and center in national politics and he had emerged as a force to be reckoned with. Stevenson and his team had watched Jack's growing visibility and power with great interest, sensing that they might be able to use Jack's new prominence and popularity to help the Democratic ticket.

CHAPTER 8

Chicago

W HEN THE DEMOCRATS opened the convention in Chicago in
1956, it was supposed to be a cakewalk for Adlai Stevenson and his
presumed running mate, Senator Carey Estes Kefauver from Tennessee.
Adlai Stevenson had run and lost against Eisenhower in 1952, but he was
back in 1956 as the nominee, due in no small part to his background as
governor of Illinois, his liberal political philosophy, and his friendship with
Eleanor Roosevelt.

Eleanor had come to be seen as the grand dame of the liberal wing of
the Democrats. Stevenson was not only her friend but also the darling of
the party's left wing and the labor movement. Known for his brilliant ora-
tory and left-wing politics, he was not a man of the people and therefore not
really Kenny or Joe Kennedy's kind of guy. Even Jack Kennedy's sudden rise
to prominence as the new boss of the Democratic Party in Massachusetts
had caught Stevenson off guard, but he quickly surmised that, as they had
with Joe Kennedy in '52, they could get support and money and use Jack's
newfound renown to help the Stevenson campaign without having to really
give anything up.

Kenny and Bobby had taken the train from Boston to Chicago, getting
there a few days ahead of Jack in order to set up their "operation," as Bobby
would later chuckle. By 1960, Bobby would know the difference between

an authentic political operation and what he and Kenny cobbled together in Chicago in '56. They chose to set up Jack's rooms at the Chicago Hilton, which was centrally located and close to the convention site. Kenny had chosen a suite of rooms for Jack, who arrived a few days later.

As they took a break in between meetings at the hotel, Kenny said jokingly to Bobby, as they watched Stevenson's people both embrace and push Jack back politically, "It just reminds me of the story of the Irish girl who worked so hard at converting her Jewish boyfriend to Catholicism that he became a priest."

Bobby just stared at Kenny for a moment in silence and then shook his head. "Where do you get this stuff anyway? I think you just make it up."

Kenny laughed, but as they began to increasingly talk to the political bosses, especially urban Irish political pros, it became quickly apparent that they preferred Jack for vice president. Kenny was intrigued and surprised, his political juices primed.

This was Kenny and Bobby's first national political convention. They arrived in Chicago as Jack Kennedy's lead operatives. Kenny teased Bobby, "Well, at least *I'm* Jack's political operative."

"What the heck does that make me?" Bobby asked, annoyed.

"His brother," Kenny jibed back.

Bobby just stared at Kenny as they walked across the convention floor. Bobby suddenly stopped. "You just enjoy annoying me sometimes, don't you?"

Kenny shrugged. "Perhaps."

"Political operative," Bobby laughed as they continued. "You know about as much about how to operate at a national convention as I do, which is to say almost nothing."

Kenny laughed. "Well, we are only here to observe anyway," he told Bobby reassuringly.

Kenny could not have been more wrong.

As they made the rounds, talking to political professionals, one thing became increasingly clear: There was great unease with Stevenson's presumed choice of running mate. Everyone assumed it to be Carey Estes Kefauver, the senator from Tennessee, seen as a good balance for a ticket headed by Adlai Stevenson of Illinois.

The northern political leaders, mostly Irish, had heard more on the inside track about how attractive Jack Kennedy might be as a candidate. They, and even some of their southern counterparts, saw Kefauver and Hubert Humphrey, the fast-rising senator from Minnesota, as dangerously liberal.

Jack may be just the answer to Kefauver, they began to murmur, whispering in Kenny and Bobby's ears. Kenny and Bobby especially liked what they were hearing, but were they serious or simply using the Kennedy team as leverage to have more weight and pull with a Stevenson/Kefauver ticket? Kenny did not know, nor did Bobby, and they completely forgot or ignored Joe Kennedy's sound political advice, back at the Cape during dinner, before they had left for Chicago.

Joe had warned them, "Don't be used!" Having just come off the victorious state convention, Kenny and Bobby were quite sure they were in control and not being used.

"If anyone was using anyone," Kenny ventured, "we are using them to push Jack forward."

For once, Kenny's steel-trap political instincts were offtrack. This was his first national political experience. Both he and Bobby were inexperienced and naive, not understanding there was a world of difference between state and national politics. The stakes were much higher.

As the momentum began to build, Kenny and Bobby decided it was time to talk with Jack. They hurried back to his suite at the Hilton but found it jammed with people. As usual, Jack was several steps ahead of them. With no place to talk privately, Jack, Kenny, and Bobby had a hurried meeting, squeezing into the small bathroom of Jack's suite.

Bobby let Kenny lay out the conversations they had been having in private across the convention floor and in various hotel rooms and bars. "The northern political bosses want you, not Kefauver. They think a Stevenson/ Kennedy ticket is a winning ticket in November."

Jack was intrigued. His competitive nature was flowing, maybe a bit in overdrive, and what Kenny and Bobby were telling him was what he had been hearing all along. It also echoed what Chicago native Sargent Shriver, husband of Jack's sister Eunice, had been hearing from his sources.

For his part, Bobby would later admit to being uneasy, but not wanting to be out of step, he had kept silent.

At the end of their briefing in the Hilton suite, Jack nodded. "Let's do it," was all he said.

Kenny was delighted. Bobby, not so much. His first thought was of Joe Kennedy.

"Dad is not going to be happy!" was Jack's only comment, as he authorized Bobby and Kenny to essentially force their way onto the Democratic ticket. He knew Stevenson did not want him, but Jack suddenly wanted the slot.

When they had last seen Joe, as he headed for much-needed and deserved vacation in the French Riviera, he had made clear that they were going to the convention to learn and nothing more. "Don't get any stupid ideas," Joe had warned them. A message directed mostly at Kenny and Larry, whom he still distrusted. Kenny had shrugged.

"It will be interesting, Dad," Bobby had replied, jumping to Kenny and Larry's defense. "We will learn a great deal."

"Don't make it too interesting," Bobby's politically savvy father had warned before leaving for the long-planned holiday.

With Joe Kennedy on his way to France, the guys felt that his absence left them with a bit more freedom to act as they saw fit. However, Joe's keen sense of presidential politics, something Kenny had picked up firsthand in those late-evening chats on Cape Cod, should have been something Kenny anticipated. He recalled later how surprised he had been at the Old Man's grasp of the national political pulse.

Joe thought it would have been political suicide for Jack to even consider the number-two spot. He told this to Jack and Bobby. He made his position clear. He told Kenny. He told Larry. He knew they would not listen, but he suspected Jack might, and even if Jack didn't, he expected Bobby would. This turned out to be a miscalculation on Joe's part.

In addition to Joe's conviction that Stevenson was not the right guy, he also never meant to have Jack run for vice president, period. Jack was supposed to sit tight till 1960 and go for the top of the ticket. Joe had correctly surmised that Stevenson would go down in flames before an Eisenhower/Nixon ticket and he guessed correctly again. It was too early. This was not Jack's year. Joe must have figured that everybody was on the same page as he boarded the boat and left for Europe, blissfully unaware that Jack had no intention of taking his father's advice.

It was only later that Kenny would admit that maybe Joe had been right—maybe they should have known better. He should have remembered Joe's words about Stevenson and national politics. Kenny had even reminded Helen of his sense that Joe knew more about Stevenson than he said, some secret knowledge on which he was basing his opinion.

Despite Kenny's better judgment, the mutual admiration he and Joe had shared on those nights had vanished after Kenny and Larry insisted on continuing to build Jack's statewide organization and Joe had again tried to undercut their position. They had pushed Jack into state political battles that his father had wanted his son out of. The Murphy loss was at the top of Joe's list of stupid things in which Kenny and Larry had unnecessarily involved Jack. So here they were, the old animosities from the early days of the '52 campaign alive again, yet in his gut Kenny knew the Old Man was probably right. Still, he overrode it. Kenny had made a mistake that was rare for him: He had allowed his emotions to dictate his political decisions.

And for his part, despite allowing Kenny and Larry to look like the bad guys, Jack had enjoyed winning control of the Massachusetts Democratic Party. The political fight itself he found distasteful, but the victory he liked.

He figured that was what he had Kenny and Larry for, to get into tough political fights and win them for him. They had done so on the state level, so why could they not in Chicago as well? Jack knew how to play political hardball, even if he did not enjoy having to do it. Initially, he may not have been interested, but once Stevenson, sensing the growing momentum to push out Kefauver in favor of Kennedy, had hung out the possibility of a VP slot, then pulled it back, Jack's competitive streak kicked in. Had Joe been consulted, which he wasn't until later, he would have seen Stevenson's move for what it was, a political ploy. He was laying out the possibility that he might consider Jack, doing so with the sure knowledge, or so he thought, that Joe would never allow Jack to run for the number-two slot in Chicago. When Jack went for it, nobody was more surprised than Stevenson, who quickly moved to squash it.

The truth was—and everyone, particularly Stevenson, knew—that Stevenson had arrived in Chicago with a major handicap. He needed help and support from the big-city Democratic bosses, several of whom were Irish Catholics. They saw Stevenson as an egghead liberal with no feel for the needs of the rank-and-file voters in their towns and cities. They distrusted him.

Stevenson found young Jack, as the leader in Massachusetts, to be an interesting combination of old and new politics. Stevenson felt Jack could be used in a manner that would help Stevenson's campaign with the urban Irish Catholic bosses. The problem was that when Stevenson built Kennedy up, Jack suddenly began to gain a momentum and popularity among the delegates that the Stevenson people neither wanted nor had expected.

In those early hours, in the excitement of the political chase, Jack, after some urging by Kenny and Larry, had decided to throw a breakfast for the New England delegates at the Hilton Hotel.

Fresh off his political and physical recovery, Jack believed that breakfast could bring the New England delegation together in a cohesive body to work alongside each other and take the same positions. He believed they could have more strength that way. With the help of his brilliant scriptwriter, Ted Sorensen, his speeches increasingly reflected his intentions.

To an outsider it seemed the path that Senator Kennedy was following was what Kenny called "the route of regional leadership. This was a strategy both he and Senator Saltonstall had been really the chief sponsors of." Kenny explained, "If we go back to 1955, there were no other significant Democrats in the New England delegation."

The only other one was House Speaker John McCormack, who did not have the force of personality to move the delegation in that manner. So Jack, with the help of Saltonstall, Ted Sorensen in Washington, and Kenny and Larry back in Boston, "sort of assumed this leadership."

This had not only strengthened his position as he entered Chicago; just as importantly, it continued to raise his profile and extend his political power base.

The power breakfast included Governor Dennis Roberts from Rhode Island and former Massachusetts governor Dever. Ed Muskie, who had by then been elected governor of Maine, was there. Muskie was a significant but volatile and independent force. He made most of the established politicians uneasy, not because they saw him as any kind of national threat but because they found him politically unpredictable. Governor Ribicoff of Connecticut was there and would ultimately become a critical player for Jack in the run-up to 1960.

This strategy can be traced back to the Irish Brotherhood's larger plan to make Jack chairman of the Massachusetts delegation. In that role and as de facto chairman of the New England delegation, Jack would represent a significant number of electoral votes.

All this came about two days before Stevenson's nomination. It was a position Jack had not planned on being in, but once it happened, he intended to make the most of the role and his newfound power. This was exactly what made Stevenson and Kefauver so damn nervous.

As Jack rose to give his speech that morning at the Hilton, Kenny stood leaning against the far back wall, watching, his arms folded. He was focused, intense. If Jack hit this one out of the park, they would all see what he saw, a national political figure who could go all the way. Kenny was sure that if Jack did well, they could begin to build on the momentum that was gathering, pushed largely by the northern political bosses. Jack's theoretical role at the breakfast was to determine how many votes he could deliver for Stevenson, but a possible run for the vice presidency formed a subtext behind Jack's words.

Kenny sensed that Jack wanted the number-two slot. Jack's reasons may not have been entirely clear, even to himself, but once his political juices were flowing, Jack Kennedy was unstoppable. Kenny could hear in the clipped tones and cadence of Jack's speech that he had made the decision to run.

Quite by accident, Bill Green from Pennsylvania was standing near Kenny and watching Jack speak. Green shook his head and whistled between his teeth before leaning over to Kenny and saying what was obvious to any observer: "The charisma of this guy is fantastic! Truly amazing to watch him transform a room, not just with this speech, but you know, look at him." Kenny did not need to be told. "Look at the way he works the room, the way he walks around the room, shakes hands, like he knows everybody! Astounding!"

Kenny smiled. He enjoyed watching the old political establishment overcome with awe, observing Jack in action. Jack's charisma was not news to the Brotherhood: For them, Jack had long represented the future of the country, not Adlai Stevenson, Estes Kefauver, or even Bill Green.

Jack made every one of these old-time pols and delegates feel as though he alone was the most important person in the room. As he watched, Kenny could not help but think that maybe they should just go back to focusing on 1960 and the top slot. Maybe, Kenny thought, Joe was right. They should wait.

The truth was, the New England delegation was not alone in its respect for Jack Kennedy. As he worked the convention, many people approached Bobby and Kenny and told them they had read about Jack and seen him from a distance but that this was their first up-close-and-personal chance to see him. They were almost starstruck; it was Worcester, numerous teas, and the clambake all over again. When Jack was well, not in pain, he could turn it on with full force, like a light switch. Kenny had increasingly come to believe it made Jack nearly undefeatable.

Many began to wonder whether they had the right man at the top of the ticket. Stevenson was no Jack Kennedy. This handsome, young, tanned, well-spoken fellow was captivating, exciting, new, and different; the buzz began to build at the breakfast, just as Kenny had hoped. Governors Dever, Dennis Roberts, and Ribicoff realized, for the first time, that they in fact had become the political army of this young up-and-coming politician who could be headed for the White House.

They saw him as someone who could handle himself with both the voter and the political pro. For the first time, they began to think not of their own political ambitions so much as the potential Jack represented. Maybe, they thought, this was our guy.

Stevenson was convinced that he needed a southerner for his ticket. He had not planned to pick Jack, but he was well aware of his need for Joe's donations to his campaign. He had no intention of pissing off the Kennedys, though he thoroughly disliked Jack's father and frankly thought the son was an arrogant, unprepared upstart surrounded by a bunch of inexperienced Irish kids, but he still had to be careful with Joe. The truth was that Stevenson had rather enjoyed rebuffing Joe back in 1952, when Joe had tried to help Stevenson's doomed campaign. Stevenson's folks had made it clear: Your money is welcome; but you, not so much.

The question for Stevenson and his people had not changed: How do we duck his son, keep him off the ticket, but not piss off the father so that he keeps writing checks to the party? Running against an incumbent like

Eisenhower would be tough enough, even if the old soldier seemed vulnerable after his recent heart attack.

Money. Money was always the issue for the Democrats. Joe Kennedy had lots of money. Of course, because Stevenson's own relationship with Joe was so frosty, he was unable or unwilling to pick up the telephone, call Joe, and just say straight out, "Look, I've committed myself to Kefauver, and you've got to explain it to Jack." Poor Adlai had no idea that, if he had done so, he would have found himself oddly allied with Joe in wanting to keep Jack off the ticket.

Stevenson, for his part, wanted to use Jack's youth, charm, and good looks to help him win the White House, but not so much that he wanted Jack for vice president. Ultimately, Stevenson wanted Jack's help without actually giving him anything in return. So he figured he had to avoid making a decision, leaving the picking or rejecting of Jack as a vice presidential nominee to others in the party.

Stevenson knew better than to put himself in the middle of a battle between Kefauver and young Jack Kennedy. He did not want Kennedy on his ticket, but he also was not about to say that publicly. He sensed the growing Kennedy momentum. He needed to stop Jack cold without appearing to do so, not because he gave a damn what Jack thought but because he certainly did not want to offend Joe Kennedy and his checkbook any more than he already had.

Instead, Stevenson and his people decided in a politically savvy move that, rather than be put on the spot with a decision on the vice presidency, they would open the vice presidential nomination to the full floor of the convention. This would force Kennedy into a battle with Estes Kefauver, who, though having lost in the primaries to Stevenson, nevertheless already had an organization in place and favors owed to him.

"Let the delegates decide," Stevenson declared.

Jack, Bobby, and Kenny saw the strategy for what it was—a blatant attempt to avoid picking Jack. Bobby was livid. Jack became more determined. Kenny liked all the action.

But Kenny was also furious. He refused to see that he was pushing Jack and making emotional decisions instead of relying on cold political judgment. If Kenny had really stepped back, he would have seen the cliff they were all about to collectively jump off, courtesy of a well-timed push by the Stevenson/Kefauver ticket.

But Kenny was with Bobby on this one. He was angry as hell. Fuck Stevenson. *If he does not have the guts to play it straight with us, then the hell with him*, Kenny and Bobby figured. *Let's go for it*, they thought, *and fight to get Jack that number-two spot.*

Although Stevenson was not the most thrilling candidate on the planet, Jack was now beginning to be seen as a new kind of Democrat. He hoped by playing a supporting role he would at least expand his own reputation on a national level.

At the same time, Jack was a little pissed at the way the Stevenson camp had treated him. Jack began to relish the idea of throwing his hat in the ring. He decided he was running for the vice presidential nomination.

"How are you going to tell your father?" Kenny asked.

"I'm not," Jack answered with a shrug as they sat on the end of the bed in Jack's hotel suite. "Bobby will tell him."

Bobby grimaced and picked up the phone, putting in the long-distance call to France.

"He's not going to be happy," Bobby warned.

"That's why you get to tell him," Jack told his younger brother with a chuckle.

Bobby had been right about his father's reaction. Joe exploded in a way that only he could when Bobby delivered the news. When Bobby hung up the telephone, he sat back for a moment on the bed, his face ashen. "Boy is he mad!"

After Joe calmed down and realized they were too far along in the thing, he wanted Jack to win the vice presidential nomination. Kennedys didn't lose, not yet anyway, and Joe and Jack did not intend to be the first.

Stevenson tried to avoid this whole mess and to keep Joe Kennedy's donations rolling in, without having to give ground and bring Jack Kennedy on as VP, by giving Jack the task of formally nominating Stevenson for the presidency. Stevenson wrongly figured that that would be enough for Jack. Jack, and Joe for that matter, even from the French Riviera, saw the move for what it was: a way to keep Jack on the sidelines.

The move failed. Jack and his Irish Brotherhood would not be so easily dissuaded nor dismissed. Jack had captured the imagination of the delegates with his "movie star presence, personality and good looks, which made him an instant celebrity," as *The New York Times* reported. He was a "political breath of fresh air," and the delegates felt invigorated by him.

None of this made either Stevenson or Kefauver happy, especially when it was evident that Jack would not back down. Only Henry Cabot Lodge of all people would have understood Stevenson's complete dismay. What was the deal with this guy? Did Jack Kennedy, so inexperienced on the national stage, really believe that he could simply walk in and take over the convention, walk away with the number-two slot?

Well, actually, yes, he did. Just as he had in 1952, when he had the right stuff to beat Lodge, beat back the Eisenhower tide, and become senator. He had not come here to run, but once he made up his mind, he posed a formidable threat to the establishment and the way they had expected the convention to proceed.

The "vaunted Kennedy organization," as Kenny and Larry joked about it later, worked all through the night in their suddenly invented headquarters at the Palmer House down the street from the Hilton, deciding what possible next steps to take.

In the meantime, back in Jack's suite, Bobby began making calls and trying to build up support. "Jack was in," he explained to anyone who would listen. Kenny and Larry joined him later, as people hurried in and out of Jack's suite trying to figure out who they knew, who might be helpful, and who owed whom a favor. Kenny looked up from his improvised desk, a coffee table in the living room, and caught Jack's eye.

Kenny later recalled how Jack sort of leaned against a bedroom doorjam with an amused, almost detached look on his face. "He was almost whimsical," as he suddenly discussed his prospects.

"This is a hell of an organization we have here, isn't it?" Jack said, almost joking, easing himself out of the chair. "Besides ourselves, I gather we all know one other guy, who happens to be the same guy, who will vote for me. So if my count is right, that makes maybe five, six delegates we can count on!"

Everyone laughed. In the end, though, Jack and his disorganized Kennedy organization would come a hell of lot closer than he imagined, and it would make Stevenson's people very uncomfortable.

As the momentum began to build, there were two meetings going on at the Chicago Hilton. Kenny had arranged for Jack to have a big suite, which contained one large room with three smaller bedrooms off of it. Each bedroom contained a different group that represented various political factions, all of which were needed for Jack to win the nomination. In one of the bedrooms was a group of old New England pros. These included Governor Roberts, former Governor Dever, longtime Kennedy associate Judge John Fox, state senator John Powers, Massachusetts chairman Pat Lynch, Governor John Bailey, an experienced politician from Connecticut, and finally Governor Ribicoff. Carmine DeSapio, the leader of New York's Tammany Hall, was supposed to be in there but had been prevented from entering the suite. He claimed later to Kenny that "nobody had recognized him or let him in."

Jack later angrily mentioned this to Kenny, who found it hard to believe, though in the confusion it certainly was possible that some newcomer to the Kennedy staff might not have recognized DeSapio. He, like so many others in that first bedroom, represented another era to many of Jack Kennedy's men. Not one to be denied, somehow DeSapio did manage to get a message to Kennedy that he wanted to talk to him. Kenny hastily arranged a few minutes in the hallway by the elevators.

In another room of the suite was tough, no-nonsense Boss Daley, mayor of Chicago. Kenny told him what Jack was thinking. "He wants to go for the number-two spot." Daley nodded, puffed on his cigar a moment, and smiled. He already knew what Kenny was just finding out. "I know," he said with a laugh.

The mayor had pulled Jack aside early and put it as plainly as he could to Jack, politician to politician. "Why not you?" Daley had asked Jack as they discussed the vice presidential candidates. Jack had smiled. Daley had understood at once. As things turned out, Jack was the only one in the room who had a full picture of the situation of who stood with whom. By 1960, Bobby would be firmly in charge, cognizant of every detail relevant to Jack's success, but in 1956 the entire operation was unscripted and they were unprepared. Despite not having a full picture or control of the situation, Jack and the Brotherhood decided together to try to move ahead.

They began with the Jack's office staff, many of whom had regular contact with politicians. Ted Reardon, for example, had been in Washington since 1945. He definitely knew some people.

Unfortunately, his staff knew the same people Jack and Kenny knew. Bobby, on the other hand, knew a lot of senators from his time on the Committee on Government Operations. Kenny felt sure that Bobby's connections could become a powerful card for them.

The key senator as far as they were concerned was John McClellan, the powerful Democrat from Arkansas. Kenny, who would later work for Bobby on the McClellan Committee, had never met the famed Senator McClellan until this time. Kenny had seen McClellan on television during the McCarthy committee hearings and had come away very impressed. McClellan came across very well on television with his judicial tone and temperament.

Kenny was excited to meet him. He considered McClellan a real power in the southern delegation and certainly in the Arkansas delegation, the kind of powerful southern senator who could turn the tide in Jack's favor.

Bobby and Kenny went to see him in his suite. They had a drink with him. Kenny laughed later when he told Jack the story. McClellan had a couple of good old boys from his home state visiting with him in his hotel suite. One was a local district attorney and another a local judge. Bobby, in his normal manner, was quite straightforward. Tough, direct, and abrasive.

Jack needed McClellan's help. Would he offer it? While Bobby began to broach this crucial question, Kenny watched McClellan's wife. Mrs. McClellan would occasionally jump in with some story that had no real general bearing on the conversation. What struck Kenny was how unserious she was about it all. Kenny found it an odd reaction. He was not sure if she was laughing at the conversation or at them. Her behavior made him uneasy. He and Bobby were missing something. What, though?

They kicked around the possibility of Jack going for the VP spot and how critical McClellan's support could be. Senator McClellan continued to chat, tell stories, and recall past battles. He repeatedly evaded Bobby's questions.

Kenny sensed McClellan was making a point. He was going somewhere with this, but Kenny had not a clue where. He kept his mouth shut. His political antenna was on high alert, and he just listened. Bobby on the other hand was growing increasingly frustrated. Bobby was direct. Small talk had never been his strength. The conversation continued to skirt around the edges, and Bobby had finally had enough. He shot a look at Kenny. Kenny smiled. He knew Bobby. Bobby wanted an answer.

Bobby asked point-blank, "What can you do to help? Can you help or not?"

Kenny winced.

It was a risky thing for Bobby to do. While it was obvious that McClellan was for Jack, he had still not made any commitment. By asking so directly,

Bobby had put himself and McClellan on the spot. After a moment of awkward silence, McClellan sipped his drink and took a long drag on his cigar. He looked thoughtfully out the hotel room window, and his wife let loose one of those disconcerting gales of laughter.

Kenny knew something was wrong. He and Bobby had misunderstood something. Then, suddenly, McClellan leaned back in his chair and began a story. He did not like Kefauver and pointed out the reasons why not. He also disliked Hubert Humphrey and Albert Gore, the other senator from Tennessee. Again, he ticked off the reasons why they did not help the ticket. By process of elimination, he would like to be for John Kennedy.

So Bobby knew, or at this point assumed, he had been correct to approach him. McClellan went on to say he liked Jack. That he also liked their father, Joe, adding that in many ways he was in the minority in that regard. In fact, he surprised Bobby when he told him he had known the Old Man for years and liked him very much. He liked Jack's general demeanor and thought his war record was impressive. He thought Jack handled himself well and had real potential. McClellan made clear he believed Jack would become a distinguished senator. Bobby was pleased.

Kenny remained quiet. He noticed that McClellan said not once, but twice, that Jack would make a distinguished senator, which was an odd thing to say when you were asking for support to run for the vice president slot.

Still, Kenny kept his mouth shut.

Despite all the accolades, McClellan had yet to offer any assistance. He had yet to say what he could do to help. In fact, he had been superbly vague throughout the entire conversation. No specifics.

That kind of shit always made Kenny nervous. He waited.

Bobby sensed none of Kenny's anxiety, so he broached his next question without any of the hesitation that had been in the edges of his voice when he first asked for the senator's help. "How much assistance can you offer?" Bobby asked hopefully. He took out a notebook, prepared to write down McClellan's answer.

John McClellan hesitated. He took a long, deep drink, followed by another drag on his cigar. McClellan, who Kenny later came to understand had never answered a question directly in his entire political life, began to speak for no apparent reason about Oral Faubus, who was then governor of "the great state of Arkansas," as McClellan put it.

Senator McClellan's description of the man was a rambling one and quite difficult to follow. A look of frustration and then puzzlement crossed Bobby's face. Kenny would later learn from firsthand experience, working with the McClellan Committee, that McClellan's capacity for circumlocution was incomparable. Kenny listened very carefully and gleaned the sense of what McClellan was trying to say.

It was not good news. Not at all. First, McClellan pointed out that Orval Faubus was a left-winger. Faubus had gone to the Commonwealth College with the communists, and McClellan suspected that Faubus did not have the proper approach to "the Negro issue." Faubus, he felt, was a little too liberal. The other men in McClellan's suite joined in quite adamantly, saying that they felt he had "liberal tendencies" toward "the Negro question."

At the end of the conversation, Kenny developed the clear impression that John McClellan had no votes whatsoever in the Arkansas delegation. All the votes were in Orval Faubus's hip pocket, and if Bobby Kennedy wanted any votes from Arkansas, he should go talk to Orval Faubus. McClellan then pointed out that Faubus would probably not be for Jack Kennedy, because Jack Kennedy was too conservative for him. If Faubus was supporting anyone, it would more than likely be Kefauver or Humphrey.

Bobby sat stunned. McClellan then said he would do whatever he could do. He would talk to whomever he could, but in most delegations it was indeed the governors who controlled the votes. Bobby and Kenny were shocked. "Son, United States senators haven't got any votes in those delegations. But thank you for thinking of me," McClellan said.

Kenny rose, thanked them, and tapped Bobby on the shoulder. "Put the notebook away," Kenny said. "Let's go."

Kenny had opened the door and almost stepped into the hallway when McClellan called them back in. McClellan told Kenny to shut the door. What he told Bobby and Kenny next was something they would never forget, and it would make all the difference in 1960. He was giving a couple of "wet behind the ears" kids a political lesson of a lifetime.

"In the future," McClellan began, "if one was interested in delegations and their votes, they better find out who has the power in the delegations and stop reading the newspapers. You can't just arrive at the convention and expect people to switch sides because your fella is so wonderful. You gotta do your homework, talk to the governors, the state reps, the party leaders; these people have been sized up, lined up, and courted for months. Just because you know a few high-profile, important fellas, a few senators or judges is not going to change things. Next time you gotta have this all done before you step off the train."

Kenny and Bobby then left McClellan, dismayed and dejected. Kenny wasn't sure whether Bobby was surprised to learn that the senators had no power and were thus useless to them or just stunned and perhaps annoyed that McClellan had taken so long to basically tell them no.

"Just politics," Kenny would say to a frustrated Bobby over a drink later to recover their composure. "He thought we should have been savvy enough to know. He'd be right. We looked like a couple of kids, still wet behind the ears. We deserved it."

Bobby had shaken his head. He found it hard to share Kenny's ability to keep an emotional distance from such events. Nobody in their organization, if you dared to call it that, knew anybody on the state level outside of Massachusetts—the governorships or anything remotely close. They knew senators. Not the state officials. If McClellan was right, and he was, these state relationships were what mattered. And of course he was right. They had not lined anyone up; this was all "seat-of-the-pants politics," as Kenny said. Though they now knew it was a lost cause from a numbers perspective, for dignity's sake they fought on.

There were other problems. Liberals didn't like or trust Jack Kennedy. They were led in their opposition by former first lady Eleanor Roosevelt, who disliked Jack. She felt he had not taken a strong enough stand opposing Joe McCarthy. At the 1956 convention her opposition to Jack proved devastating, and there was not a thing they could do about it.

By 1959, Eleanor Roosevelt would have even more reasons to dislike Jack Kennedy, but that was a future day and a different fight. Eleanor stood firmly against Jack now, and their problems with her would only redouble as they approached 1960.

The Brotherhood's final problem was labor and the AFL-CIO, led by Walter Reuther, who was close to Hubert Humphrey and who eyed Jack Kennedy with suspicion. Reuther's group had control of the key Michigan delegation, among others. They had no use for Jack Kennedy, and the brotherhood was going nowhere without Eleanor Roosevelt and Walter Reuther.

"It was very clear that they were opposed to us," Kenny later reflected. "My thought now, looking back, is that they were in on the deal and committed to Kefauver. I believe this was done through prior arrangements."

Labor was also disinclined to support Kennedy because of the McCarthy situation. Both labor and Eleanor Roosevelt firmly believed that Jack had ducked and run when he could have stood up to McCarthy. They saw him as suspect and a convenient liberal. In fact, Eleanor confronted Jack at the convention, attacking him for ducking the vote on McCarthy and embarrassing Jack in front of many of the delegates. They felt that Kennedy was too conservative to begin with. The fact that he had not stood strong against McCarthy, well, that made them deeply suspicious. This would prove to be such an issue and, as Kenny called it, "a political problem" that by the time Kenny hit Washington to work with Bobby on the Rackets Committee, one of his most important jobs would be to fix this problem and, as Jack later told him, "fix it now." They would not make the mistake of arriving in Los Angeles in 1960 without this solved, but that was then and just now they were still dreaming of '56.

The truth was, Walter Reuther was very concerned about Jack's role, or nonrole, nonvote on McCarthy and his conservative background. He quietly confided to Eleanor that he was also suspicious of Jack's support among big-city people like Daley, and Reuther wondered how deep such support actually was. Add all this to indications that there was support from some southerners, and labor and their allies immediately became wary.

They were probably in on some kind of pact with Stevenson, or else they would have chosen Humphrey and not Kefauver. Kefauver was not their kind of senator. It would turn out that Kennedy correctly suspected a backroom deal here. In addition, Reuther's perception, though incorrect, was that Senator Kennedy was not a supporter of or strong on labor. It was a damning perception and one Kenny would have to correct before Jack ever had a chance in 1960. This would become a critical issue once more two years later during the McClellan Committee hearings.

Their final problem at the convention was the third rail for the Kennedy team, and nobody wanted to address it publicly. It was the Catholic issue, the issue that would not go away. America had never elected a Catholic. None of their opponents wanted to say it outright, lest they appear bigoted; still, the fact was unavoidable even if it remained unspoken: Jack Kennedy was not only impossibly young, brash, and Irish, but he also was, worst of all, a Catholic.

In a tight election against a strong incumbent such as Eisenhower, many political leaders felt Jack's Catholicism was a liability. In the America of the 1950s, Protestants, not Catholics, elected presidents.

The Catholic issue would never be vanquished completely. This being 1956, they were not even close to understanding how hard it was going to be to overcome. In the end, all these issues, lack of time, lack of organization, problems with the liberals, and Jack's Catholicism combined together to defeat Jack. The final vote tally was 75,512 for Kefauver to Jack's 589.

When it was over, Bobby and Kenny were still smarting. Stevenson had wisely put the choice up to the delegates, and when it appeared that the Kennedy forces were getting too close, conveniently for Kefauver's team, which had been more organized and was in control of the tally board that counted the votes, "the board went black," as Kenny angrily summarized over a beer with Jack and Bobby at the pub later. What that meant, though Bobby and Kenny could not prove it, was that Kefauver's forces had shut the electronic tally board down. This meant only one thing: a voice vote from the floor, which Kefauver could not lose. "He was more organized; well, he had an organization and we did not. He had the floor covered like a carpet, because he had the people and the organization, a way to reach them, and we simply did not. Bobby and I were forced to run across the floor trying to find people in that throng. Kefauver had wisely flooded the floor. We could not, because we did not have the organization or the people to flood it with." In the end, Kenny growled to Bobby and Jack, "We were jobbed!" Bobby demanded Jack fight it. "We all know Kefauver's people illegally shut that board down when we were getting too close!" Jack may have agreed, but Kenny could see that mentally Jack had already moved on. It was over.

While not accustomed to losing, Jack was determined to make the most of it. He admitted only to Kenny and Bobby that, despite his running for the spot, he felt relieved he had lost. This was when Kenny began to understand that Jack was mentally, politically miles ahead of them; he had seen the loss coming and realized his mistakes.

By now Jack's political instincts had kicked in, and they told him he was damned lucky. He made the most of losing. Kenny watched the transition in amazement. He was learning a great deal from Jack Kennedy, and by the time 1959 rolled around, he and Jack would work hand and glove. Never again would Kenny get too far out ahead of Jack.

Jack made an appearance before the convention, making an impassioned plea for a unanimous vote in favor of Kefauver. His speech was stellar, his appearance remarkable. In losing he made himself the star. The center of attention. The man of the hour. In losing he came across like a victor; the delegates were awestruck. All because he had lost.

One Boston journalist headlined his story by declaring, "Jack's appearance rates as the one real victory of the entire convention. He was the one new face that actually shone. His charisma, his dignity, his intellectuality, and in the end, his gracious sportsmanship . . . are undoubtedly what those delegates will remember. So will those who watched it and heard it via TV and radio."

Even Joe agreed, declaring to anyone who would listen that Jack "had come out of the convention much better than anyone could have hoped for . . . his time is surely coming!"

With Kefauver on the ticket in the number-two spot, Jack was off ostensibly stumping for Stevenson, but he was really pushing himself. Bobby then joined the Stevenson campaign to learn the ropes of a national campaign. He was determined to learn everything he could about a presidential run. The Kennedy brothers and their political Irish Brotherhood had learned valuable lessons in Chicago. They would learn even more during the ensuing Stevenson campaign for president.

"Sometimes," Kenny declared, "you can learn as much, if not more, from losing than from winning."

Bobby would later declare the Stevenson campaign "the most disastrous operation he had ever seen." He made extensive notes, determined not to make the same mistakes in 1960.

Once Jack saw the political writing on the wall and saw the delegates' reaction to him, he knew he had been damn lucky. He also knew Stevenson had come off as boring, gray, and old news. Sure, maybe Jack had lost, but as he had in the lead-up to the Massachusetts Senate race in 1952, he told Kenny and Bobby that he intended to turn this to his advantage.

And so Jack was everywhere: giving speeches, making TV and radio appearances, always talking up the Stevenson ticket, but talking up himself in doing so. He marched in parades and rode in motorcades, increasingly leaving Democratic voters, as he had left some convention delegates, disenchanted with Stevenson and wondering why Jack was not the candidate. It was exactly the reaction Jack wanted to achieve. Never had anyone gained so much by losing.

As Jack sat back and surveyed the political scene in 1956, he later told his dad that he could not help but think of his older brother, Joe, who by all rights should have been there. Even as Jack saw the political tide turning his way, he was never quite out from under the shadow of his dead brother, Joe.

He shrewdly, and with more than a touch of wistful Irish melancholy, told his mother, "If Joe had lived, he would have run for the House, for the Senate, and, like me, he would have gone for the vice presidential nomination at the 1956 convention. But unlike me, he wouldn't have been beaten. Joe would have won the nomination. And then he and Stevenson would have been beaten by Eisenhower."

His mother just smiled. Like any mother who has lost a child, she could only imagine what might have been.

Kenny, in the room at the time, said little. It was a rare moment of reflection for the Kennedys, and he felt it was not appropriate to intrude.

In later years, when Jack and Kenny would sit around the White House, winding down after a stressful and busy day, Jack would, upon occasion, reflect on events, both planned and not planned, that brought them to this moment in his career.

Kenny said to Jack, "Losing that vice presidential nomination was the best thing that ever happened to you. Without it, you would never have won in 1960."

Jack laughed. "Fate," Jack said, "is a funny thing."

"It was only later," Kenny would explain to journalist Sander Vanocur, "that the significance of this moment became clear."

"You would think we'd have known that," Kenny remarked later, "but in the moment we got very caught up in it. We never made that mistake again. Though our instincts were wrong, as I said before, it backfired beautifully for the senator, setting him up beautifully for 1960, but certainly not because we planned it that way. That is the beautiful thing about politics: It is always unpredictable."

◆◆◆

AFTER WATCHING THE disaster of the Stevenson campaign, the Irish Brotherhood would come to believe that the Chicago convention was the most significant turning point in their professional careers.

As they crossed the country, ostensibly for Stevenson but in reality to set the stage for 1960, Jack told Kenny and Dave Powers about one of the most important lessons he had learned from his loss in 1956: "I've learned you don't get far in politics until you become a total politician. That means you've got to deal with the party leaders as well as the voters. From now on, I'm going to be a total politician."

Kenny had to have smiled. This was the Jack Kennedy he saw in mid-June 1955, during that first clambake at the Kennedy compound. Jack Kennedy had made up his mind. There would be no turning back now, no matter what doors they had to kick in to see the inside of 1600 Pennsylvania Avenue.

CHAPTER 9

Washington Interlude

OTHER THAN THAT one moment of anger at the pub, which in retrospect Kenny thoroughly enjoyed, the Kennedy forces had decided to take their loss in stride. Kenny hated admitting it, but Joe had been right. Stevenson could not beat President Eisenhower. Had Jack won the nomination for VP, he would have gone down with Stevenson. In the end, they were content to depart the convention with most of the delegates comparing Jack to Stevenson and wondering if perhaps they had made a mistake in their choice for the presidential nomination.

Jack had already decided to make the most of the opportunity fate had presented. Kenny suspected that Jack had made the decision the second he knew he was licked in Chicago in '56. Jack was not, Kenny was fast learning, a man to waste time on might-have-beens. Mentally and politically he had moved on. Despite having been outmaneuvered, Jack had seemed to glide through the convention and the presidential campaign with the same intrepid profile that had won him a Senate seat in '52. He was everywhere and anywhere campaigning for the Democratic ticket. Maybe he was the good political solider or maybe, just maybe, he was stocking up political IOUs. In contrast, Stevenson's campaign lurched uncomfortably forward with a candidate who seemed at best ill at ease and at worst slightly contemptuous of the entire convention process.

As historian Robert Dallek noted, "Jack seemed to be everywhere, exuding charm, offering sensible pronouncements, and muting his competitiveness and ambition for greater national recognition with self-deprecating humor."

In the end, Jack received slightly over twenty-five hundred speaking invitations from all over the country. He accepted about 150 of them, as Kenny remembered, traveling across twenty-four states.

With Kenny in tow, they began what was, no question, an early step toward 1960, designed to bring Jack into the key primary states. On this speaking tour, Jack's implicit goals were getting his name out there, shaking as many hands as possible, doing television appearances, and remembering the name of every political leader or official who might be of some importance.

Bobby, on the other hand, had the unpleasant job of spending time with the Stevenson campaign and the candidate himself. One trip with Stevenson brought Bobby to Boston, where Kenny met his old friend for drinks.

Bobby was appalled at the Stevenson operation, saying to Kenny, "You wouldn't believe it. This is the most disastrous operation you ever saw. He gives an elaborate speech on world affairs to a group of twenty-five coal miners standing on the railroad tracks in West Virginia."

The campaign was apparently an utter disaster. It lacked focus, organization, any coherent plan of action, and, most important, an enthusiastic candidate. Kenny and Bobby concluded that the campaign's "basic problem was that Stevenson had an intense distaste for politics and politicians."

This was not the best approach to winning the White House. The experience taught Bobby a useful lesson: ultimately what not to do in a presidential campaign. Bobby emerged from the Stevenson campaign with several yellow note pads covered in his characteristic chicken scrawl. He would take notes about anything and anyone he thought important, not necessarily to help Stevenson (it was far too late for that) but with an eye toward his brother's run in 1960. On Election Day, in November 1956, Eisenhower defeated Stevenson, and Bobby stowed his notebooks away in anticipation of the national campaign to come.

With the election of 1956 in the rearview mirror and President Eisenhower assured of four more years, Bobby was heading back to Washington, DC, eager to return to his own life and to accept his new post, which began in January 1957. It was a job he was terribly excited about, though up until now he had kept the details to himself: He would be chief counsel for the United States Senate Select Committee on Improper Activities in Labor and Management, chaired by their old friend from Arkansas Senator John McClellan, the very same one who had given Kenny and Bobby a tough political lesson at the Chicago convention.

The McClellan Committee, as it became known, and which was later widely known as the Rackets Committee, would prove a perfect fit for Bobby Kennedy's determination and prosecutorial skills. Taking the job was not without major political and, as it turned out, personal risks as well, but Bobby knew well enough that while Kenny would support his decision, his father would be less than pleased. This understated the situation: Joe was pissed when he found out.

Bobby got a chance to tell his father and brother of his decision in December 1956, over the Christmas holiday. His father's reaction was even worse than Bobby had feared. Joe and Bobby had what Bobby later described to Kenny as "a brutal argument," but Bobby was determined. Even the attempt to dissuade Bobby by Kennedy family friend William O. Douglas, a man Bobby much admired, fell on deaf ears.

Bobby had made up his mind. He would be there when needed for Jack, but in the meantime he planned to follow his own path. Joe Kennedy foresaw in Bobby's decision potentially disastrous consequences for Jack's political future. Jack would need labor. The 1956 convention had shown how much labor and their liberal friends already distrusted Jack. Bobby leading an investigation into their business dealings and potential misman-agement would not help the situation much.

Bobby disagreed. He saw this as an opportunity to employ the Kennedy name in a fight for justice on behalf of the underdog. For a man who saw life in black and white, with precious little gray, this was the ideal opportunity to serve.

Bobby, however, did admit to Kenny that "if the investigation flops, it will hurt Jack in 1958 and in 1960, too . . . a lot of people think he's the Kennedy running the investigation, not me. As far as the public is concerned, one Kennedy is the same as another Kennedy."

Kenny was not a fan of McClellan, especially after the senator's aloof performance and lack of support for Jack in Chicago, 1956. All the same, Kenny, who had been vehemently opposed to Bobby's stint with the McCarthy Committee, found John McClellan and his subcommittee welcome relief this time around.

Ralph Dungan, a Philadelphia-born lawyer with an Irish background and strong political connections, had joined Jack's office as a legislative assistant working with Ted Sorensen. Dungan remembered when Bobby joined the McClellan Committee and the first time he understood just how powerful and important Kenny's role was with regard to Jack and his family: "Jack's decision to join the McClellan Committee was certainly important. I was aware of where things cut in the Kennedy family. I can infer without ever having been in on the discussions, which I'm sure occurred between him and Bobby and Ken O'Donnell and the Old Man, that more than likely, this was decided in a family powwow — the decision would be taken with just these guys present. The arguments would go somewhat [like], 'You're going to get all this national publicity and television exposure.' Plus, though Jack did not have the kind of crusading Irish Puritanism of Bobby, he had the crusading fighting spirit of the immigrants overall. He did not like to see the little guy stepped on." In the end, Jack had joined the committee largely, he told his father, to support Bobby's decision, and, sure, Bobby had asked him to join as a favor. Maybe. But Kenny and Jack saw political opportunity as well as peril. The truth was, it was done now; Bobby had made the decision. The key now was to make it work for Jack's benefit.

When Kenny came to work for the McClellan Committee, little would happen to change his dim view of McClellan. Still, it was not McCarthy, and that was good news. Committee work would keep Bobby's taste for fighting injustice satisfied without getting him into too much hot water or screwing things up too much for Jack. This at least had been Kenny's view from the safe distance of the Kennedy political offices at 122 Bowdoin Street in Boston.

Kenny understood all too well the potential political pitfalls involved for Bobby and for Jack. Yet Kenny, despite having more influence over Bobby than Joe and knowing better than Jack what made Bobby tick, did not even bother to try to dissuade Bobby from taking the job.

Unlike Bobby's stint with McCarthy, there were no arguments, battles, or long, drawn-out discussions and weeks of cold silences between Kenny and Bobby. While Kenny perceived there might be some problems with McClellan's committee, given labor's perception of the Kennedys, it was still a better choice than it might have first appeared to be.

While there was indeed no real worry that Jack might not win in his upcoming 1958 Senate race, the Irish Brotherhood needed to pull off a disproportionately big win as they eyed 1960 in order to convince any remaining skeptics among the national political elite of Jack's viability at the polls. The postconvention bounce and glow from 1956 had set Jack up beautifully. But political leaders were now looking toward Richard Nixon, Eisenhower's VP, as a sure bet in 1960, and this made them all the less sanguine about Jack Kennedy's staying power.

Sure, he had been in the spotlight at the Chicago convention and certainly during the national campaign four years previously, but compared to Stevenson, they argued, who wouldn't shine brightly? Spotlights fade, however.

Nixon was a pro, a seasoned politician. He knew the ropes, had plenty of executive experience. Kennedy was young and green. While he had proven himself smart, handsome, charming, well versed in international issues, and a great speaker, he nevertheless had no major legislative accomplishments, certainly not when compared to Nixon.

As if those concerns were not enough, Jack had three further problems: He was Irish, he was a Catholic, and his father was Joe Kennedy. The outright opposition to Joe Kennedy on the parts of Eleanor Roosevelt, Walter Reuther, and labor in general made these entities natural allies of Hubert Humphrey, the Minnesota senator who was eyeing the race himself.

As if these people needed yet another reason to oppose Jack Kennedy's political aspirations, they now found one in Bobby Kennedy, chief counsel for Senator John McClellan's committee on mismanagement in labor. This was a committee Eleanor Roosevelt, the Reuther brothers, and other labor interests despised on principle. Bobby's job, as they saw it, was to allow the government and big business to stick their noses where they had no business being. Bobby's background with McCarthy was the worst of all. Eleanor Roosevelt, in particular, found this association unforgiveable.

After all, Bobby had worked for McCarthy, who had been a friend of Joe Kennedy's. When the Senate gathered to vote to censure McCarthy, Jack was conveniently nowhere to be found. In addition to having worked for McCarthy, Bobby had earned at the 1956 convention a reputation for arrogance, brashness, ill-tempered behavior, and downright pushiness as a result of his efforts on behalf of Jack's failed struggle for the VP slot.

Eleanor Roosevelt had other reasons for distrusting Jack Kennedy and his candidacy. She detested his father; she not only saw him as a reactionary, but she also believed he was trying to buy the election for his son. She believed that Joseph Kennedy had an "odor of corruption" that threatened the Democratic Party and that he was, as she put it, "the real power behind his son." She made clear that she wanted Adlai Stevenson, who had lost to Eisenhower in 1956; but she believed he had earned the mantle in 1960. Most important, she trusted Stevenson and felt no such trust for Jack Kennedy, his father, or his brother Bobby.

Walter Reuther, who was, as Kenny said, "terribly close" to Eleanor, was easily influenced by her views on Jack, and that, added to his own belief that the activities of the so-called McClellan Committee represented a real threat to labor unions in the country, made gaining their support and trust both difficult and yet essential if Jack was to win in 1960.

Many viewed Bobby as "a young kid who did not know his place," as one pol had described Bobby to Kenny after Chicago. Kenny had laughed. Bobby hadn't known his place since the football field at Harvard. After all, he'd pushed himself onto the team through sheer determination. It was a quality that did not much bother Kenny, and it was one of the reasons he had wanted Bobby to run the '52 Senate campaign. He knew Bobby would be crucial in 1960 as well. But Kenny also knew full well that diplomacy was not one of Bobby's strengths.

All these issues were swirling in the background as Larry and Kenny began to plan for the 1958 Senate race. They needed to prove Jack's viability through sheer vote count, something professional politicians could understand. They would need to demonstrate with a major win in the 1958 Senate race that events of the past year had not been just a political fluke or a flash in the pan. They had to demonstrate that Senator John F. Kennedy was a national political figure who was here to stay and that, as such, he was a viable contender for the nomination in 1960.

This is where Kenny's mind was when Bobby called him to request his help with committee work in DC. It caught Kenny off guard, though it shouldn't have. When Bobby first went to Washington and as Kenny and Larry built the Kennedy organization, Bobby and Kenny would speak fairly regularly, at least a couple of times a week, about politics. And since they had left Chicago, they had been in touch even more than previously, almost once a day, sometimes twice a day. They both now understood that Jack was headed for the White House in 1960, and while Bobby might be sidelined in Washington by his own choice, there was no question they were in conversation regularly about a potential presidential campaign for Jack.

Increasingly though, Kenny noticed that their conversations were more and more about Bobby's work on the committee. The task was becoming formidable, if not dangerous, politically and otherwise. Bobby was increasingly concerned.

"Not for himself," Kenny explained. Bobby didn't care or worry for a moment about himself. "Rather that he might screw things up and hurt Jack's national prospects."

So when Bobby requested that Kenny come down to Washington to work with him, Kenny was both taken aback and displeased. He thought that Bobby had understood his role was with the Kennedy organization in Massachusetts. In winning, they had finally overcome tremendous odds, not the least of which was opposition from the Old Man and Morrissey's meddling and crises such as Jack's health scare, in order to get the Kennedy organization up and running in the senator's home state. They were on the verge of having the organization fully functioning and developing it into a force to reckon with in Massachusetts politics. From Kenny's point of view, "this was just damn lousy timing," and he told Bobby so.

Kenny was inclined to say no until Bobby made clear that it was more than just the McClellan Committee that concerned him. If things got bad, and they just might, the committee could hurt Jack with labor, damage his national reputation. Bobby needed Kenny's help now.

"You talked to Jack, right?" Kenny asked as he sat on the edge of the bed in his bedroom in Winthrop. "Your brother is fine with this?" He was frankly surprised that Jack thought this was a great idea. Kenny assumed, wrongly as it turned out later, that if Bobby was making such a request, then the brothers had already talked about this.

Kenny said yes, under the impression that it was a request from Jack as much as Bobby. Somehow Kenny got the distinct impression that Bobby had replied in the affirmative, that he'd spoken to his brother. When an infuriated Kenny later pressed Bobby on the point, Bobby shrugged. Maybe he'd misled Kenny. But it was done now, so they might just as well get on with it. Kenny was not amused. As it would turn out, Jack was even less amused.

"I was to find out later," Kenny laughed, "that Jack had nothing to do with Bobby's decision to bring me to Washington and was frankly none too happy to see me there when I arrived."

BOBBY HAD COME to the McClellan Committee after having served a turbulent and well-documented stint with the McCarthy Committee—a position Kenny had vehemently opposed and a job that had put their friendship to the ultimate test. It was a decision that would haunt Bobby for the rest of his life.

The committee, run as it was by Joe McCarthy and Roy Cohn, was terribly destructive, mean-spirited, and replete with a horrendous partisanship that persecuted people and did real damage to their lives, careers, and the U.S. senatorial institution itself.

"Joe McCarthy," Kenny said, "was a vicious, sorry excuse for a human being and had no business in politics. He was a hater. Haters can only survive so long on the national political stage. The entire episode was a disgrace."

On the McCarthy Committee, Bobby had been exposed to what he thought were some very grave violations and abuses of the authority of congressional committees. He was very sensitive about this and was determined that the McClellan Committee would get it right. From the start of his role as chief counsel with the McClellan Committee, Bobby was very meticulous about witnesses and very concerned about the content of their characters—partially out of innate kindness but also with an eye to what his appearance as a prosecutor projected to the American people. The power and position had been abused in the past. Bobby wanted to establish a different public face for congressional committees because he felt strongly that they could make a positive contribution to society.

Bobby planned to show that committees could go after those who broke the law without individual committee members being perceived as doing so themselves. During his tenure on the McClellan Committee, Bobby was under scrutiny. He was under serious political pressures of a kind he had never experienced before, and perhaps he felt a bit over his head. He did not want this to blow up in his face, which would hurt Jack terribly, perhaps destroy his chances for 1960 completely.

"This," Kenny explained, "is what I stepped into when I came down to Washington in early 1957."

What made the situation more complicated was that while Jack Kennedy had reluctantly agreed to serve on the committee, in no small part to support his brother, he had no idea how far out on a limb Bobby felt he had taken the Kennedy name. Nor did Jack fully understand the political pressures Bobby felt himself to be under.

Kenny was about to learn a vital lesson about the relationship between Jack and Bobby, a lesson that would be of critical importance in solidifying his leadership of Jack's Irish Brotherhood. It would make him indispensable from here forward.

Once Kenny arrived in Washington, he went straight to see Jack. When he strolled into Jack's outer office in the old Senate Office Building, he greeted Mary Gallagher, who had worked for Kenny at the paper company Hollingsworth and Whitney. She was Italian but had married an Irishman. Kenny had found her efficient, smart, and savvy. He had strongly recommended that Jack take her with him to Washington, which he had indeed done. Jack thought she was terrific, "even if you did suggest her," he had teased Kenny. "Hi, Mary. He is expecting me," Kenny assured her after some good-natured teasing back and forth. She did not doubt Kenny. He was not someone who made up excuses to see the senator, but given who Kenny was and his close relationship with Senator Kennedy, it was unusual that the senator would not have carved out more time on his schedule to see Kenny.

When she went into the senator's office to tell him, the senator's frosty reception told her something was wrong.

"He's not happy," she whispered to Kenny as he strolled toward the lion's den, leaning forward to reassure her.

Kenny whispered, "Don't worry. If he gets mad, I will just blame Bobby."

Kenny did not think Jack would know exactly when he was coming, but he was sure Bobby had cleared it with him. It would turn out to be a bit more complicated than that. Kenny found out later from Bobby that Jack had actually been told only a few nights before at a dinner party at Bobby's Hickory Hill estate that Kenny was coming down. Jack was furious. But Bobby was Bobby. Even Jack had to come to grips with that.

After a moment of icy silence, Jack wanted an answer to the obvious. "What the hell are you doing here?"

Kenny could tell by Jack's cold stare that Jack was neither kidding nor amused.

"I assumed Bobby spoke to you."

"About what?" Jack demanded.

"About my coming down here to work with him at the committee."

Jack stared and said nothing, restraining his fury while Mary brought them coffee. The two men sat silently until she was safely outside the door. Kenny jumped in quickly, not inclined to give Jack another chance. "Don't you two talk to each other?" Kenny asked incredulously.

"No," Jack replied immediately, the answer catching Kenny off guard. "We talk through you. That's your job, don't you get that?"

Kenny suspected that Jack's anger was in no small part due to the fact that he felt Kenny was *his* friend. It was a funny quirk that Kenny would come to see more and more in the Kennedy family: They were competitive with each other even in their relationships with friends and staff. Jack was admittedly angry because Kenny had not asked. Had not called him first.

Actually, Kenny had not understood these internal dynamics of being a Kennedy, but he sure as hell did now. It was a mistake he would not

make again. He quickly moved the discussion from the committee itself
to politics.

Kenny pointed out to Jack that his role would be much more than supporting Bobby and helping him get organized. He could also work the labor
side at the same time.

"How?" Jack wanted to know, leaning forward to sip his coffee, despite
a grimace of pain.

"I can talk to them," Kenny explained, "and get them to understand the
difference between Bobby and the senator. Give them a face, a person, a
voice they can reach out to on a national level."

"You think they know the difference between one Kennedy and the
other?" Jack wanted to know.

"Maybe not now," Kenny went on to explain, but that was why having
him as a point person was key. He and Larry O'Brien had set up a similar
situation in Massachusetts. People eventually came to see them as honest
brokers who could not only speak to the senator for them, but who, when
needed, also spoke for the senator himself.

Jack nodded. Kenny made clear that he and Larry would be in touch
every day while he was in Washington. Nothing would be left to chance
or go unfinished. If Larry needed him in Boston, Kenny would go. At the
end of the day, when Bobby didn't need him anymore, they'd shut the
door of Kenny's office at the committee and it would be Jack Kennedy's
Washington political operation.

Jack admitted that this all made some sense, as long as Kenny fully
understood what his priorities were. Bobby's needs, no matter how important, could never get in the way.

"But when it is finished, straight back to Boston. Do not forget the real
goal here is 1958 and viability in 1960," Jack said.

Kenny nodded and turned to go. Jack called him back. This conversation, Jack said to him, was between them. He did not want his brother
to think he was second-guessing him. Kenny understood but suggested

perhaps they should talk with each other directly in the future. Jack pointed toward the door.

Kenny laughed about it later. Jack was not particularly pleased, but the decision was one they would all have to live with, at least for the moment. Still, Jack had heard Kenny clearly. Increasingly their relationship would grow ever closer, ensuring such miscommunication would not happen in the future.

As Kenny headed out the door to find Bobby, he shook his head. He found himself once again in a strange position, vis-à-vis the Kennedy family. He had not planned to become the sounding board for both brothers or their go-between guy, but here he was. Maybe that was his role. The mechanic. The guy who got the job done. He didn't yet know for sure, but he planned to have one straightforward conversation with Bobby, making clear he did not appreciate being the middleman.

For his part, Bobby couldn't have cared less how Kenny felt and didn't even listen to his complaints. He pointed out that Kenny had done him a similar favor in 1952, by going directly to Jack to bring Bobby in to run the 1952 campaign. So maybe now they were even.

The first people Kenny met in his new role were Angela "Angie" Novello and Carmine Bellino. Angie was Bobby's personal secretary and, as Kenny dubbed her, "Bobby's minder." An attractive, smart woman originally from New Jersey, she had been working for another Senate committee when Bobby met her. They hit it off immediately, she later joked with a touch of irony. Angie thought Bobby was brash and arrogant and didn't know his place. He thought she was smart as hell and just what he needed as his right hand at the committee. So he gave her the job as his secretary. The only problem was that Angie had not asked for the job. In the end, as Angie explained, "he was so persistent I gave in, but we agreed that it would be a one-month trial period. If I did not like him, I could leave and he would help me find another job." As it turned out, Angie stayed with Bobby all the way until Los Angeles in June 1968.

Angie, who eventually got to know Kenny well, admitted to him later she'd been less than thrilled with Bobby when she first met him, finding him very pushy.

"I did not want the job," Angie laughed, "but suddenly here I was. Working for the committee and Bobby."

Kenny chuckled, explaining that her experience was not unique. "Bobby has a way of hearing yes," Kenny explained, having just had a similar experience, "even when you say no."

Angie was somewhat relieved. She thought it was just her. And, "when Kenny arrived," Angie explained later, "absolute organization descended upon us. Suddenly, I could see over the top of my desk! Everything just fell into place, and I felt perhaps it was going to be okay."

Along with Angie came her brother-in-law, Carmine Bellino. Bellino was a brilliant accountant and would turn out to be a key player, perhaps one of the most important people on the McClellan Committee, though Kenny could not have surmised this when he shook his hand that day. The handshake was weak, trembling. And Bellino looked every bit the accountant.

Kenny intended to bring more than order to the chaos of the McClellan Committee. He intended to use it as a platform to demonstrate to labor that, despite their misgivings, Bobby was not "out to get them," that he was, in fact, on their side and could be trusted. In turn, Kenny hoped, they could and should trust Jack. Kenny wanted to convince labor that while the committee, with Bobby as chief counsel, certainly intended to go after corruption and abuses in the labor unions, they were targeting the bad guys: the Dave Becks, the Jimmy Hoffas, the Jimmy Crosses—not the good guys, not the Reuther brothers, the Gossers, and others like them.

In many ways, Kenny felt the contrasting style of the Kennedy brothers would serve the committee well, where Bobby could be brutally direct, prosecutorial, at times moving from relentless questioning to outright belittling of witnesses—all of which further enhanced a growing perception that Bobby was ruthless and would stop at nothing to win.

Jack Kennedy, on the other hand, proved, as Kenny said, "deft at moving witnesses in the direction he wanted them to go. He was always restrained, polite, never belittling, but always direct. Armed with all the facts before ever beginning his questioning, he never assumed anything. He knew well before he asked the question the answer he was looking for, and inevitably got it."

Helen teased Kenny over the phone that evening of his first day in Washington, as they chatted from his temporary perch at the Mayflower Hotel on Connecticut Avenue. "You mean to say, the committee is not targeting the labor guys you need for Jack in 1960."

"So cynical," he teased her in return. But this was closer to the truth than Kenny cared to admit. The cold, hard political reality of the time was that you could not be elected as a Democrat without the unions. The Irish Brotherhood had learned this the hard way at the 1956 Chicago convention. Kenny had to convince Walter Reuther and the AFL-CIO that Jack and Bobby could be trusted. By convincing labor, they would convince Eleanor Roosevelt and the liberals that Jack Kennedy should be the nominee in 1960.

But that was three years away. Right now, Kenny had to begin somewhere, so he began by reaching out directly to Walter Reuther's guys at the United Automobile Workers union, the guys who had run from Jack as quickly as possible in 1956.

Whatever Kenny did in his new role at the committee, Jack was clear that he did not want to tangle with UAW politically. They were an incredibly potent political power that Jack, Kenny, Bobby, and Larry knew they would have to deal with to win in 1960. The truth was that the UAW had opposed Jack in 1956 as the vice presidential candidate because of the deal they had struck with Estes Kefauver. Bluntly, they had told Kenny and Bobby at the time in no uncertain terms that they did not feel John Kennedy was the kind of liberal leader they sought.

The Taft-Hartley Act of 1947 was widely seen by the press as the cause for the unions' lack of support for Jack in '56. Liberals viewed this law, passed over Harry Truman's veto, as an attempt by business and the Republicans to demobilize the union movement, undermining unions' rights to strike and attacking their right to free speech. As a member of the House, Jack had voted against the Taft-Hartley Act. Even though the unions knew this, the ultimate passage of the law became an easy out for them.

"They opposed you," Kenny explained directly to Jack, "because they did not feel or believe that you are a traditional liberal. They felt your father was and remains a reactionary. They feel uncertain and suspicious of your position and views on McCarthy. They have every reason in the world to believe that you, John Kennedy, a rich Irish Catholic, would be a conservative."

Kenny continued, "The depth of their opposition to you can be found in their belief that you could not be trusted to vote with them on all issues at all times. When it comes down to it, from their perspective, you are a reactionary and a conservative just like your father."

In other words, their suspicion of Jack had hardly changed since Chicago in 1956. This was not what Jack wanted to hear. And Bobby's committee role was certainly not going to help the matter in the least.

"Fix it," Jack had ordered Kenny.

It was not an easy task, but in many ways nobody was more suited to accomplish it than Kenny. Kenny's background converged with those of the working-class tough guys that surrounded the Reuther brothers and filled the ranks of the UAW. Like Kenny, they were from blue-collar families who understood the value of a dollar and understood the plight of those who toiled in the difficult, often dangerous jobs that the unions sought to protect. Kenny knew well the risks these people took simply to feed their families, and he shared with them a healthy skepticism and distrust of management and the business interests they represented.

In time, the UAW would find in Kenny someone they trusted, a man with no ego whose word was his bond. Importantly, he spoke for John Kennedy, and if Kenny gave you his word, he gave it in the name of Jack

Kennedy. It was a power that would be critical to Jack's success with the labor movement.

But that was a few years away. Right now, Kenny was looking for a way in the door, someone within the UAW who would lend him a friendly ear. He finally found him in the person of Jack Conway, Reuther's right-hand man, though their first meeting would get off to an inauspicious start.

The truth was that the UAW was totally opposed to Jimmy Hoffa's heavy-handed union politics. Reuther and his colleagues had no truck with labor leaders who used their positions of power and influence for personal gain. Their real opposition to the McClellan Committee lay in their principled stance against government interference in labor management. This principle was far stronger than their dislike of or disgust with the Jimmy Hoffas in their ranks.

Kenny explained later, "The UAW did not, as has been misconstrued by the press, view the McClellan Committee as a weapon for bringing down Jimmy Hoffa and Walter Reuther. I did not detect any of that, at any time, in their conduct. I think they probably felt, which they do to this day, that the government ought to leave labor entirely alone. They felt strongly that it was up to the unions to police themselves and that the individual labor unions should clean themselves up, and they resented the hell out of the government intrusion. That principle extended even to the Teamsters Union."

Kenny would come to understand, as he put it, that "there was no individual interest of theirs in this investigating committee, except to be opposed to it on the basis that the McClellan Committee was allowing the beasts of management and business, their ancient enemies, to influence government actions directed at the unions."

Amid this "ancient" conflict, Kenny was tasked with balancing Bobby's need as chief counsel to bring corrupt union members to account against Jack Kennedy's wish to be elected president. To do so meant that Kenny had to solicit the support of the very labor unions Bobby and his brother were now investigating. It was a Herculean labor for which Kenny himself had no organizational support to draw on.

CHAPTER 10

The McClellan Committee

O N THE OPPOSITE side of labor's dispute with the McClellan Committee, the Irish Brotherhood faced an entirely different problem.

Kenny noted to Jack one evening that he had come firmly to believe that "the management/business group was almost violently pushing this investigation, as they believed it was a way to topple Walter Reuther. They were more worried about Walter Reuther than about Jimmy Hoffa."

Bobby was caught squarely in the middle of this very public fight. It was this deepening political quagmire that in part prompted Bobby's call to Kenny. The other reason Bobby needed help was that Jimmy Hoffa had just ascended to the top of the powerful Teamsters Union, with the help of organized crime, making him an even more formidable opponent.

Hoffa cared little about those he trampled on in search of power, and he cared even less about associating with the mobsters who kept him in power. Angie Novello remembered the so-called union men who worked with Hoffa wearing loud, expensive suits, too much jewelry, and more perfume than most women. Jimmy Hoffa, like Bobby, was relentless in pursuit of what he wanted.

The McClellan Committee's immediate focus, and what it became most known for, was a series of epic battles between Bobby and the

Teamsters Union. Hoffa had never crossed swords with someone quite like Bobby Kennedy, and the results were dramatically unpleasant, leading to explosive moments both in and out of the hearing room. What concerned Kenny and Jack, however, was the degree to which Bobby personalized the battle. They found Bobby's obsession with Hoffa disturbing, and while they shared Bobby's judgment that Hoffa and his mob associates were bad news, Kenny and Jack agreed that Bobby's approach lacked decorum and was, as Kenny put it, "entirely too personal."

Jack's involvement in the hearings contrasted sharply with Bobby's. His exchanges with the teamsters were noteworthy for what they were not. If Bobby's idealism and enthusiasm had gotten them into this thing, Jack's cool detachment and mental acuity would be put on display for the national press and the nation in order to mitigate Bobby's vociferous depositions. Jack came across as smart, in control, and well versed in labor politics. On almost every occasion, Jack's grasp of the issues at hand compared with his antagonists was impressive, and his rapid-fire cross-examination of his opponents was extraordinary.

Kenny remembered watching Jack in action. "Everyone (every Democrat anyway) knew that Jack would be a candidate for president in 1960, and everyone had their own agenda. Jack was out there alone. When he went after these witnesses, he knew no Democrat would step up to rescue him."

Jack would have to play this one out all the way through to the end. "And he did so," in Kenny's view, "brilliantly."

Battling Jimmy Hoffa and the teamsters, however, was relatively easy. Their known mob connections made them appear like natural villains in the press coverage. But with the Republicans pushing hard for an equal investigation into the UAW, things became less cut and dry. Bobby was against a UAW investigation, not for political reasons but simply because he questioned the legal case the Republicans made for opening an investigation in the first place.

The management and business side of the dispute viewed the McClellan hearings as an opportunity to expose Walter Reuther for what they truly believed him to be: a communist. They were sure that Reuther was using the UAW as a front for his ultimate goal of gaining a foothold in the American political establishment. In addition to abuses and mismanagement, business management was sure that the McClellan Committee would find communism rampant within the UAW. The paranoia of the managerial class in the late 1950s had them convinced that Walter Reuther and his labor-organizing brothers, Victor and Roy, were transforming the UAW into a vicious Stalinist organization. As examples, business interests cited the reported beatings of people who had opposed Reuther and indicated that they had evidence that these beatings were carried out at the direct instruction of the Reuther brothers.

Bobby wondered aloud to Kenny, Jack, and Senator McClellan whether an investigation into the UAW actually fell within the purview of the committee. This was too convenient for the Kennedy critics in the press, who hammered Bobby and Jack daily for going after Jimmy Hoffa and the teamsters with incredible zeal while leaving the UAW and the Reuther brothers, strong Democratic allies, alone. The press declared with vehemence that the Kennedy brothers intended to further Jack's political ambitions by going easy on the Reuther brothers and the UAW.

For his part, Senator McClellan told Bobby and Kenny that he considered Walter Reuther to be, if not a communist then at the very least akin to one. But McClellan, in respect for Bobby's judgment, had held off the UAW issue for a period of time. Kenny recalled how, at last, "the pressures from the press continued to build to a point where Senator McClellan, whose entire sympathy was with the business community, simply could no longer take it. More than anything else, Senator McClellan resented being depicted as 'a tool of the Kennedy brothers.'"

McClellan finally felt that he had to go ahead with the investigation into the UAW. Jack and Kenny discussed it at length, and they recognized that they could no longer avoid a confrontation with their powerful union allies. Jack simply could not disagree publicly with McClellan on this point. If Jack were to oppose McClellan, Jack would cause the opposite of his intended effect, merely amplifying cynical newspaper coverage of his motives and subsequently increasing pressure on McClellan to target the UAW.

When they saw Senator McClellan weaken, Republicans were only confirmed in their belief that Bobby Kennedy could not be trusted to conduct a fair investigation. Senator Kennedy was also suspect.

"This was," Kenny remembered, "the lowest point for Bobby. Bobby was really vilified here as someone who could not be trusted. Senator McClellan, in his usual fashion, agreed to agree with both sides, leaving everyone unhappy."

If the situation was not tense enough, it was about to become even more so when Joe Rauh, counsel for the UAW, contacted Bobby Kennedy.

"He is not a very happy fellow," Bobby reported to Kenny as they sat in Kenny's cramped office, after Bobby had hung up the phone. Bobby was shaken.

"Can you blame him?" Kenny teased. "A lot of people feel that way after they talk to you." Bobby made a face at Kenny. This was not a time for humor.

There was certainly nothing to laugh at from the UAW's perspective. Rauh indicated that he would like to see Bobby about the upcoming hearings, telling Bobby in no uncertain terms that he was not pleased and thought this entire investigation was an imposition of government control and political game-playing. Rauh admitted later to Kenny that during that phone call he was very upset, making clear that he felt Bobby was personally behind the investigation. In response, Bobby had been stunned, angry, and overly defensive. He had not wanted these hearings in the first place, but now that they were under way, he intended to pursue them with his normal zeal for correct procedure and the rule of law. This was not what Rauh wanted to hear.

Kenny's time at the McClellan Committee had been well spent. He had become, as he put it, "a bit of an expert. I had really done my homework. I'd undertaken this with some political calculation in mind, but afterward I became totally convinced about who was right and who was wrong in the conflict between labor and government."

If Joe Rauh had hoped Kenny would put a stop to the UAW hearings, though, he was ultimately disappointed. While Kenny confided to Rauh his belief, shared with Jack, that the hearings were being used to facilitate Republican grandstanding, Kenny also made clear that there was little either Bobby or Jack could do about it. Senator McClellan had ordered the hearings, and all Kenny could promise was a fair shake. Still, if it would help, Kenny would arrange a meeting with Bobby.

The first engagement that Kenny recalled was when Jack Conway, Reuther's strategist, and Dave Rabinowitz, a UAW lawyer from Sheboygan, Wisconsin, requested a meeting with Kenny directly. They had been told that Kenny spoke their language and, more important, that he spoke for Jack. They figured that even if there was no negotiating with Bobby, Kenny would listen to reason.

Kenny recalled pressure building into late winter 1957 for the UAW hearings. "Bobby Kennedy and I went and met Dave Rabinowitz and Jack Conway in the afternoon in Bobby Kennedy's cramped, messy office in the old Senate Office Building. Bobby was from the beginning very cold and unpleasant with them. It was a brutal directness, a cold and confrontational style he employed often at the time. Personally, I felt he often did this unnecessarily. This was one of those times. I was not pleased and did not think it would help the situation."

Kenny later accused Bobby of either not thinking politically or not thinking at all.

"Bobby told them quite coldly that he had been ordered to investigate and that he would conduct the investigation in a forthright fashion, that all the witnesses he thought should be called would be called. Bobby indicated that he had read everything very carefully and he indeed had. Bobby always did his homework."

Kenny had also read all the committee documents pertaining to the UAW but did not come to the same conclusions as Bobby. Perhaps he had been influenced by the critical importance of the UAW to Jack's political future, but Kenny also believed that, in comparison with Jimmy Hoffa, who was up to his neck in mobsters, graft, and corruption, the UAW was being targeted by McClellan for purely political reasons.

Bobby did not agree. He felt the UAW had in fact committed some improprieties. "The one piece of advice that I would like to give to you is that you should come before this committee and not lie to us," Bobby said. You should be cooperative. You should always be truthful and forthright in your testimony."

Conway and Rabinowitz were growing angrier by the moment as Bobby went on to say, "You should not invoke the Fifth Amendment if it can be avoided, as that always connotes guilt. Despite your feelings toward me and this committee, the Senate committee will be fair in their judgment of your problems if you in fact told the truth and were honest at all times."

"I've looked over the situation carefully," Bobby continued, "and while I am aware that this does not fall into the category of my other cases, I still feel it of necessity that the UAW should be called before the committee." Bobby went on to say that they should not impede the investigation in any way; but he also wanted to be clear that they would be treated like any other union that came before the committee.

Kenny groaned as Bobby finished his instructions to the union representatives. By the look on Conway's and Rabinowitz's faces, Kenny understood that Bobby's approach had just made gaining their support for Jack Kennedy in 1960 a hell of lot harder.

Conway and Rabinowitz were upset at the manner in which Bobby spoke to them—Rabinowitz less so than Conway. Conway was a tough man who had worked his way up through the ranks and saw Bobby as some snot-nosed rich kid trying to score political points by pushing around the UAW.

Kenny tried in vain to point out that this was hardly the best approach to take with Bobby, but Conway was too enraged with the investigation and with Bobby's tone to hear him. Conway made clear to Bobby, in an equally cold and very tough manner, that he felt the committee was strictly an instrument for punishing labor, expressing his disgust with McClellan's exploitation of the UAW for political mileage.

By now both men were standing, and Kenny rose as well, just in case Conway decided to take a poke at Bobby, which was not entirely out of the realm of possibility.

"Conway told Bobby point-blank and with great hostility," Kenny recalled to Jack later, "that nobody in the UAW would lie to Congress or the committee, but he also told Bobby quite angrily that the UAW would not under any circumstances cooperate with the committee or with Bobby or with his investigation. The union would do what they had to do to protect themselves and their members from a prosecutorial committee and chief counsel, 'Meaning you,' Conway said, pointing at Bobby, should his intentions be missed. Conway felt the committee was abusing its congressional powers and authority."

"You and your committee are on a witch hunt against labor," Conway said, nearly spitting out the words. "You're not just after us but all of labor, including the teamsters." Rabinowitz tried to calm Conway, but it was too late. Conway went on to tell Bobby that he was not happy with the committee and felt that Bobby was personally responsible for not only the hearings on the UAW but also the attacks on the teamsters as well. Conway then made it as plain as possible that Bobby's action and attitude in this and other labor matters amounted to a price his brother would pay in 1960.

With that, the meeting came to a dramatic close. Bobby was furious at Conway for attacking him personally and for invoking his brother. What made Conway's attack even harder to stomach, though, was the fact that Bobby had resisted McClellan's hearings on the UAW in the first place, though he never said this to Conway, fearing it would sound disloyal to Senator McClellan. It fell to Kenny to give Conway and Rabinowitz the background later.

Sitting with Bobby afterward, Kenny handed him a beer and tried to lighten the mood. "Well, that went well."

Bobby shook his head. "I am worried that by doing my job, in fact I will be hurting Jack's chances for 1960."

Kenny pointed out it was a bit too late to start thinking like that. But Kenny believed that Jack's future "always played in the back of Bobby's mind, though it never impeded or changed his actions, either with this committee or in later conflicts, much to everyone's frustration. Bobby was always his own man, whether you agreed with him or not." It was a quality that Kenny found both admirable and infuriating in equal measure.

Kenny admitted later, "There was no question in either my mind or Bobby's that this was the most ridiculous set of congressional hearings that had been held by this committee, especially in comparison to the very serious work we had been doing previously. In the end, the hearings became almost ludicrous before they were through. However, neither Bobby nor I could say this to Conway, so Bobby took quite a hit verbally from him. Given Bobby's hostile approach, though, this was not surprising."

For a first meeting, at least from Kenny's perspective, things could not have gone worse. On the other hand, Jack Conway was the first union official who seemed to really make an impression on Bobby Kennedy. As Kenny remembered, "Bobby was really quite struck by the fact that Conway looked completely different than what he had grown to expect in previous hearings from a labor union guy. Jack Conway did not come in with pearl studs in his shirt, an expensive suit, cashmere coat, and bathed in cologne. Conway was obviously a real union leader, and he was going to fight the committee on principled grounds. He was a guy's guy. He was very impressive to both

Bobby and me in terms of the way he was able to articulate his views and his union's positions. He had no fear whatsoever of the committee, which also impressed both Bobby and me tremendously. He was not a thug. He was a genuine union fellow."

Kenny, trying to find a way to mend fences between labor and the Kennedys, decided that Conway at least was a good place to start. Conway was exactly who he appeared to be, and he might be Jack's in with the UAW, despite their less than auspicious first meeting.

Kenny felt Conway had spoken truth to power, that he had stood up to Bobby in defense of himself and his union. Unlike others they had dealt with in the past, Conway was at least honest. Angry but honest, as Kenny described him to Jack.

Kenny made clear to Jack that he "believed the UAW under the leadership of Reuther and Conway was an upright, decent union, which had made some mistakes but overall was led by good men who were simply seeking better wages, benefits, and working conditions for their men. They made clear that they were not going to be put upon or used by either a congressional committee or company management."

Kenny needed to figure out how to balance Bobby's obligation to follow through on the hearings with Jack's need to ally himself with the UAW. Conway, Reuther, and the rest of the UAW leadership needed to believe that the Kennedys were not siding with the Republicans and big business in an attack on labor. They were not out to get the unions in general but were only after those who were corrupt. The challenge was conveying this to Conway and Reuther, who after this first meeting were even less inclined to trust anything that came from the Kennedy brothers.

All three men were convinced that the Republicans' strategy was an attempt to damage John Kennedy and to adversely affect his relationship with labor, which the Republicans well understood would be crucial to Jack's presidential ambitions. In the end, Kenny felt the best strategy was a direct one. He would set up dinner with Conway and Rabinowitz.

So a few nights later, at Duke Zeibert's restaurant near Connecticut and K Street in Washington, DC, within walking distance of the White House, Kenny, Conway, and Rabinowitz discussed the hearings at length. As dinner wrapped up, Kenny was confident enough to have Bobby join them.

Kenny, now having the lay of the land, over drinks with Conway before the dinner, began to get the UAW to listen to Bobby's viewpoint. Kenny felt his job was to get Conway to meet and see the authentic Bobby Kennedy, not the media-created individual. Conway and Rabinowitz were surprised because the Bobby Kennedy the media wrote about and the person they had met the other day was unfair, bloodthirsty, and ruthless. They were stunned to see that he was a regular guy, who could be tough when necessary but fair-minded and not intent on destroying the unions in this country.

"Kenny," Jack joked, "often made a better case for Bobby than Bobby did for himself."

While getting Jack Conway and Bobby to at least listen to each other and understand each other's problems was in no way a solution to Jack's larger political problem, Kenny felt good that he had at least opened a line of communication. They were talking to each other instead of at each other, even if major disagreements would remain for some time.

The UAW leadership was beginning to understand that Bobby and Jack viewed the McClellan investigation of the UAW as a political problem, just as the union itself did. The Reuther brothers and the UAW slowly realized that they were being used as a political football to do as much damage as could be done to Jack Kennedy's presidential aspirations. Kenny reflected on this fateful dinner: "I think within an hour that Dave Rabinowitz, even more Jack Conway, admitted they got the surprise of their lives when they met Bobby Kennedy that night for the second time. While they came away still not liking him personally very much, they were more convinced that all Bobby Kennedy wanted was to be fair. This time Bobby was more controlled. He was less biting and more willing to both give and take.

"Bobby made clear that he had no control over the hearings, that they were in fact a political exercise, and his candor on that point surprised them; but since we were now in a position where the hearings were going to be held no matter what, Bobby made clear that the hearings would be even-handed and the union would be treated properly."

While this did not mean that the UAW would support Bobby's brother in a potential presidential campaign, it did mean they understood where Bobby was coming from. More importantly, the UAW had no intention of being used in this way by the Republicans or even by well-meaning Democrats.

"What was fascinating to me as the meeting unfolded," Kenny said, "was that Bobby and Conway began to realize that neither was the person that they had perceived the other to be.

"It became evident to both men that they had been dealing with stereotypes of each other's character. You could not help but see after a while that Jack Conway was an honest union leader. This really struck Bobby. He was shocked by the difference between teamsters Hoffa and Jimmy Cross and men like Conway and Rabinowitz. Bobby had given up hope that there were any honest union men left in any of these organizations. Conway and Rabinowitz were equally shocked that Bobby Kennedy was not this ruthless, unhinged dismantler of unions. They saw, as Bobby talked, that he was faced with real political problems of his own. They were also surprised to see he was very familiar with the UAW and had done his homework."

As Kenny noted later to Jack, "In the end, both men had, to some degree, overcome their misperceptions of each other. They could then begin to talk as equals."

As they turned to leave, Bobby suddenly said to them, "If you have a problem or something comes up, if you find out something that you think I should know, come to me. My door is always open."

This surprised them, but they felt he was sincere. According to Kenny, "Bobby told them they could reach him whenever they needed. Even going so far as to give out both his and my home phone numbers should they need to talk to either one of us. This was the Bobby Kennedy I knew"—and the one Kenny wanted the union men to know and come to trust.

For their part, Conway and Rabinowitz walked away somewhat relieved, extremely surprised, and feeling that Bobby Kennedy was going to be fair with them, which was the best they could hope for in a bad situation.

Perhaps the first thing all parties understood, beyond the fact that hearings were going to be held, was that they were dealing with a common enemy: the Republicans. Kenny hoped to use this to forge a bond, even a tentative one, between Jack Kennedy and the UAW.

Bobby and Kenny's initial strategy was to go directly to the senators on the committee and challenge the need for the hearings. At a closed-door hearing, in which Kenny sat next to Bobby, the two could not have been clearer. "Bobby told them in his view that they were making a grave mistake, that the hearings would end up being an embarrassment to the committee, and to the Republicans especially. He told them he believed firmly that while hearings needed to take place, this was in fact the wrong committee to hold them. The senators listened quietly and I think the Republicans, led by [Senator Barry] Goldwater, appreciated Bobby's view and wanted to think about it." Republican senator Karl Mundt, however, who really did not like Bobby or Jack, leaked to the press that Bobby had tried to kill the hearings.

Once the story hit the newspapers, all hell broke loose, and the committee reconvened. Everyone agreed now that they had no choice but to hold the hearings. In the end it was Senator Kennedy who offered the motion to convene the hearings. Politically, it was the best move he could make under trying circumstances.

"We had to make the best out of a bad political situation before it got worse," Bobby said later.

With that unceremonious start, the hearings on the UAW and Walter Reuther were under way, but, as Kenny remembered, "Nobody was particularly happy about it"—least of all Jack and Bobby Kennedy.

With Jack's profile steadily on the rise since 1956, what they could hope for at this early stage was that the unions, in the end, actually grew to like John Kennedy. It was a situation that could easily have played out another way, if Bobby and Kenny, with Jack's approval, had not handled themselves and the situation correctly.

At this point, Kenny and Bobby in Washington and Larry O'Brien, who had remained in Boston working the political operation, were well aware that Jack was always in the top polls; between '56 and '58 he was always in the top four. The Republicans, of course, assumed that John Kennedy would be a candidate for the nomination; however, none of the Republicans, and certainly few Democrats, believed he would win the nomination. There was a lot of speculation about him, but underlying any discussion about John Kennedy's potential candidacy was the conventional wisdom that the Democrats would not nominate a young Catholic senator from Massachusetts who was related to Joe Kennedy. This would be political suicide on the part of the Democrats.

"Of course," Kenny noted later to Sandy Vanocur, "the rap became that the Kennedys were trying to use the hearings to protect their labor allies. The reality was they were not allies of the Kennedy brothers, at least not going into the hearings. If anything, the UAW disliked and still distrusted the Kennedys." Kenny's job remained to change that scenario.

Kenny made clear, "Jack was under attack from all sides, including but not limited to other ambitious Democrats, the Republicans, and the unions that had an image of him not in the least bit connected to reality. I don't think anyone understands that we faced obstacles of every size and variety at every turn. Everyone was distrustful, suspicious, and wanted to prevent John Kennedy from going any further. We were once again the outsiders trying to find a way in." Some observers and historians would later argue, though, that Jack, Bobby, Kenny, and Larry were at their best politically under those circumstances.

In the end, Kenny said, this was all made easier by the Republicans on the committee, who felt Jack and Bobby were vulnerable with the

UAW. In their zeal to assure an outcome detrimental to Jack Kennedy, they made a series of mistakes that would provide Kenny the opening he needed and allow Jack Kennedy to open a door with the UAW. Without the Republicans' mishandling, this might have been much harder to obtain. Later, Kenny would joke that the best friends they had during those hearings were the Republicans, who simply could not help overreaching. Of course, Jack was ready to take advantage of their stumble, but in no small sense that credit was shared by Bobby and Kenny.

The Republican tactic was clumsy but clear. They were hiring people on the side to deploy against Bobby Kennedy. One of the committee's former employees, Vernon L. Johnson, who had been fired for withholding evidence, was now out investigating privately, trying to gather information to embarrass Bobby and Jack Kennedy—not necessarily to embarrass them personally, but to embarrass their witnesses.

The strategy was that by calling into question Bobby and Jack's witnesses, rather than personally attacking them, it would provide a public impression that the Kennedy brothers were not doing their homework. This strategy was to prevent the Kennedys using the hearings as a strictly public relations tool to get Jack into the newspapers.

"Furthermore," Kenny said, "the Republicans hoped such a strategy would make the Kennedy brothers look as if these hearings were all simply a ploy to promote Jack's political ambitions."

The Republicans on the McClellan Committee had initially hired Johnson to investigate a UAW local. Kenny found out that Johnson was turning over only information that management gave him while discarding or destroying any information from the union membership that might have been in the committee's favor.

When Kenny brought this to Bobby's attention, a private hearing was held, and Bobby unceremoniously fired the man. Nobody on the committee objected to the decision, and all expressed horror and outrage at the gross violation of Senate rules.

Shortly thereafter, Kenny made a brief visit to Boston to consult with Larry O'Brien on Jack's upcoming Senate reelection in '58. On his return to DC, no sooner had Kenny strolled into Bobby's office and said hello to Angie than a clearly angry Jack Conway charged into the room.

Kenny's first thought was, *Now what has Bobby done?*

But Conway's explanation surprised Kenny. "You said if we ever had a question to come to you. Well, here I am. There is this guy who says he is a member of the McClellan Committee. He came into our office and wants access to all this closed material and says that you and Bobby Kennedy sent him."

Kenny was stunned. Bobby, Kenny, Conway, and Rabinowitz had agreed to share information, no surprises, everyone making sure everyone else was in the loop, so from the start Kenny was suspicious.

They had come to this understanding in order to prevent the Republicans from playing Bobby and the unions against each other to gain a political foothold. Kenny had struck the arrangement, and taken responsibility for it, which he felt was his role. That way if any heat came, it would not be directed at Bobby. The truth was, as Conway and Rabinowitz would find out, when Bobby and Kenny made a political promise, they kept it. Kenny quickly asked Jack Conway for the man's name. Kenny was assuming Bobby had sent this guy.

Conway replied, "Vernon Johnson." Kenny was stunned and asked Conway to repeat it. Kenny thanked Conway and told him to deny all of Johnson's requests.

Then Kenny called Johnson on the telephone and said, "Vern, I do not want to hurt you, but there is a subpoena in the mail for you. I just want to know physically where you are, and I will send someone right over with it. Senator Kennedy wants you before the full committee tomorrow morning to explain your actions."

"Unfortunately for Vern, and fortunately for us, he was not a very bright fellow and was caught rather easily," Kenny noted. It simply never occurred to him that somebody might check with Bobby Kennedy's office and verify his credentials. Kenny knew somebody had to be paying him, so he said, "Vern, I know you have no job and no money, so who is paying your expenses?" Vernon said to Kenny straight away, "Oh, well, Kenny, Senator Mundt is paying my expenses, but you aren't supposed to tell Bob or Senator Kennedy, okay?"

"I said, 'Fine, Vern.' Then he said to me, 'I'll get paid for all this stuff they've had me doing, won't I? Ask Bob about that, because I really do need to be paid for this.'"

Kenny agreed. "Sure, Vern, you can raise that yourself with Bobby tomorrow morning at the closed hearing. In fact, why don't you ask Senator Kennedy that question when you are testifying first thing tomorrow morning? Stay right where you are; the subpoena's on its way."

"I just hung up the phone and shook my head," Kenny recalled. "I didn't know who was dumber: Johnson or Senator Mundt for hiring such a dope."

Armed with information that caught the Republicans in the act of tampering with evidence, Kenny and Bobby quickly tracked Jack down and brought him up to speed.

The next morning, at the closed committee hearing, Jack wasted no time and jumped right in: "I have received information that you have hired a private investigator to impersonate officers of the United States Senate, which is a violation of every rule that governs congressional committees. These investigators are going around to people and saying that they are officers and using our names and this committee's authority, the Senate's authority, to obtain unauthorized material from union locals. This committee is not authorized to obtain such material under the scope of our operations. Furthermore, this material is not relevant to any current or past investigations."

His statement was greeted with stunned silence. Finally, Senator McClellan said, "Well, Senator Kennedy, if what you are saying is true, it is a clear violation of the rules of the Senate. Can you name a name?"

For the first time since he had been working with John McClellan, for whom he had little respect, Kenny said the man finally seemed very angry about something. "McClellan may not have been terribly brave about a lot of things," said Kenny, "but he loved the rules and regulations that governed the Senate. This to him was outrageous."

Looking right at a very pale Senator Mundt, who sat there fiddling with his pipe, Senator Kennedy said, "Yes, I can."

Then he let the silence build a moment before saying, "The staffer's name is Vernon Johnson, and he was fired by the chief counsel with the full agreement of every member of this committee for illegal activities and poor performance."

Senator McClellan said, "Well, what do you mean? What is he doing now?"

Of course, McClellan thought he was going to name the senator responsible, but Senator Kennedy was too smart for that. He did not want it to look as if he were on a witch hunt or that it was a purely political attack on his part. Jack continued on and explained what Johnson had been up to.

Senator McClellan listened and, growing angrier by the minute, finally asked, "Well, who hired him?"

Then Bobby broke in and said, "Mr. Chairman, perhaps you should ask who's paying him instead of who hired him."

Senator McClellan looked at Bobby and said, "What?"

Bobby said, "With all due respect, Mr. Chairman, I think the real question is not who hired him, but rather who is paying him." Bobby and Senator Kennedy knew that if they allowed the question to be who hired him, then the Republicans would find some fall guy staffer they could then ship off to the Republican Committee and pretend to look clean again.

But Bobby had confirmed that the actual paycheck was coming from Senator Mundt. Vernon Johnson, again not too bright, had happily showed the stubs to Bobby and Kenny, assuming this meant that he would continue to get paid.

Senator McClellan said, "Okay, you are right. That is the right question."

Kenny and Bobby later joked with Jack that Senator Mundt was, as Kenny put it, "not too bright, either, so maybe it never occurred to him that Johnson had told Bobby the truth, because to Bobby and Senator Kennedy's astonishment, Senator Mundt then said, 'Hmm. I think the chief counsel is absolutely correct. That is a very good question. We need to find out who is paying this fellow.'"

With the door opened, Bobby then said, "Senators, I would like to ask Ken O'Donnell, one of my staff, to answer that question, as his research has gotten us the answer that we need."

So Senator Mundt turned to Kenny, who was sitting next to Bobby, and said, "Fine," puffing his pipe. "Fine, Mr. O'Donnell, tell this committee who is paying this fellow."

"Bobby and I just stared at each other for a moment," Kenny recalled. "I think he was as amazed as I that it could be this easy. And I said, 'Senator, I would be happy to answer that question. You are, sir.'"

By now, all the senators were staring at him, and Mundt said with another puff, "Hmm, hmm, how did you determine this, Mr. O'Donnell?"

Kenny said, "I talked to Johnson, interviewed him yesterday, and he gave me his pay stub."

Silence.

Mundt continued puffing on his pipe to cover his dismay. "That, young man, is a very interesting story. He told you this, Mr. O'Donnell, he showed you this, did he? He said this to you under subpoena?"

Kenny replied, "Yes, Senator Mundt, I have his whole testimony right here."

McClellan, who was furious, interrupted and said, "Yes, and I signed the damned subpoena, and he will be here tomorrow morning to testify!"

Senator Mundt said, "Hmm, well, that is very, very interesting. We really should look into this matter."

"With that," Kenny remembered, chuckling, "Senator Mundt got out of that room so fast your head would have spun."

The next morning, before Johnson was to testify, the hearings into the UAW locals were brought to a sudden halt, and a third set of hearings the Republicans had scheduled were also canceled.

Of course, Johnson mysteriously couldn't remember who hired him, the pay stub with Mundt's name on it vanished, and suddenly Johnson accepted a wonderful job far from DC.

"Probably East Alaska," Jack joked later. As was the Senate way at that time, and still is to a degree, the matter was handled within a private, clublike atmosphere. There were no public hearings about it, and the public never became aware of what Mundt had been up to. This was irrelevant, at least from Kenny and Bobby's perspective. The important takeaway was that Jack Kennedy took a political situation that could have done him real harm and turned it swiftly to his advantage—and the Republicans knew it.

It was evident that the Republicans perceived him to be a potential threat and would do all they could to damage him in advance of the presidential race. But now they would have to think twice about it.

And the Democrats? Many had their own ambitions or favorite-son candidates. They were happy to allow the Republicans to do their dirty work.

Kenny remembered that this strategy "was typical of the kind of tactics the Republicans used to discredit the unions. The real untold story here is the gross impropriety and really illegal activities the Republicans used to attack the Kennedy brothers with the underlying motivation that they feared Jack would get the support of the unions and the UAW."

Of course, Jack was happy to be perceived as an ally to the UAW, but he was savvy and realistic enough to recognize the distance between performances in hearings and actually gaining UAW support in a national campaign.

Kenny and Larry thought both Kennedy brothers had handled the situation beautifully. Kenny said later, "I have to say in all candor, never did either brother complain or take any of these internal disputes public. They handled problems as they arose and never, and I mean never, let it dissuade them from doing the job they were both on the committee to do. That impressed the hell out of me and the unions."

Jack Conway later told Kenny that this made a strong impression on the UAW as well.

It was during this period that Jack's, Kenny's, and Bobby's families began to grow. Caroline Bouvier Kennedy was born in November 1957, much to Jackie and Jack's relief, after losing one baby and fearing that Jackie might never have children. Caroline brought a particular joy and renewed confidence to Jackie.

This period also saw Jackie and Jack move from Hickory Hill to a Federalist brownstone in Georgetown. Hickory Hill had come to symbolize so much sadness for Jackie that the change did the couple a lot of good, as Kenny recalled. Hickory Hill was sold to Bobby, for whom the sprawling estate was well suited to his growing brood, which was soon joined by Michael LeMoyne Kennedy on February 27, 1957.

As for Helen and Kenny, Helen happily made the move from Boston to Bethesda, a suburb of Washington, DC. Nancy Sheridan helped locate a perfect rental home for the O'Donnells. Nancy was the wife of Walter Sheridan, another of Bobby Kennedy's investigators on the McClellan Committee. Walter would go on to be the key man in Bobby's relentless, obsessive pursuit of Jimmy Hoffa.

Around this time, Kenny and Helen also welcomed their own addition to the family. Mark Francis O'Donnell was born in 1956 and joined Kenneth Jr. and twins Kathleen and Kevin to round out the growing O'Donnell tribe.

Ironically, just as Helen got herself and her family settled into their new life in Bethesda, Kenny would soon be headed back to Boston.

It was now early June 1958, near the end of Kenny's work with the McClellan Committee, and Jack called Kenny over to his office.

"Get back to Massachusetts," Jack said. "I need you to take charge of the 1958 Senate campaign. You should have been there six months ago instead of wasting your time in all this nonsense. It's time."

Kenny gladly closed this chapter in his political life, heading back to Boston to rejoin Larry O'Brien and take the reins of the 1958 Senate campaign. They had survived another attack on Jack Kennedy's political viability, and while a long way from securing the UAW's endorsement, they had at least opened the door for union support in a national election. Kenny now had a way in. He was sure that was all he and O'Brien needed, and this alone had been worth his interlude in Washington, DC.

CHAPTER 11

The Landslide

AS KENNY WOULD recall later, "1957 was one of the happiest years. It was the lead-up to '58 and the huge reelection victory that secured his run in '60; it was the year Jack won the Pulitzer Prize for *Profiles in Courage*, edged out Estes Kefauver for a seat on the Foreign Relations Committee, which he enjoyed on several levels, but most importantly, [it] was the year his first child, his beloved daughter Caroline, was born."

"Never," Kenny said, "had I seen someone so thrilled to be a father." After Jack's health scare, marriage difficulties, and Jackie's two difficult and unsuccessful pregnancies and the loss of a stillborn child in 1956, it all seemed to turn around in '57. They moved out of the large estate at Hickory Hill with its pristine, sadly empty nursery.

"The house had seemed," Kenny said, "to bring them no luck. Jackie was miserable, and Jack had been driven to distraction by the morning and evening commuter traffic." It was a house built for a growing family and children. The empty bedrooms seemed in some manner to mock Jackie, so they sold it to Bobby and his growing brood, with child six, Michael LeMoyne, to be born in 1957. They chose a Federalist townhouse in Georgetown on N Street. "When Caroline was three weeks old, they moved into their new home on N Street. Jackie, their new daughter, and Jack were finally, as Dave said to Kenny, on the surface at least, happy and at peace."

Kenny was pleased. If there was more going on in the background, Kenny was unaware of it, as his relationship with the family, at least for now, remained need-to-know, though that would change as they approached the White House campaign.

For Kenny the next step was a return to Massachusetts and working with O'Brien to run Jack's reelection campaign. The 1958 Senate campaign marked several significant firsts for the presumptive chief of Jack's Irish Brotherhood. The race would mark a permanent and positive change of roles for Kenny O'Donnell. "You must understand," Kenny told Sandy Vanocur some years later, "the 1958 race was critical and indeed crucial as the precursor to the 1960 national election campaign. This was also the first campaign when I began to fully assume my role as the future president's right-hand man."

Kenny would find himself exactly where he wanted to be and in a position for which he was uniquely suited. His new job as an advisor to Jack would keep him working in tandem with O'Brien, but it would also enhance his position in relation to the senator. This new role would also mark a change in the relationship between Bobby and Kenny.

The plan for '58, as Kenny and Larry had originally worked it out, was for Ted Reardon, who had been Jack Kennedy's long-serving (some might say long-suffering) aide and scheduler, to move from the office into a full-time role as Jack Kennedy's personal and political assistant. This meant traveling with him at all times and being his political eyes and ears.

Kenny and Larry wanted to stay close to the ground and to the campaign operations in Boston. In many ways, they saw Reardon's role as a reward for his long service to Kennedy. He, like Dave Powers, had been with Jack since that first campaign in 1946.

But Ted Reardon performed this new job for a couple of days before complaining to Kenny that he simply hated it. He was much happier working in the senator's office. "Thanks, but no thanks. It was just too stressful," Ted had said.

Surprised and without any other suitable candidate, Larry and Kenny decided that they would take turns until they found someone who could assume the role full-time. Neither Kenny nor Larry had envisioned the position for themselves. Kenny felt sure that Larry would be a natural for the role and ideally suited for such close quarters with Jack.

That did not work out so well, either. Jack was miserable. He called Kenny at his hotel in Boston early one morning, asking him to meet with him at his apartment at 122 Bowdoin Street. Jack made clear to Kenny that the job was his. Period. Kenny never asked O'Brien what happened, but Kenny never relinquished that job with Jack until fate intervened. In retrospect, one can only imagine how different the outcome might have been had Reardon or O'Brien wished to stay.

In many ways, while Kenny and Larry loved Reardon, as did Dave Powers, they began to realize in hindsight that it was a good thing he had turned the job down. He was not well suited for the new role. As Jack's political hunger and ambition grew, the role increasingly required someone who was not only sensitive to political realities as they arose but also adept in political operations beyond the Senate campaign.

The role also required a fearless "don't give a damn what people think" quality and an ability to stand up to the senator and the Kennedy family no matter what that Kenny seemed, for better or worse, to possess. In addition, Jack required someone in whom he had absolute trust, but also someone who had no fear of Jack. In other words, someone who could shoot straight with Jack, without fear of reprisal or retribution. Kenny fit the bill perfectly.

Kenny and Jack shared, from the beginning, a mutual respect founded in their war experience and their common distaste for sentimentality.

"Kenny was a guy's guy," said his old friend William "Bill" Connors, "who came right at you. No holds barred. You knew where you stood with Kenny, like it or not."

Jack was the same sort of man, so the two seemed beautifully suited to work together, spending long hours on the political hustings under enormous pressures without, importantly, driving each other nuts.

Kenny also kept his mouth shut. Any conversations he and Jack had stayed between them. That was another quality Jack would come to absolutely appreciate.

"Kenny," another pal noted, "also was a political guy, so it allowed Jack to be the candidate and Kenny to cover the political angle, then transmit that information to O'Brien, Bobby, or the father, whomever needed to know in order to act." The truth was a lot simpler than all that because Jack had begun to trust Kenny's instincts and was comfortable around him. In the end, that was all that mattered.

Some found Kenny's approach intimidating, but he had just the persona Jack needed. He also seemed to have no personal ego and couldn't care less about anyone else's opinion, with the exception of Jack.

"Kenny," Vanocur recalled with a chuckle, "didn't give a damn who liked him or who didn't. He was his own man. Always. I'd never seen anything like it in politics."

Kenny took great pains to ensure his independence. As he explained later, "It is important to understand that during this entire period, from my first involvement with Jack Kennedy right through the '58 campaign, I was never a paid staffer. I never wanted to work for the Kennedys, and by that I mean get a paycheck. I felt it would change the relationship. Helen was in complete agreement with me from the very beginning. It gave me the ability to speak my mind with Jack Kennedy. I know it made me more comfortable. I know he appreciated it, and it made him more comfortable. He knew he could speak his mind with me with no fear. I actually did not start getting paid for my work with Jack Kennedy specifically until the White House, and that would be January 1961, after the inauguration. At that point, it was more than appropriate. We were both comfortable then, because in truth, I was being paid by the American public, not President Kennedy."

The decision not to be paid put Kenny in a unique and powerful position within the Kennedy organization. It brought him deeply into their inner circle and garnered a respect from them that no staffer would ever attain. Joe Kennedy, who had been suspicious of Kenny from the beginning, was impressed.

This tough decision must have placed burdens on Kenny's home life. But Jack never wondered about Kenny's real or imagined agenda. Kenny never worried that telling it like it was might get him fired. This sense of freedom in their relationship cemented an honesty and trust that would only build in the years to come as they spent increasing amounts of time together. Jack, who was not given to trust easily, came, by the end his life, to trust Kenny utterly and completely.

Jack later said, "I never doubt Kenny. His loyalty to me is absolute. I trust him completely. We may disagree at times over politics or people. He is not always right, nor am I. But I always know he has my back and always will. He always calls it like he sees it. I appreciate that."

This faith Jack placed in Kenny led to another unofficial title for Kenny. The press would dub him "the ultimate insider." You knew, said one Washington reporter, "when Kenny spoke . . . he spoke for Jack. You could take it to the bank. He never lied or misled. He always played it straight with us, whether it was answering a question or telling us to go to hell. We respected that." His agenda was Jack's agenda.

Kenny and Larry's strategy for the 1958 Senate race was a simple one: use the Kennedy machine to scour every corner of Massachusetts for a vote. The goal was to run Jack as if this race were in question and everything depended on each vote. They had to get the vote out and build up the vote count. This was not an easy task in an off-year election against a particularly weak, nonpolarizing opponent, Vincent J. Celeste. Celeste was a Republican whom Jack had faced in the House in 1950 and had already beaten once. Later, Celeste would correctly point out that Joe's money made a serious bid by any candidate against Jack difficult. While that was certainly true, Kenny and Larry believed that the sheer number of registered Democrats in the state who were inclined to back Jack against any Republican was another key element in Jack's success.

Kenny and Larry, having taken over the Massachusetts state party, had spent the time between Jack's election and the '58 race making sure Jack's reelection was as preordained as possible. They intended to establish a sense of inevitability to Jack's reelection, while at the same time working to keep Jack's involvement to an absolute minimum. Nevertheless, they worked tirelessly to give the voters the impression that Jack's presence was everywhere in their state.

The Irish Brotherhood could hardly have kept their political operation humming across Massachusetts without the healthy budget afforded to them by what Kenny referred to as "the Old Man's purse strings." In the end, Kenny noted that Joe spent something in the neighborhood of $1.5 million on Jack's reelection campaign. Such an amount of money, in 1958 dollars, was unheard of for a race not in question.

Such expenditures in grassroots organizing, advertising, and overhead allowed Larry and Kenny the resources they needed to build the Kennedy machine and put it into operation as they had long envisioned it. This time, however, they did so with an understanding between Joe, Jack, and the Brotherhood that the Kennedy machine was being well oiled with Joe's cash in preparation for running it nationwide.

This was about a lot more than Massachusetts. Their goal of a landslide victory for Jack, once achieved, cemented his position nationally and placed him exactly where they had hoped it would: on the radar screen of the national media.

Kenny and Larry also made sure that at every opportunity the media, both print and fledgling television, were in tow. They wanted to expose Jack as much as possible on the national stage, not only to convince national party leaders of his viability. It was also to expose the nationwide audience to this young, handsome candidate with a beautiful wife and child. This exposure was accompanied by design with a sense of inevitability and Hollywood-style glamour that had not been seen before in national politics.

Kenny had just seen the effect that the Kennedy panache had on the crowds in Chicago in '56 as Jack gave his concession speech, which turned into, in many ways, an eventual victory speech for Jack. Kenny and Larry were in full agreement here with Joe Kennedy, that getting Jack and Jackie out there in the public eye, not just in Massachusetts but nationally, was of critical importance. They approached every media outlet they could think of. The strategy worked in the end, but not without a few funny slipups.

At one stage of the campaign, Rowland Evans, a reporter from *Time* magazine, and two other reporters were all doing profiles of Jack. Evans's piece was for the cover of *Time*, thus his traveling with the candidate had taken on a special importance. The public relations value of a *Time* magazine cover was not to be underestimated.

Because Kenny and Larry had sought to keep Jack's physical role and involvement in the campaign to a minimum, whenever they did have him, the schedule was jam-packed, with no room for error. For the most part, all went according to plan. But not always.

One particular campaign stop, Kenny recalled later, involved a trip to Quincy, Massachusetts. Kenny had personally made the choice for Quincy, feeling it would showcase what he and Larry later jokingly called the "vaunted Kennedy machine in action." The trip actually would teach Jack, Kenny, and Larry that they still had much to learn before they were ready to take this show national.

From the moment they arrived, everything went wrong. For some reason the Kennedy secretary, Jack Curley, a young, efficient lawyer and vet who exemplified the new wave of Kennedy recruits, had gotten it into his head that they were arriving at 10:00 a.m., but instead the candidate and his entourage arrived at 9:00 a.m., an hour early. When they arrived, media in tow, there was no Kennedy secretary to meet them. There was only confusion.

Kenny's main concern was that the savvy and experienced Evans from *Time* was there along with a reporter from *The New York Times* and a few people from the Boston press. The last thing they wanted was some headline written in a national publication saying, as Kenny imagined it, "'This is amateur hour and Kennedy has the most confused, screwed-up campaign organization on the planet.' Not a good piece as you prepare to run nationally."

Evans had only the one day, so whatever impressions he took away from this day's events would comprise the entire story.

But Kenny and Jack improvised quickly with a tour of the Quincy shipyard, much to the surprise of the superintendent who ran it. Once they knew they were in trouble, Kenny sprinted ahead, getting to the shipyard and explaining their dilemma. The fellow, eager to please the senator, wanted to help, but it was Saturday, and there were at best only one hundred men around. Not to be deterred, Kenny suggested that the senator could inspect a ship. When the entourage arrived, Jack shot a nervous look toward Kenny, who walked quickly up to Jack announcing, "Senator, this is the ship you were to inspect."

"That's right, Kenny," Jack replied, no doubt with great relief. "We are going to inspect a ship here."

With that, Jack, with Kenny in tow and the press clipping at his heels, inspected the ship from bow to stern. After this, and still with no Kennedy secretary in sight, the group quickly headed to the local mall, where Jack and Kenny leaped out of the car, showing Jack's "grace and vigor," as Kenny recalled it, laughing. The reporters were impressed with how rapidly Jack moved through the mall, shaking every hand, even climbing over barricades to greet people with his familiar Boston accent: "Hi, I am Jack Kennedy!"

Kenny and Dave Powers chuckled afterward. Kenny said, "If only the press had known that we were moving so fast because the day was a complete disaster, the schedule was blown to smithereens, and we were making it up as we went along!"

Kenny recalled that much of the day went like that, racing with Dave from made-up event to made-up event, "hoping that we would not get found out."

Later that night, when Kenny joined the reporters for drinks at the pub, not far from Jack's Boston apartment, "the press marveled at how terrific the senator was on his feet, how healthy he appeared to be, which was not what they had heard, and how organized our operation was."

One reporter even noted, "You have days like this on the national campaign, you're headed to the White House! What a terrific operation!"

Kenny said that he and Dave exchanged a glance and downed their beers as fast as possible. Later, when Kenny rejoined Jack back at the apartment, he filled him in on the unofficial reviews of the press corps.

"He shot me a look," Kenny said. "'Next time,' he asked, 'should I plan my own schedule and advance myself? It seems you and O'Brien have a bit too much on your plate to make sure this campaign runs well. I would not want to overburden you.'"

The point, while made in jest, was clear. Don't screw up again. And if you do, try not to do it with the national press in tow.

It was during this critical 1958 campaign that Jack discovered perhaps his best-kept secret political weapon in Jackie Kennedy. Kenny had seen little of Jackie since Helen's party for her at the Parker House in Boston and the wedding in Newport. When Helen would ask him about some article or puff piece on Jack and Jackie or the birth of their daughter, Kenny would glaze over or run for the door.

Kenny liked Jackie well enough. She seemed fine as far he knew. She just didn't talk politics, and so Kenny had no need to spend a lot time chatting with her on the rare occasions when their paths crossed. He would not have known what to talk to her about anyway. Kenny was comfortable with someone like Helen: charming and attractive but also able to talk Harvard football and poll results in Ward 6 in Boston, and able to throw a hell of a good pass just in time to beat Bobby and Ethel during a game of pick-up at Hyannis Port.

Jackie, as Kenny was about to find out, was an entirely different creature. Like Kenny, she did not give a damn what other people thought of her or her actions. She did what she wanted, a trait that both Jack and Kenny would alternately admire and, especially during the White House years, find maddening.

"The president," Kenny said, "would ask Jackie to do such and such, which she did not want to do. She'd 'yes' him to death, then do exactly what she wanted. It drove him crazy at times, but Jackie was always her own person. Always."

What Kenny had heard about Jackie was not necessarily encouraging. He knew secondhand from staffers in Jack's office and some political wives that she was "a difficult girl and sort of a snob," that she, in fact, did not like politics and did not even like Jack Kennedy being in politics. Kenny remembered hearing all this in the background, but he couldn't have cared less. It had nothing to do with him or his role in Jack's political career.

This was all in Kenny's mind early one morning when Jack told him over one of Dave's wonderfully cooked breakfasts at the 122 Bowdoin Street apartment, with some mischievous delight, waiting to see Kenny's reaction, "Jackie wants to campaign with us. She is going to join us on the swing through Haverhill. This will be her first, and I want you to show her the ropes."

Kenny was horrified. "She's a woman," was all he could think to say.

Jack stared at him, no doubt enjoying Kenny's discomfort, and said, "Nothing gets past you."

Jack was clear: the next day Jackie would be joining them. Kenny knew when he'd lost the argument. That night he went home and promptly called Helen at their new house in Bethesda, just outside of Washington, to complain. He didn't know what to do with a woman, he said to her. Helen, surveying her home, which was by then filled to the brim with four children, quipped that he seemed to have figured it out fairly well in the past. Kenny was not amused.

"I've been told," he complained to Helen, "she's difficult."

"By whom?" Helen demanded.

Kenny said that Joe Kennedy had called him that very afternoon and said she was "a difficult, fragile china doll who might not be excited about shaking hands with Vernon Clearly of Taunton." Helen laughed. "This is the same Joe Kennedy whom you ignore 90 percent of the time, but this time he's got to be right." Kenny felt that Helen simply was not appreciating his plight, so he forged on.

If that was not bad enough, Bobby called Kenny to ask him to please "try to have some manners. I mean you really should try to have some manners and be nice; she's very fragile. You don't want to frighten her. She's never dealt with anybody like you," Bobby said worriedly.

"I've never dealt with a woman like that," Kenny protested to Helen. "What does that mean, 'Have some manners and don't frighten her'?"

Helen laughed. "Maybe your brother Cleo will pinch-hit for you," she replied, completely unsympathetic and obviously enjoying his discomfort.

Kenny was horrified. He had no idea how he was going to handle such a situation. Hardball politics with the Dever people he could deal with; toughing it out in Chicago with Kefauver's fellows, that was okay; tossing a guy through a window or over a bar, that was fine. But how the hell do you talk to a china doll?

Before they hit the trail the following day, just as they climbed into the car outside the Kennedy apartment on Bowdoin Street, Jack pulled Kenny aside, whispering so that Jackie would not overhear them. "Jackie doesn't like campaigning, and she doesn't like politics or politicians. You have to be careful with her. She is a rather delicate flower."

Kenny couldn't take this anymore. "A delicate flower?! Jesus!" was all he could think of. "Does she know what you do for a living?" Kenny asked, half to himself.

Jack shot him a dirty look. As they climbed into the car, Kenny thought to himself, *The McClellan Committee doesn't look so bad just now.* Maybe he should have stayed in Washington with Bobby!

Later, after Jackie and Kenny became close and formed a deep and trusting friendship that lasted for years after Jack's death, they would laugh about this first substantial meeting.

"Massachusetts politics constitute a rather rough variety of politics," Kenny recalled. "I felt when Jack told me this about her that in fact this was not going to go very well. We had a day trip scheduled, and particularly during a trip like this, you never know what you are going to run into. So I was very concerned about how to handle Jackie. I wanted her to be happy and content. I wanted it to be a good day. My main concern was I did not want her to fall apart, start crying, and cause any trouble for the candidate. I would not have known what to do with a sobbing, hysterical woman."

"I was astonished when I met her," Kenny laughed later. "Larry and I were prepared for a very high-strung, fragile, demanding china doll who couldn't cope with anything. This is what the buildup had been. We did not know what the hell to expect. Well, I recall the day vividly because she was the most pleasant, sweet, beautiful, elegant child, and very funny. I found her to be that way from that point forward. She was and is simply a delight as a person. She never raised her voice. She never once complained. She was not enthusiastic, but she never complained. In truth, most politicians' wives are not excited about this aspect of their lives, either, but most are phony and put on a big show. She never did that. She did exactly what you asked of her, but she was never a faker about it. She was not terribly interested in meeting the local politicians, whose big excitement was describing their local shoe factory. It wasn't that unusual to not want to listen to some of those fellows. Half the time, I didn't want to listen to them, either. I admired the fact that she wasn't a phony. I noticed that the locals also seemed to admire the fact that she was not a faker. She was beautiful. Beautiful in a sense that these fellows were not accustomed to seeing. Jackie was very elegant and classy. Unusual, not your regular politician's wife, but then Jack Kennedy was no average politician. She would travel with Jack, and he would introduce her. She would say a few words and knock everyone dead. All she had to do was say hello, and these average fellows were captivated. It really was a foreshadowing of the future. This was before she had become completely transformed, but you could see that it was coming."

"Over drinks a few days later, I asked the senator, 'Have you actually met Mrs. Kennedy?' He looked at me astonished and asked what I meant. I told him of our experiences, and I said, 'Senator, she is anything but fragile; she's smart as hell, capable, funny, and has a keen political instinct that in certain situations was better than ours. But fragile flower? No.'" Jack nodded, but Kenny sensed that he was surprised. Jack was beginning to understand that if he could persuade her, Jackie could be a useful asset on the campaign trail.

There is one trip in particular that Kenny recalled as marking the beginning of their relationship, or the start of Madame La Femme, as Kenny had dubbed Jackie.

This was a standard political trip for the Kennedy operation to Western Massachusetts's industrial towns. This trip would be different, however, because it marked their first political trip with Jackie. And because it was her debut, Jack in particular was, as Kenny put it, "a wreck." Kenny and Larry wanted her to be happy, mostly because they wanted her husband to be happy.

"We were all very hungry," Kenny recalled, "so we stopped finally for lunch. One of the things that we did during the campaign was we always took two hours for lunch. We did this throughout Jack's career. This was one of the things that we always paid great attention to and made sure to take a full two hours. It was very important for Jack's health.

"We really held our Kennedy secretaries throughout the state to this routine. It would also later be an important part of our national schedule. We did it in the 1960 campaign, and we were very tough with everyone about it. Joe Kennedy was the one who first spoke to me about it. He asked me directly for this one concession and said for his son's health it is important that he eat properly. It was one of the only concessions I made to Mr. Kennedy. I will say I did so with great pleasure, though, because I felt he was quite right."

Kenny still was not fully versed in Jack's health issues, but the recent health scare in 1955 had given him enough information to know the well was far deeper than it appeared.

Kenny could see that Jackie was laughing generally at the entire operation. She was not quite able to figure out what all these maneuvers were about. She didn't know any of the players or understand the purpose of it all. It was evident that she thought it was all a bit silly.

"We were in the back room in a restaurant. John Lenihan was there. He was our secretary in Haverhill. We were all seated around this table, having our lunch: steak, baked potato, glass of milk, and chocolate cake for dessert. That was really our standard lunch, always prearranged in advance, so we could just sit down and order it. Jackie was terribly amused that we all ate the same thing every day. But it was what the senator wanted, and so that was that.

"Senator Kennedy was giving me his usual twenty-five instructions: 'I want you call so-and-so. Then call that SOB down there and tell him to do such-and-such. Call this fellow over there and tell him to do this.' I had my pencil and my usual notebook, which was really the back of an envelope. I wrote down every single thing he said and made a list.

"Jackie was eating, sipping her drink, and watching me intensely. We got all through the list, and Jackie said, 'I have always wondered what exactly is it you do with all those things Jack tells you. You keep writing them all down, but I have never actually seen you do anything with any of the items on the list.'

"Senator Kennedy had decided, since Jackie was with us, to relax a bit, and so he had ordered everyone at the table a glass of wine with lunch. I thought it was quite funny that she should notice this, and I said to her, 'Well, you know what I do with them? I wait until he calms down, and then

I only do what I think is important, and I throw the envelope out.' Jackie burst out laughing.

"'I knew that!' she declared. 'I just guessed.'

"Jack was less than amused. While he likely understood my routine better than most, he was as nervous as a schoolboy and obviously was trying to impress his wife.

"He was furious. 'You son of bitch,' he barked, 'I bet that is just what you do!'" Kenny tried not to laugh, suddenly realizing for some odd reason that Jack was really trying to impress Jackie.

"Oh, Jack," Jackie said, putting her hand on his arm to calm him down. "He's just teasing you. Relax. It's all supposed to be good fun."

Kenny watched as Jack immediately returned to his good-natured, teasing self and laughed.

"You SOB," he said again to Kenny as they rose to leave. "I have no doubt that you do exactly what you want, no matter what I say."

Kenny laughed, lagging behind as they left the restaurant to return to their cars. He caught Jackie watching him and pretended to throw the envelope away. He laughed instead, stuffing it in his suit coat pocket. It was the first time Kenny had been exposed to Jackie's charming side, and Kenny was utterly captivated.

Kenny told Vanocur later, "She had not yet made the full transformation into this enormously popular national figure, but you could see the potential was there. For the first time, I also saw just how important she was to the senator. Her good humor and wonderful perspective kept him levelheaded, and in politics that is critical for a candidate."

It was clear to the Irish Brotherhood that Jackie was a political asset. Kenny took note of it for the future, though this was not something he needed to write down on an envelope.

The campaign that Kenny and Larry designed was, as Kenny described it, "as nearly perfect in planning and operation as an election campaign in an off year could be."

•◆•

As the campaign got under way, the first order of business for Kenny and Larry was to bring together the Kennedy secretaries from throughout Massachusetts. This would, in essence, be a copy of the 1952 race, but with clearer footing and more political cards in their deck, Kenny and·Larry were determined to run up the numbers. They instituted the same card system they had in 1952, bringing in the girls, led by Helen Lempart and Kenny's younger sister Justine O'Donnell, to update the system; this also meant pushing the Kennedy secretaries hard. While money wouldn't be an issue, access to the candidate this time round would be extremely limited, so Kenny made clear that days were to be jam-packed and that each event needed to bring in the votes as well as pound home the Kennedy sense of inevitability.

"The truth was," Kenny and Dave recalled, "While [Jack] was running for reelection as senator for Massachusetts, Kennedy was still carrying on his national campaign for the 1960 presidential nomination, making appearances at political gatherings all over the nation. This meant the time he could give to personal campaigning in Massachusetts was limited. Actually, he spent only seventeen days in the state between the September primary and the November election."

Kenny told Vanocur, "He and O'Brien had worked out the schedule for the senator from September to November during the lull in campaign in the summer months. Jack, Jackie, and Caroline had been in Europe, ostensibly on a tour for the Senate Foreign Relations Committee. He was due to return on a ship that would dock in New York on primary day in Massachusetts; both Kennedy and Furcolo were running unopposed on the Democratic ticket. "The schedule was so tough that Kenny admitted later that he dreaded showing it to the senator. They had already given it to Joe, who had joined them at the dock to greet his son. Upon reading it Joe exploded. "What are you trying to do, kill him?!" he roared.

Kenny had shrugged. "Given the limited time we have with him and the numbers we need to run up, it is what we have to do."

When Jack and Jackie got off the boat, he took the schedule from Kenny, and with that computer-like mind of his, he looked it over immediately. Handing it back to Kenny, all he said was, "Looks good."

Joe was appalled, but Jack and Kenny were more worried about the primary vote that day. While such a vote was always light in off-year elections, Furcolo was far ahead of Kennedy in the totals and that was not good, particularly in the Italian districts.

There was also some anger among teamsters, longshoremen, and other labor unions over the Saint Lawrence Seaway and Bobby's role at the McClellan Committee; since Kennedy was running unopposed, they decided to blank the ballots, "which," Kenny said, "substantially dropped our numbers." The light turnout and disappointing numbers in the primary made it easier to get Jack to agree to the schedule, and while both Kenny and Larry well knew that a light primary does not necessarily mean anything for November, they were still disgruntled and concerned. These were not impressive numbers for a candidate rumored to be running for the White House in 1960.

"We cannot," Larry said, "take any chances. It must be an all-out press." And so it would become.

The '58 campaign would "follow really a small-scale model of what we did nationwide in 1960 and had one attractive feature that was unfortunately lacking in the later presidential campaign: We had Jackie Kennedy, who was able to accompany her husband on several of his long days' journeys. Local politicians went nuts over her," Kenny said. "Trust me, there are lots of homes around Massachusetts with pictures of Jackie taken during the '58 campaign. It was but a small inkling of what would happen in the White House."

By now Kenny had gotten used to Jackie and her style. He was quickly learning firsthand what a powerful political weapon she could become.

Jackie, Kenny believed, had been key to their success in 1958. He would come to very much regret that she would not participate in '60, which is why her agreement to help in the '64 campaign had been a source of such excitement. But, still, Kenny and Jackie's early meetings in '58 were not without their bumps in the road.

If Kenny called Jackie Madame La Femme privately, she called him "the wolfhound"—for his serious demeanor, intimidating style, and fierce protectiveness of Jack. The nickname also referred to the fact that every time Kenny arrived, Jack had to return to work.

But, from the 1958 campaign forward, Kenny and Jackie would learn to dance around the political realm, both knowing that in their own way they had Jack's best interests at heart. For instance, Kenny and Jackie often joked later about another humorous incident from the '58 campaign.

Kenny and Larry had been sent to Haverhill, Massachusetts, with Jackie in tow. The community was largely French, with many members still speaking French. Both Kenny and Larry believed, correctly as it turned out, that Jack would carry the area by overwhelming numbers. They also felt that Jacqueline Bouvier Kennedy would be a smash hit!

The schedule called for a tea at the local church parish's school hall. Unfortunately for Kenny and Larry, the local Kennedy secretary had gotten the day wrong. When Kenny and Larry arrived with Jackie, on what would be only their second trip with her and her first trip without Jack, there was no one there but a few nuns and the parish priest.

As they walked into the room, used mostly for recitals and practices for the schoolchildren, they were expecting a large crowd. Even though Kenny, Larry, and Jackie had arrived a day early, the kitchen staff at the church had made enormous urns of hot tea, surrounded by delicate white-and-pink teacups. To make matters worse, each of the tables was piled high with mouthwatering small tea cakes, carefully frosted to reflect the flags of the United States and French Canada. The pièce de résistance was the piano player, an older nun who had been long retired but who loved the Kennedy family and was brought back especially for this grand occasion.

The idea was for Jackie to meet and greet the enormous crowd that no doubt would soon arrive and then address them in French about the importance of supporting Jack's candidacy for the Senate. Jackie immediately began chatting with the priests and the nuns while waiting for the crowd. She looked elegant in a classic navy cloth coat, gloves, and pillbox hat. Kenny watched admiringly as Larry watched the huge clock over the doorway tick away the time. Still no Kennedy secretary and no crowds.

Larry finally sidled over to Kenny. "It's been a half hour; something is wrong." Kenny, brought back from reverie, looked up at the clock. "Shit!" the wolfhound exclaimed loud enough for Jackie and the priests and the nuns to hear. The room remained mostly empty. Kenny realized he was going to have to improvise to avoid a disaster in front of Jackie.

Jackie shot Kenny a disapproving look. He shifted his weight uncomfortably and waved, turning to Larry, "Call the SOB!"

As Larry left to call, Kenny took action. Not knowing what else to do and wanting it to look like something was happening, Kenny ordered the nun to begin playing.

"Play what?" she asked, concerned.

"I don't care! Anything," the nonmusically inclined Kenny said. "'Danny Boy'!"

The nun stared at Kenny, puzzled. "I hardly think that is appropriate for an afternoon tea," she replied, looking at him sternly.

It reminded Kenny of his parish in Worcester. He didn't like the look then and he did not appreciate it now, either.

"Play anything you want," Kenny snapped as he suddenly began pouring tea into the cups and stuffing pastries in his pockets.

Just then, Larry returned, breathless. He stopped and watched Kenny, puzzled for a moment. "What are you doing?" he asked, almost afraid to get the answer.

"Start drinking some tea and stuff some of these pastries in your pockets, Kenny barked to Larry. "You as well," he said to the sister, shoving a plate over to her at the piano.

Larry obliged at once. "And why are we doing this?" he ventured to ask as he began stuffing the cakes in his mouth.

"Jackie keeps looking over here, and she is trying to head this way. I want it to look like somebody's been eating and drinking the tea."

Larry surveyed the empty room, save for Jackie and about a dozen nuns. "Who exactly is she to think has been eating them?" Larry asked through a stuffed mouth.

Kenny looked up from his hands full of cakes. "Shit, here she comes." Kenny heard a distinct disapproving hiss behind him.

"Sorry, Sister," Larry said, spitting cake out as he spoke.

"Dance," Kenny ordered.

"What?" Larry asked, incredulous.

"Dance," Kenny ordered. "I will be right back." Kenny began dancing across the room toward the door, cake in one hand, teacup in another, and sort of waved as he headed out the door. Jackie came to a full stop watching him, puzzled, amused, or perhaps frightened; it was hard to tell from her expression. She then turned to watch Larry, who waved while dancing clumsily from side to side and sipping tea. She looked past him toward the nun, who was dutifully playing while taking occasional breaks to stuff cake in her mouth.

Jackie stood elegantly but with the most puzzled expression on her face.

She admitted to Jack later that she really did not know if this was standard fare or perhaps the vaunted "wolfhound" and his partner in crime, O'Brien, were having a breakdown and perhaps she should call her husband?

Before she could decide, Kenny returned, still holding the cakes and teacups, followed by an older nun, who turned out to be the school principal, and a sea of giggling girls, not one of whom could vote. Also along was the gardener, and Kenny had managed to round up a few passersby, which included women with baby carriages.

As they all converged in the room en masse, the schoolgirls' giggles and squeals at the sight of the food reaching an ear-splitting level, they all spied Jackie standing in the middle of the room. For a moment, all parties surveyed each other in silence. That is when, teacup in hand, Kenny began dancing with the principal, while Jackie watched in amusement. Then Kenny got to Larry and began to dance. The girls giggled, took this as sign, surged past this beautiful lady—with no idea who she was—and headed for the food!

Kenny and Larry kept dancing as Jackie approached them, hands clutched behind her back, purse in her hand. "Do you think she will hit us with it?" Larry asked as he two-stepped badly with Kenny.

Kenny watched her approach. "No, but I am dreading what she is going to tell her husband!

Larry was watching Jackie and said, "Stop leading, Kenny!"

Despite their best efforts to dance away from Jackie, who was a superb athlete, amateur ballet dancer, and horsewoman, Jackie solo-danced right up to them. Escape was impossible.

"The jig is up," Kenny said.

"Thank God!" Larry said with relief. "You were stepping on my toes. I don't how women do this!"

Kenny glared at Larry.

"Kenny," Jackie inquired in her elegant, whispering voice.

"Yes, Mrs. Kennedy?" Kenny replied as if this were all perfectly normal. "Anything wrong?" he asked over the din of screaming schoolchildren.

"I don't want to hurt your feelings," she said, her deep brown eyes locking with his, "but shall we both save ourselves further pain and embarrassment and simply admit your event is a failure? Besides," she said, looking at the two of them with their overstuffed pockets, cakes bulging out of each one, "I really don't think either one of you could stuff another cake in your suit pockets or drink more tea. Shall I just take it from here?" she asked with a tone that said, *Let me show you how it's done.*

Sheepishly, Kenny and Larry agreed. With that Jackie turned to go but stopped short and looked back. "Besides," she added, "I really don't think I could stand watching you stepping on Larry's toes any further."

Kenny grimaced.

"Follow me," she ordered.

From there they followed her to the monsignor, who was trying in vain to corral the girls away from the cakes.

Jackie whispered something in French, and before they knew it, they were sitting in the monsignor's private den in the rectory. Jackie requested a beer each for Kenny and Larry. She had a glass of wine with the priest as they spoke in French. Kenny had no idea what they said; he did not ask, but he could tell that the beer tasted good.

As they climbed back in the car later, Kenny said little. What could he say? She was obviously going to complain to her husband and there would be hell to pay.

Finally, after a painfully quiet trip they met Jack back in Boston at John Fox's place for dinner. Dave had already ordered it: steak, baked potato, salad, and chocolate cake. As they entered the back room, Jack rose, pain briefly evident on his face, but it was quickly replaced with delight at the site of Jackie.

"How did it go?" he asked, excited, shooting Kenny and Larry, who'd hung back, an *it better have gone well* look.

After a pause as Jack pulled out a seat next to him for his wife, she smiled broadly and met Kenny's steady gaze. "It was wonderful, Jack," she exclaimed. "Just the most unique experience I've ever had. I also was exposed to Larry and Kenny's hidden talents. They certainly have panache."

Kenny smiled and in a rare moment pulled the waiter aside and ordered two beers.

"Thanks," Larry said,

"Get your own," Kenny said. "Those are for me."

Jack, sensing something was up, looked to Kenny for an explanation. Kenny simply smiled and downed his beer. Jack let it go, but as dinner came to a close, Jackie again piped in, "Jack, darling," she said with a smile at Kenny, "I don't think Kenny or Larry need any cake. They've brought their own." Jack looked over at Kenny, puzzled.

Kenny suddenly remembered all the cakes in their pockets, now stale and stuck together as he and Larry pulled them out of their pockets and put them on the table in front of them.

"For the kids," Kenny said.

Jack looked at him skeptically. "You are going to mail the cakes to Washington?"

Powers, sensing pending disaster, not for the first time, quickly stepped in with one of his stories, changing the subject. "You can tell me what happened later," Dave chuckled as they headed to the car.

It was days later, when sitting with Jack at lunch during a jam-packed critical campaign day, that Kenny got confirmation that Jack had heard the whole humorous and disastrous story.

As Jack was looking over the afternoon schedule and Kenny and Larry were diving into their steaks, Jack suddenly asked, "Larry, how are your feet doing?"

Larry looked up, puzzled for a moment. "Fine," he said, confused.

Kenny stopped chewing and looked at Jack, waiting for the explosion, but instead he got an amused look.

"Good," Jack said, "because I hear Kenny has two left feet."

Nothing more was said until years later in the White House, when Jack humorously admitted to Kenny that Jackie had told him the entire story with great relish and spared no detail.

In the end, as it turned out, Jackie had convinced the monsignor to endorse Jack from the pulpit at every Mass and to do so in French.

As things turned out, Jack would carry the district overwhelmingly.

There were some changes to the '58 campaign that Kenny and Larry did not like, but they were dictated by Joe. It seemed to Kenny anyway that it was the senator's way of appeasing his father. For instance, rather than set up Kennedy for Senate headquarters across the state as they had in 1952, Jack decided they needed to work out of single headquarters on Tremont Street in downtown Boston. Kenny, whose entire focus was running up the numbers, was dismayed. In addition, this time around there was no Bobby. He was busy writing his book *The Enemy Within*, about his days at the McClellan Committee, and wrapping up the committee in preparation for 1960.

The 1958 campaign would be organized differently than the one in 1952. The role of campaign manager would fall to Jack and Bobby's younger brother, Teddy Kennedy, who was, Dave said, "getting his baptism by fire," and Steve Smith. Steve, a New Yorker, was newly married to their sister Jean Kennedy, and it was Steve who was really in charge of the day-to-day operation. He was new to the Kennedy organization and family for that matter, but Kenny and he immediately hit it off. Smith was low-key, sharp, and excellent with money and numbers. Kenny found him to be a no-bullshit kind of fellow on whom he could always rely to give him straightforward feedback and advice. It was the beginning of a relationship that would simply strengthen over the years.

"Steve is," Kenny said, "smart as hell, great political insight and instincts, his own man, so I could approach him with issues regarding the senator and the family that I could not discuss with others. I knew whatever we discussed would go no further."

Steve, Kenny learned, could always be trusted to keep any and all conversation private.

There was one particular incident that stood out for Jack Kennedy during '58 on these jam-packed campaign days. Jack would make a point of moving into the crowd, shaking hands and talking to voters. After one seemingly successful event, where the crowds had roared and surged around Jack as they left a factory, Kenny noticed that Jack seemed troubled.

"What is it?" he asked, puzzled by why such a great crowd might leave the candidate troubled.

Jack stopped and winced for a moment in pain before climbing into the car. "Half those people," he said, "were not registered to vote."

Kenny stopped. He had not checked, just assumed. Jack put up his hand to indicate that that was not his point. His concern, a focus that he would take into the White House, was that all these nonregistered voters in essence had no voice in the democratic process. It bothered him deeply. As a war vet, who had fought for these cherished rights, it bothered him that given the opportunity, people would not choose to register and vote.

"It bothered him deeply," Kenny said, "that there were millions of people, particularly in black populations, who could cheer a candidate but not vote for him."

Jack tasked Kenny with refocusing the Democratic National Committee once they were in the White House. "At the time of his death," Kenny recalled, "in the 1964 campaign he wanted the Democratic National Committee to have two main functions only: to raise as much money as possible, and to spend most of it on registering voters, particularly in poor and minority areas." President Johnson would carry this policy forward, going as far as to appoint Kenny executive director of the Democratic National Committee, a job he took on in addition to his normal duties for President Johnson. Jack, Kenny reasoned sadly and later told Jackie, "would have been pleased."

Foster Furcolo, who in '52, '53, and '54 forward had been battling Jack for primacy in Massachusetts politics, now saw the writing on the wall. He was eager to be governor and wanted to tie his campaign to Jack's. Steve Smith, no doubt quietly amused given the history of distrust and dislike between Furcolo and Kennedy, agreed, but only if Furcolo would pick up the cost of all the billboards, pamphlets, and advertising. Furcolo, seeing the inevitability of a Kennedy win in November, happily agreed.

Kenny told Steve, "That alone gets my respect for you forever!" The two men chuckled. Despite having only one central headquarters and not paying for the advertising, the Kennedy campaign was nevertheless the most expensive Senate campaign up until that point. With an eye toward 1960, Joe Kennedy was taking no chances.

As Election Day dawned, though Kennedy's victory was never in doubt, Kenny, Larry, and Dave felt the pressure to deliver a landslide victory. Their opponent, Vincent J. Celeste, was no real threat to Jack, but as Jack noted to Kenny and Dave on Election Day, "If we don't get a majority of more than five hundred thousand, Celeste will be the real winner."

To win by such a margin meant that they would need at least two million people to go to the polls, not an easy task in an off-year election.

Yet Dave Powers was confident, noting later to Kenny that "nearly everybody in Massachusetts, Republicans and Democrats alike, had been thrilled by Jack Kennedy's performance at the 1956 Democratic Convention in Chicago."

He was sure that meant they would come out and vote. The operation they put together in Jack's 1958 Senate race was an expanded, more efficient effort than in his first Senate campaign in '52. This time Kenny and Larry, having learned from experience, made sure to get out the vote as much as possible.

This included, as Kenny put it, a two-channel approach: "the senator making personal appearances in as many towns and cities as possible, as well as large numbers of volunteer workers enlisted for door-to-door canvasing in every community."

This would include some three hundred thousand signed pledges to vote for Kennedy. It would also involve an extraordinary effort of sending out 1,240,000 copies of a tabloid-style newsletter describing the senator's past accomplishments and future aims.

On election night, all that personal outreach paid off. Close to two million people—1,952,855 to be exact—actually went to the polls and voted.

It was an off-year-election record. Jack would receive 73.6 percent of the votes, giving him 1,362,926, which provided an incredible 874,608 margin over Celeste. It would turn out to be the biggest majority by which any candidate had won the Senate in Massachusetts and the largest majority won by any senatorial candidate across the nation that year.

Kenny said with satisfaction, "His showing was much better than even he or we had hoped for. His victory attracted much attention all over the country, and he came out of the 1958 election a much more prominent candidate for the presidency."

At Joe Kennedy's apartment in Boston on election night, the Brotherhood watched the returns with Jack and Jackie, a mixture of anticipation and excitement in the air. By 2:00 a.m. it was over, and Jackie and Jack returned home.

Joe, Kenny, Larry, and Dave stayed up a bit longer to talk. "It was not that we weren't excited," Kenny said later. "We were excited, but we were already thinking about the next ball game."

They had succeeded in demonstrating that Jack could achieve a big win at home, putting him on the national map as a viable candidate for the presidency. This was done for the voting public across the nation, but also for the party leaders, who watched Jack's team stack up an impressive set of numbers for an off-year election. The plan for 1960 was coming together.

CHAPTER 12

The Kennedy Kickoff
in Palm Beach

T HE EVENING OF the 1958 Senate victory, Kenny, Larry, and Dave stayed up late into the night with Joe Kennedy. Joe was still amped up from his son's victory, not as much from the landslide as from seeing his presidential dreams for his son come that much closer to reality.

Just before Jack and Jackie took off around 2:00 a.m., Jack turned to look at Kenny and Larry. Kenny thought Jack appeared almost wistful, as if he knew he had one foot in a part of his life that was coming to a close and his other foot planted firmly in the future.

The dream Jack had long pursued promised to include exhausting battles but also the hoped-for victory that would bring him to 1600 Pennsylvania Avenue. He said none of that, of course, but just nodded a thanks to Kenny. Kenny nodded back, the elation of victory tempered with the reality of the task ahead.

Kenny waited as the various Kennedy family members departed, saying goodnight to their father. They were all headed back home, going their separate ways after Jack's record landslide. But before the Irish Brotherhood could leave, Joe invited them to sit, and another round of drinks was poured.

"We had had some disagreements with him during the campaign. Mr. Kennedy has never been noted for his willingness to brook disagreements from those he considered young kids, which is how he viewed Larry and me, who in his view were still wet behind the ears. In the past, his sources of information about our conduct during the campaign had not always been friendly to us, but that had all changed by now," Kenny recalled.

Before they sat and toasted, Joe put his hands on each of their shoulders, something he had never done. Kenny was startled, recalling, "He was very profuse in his congratulations to both of us."

They toasted to Jack's future before getting down to brass tacks about the next steps in the plan.

From Kenny's perspective, "The father could not have been warmer, kinder, or more grateful now that everything had turned out well. The test had always been the score at the end of the game, as far as he was concerned. As the son of a football coach, that was an approach I completely agreed with. Frankly, to my surprise, he left me with a very warm feeling toward him. I am sure Larry felt the same way. We continued that relationship from that point forward and our approach toward the coming campaign. We never again returned to the difficult prior relationship. We had all come to an understanding. The focus now was the score at the end of the next game. We were all aimed at 1960 and the campaign for the presidency."

The campaign for 1960 had really begun in earnest that evening in Joe Kennedy's Boston apartment after the '58 returns had come in. Kenny left there that evening completely clear that he, Joe, and Larry were on the same page. There would be no more wasted time in turf battles with Jack's father.

◆◆◆

WITH THE SENATE campaign wrapped up, Kenny headed back to Washington at Bobby's request to help clean up some issues related to the McClellan Committee. Kenny was not happy about the assignment. He told Joe the evening of the Senate victory that he was eager to get the campaign under way. Joe agreed. Yet he pointed out to Kenny what Kenny knew already. The labor vote was key to Jack's success.

At the moment, Hubert Humphrey had the labor vote wrapped up, and the hearings had done little to help the UAW's views of Jack. Eleanor Roosevelt still strongly opposed Jack, and she had sway with Walter Reuther and the UAW. That relationship had to be broken, in Joe's view.

Kenny of course agreed, and though he was unhappy about it, he recognized that it was important that Kenny help Bobby wrap up work with the McClellan Committee successfully, transitioning these contacts as much as possible to Jack's national campaign. Kenny knew Joe was right, though he'd much rather be setting up for 1960.

This period of time right before the '60 campaign began in earnest and was very difficult for Kenny: "I really felt a sense of confinement. I was eager to get under way with the presidential campaign. I felt we were wasting time. Bobby was also eager to get under way, but his mind was really on finishing off the work of the McClellan Committee. He was worried about getting the bill successfully passed in the Congress and working on his book *The Enemy Within*.

"We would have conversations about the upcoming campaign, but often these conversations were sort of hit or miss." Kenny felt there was little left for him to contribute to the McClellan Committee, and it was time for his considerable energies to focus on the national campaign.

Ruth Watt, then a secretary at the McClellan Committee, remembered this time very well: "The work of the committee would go on during the day, but Kenny would have his door closed. We all knew that he was working on the presidential campaign for Senator Kennedy. During the day, it was the McClellan Committee, but at night when the door closed, it was Kennedy for President headquarters."

By the time of Jack's reelection in 1958, Kenny and Jack had spent so much time together that their relationship had begun to evolve. They were developing a system of understanding each other, originating in long stretches of time spent in proximity to one another that often did not require words. It was during this period that Jack indicated to Kenny that he had made up his mind about 1960. While he never said directly to Kenny, "The campaign starts on this day," he did not need to say a word. They both knew the campaign had begun with his victory in 1958. In some ways, Kenny came to believe the campaign had really begun in 1955, when Jack, having survived several close calls with death, had made the decision to become a "total politician," as Jack called it.

Kenny said, "Jack and I spoke, at this point, literally every day and often several times a day and evenings. He would call me on one matter or another. We would discuss strategy and the next step, primaries and so forth. So the 1960 campaign was just assumed. Often he would have a congressman or senator over for meetings in his office and ask me to sit in on those meetings so he could discuss them with me afterward. This became a regular feature and would naturally continue to be my role in the White House. We never discussed any of this outright. My role simply emerged.

"The senator would call me up to his office and introduce me to these fellows. He would then say to them, 'This is Kenny. Senator or Congressman So-and-So is having this problem. I want you to help him.'

"He would then turn to them and say, 'You should feel free to call Ken O'Donnell directly. He will do whatever it is that you would like him to do within reason and will help you with this problem or that problem. He really speaks for me.'

"This would happen on a regular basis between the months of January and March. The senator and I would talk almost every day and casually discuss the possible political implications of certain moves, certain legislation, certain personalities, and so forth. He would discuss; I would listen and perhaps have some comment. These discussions became a regular daily feature of our relationship. This strategizing sort of emerged and began to take shape as we went along."

Kenny's new, powerful role would continue to evolve throughout the campaign. Jack would also learn that Kenny's keen political antennae could serve him well on many fronts, the labor front in particular.

The Kennedys' prickly relationship with the UAW was very much on Jack's mind as the McClellan hearings came to a close. As Kenny remembered, "The senator was quite aware by this time that I had established a close working relationship with the United Auto Workers people, and especially the leadership team around Walter Reuther. They told him that I had been rather kind to them, especially in light of the rocky start of their relationship with Bobby and the committee. They appreciated that very much. They recognized that I had worked hard to gain their trust, and this naturally pleased Jack a great deal. The truth was, he had no one else on his staff who had contact with them to the extent that he thought would be necessary. I would say in fairness, though, that Ted Sorensen, because of his intellectual qualities, had some working relationship with them. They respected Sorensen and Ralph Dungan."

Ralph Dungan, another Irishman, had joined the Kennedy office in Washington in 1957 as part of Ted Sorensen's operation. Dungan was politically connected, an attorney from Philadelphia, who became close to Kenny and in some ways part of the extended Irish Brotherhood.

Kenny recalled, "They liked him very much. However, in a cold, political judgment, they were not about to discuss any of their problems with any of these fellows."

The discussions between Kenny and Jack at this point were casual, and he certainly did not reveal his plans, in part because he had not quite formulated any. He would leave that job to Bobby, Kenny, Larry, and brother-in-law Steve Smith.

Smith was from Bayport, New York. He hailed from a wealthy New York family that could hold its own against the Kennedys. Kenny would eventually become close to Steve, respecting him not only for his business savvy but also for his genius with raising money on the campaign trail and making just the right political connections. Also, like Kenny, Bobby, and Jack, Steve was low-key, smart, funny, and tough as nails. He had married Jean Kennedy in May 1956 and moved into managing the Kennedy family financial operation in New York. He fit in perfectly with the team Jack had already assembled and would prove essential to Jack's strategy in 1960.

Kenny would say later, "Success would have been impossible without the help of Steve Smith. He was one of the most underappreciated guys in the Kennedy operation."

Like Jackie, with whom he would establish a strong friendship, Steve always remained his own person within the powerful Kennedy family. Like Jackie and Sarge Shriver, he refused to be pulled into the Kennedy family undercurrent and always could be counted on, as Kenny said, "to provide cold, practical, and completely unvarnished answers to your questions." Kenny came to value Steve's insight and advice greatly in the campaign ahead.

In April of 1959, Jack called Kenny to his office. Kenny went in, expecting it to be a meeting with another senator, congressman, or union official who Jack felt should meet Kenny, Jack's point person, voice, and right hand.

But there was no one there but Jack, who seemed focused, intense, and mentally taut. Tanned and wearing a well-tailored blue suit, Jack appeared to Kenny as if he were in campaign mode. Kenny had seen this persona at the first Kennedy clambake and many times during the '58 campaign. Kenny knew, without Jack having to say a word, the time had arrived.

"Kenny," Jack said, "I am calling a meeting at the Kennedy family home in Palm Beach. It is time to take the next step."

Kenny nodded. "Got it," was all he said. Kenny knew what to do from there. They both did. They did not need to discuss it.

Kenny immediately arranged to meet with Bobby later that day at the McClellan Committee office. He told Bobby that he was relieved. "I've been chomping at the damn bit," Kenny said.

Bobby replied, "We ought to get going on this thing down at Dad's house and discuss what our problems are and what needs to be done. It is just going to be Jack, you, myself, my dad, and Ted Sorensen."

Kenny said to him, "Fine, but don't you think you ought to have Larry come down as well? We are going to eventually need him in the campaign. He has excellent judgment, the professionals have great respect for him, and he has worked his ass off. He is a good man."

Bobby considered and said, "Yeah, that is a great idea. You take care of it."

So Kenny called Larry and asked him to join them. After the 1958 campaign, waiting for the presidential campaign to begin, Larry had once again returned to private practice in Springfield, Massachusetts. Larry agreed to come down at once. "He came down to Washington," Kenny remembered, "and then Larry and I flew down together. The senator and Bobby went down ahead of us, and Larry, Sorensen, and I went down a couple of days later.

"It was blistering hot. Larry being black Irish like myself did not take the sun too well. He got completely fried and ended up not being a very cheerful companion for the three days that we were down there. He did not appreciate our teasing him about it either; that did not stop us, though," Kenny said with a good-natured laugh.

"Sorensen, Larry, and I stayed at the same hotel, not far from the Kennedy family home. Quite a pleasant place. We were also joined there by pollster Louis Harris. I recall this because we went to dinner with him one night. I had never met him before, but Bobby had invited him. He had his polls with him."

Perhaps the second-funniest moment after Larry O'Brien's sunburn came when Ted Sorensen began, as Kenny joked, "channeling his inner Jack Kennedy."

At dinner, Ted Sorensen ordered a daiquiri and began talking with a distinct "Kennedy accent," which appeared with the drink. He had never had one before, and Kenny and Larry couldn't believe it; nor could they resist teasing Sorensen unmercifully.

Kenny laughed about it afterward. "Of course, Senator Kennedy drank daiquiris, so Larry and I gave Ted a hard time. We told him we presumed all the vices were catching. I recall he got quite defensive. It was very funny."

Ted Sorensen did not find Kenny very funny at all and quickly told Jack, who, as Kenny said later, "dissolved with laughter listening to Sorensen's silly complaints." The incident, though humorous, underlined the continuing tension between the O'Donnell and Sorensen wings of the Kennedy operation. If Kenny was Jack's political genius, Ted Sorensen was his brilliant wordsmith. Jack needed both to be successful. It is a testament to both Kenny and Ted that they put their personal views of each other aside to help Jack succeed and win in November 1960.

It was a testament to Jack Kennedy that he was able to keep both men working together like a finely tuned team in harness to help make the victory possible. It is also worth noting that despite their dislike of each other, when Kenny died some years later and I, his daughter Helen, needed help, Ted Sorensen was the first man at the door, saying simply, "Your father and I never liked each other, but we respected each other's talents. How can I help?"

It was Jack Kennedy's strength and wisdom in bringing together the right team. In many ways, Kenny and Ted had rivaling teams, each loyal to their captain, but in the end, they all remained loyal to Jack, and that was the key to Kennedy's success in '60.

Despite Kenny and Jack's good humor, the purpose for their visit to Palm Beach was deadly serious. They had to decide on strategy and under what conditions Jack would launch his presidential bid and what primaries he would enter. The next day the meeting started early and was expected to last all day. Once everyone settled into the huge living room of the Kennedy family's Palm Beach mansion, the discussions began in earnest.

The group was deliberately small and included only the Kennedy inner circle: Joe Kennedy Sr., Jack, Bobby, Lou Harris, Ted Sorensen, Larry, and Kenny. Kenny and Larry said little during the meeting, mostly listening,

▲ My father, Kenneth "Kenny" O'Donnell. © JOHN F. KENNEDY PRESIDENTIAL LIBRARY AND MUSEUM

➤ Joe Kennedy and John
F. Kennedy, England 1938.

➤ New Congressman John
F. Kennedy at Bunker Hill
Monument. 1946.

◄ Special Assistant to the President David Powers accepts a portrait of President John F. Kennedy. 1961.

© CECIL STOUGHTON. WHITE HOUSE PHOTOGRAPHS. JOHN F. KENNEDY PRESIDENTIAL LIBRARY AND MUSEUM

▼ Special Assistant to the President for Congressional Relations Lawrence "Larry" O'Brien.

© ABBIE ROWE. WHITE HOUSE PHOTOGRAPHS. JOHN F. KENNEDY PRESIDENTIAL LIBRARY AND MUSEUM

▲ John F. Kennedy with Henry Cabot Lodge Jr. JFK upset Lodge in the 1952 Massachusetts Senate election. © JOHN F. KENNEDY PRESIDENTIAL LIBRARY AND MUSEUM

▲ Photo booth shot of John and Jackie, possibly taken during their honeymoon in 1953.

▲ Jackie and John on their honeymoon in Acapulco, 1953.

◄ Kennedy siblings at the wedding reception of Jacqueline Bouvier to John F. Kennedy, Hammersmith Farm, Newport, RI, 12 September 1953. (*clockwise from left*): Robert F. Kennedy, Patricia Kennedy, Eunice Kennedy Shriver, Edward M. Kennedy, Jean Kennedy, John F. Kennedy, Jacqueline Bouvier Kennedy.

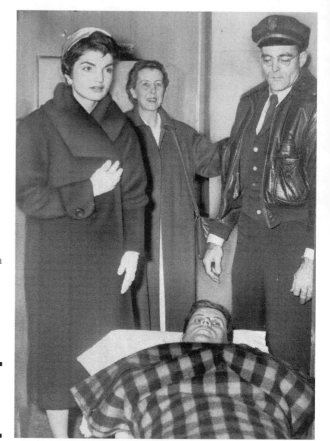

➤ John F. Kennedy leaving on gurney from hospital following spinal surgery, as his wife Jacqueline stands over him, 1954.

© DICK MARSICO, NEW YORK WORLD-TELEGRAM AND THE SUN NEWSPAPER PHOTOGRAPH COLLECTION

▼ Robert Kennedy and John F. Kennedy at the Mclelllan Hearings. 1957.

© CORBIS

◄ Joe Kennedy, Sr.'s Palm Beach Estate. 1961.
© ROBERT LEROY

⌄ John at Hyannis Port. July 1960.
© JOHN F. KENNEDY PRESIDENTIAL LIBRARY AND MUSEUM

▲ The Irish Brotherhood.
(*standing, from left to right*):
Hy Raskin, Pierre Salinger,
Sargent Shriver, Larry
O'Brien, and John Bailey;
(*seated from left to right*),
Kenny O'Donnell, Robert
F. Kennedy, and Steve Smith.

➤ Kenny and Bobby.

▲ John and Jackie campaigning in New Hampshire, 1960.
© JOHN F. KENNEDY PRESIDENTIAL LIBRARY AND MUSEUM

◄ President John F. Kennedy with Vice President Lyndon Johnson.
© JOHN F. KENNEDY PRESIDENTIAL LIBRARY AND MUSEUM

▼White House Press Secretary Pierre Salinger. White House, Washington, D.C. 1961.

▲ A Kennedy campaign pamphlet from 1960.

▲ John F. Kennedy and Richard Nixon at the Presidential Debate, 1960. © THEODORE ATKINS ARCHIVE

▲ Kennedy staff aboard the
campaign jet, Caroline. 1960.
© JOHN F. KENNEDY PRESIDENTIAL
LIBRARY AND MUSEUM

➤ John and Peter Lawford,
1960.
© JOHN F. KENNEDY PRESIDENTIAL
LIBRARY AND MUSEUM

▲ John F. Kennedy and
Frank Sinatra at a Fundraiser,
Los Angeles 1960.
© BETTMANN/CORBIS

◄ Steve Smith with Marilyn
Monroe at Private Reception
in New York City, 1962.
© CECIL WILLIAMS

➤ Kenny in his office on
a good day.

▼ Jack, Bobby and Kenny
in the Oval Office.

◄ Kenny O'Donnell with
White House Army Signal
Agency Staff Member. 1961.
© ROBERT KNUDSEN. WHITE HOUSE
PHOTOGRAPHS. JOHN F. KENNEDY
PRESIDENTIAL LIBRARY AND MUSEUM,
BOSTON

▼ John F. Kennedy visits
82nd Airborne Division at
Fort Bragg, North Carolina.
President Kennedy (*left*);
Press Secretary Pierre
Salinger (*center*); Kenny
O'Donnell (*right*).
© CECIL STOUGHTON. WHITE HOUSE
PHOTOGRAPHS. JOHN F. KENNEDY
PRESIDENTIAL LIBRARY AND MUSEUM

▲ *From left*, Ted Kennedy, Helen O'Donnell (my mother), Joan Kennedy, and my father at a party in the late 60s.

➤ Kenny and Jackie remained friends after Jack's Death. Late 60s.

as was their role. Larry took copious notes. Kenny took none. His photographic memory for details was all he needed. After the meeting, when Jack wanted his feedback, Kenny took center stage. His mission was to listen and, after the fact, give Jack his honest opinion on whether the other members of the inner circle were right or wrong, speaking for Jack's best interest or their own.

Journalist Ted White later described Kenny leaning against a wall, arms folded, "dark and lean . . . his expression over the next year of the campaign would alternate between quiet curiosity expressed by raised eyebrows and quiet amusement indicated by the faintest turning of his mouth into a smile."

Being Jack's eyes and ears would increasingly become Kenny's most vital role. He could hear what nobody else in the room picked up, listen for that unspoken word, the alternative agenda, the man who says one thing when he means another.

Kenny was Jack's "bullshit detector," as Bobby once said. "Kenny would give you his honest views of what he heard or saw, what he believed someone was saying when they had a secondary agenda. He gave you an answer; oftentimes it was not always what you wanted to hear," Bobby continued, "but it was critical that we hear it." Kenny said almost nothing, unless either Bobby or Jack asked him something specific.

Kenny said, "I would sit with Jack and give him my feedback on what I'd heard. I would give him my views on the issue, the people, what was said, what I felt needed to be done and by whom, or what should have been said and was not and by whom. He would listen, and then we would discuss it in depth, going back and forth. Then he would make his own judgment."

"The main thrust of the first conversation in Palm Beach was that Jack should set up some sort of Kennedy organization in Washington, DC, reasonably rapidly," Kenny recalled.

Kenny was delighted. This meant he could finally move his operation from the small office at the McClellan Committee to a proper campaign office. The main decision Jack felt he had to make then concerned the upcoming primaries. Jack indicated that he should enter all the primaries, or as many as he could.

Kenny remembered, "Lou Harris had already conducted a poll in Wisconsin. He had just completed a second poll comparing Jack with Senator Humphrey. The poll in Wisconsin showed Senator Kennedy beating Senator Humphrey substantially in Wisconsin," Kenny said. "Later I told the senator I was reasonably suspicious of these numbers. Humphrey was like the third senator in Wisconsin; the numbers did not add up."

"I wonder if they knew you were Catholic," Kenny said to Jack, raising an ominous red flag nobody had yet addressed when they discussed the poll.

Jack nodded. He was tense, staring out the window of his dad's living room watching nothing in particular on the front lawn, his mind, Kenny guessed, on the Harris poll numbers from Wisconsin. "I agree," he said. "Let's find out."

Kenny recalled that Sorensen spoke at that initial meeting quite a bit. He had really studied Wisconsin and the primaries. Kenny said, "He had done his homework, and it was impressive." But when pressed, Sorensen admitted, as did Harris, that "no, the 'Catholic thing'" had not been raised as such.

Whatever that means, Kenny thought to himself. Later he said to Bobby, "Look, they either asked the question or they didn't!"

As expected, Lou Harris spoke quite a bit as well. He had a detailed electorate breakdown, which seemed to run along religious lines, yet Kenny still believed, rightly as it would turn out, that they were missing the undercurrent of the Catholic issue.

In fact, as Senator Kennedy pointed out quite clearly, "You could win the Wisconsin primary and in fact accentuate that I am a Catholic rather than diminish it."

Kenny said later, "It was the first time [I] realized the depth to which the senator was worried about the Catholic issue. While I had been hesitant to raise it, when I saw this poll, I realized the senator was leaps and bounds ahead."

Jack's gut had told him what Kenny's caution gave voice to.

Jack continued with his razor-sharp analysis: "It just seems to me that if I could stay out of Wisconsin, I would be much better off. I do not know whether I can. I may be forced into the primary. My inclination is not to go into Wisconsin. It is a difficult state at best. I would be running against Hubert, who practically lives in Wisconsin. Minnesota and Wisconsin have about the same economic problems. Hubert is obviously on the right side legislatively of the local problems in Wisconsin, while I, as a city boy from Boston, am not going to be familiar with some Wisconsin issues at all. So on balance, I do not see any advantage to participating in Wisconsin." In the end, he went on to say that he felt "Wisconsin would be a great gamble. If I lost in Wisconsin, it would knock me out of the ballpark totally."

Jack also pointed out that in any national poll, Hubert was running far behind. "Hubert," Jack continued, "was consistently in the same political rut. He cannot break loose. It is my view that he is not considered a seri-ous candidate for the nomination by any of the professionals. But he could damage my candidacy."

Kenny said later, "Every chip that Jack laid down in his very logical and methodical fashion dictated that he not go into the Wisconsin primary. On the other hand, he held the view that Hubert and those political people behind Hubert, Stevenson, [Lyndon] Johnson, and [Stuart] Symington, would attempt to force him into the Wisconsin primary, knowing it would potentially damage, if not destroy, Kennedy's chances."

"In my view," Jack said, "if they maneuvered things in a certain man-ner, it would force me into the Wisconsin primary, because if I did not go in, then they would say that I was afraid to face the religious question head-on."

"Everybody did what they always do to the executive in charge," Kenny told Vanocur later. "Everyone laid out the problems in a very detailed and precise fashion, gave the problems to the senator, and then left. I remember starting to walk out with the others, and he said to me, 'Where the hell are you going? Oh no you don't. Come back here and help me answer these questions.'

"I turned around and sat back down. By then it was just myself and the Kennedys, the senator, Bobby, and his father. At this first discussion, we focused almost exclusively on Senator Kennedy as the candidate and the difficulties he faced. The thing that became evident immediately, and he and I agreed on this point, was that he would have to go the primary route, which meant, since the professionals saw him as a threat and an outsider, he would have to enter every single primary. This didn't change the fact of his real concern that the first primary was Wisconsin."

Jack told Kenny after the meeting, "If I am forced to participate there in Wisconsin, I could get knocked out completely." Being beaten by Hubert Humphrey, who at the national level was not even a legitimate contender, was a very daunting prospect and a real possibility.

Another important problem facing the inner circle in Palm Beach was, as Kenny said, "The cold hard reality that at this point the only national politicians in our corner were John Bailey, chairman of Connecticut's Democratic Party, and while one of the most powerful politicians in Connecticut, he was also, like Jack Kennedy, an Irish Catholic." A graduate of Catholic University of America and Harvard Law School, Bailey had become close and trusted friends with both Jack and Kenny. Abraham "Abe" Alexander Ribicoff, also hailing from Connecticut and a friend of Bailey's, had served in Congress and now was governor. He was smart, politically savvy, and tough; he was also Jewish and liberal, which at the time was not any easier politically than being a Catholic. But as of that moment, neither Bailey nor Ribicoff had yet publicly committed to John Kennedy for the presidency, though behind the scenes they were supportive of him. Once Jack announced his candidacy in a public way, Kenny told Jack and Bobby, he felt that both Ribicoff and Bailey would be with them.

"Obviously, we wanted to get the entire New England base solidly behind John Kennedy at the time of his announcement and to re-create the situation that had existed in Chicago in 1956. This is in part why we had not yet made our position clear. We wanted to get the entire base wrapped up first.

"Joe Kennedy mentioned quite a few names of people he had talked with, including Charlie Buckley, who was the political boss of the Bronx in New York, having taken over from the legendary Ed Flynn, who had built up the machine. Buckley was shrewd, smart and politically streetwise, tough, and Roman Catholic. John Kenny, former mayor of Jersey City, was well connected and had his pulse and control of much of the Democratic machine in New Jersey. Mayor Richard Daley, 'the Mayor,' as he was called, was the key to Chicago and Illinois. He had close ties to Joe Kennedy, whose business empire, the Merchandise Mart, where Kennedy in-law Sarge Shriver hailed from, had become close to the city, and he was a fan of Jack's from 1956. He was key to a victory in Illinois, but he was also Irish Catholic. None of these guys were nailed down to any degree and none of them had yet agreed to publicly support Jack. Joe Kennedy had obviously had a lot of conversations with a variety of different people, but it was too early.

They needed more ducks in a row, Kenny believed, before any of these people would commit. "Furthermore, Sorensen went through a memorandum of the potential primaries and what the technical and legal problems were going to be. It seemed to me that Ohio was basically the most imminent or pressing problem, rather than Wisconsin. This is what I said later in private to the senator. The problem in Wisconsin was in some ways related to Ohio, because if Jack were to enter into a primary in a state as large as Ohio, I was concerned that he would not be able to devote enough time or resources to Wisconsin. That was, in my view, the most immediate reason not to enter Wisconsin."

Jack and Kenny did not get into a detailed discussion of Ohio and Ohio governor Michael DiSalle at this time. But the senator had been in Ohio occasionally in the past. He had talked to DiSalle before, and Jack indicated that there were quite a few people in positions of power in that state who had suggested that he should enter into the Ohio primary.

"While I was new to this part of the discussion," Kenny recalled, "I felt instinctively it was a bad idea. We would need to find a way to secure either Ohio or Wisconsin, but we could not successfully enter both."

Kenny kept this reservation to himself during the public discussion. Ted Sorensen dominated much of this meeting, with the exception of Jack of course. But Sorensen had done a great deal of research on each primary, outlining the pros and cons for each.

Kenny said that "Sorensen was impressive. He talked and we listened, really. Then Senator Kennedy and his father would respond to what Ted said accordingly, ask very pointed questions, some Ted could answer, many he could not. But I took note of them. Bobby, Larry, and I had little to contribute; we listened carefully, but once certain decisions were taken regarding the primaries, we would go into action. Bobby discussed the labor people and the contacts he and I had made and how we would begin talking with them."

"You mean the ones that still talk to you," Jack teased his brother. Kenny and Bobby laughed. There was more truth to that at the moment than any of them wanted to consider, but it would fall to Kenny to "fix it," as Jack would say to him again.

"In general," Kenny felt, "the meeting was reasonably inconclusive. The Wisconsin thing dominated the meeting. Problems were raised and detailed analysis listened to, but clearly no decisions were made. It seemed to me that the only decision that came out of this meeting was that they would open an office in Washington, which Steve Smith would come down from New York to run around late April/May. He would begin organizing the campaign. But it was a key decision and the only thing I really wanted to hear. I was ready to go. 'Let's move forward' is how I felt."

Up until this meeting, Ted Sorensen, and to a degree Dave Powers, comprised what there was of a Kennedy organization in DC, with Sorensen

writing the speeches, meeting with people, and generally being all things
to everybody. But now the operation would grow and become more professional. The particular roles and how they would play out would be decided
later, but as had been the case since 1952, the running of the campaign
would fall mainly to Jack's ever-expanding Irish Brotherhood.

It was loosely decided, Kenny remembered, that "Bobby, Larry, and I
would all take our usual roles in the campaign at some point. Larry could
not come down right way, so it was suggested Larry might come down two
or three days a week and work with Steve. Bobby and I would remain at the
McClellan Committee, at Bobby's suggestion, because of the problems that
still existed with the unions, but I would continue my two-pronged operation at the committee; then, as soon as Bobby was able to leave the committee, he would come over and take general direction of the campaign.
There were no specific duties outlined for me or for Larry. As before, our
roles were sort of assumed. We simply were duplicating the Massachusetts
organization on a national scale. So we just proceeded along those lines.
Sorensen would continue to handle the general background work for some
of these things for now, since he was well along already. However, as Steve
Smith took over and became more and more familiar with how we operated, he would increasingly take over that role from Sorensen."

In terms of their primary strategy, more than just Ohio and Wisconsin
were left up in the air after the Palm Beach meeting. "We had barely
touched on the other primaries," Kenny said. "It was my view that we would
have to enter them all, because we had the establishment against us; this is
why I felt we had to make a choice between the two big states of Ohio and
Wisconsin. We could not enter both."

Later, back in Washington, Kenny would raise this to Jack, who agreed
completely but had yet to decide whether it was Ohio or Wisconsin.

Later, Kenny and Jack discussed the Harris Wisconsin poll in some
detail. "This was the beginning of what turned out to be a major error on
our part," as Kenny remembered it. "Sorensen decided offhandedly that we

would approach Wisconsin as a ten-congressional-district state, taking each district as if it were its own entity or state, as opposed to taking the state as whole. This became widely disseminated in the press. We were therefore forced to run the campaign in that manner. This turned out to be a mistake. It is also the only time we handled a primary in that manner and the last time Sorensen was allowed to play such a role. Because Palm Beach was our first major meeting as a campaign team, understandably most of our conclusions were rather general or casual, a mistake we would not repeat. After Wisconsin, Sorensen's role changed rather radically. Up until then, he had been running the primary ball game in conjunction with Lou Harris, in consultation with the Old Man."

When Kenny spoke with Jack about the issue, he made clear that the national campaign operation needed to mirror Kenny and Larry's Massachusetts model. This would also require changes and tweaks as the reality of running nationwide set in, but Kenny, eager to take charge of the political operation, thought Sorensen needed to focus on what Kenny felt were his strengths, and that meant, as Kenny put it to Jack, "get him the hell out of my area." Jack agreed, and to Kenny's relief, things began to change.

"It had been, up until this time, Ted Sorensen's show," Kenny explained. "Dave Powers had been involved to some degree, but his role with the senator was rather a direct and personal one, and he was no match for Sorensen. In my view, clear lines of authority and area had to be drawn. You cannot have a campaign with too many chiefs, and you also cannot have a successful campaign without clear lines of authority.

"Sorensen would devote himself to speech writing and the senator's office, which were his strengths and where he was simply masterful and untouchable. Steve Smith would now come down to Washington and take charge of the day-to-day operation and its finances. A PR man would be found from within our own ranks, taking that burden from Sorensen, and Larry and I would work on moving the Massachusetts political operation to a nationwide model.

"O'Brien, as soon as his business situation could be straightened out, would spend as much time as possible in Washington. Smith would find an office and get the place staffed up. In the meantime, I would split my time between the McClellan Committee, cleaning up some matters, and working on the campaign full-time directly with the senator.

"In the end, there were no final decisions made about primaries or what the candidate would do next. As far as the public relations and press aspect of it was concerned, the senator made clear he would handle that himself in conjunction with Sorensen until our new man was found. Sorensen would continue to have great influence in this area until the press operation was established, and establishing this meant finding someone who fit in with the Kennedy organization. We finally found just the right fit in another McClellan staffer: the affable but shrewd Pierre Salinger, a San Francisco native and the son of a French Catholic journalist."

Jack Kennedy's presidential dreams were beginning to take shape, and no one was happier to get the campaign under way than Kenny O'Donnell and his political "Irish Mafia."

CHAPTER 13

Going Nationwide

W HEN STEVE SMITH, in late April of 1959, moved down from his beloved New York City and opened the Kennedy campaign offices at the historic Esso Building in downtown Washington, DC, there was no fancy signage indicating the site of Kennedy headquarters. There was only a simple sign on the door that read STEPHEN E. SMITH. For Kenny, the move was welcome news. It was the first official step in the launch of this important phase of Jack Kennedy's political journey and, by extension, his own.

Kenny would come to consider Pierre Salinger, who would the handle press, almost as a younger brother. Salinger had been working at the McClellan Committee and had made himself memorable from his first meeting with Bobby. Bobby and Ethel invited Pierre to dinner one evening at their home in Hickory Hill. At that time, neither Ethel nor Bobby drank. "No problem," Pierre assured them good-naturedly. Then he opened his briefcase to reveal stowed away, in case of such emergencies, a lovely bottle of red wine. When Kenny heard the story he roared with laughter. Pierre was his kind of fellow.

While Pierre's loyalty would prove to be absolute, he was not without his issues. Kenny recalled, "The problem with Pierre was twofold: Like all of us, he was quite young and inexperienced on a national level. He also completely lacked national press contacts. Right from the beginning he made a good many crucial mistakes that were fortunately caught by Senator Kennedy in time. It was a difficult period for Pierre."

Often, Kenny feared that Pierre would not make the grade in these early days, so he did what he could with his own contacts to help. While Pierre's start was rocky, he managed to find his sea legs as the organization took shape.

The next step was to bring in the office staff, led by Justine O'Donnell, a dark-haired, green-eyed beauty with a sharp wit, a keen intelligence, and a work ethic that made her invaluable to the Kennedy operation. The remaining women included a brilliant political operator from Massachusetts by the name of Helen Keyes, whose father had been a dentist for the Kennedy family. Beyond Helen, there was also Helen Lempart, Kenny's pal from Haverhill; Pauline Fluet, who would later work for Kenny at the White House, then go on to work for Steve Smith running the Kennedy family office in New York; and Jean Lewis, who came over from Jack's Senate office.

These "girls," as Kenny and Jack called them, were in many ways the Kennedy organization's backbone. Kenny said, "They were fearless, savvy, tough, smart as hell, very, very sharp, and could outwork anyone. So they were brought in to begin working on the infrastructure of the campaign. They were our secret weapon. Our first step was to put these girls to work on the card system, the same system first implemented so successfully in the '52 campaign, used again, updated in '58, and now would be used for the primary on a state-by-state basis. We had imported that from the Massachusetts Senate campaign and now planned to take it to a national level. Naturally, it was far too early and there were no delegates as such in existence."

Justine noted, "The best anyone could do was take the list of delegates from the 1956 convention. Most, if not all, of these delegates would not return, but it gave us a starting point. As with '52 and '58, an index card was created for a delegate. It would list how they had voted in the most recent campaign, their political leanings, connections, . . . likes or dislikes, relatives in politics, and any other pertinent information. We then would give these cards to the Kennedy secretaries once we had determined whether this delegate planned to return or not; if not, [we would find out] who replaced them. Then a card would be created for that person, so by the time we got to the convention in Los Angeles in 1960, the idea was every single delegate would have an index card created for them. We also recruited both of my other brothers," Justine chuckled. "My older brother Cleo Jr. and younger brother Warren were persuaded to put their careers on hold and join the campaign, not that Kenny gave them much choice in the matter. But the core of the campaign began to come together."

Ralph Dungan, Jack Kennedy's legislative aide, agreed with Justine's assessment of the early days. Dungan himself began to move into a quasi-role with the campaign, one foot in the Senate office and the other in the campaign office.

As Dungan recalled, "Steve Smith came down and set up offices at the Esso Building around late April/May after the meeting in Palm Beach. I was not part of that meeting but knew from Sorensen that it marked the unofficial kickoff. I was not really in the inner circles of the political planning group among the Washington unit. That was Sorensen, O'Donnell, Bobby, Steve, the Old Man, and sometimes O'Brien. That was it. They were the decision makers."

The focus was largely on organization in these early days of the campaign, which meant duplicating the system Kenny and Larry had established in Massachusetts, moving it to Washington, and expanding it for the national presidential campaign.

Kenny and Larry were to find out later that not everything in their system would translate or work as well in the national arena. The political stage and players proved very different. The Irish Brotherhood would discover their grassroots approach now had to include the national party organization and its leaders.

"Our approach in Massachusetts," Kenny said, "had been to go the grassroots level only, because we knew we had no chance with the party regulars. We had to really kick the door in by going to the people directly. We expected to have to do the same thing on the national level as well. But we would learn that we needed a two-pronged approach to be successful. In the national political arena the grassroots approach might win primaries but not get you the nomination. But we had not gotten to this stage yet."

"However," Kenny added, "once we began to understand that, we adapted as quickly as possible. The key to any successful political operation is the ability to adapt to changing circumstances as quickly and effectively as possible. That had always been our strength."

Bobby left the McClellan Committee in July of 1959 to finish writing his book *The Enemy Within*. "This period, July and August," Kenny remarked, "was a real hiatus. There is not much you can do in politics at this time of year. The Congress was out. The senator was out campaigning as best he could under the circumstances."

With Bobby off writing his book and the McClellan Committee finally coming to a close, Kenny was, as he put it, "finally able to join Steve over at the campaign full-time to set up the physical organization."

The campaign's primary strategy was still not finalized, but in these early days during the summer doldrums the goal was to get the Kennedy organization up and operational as quickly and effectively as possible. O'Brien spent much of the summer going back and forth from Springfield, where he was slowly shutting down his business operation in anticipation of a full-time role with the campaign.

Kenny recalled, "Larry and I went through all the files and became completely familiar with every state, every primary, and every individual and political person we would need to know if the senator were to enter that state's primary. These are all the unglamorous early steps of campaign organization, which, if done well, can prove crucial in the later months when you no longer have the time available to strategize."

The summer months were spent on setting up the organization and the initial core staff. Kenny took a few early but mostly inconclusive trips with Jack. From Kenny's point of view, the next most important thing that happened in the campaign was the meeting in Hyannis Port in October.

For Kenny, "this meeting really was the indication we were under way," he said. "This was the first full-blown meeting of the Kennedy for President campaign. Senator Kennedy conducted the meeting this time."

The group present at the Kennedy compound that October had expanded since that first tentative meeting in early April. This time the players, besides the core group of Joe, Jack, Bobby, Kenny, Larry, and Steve, included John Bailey, Governor Ribicoff of Connecticut, Governor [Dennis] Roberts of Rhode Island, and Hy Raskin. Raskin was a lawyer from San Francisco whom Joe had recruited. He had worked on Stevenson's campaign in '52 as deputy director and been head of the Western States for Stevenson organization in '56 before going to the Democratic National Committee, where he eventually made the transition to Jack Kennedy and never looked back.

Raskin later described his first impressions of Jack Kennedy upon meeting him in 1956: "The knock on Kennedy was he was young, he was very rich, and perhaps lacked expertise and experience, not to mention the Catholic issue. But right from the start, we saw in '56 at the convention, he had what I would call political sex appeal."

Others at Hyannis Port that October included Ted Sorensen, pollster Lou Harris, John Salter (administrative assistant to Senator Henry Jackson), and Dave Hackett, whom Bobby Kennedy had recruited to work with him at the McClellan Committee before being brought onto the campaign and eventually to a position within the Kennedy Justice Department.

Hackett, a gifted athlete and talented writer, had been a close friend of Bobby's since their prep school days together at Milton Academy. Hackett had befriended the shy Bobby, making his transition to Milton easier. Bobby's oldest son, Joseph Kennedy II, best described Hackett "as my dad's oldest and best friend." Finally, the meeting included the youngest Kennedy brother, Teddy.

Jack stood, as journalist Ted White described it, "with his back to the fireplace, facing the others as they sat, dressed in a sports jacket (which he later removed), slacks, loafers, and looking thoroughly boyish. His hair was still cut in the youthful brush cut with which the public would become so familiar, later replaced by the more mature side cut once he was president."

Jack began the meeting with a dazzling analysis of the facts and the situation now facing the fledging campaign.

"It was a detailed analysis of the campaign as he saw it," Kenny said. "He went state by state with the primaries. He discussed each primary as he had in the past, presenting a rather clear one, two, three setup. He went through Ohio, Wisconsin, and whether we had to enter one or the other and, of course, whether we had to enter both.

"He named those whom he had talked to in each state and where they stood. He listed those who were supportive and those who were leaning, as well as those who were not and posed serious problems.

"The senator then enumerated which states and issues would bother him or present problems for us. It was a complete and total rundown and lasted about an hour. It was very impressive. He then suggested that we ought to assign each person a role in the campaign. He felt the campaign had been very disorganized so far, in large measure because it was running without a head and because people did not have specific roles or assignments. They did not, in fact, know what was expected of them and when. Now each person ought to have a specific assignment and be responsible to someone and report in rather regularly as to their contacts and the results of their efforts.

"From there the meeting rather degenerated a bit. Things became rather vague as they always do in these large organizational meetings. It is very difficult to get anything too specific out of meetings with that many people in there at once.

"The first really specific thing that I recall was that O'Brien would look to the primary states as his overall responsibility. Larry should begin visiting all the potential primary states and meeting with the proper people. Then Larry and I should have battle plans drawn up for each state. We should know the laws and filing dates for each state. Sorensen had done some of this, but he could use some help there, and so those assignments were given out. The battle plan should outline the issues, potential supporters, detractors, and the major problems we faced with issues, people, supporters, logistics, deadlines, size, and so forth. The senator also indicated I would continue in my role with him, which was, as Bobby joked, 'whatever Jack wanted it to be.'"

From there, the meeting moved to a discussion of the primaries. Questions remained about the best approach. As Kenny recalled, "We discussed the ones of interest to us: Wisconsin, Ohio, Indiana, and Maryland. The senator took on Ohio almost as a personal chore, indicating he and I would deal with that situation. He took the same approach to California also, though that was a ways off, so not a priority."

From there, Bobby asked John Salter to look into the western states. Abe Ribicoff and John Bailey were asked to continue doing what they were doing, which was trying to tie down the New England states and keep them together as a Kennedy bloc.

New York was largely left to, as Kenny said, "the capable hands of Mr. Kennedy, Steve Smith, and Senator Kennedy himself." It was Kenny's memory that Joe Kennedy and Steve Smith, whose connections ran deep in New York, took on the complicated issues in the Empire State.

"Illinois," Kenny recalled, "was another primary state discussed, though at this time it was not assigned to anyone. We went through the problem in Pennsylvania. We all realized that at this point there was only one person who could talk to Dave Lawrence, who was governor of Pennsylvania, a Catholic, and critical to our plans, and that was the candidate himself. It was too early to do that just now, though. New Jersey was not assigned to anyone; in fact, whatever contacts there were in New Jersey came from the senator and his father. So that was also left alone for the present and would be assigned later. The decision as to whether Bobby wanted to handle the southern states himself or get someone to handle it was left in his hands."

The reason for this, of course, was that Bobby was the only one who knew anything about the South due to his extensive work with Senator McClellan. Kenny was not assigned to anything specifically. When he asked, Bobby shrugged and pointed to Jack. Kenny nodded. His role was now set. With that, Jack's campaign was off and running.

"During these discussions," Dave Powers said later, "Senator Kennedy did not dwell on the problems either he or the campaign faced. He outlined them in his very straightforward manner but did not dwell."

Kenny agreed. He felt that Jack "simply cited potential problems and then determined how to address those problems. But we had two immediate and key problems. The first was that the Kennedy organization was not in shape yet." As Kenny told Jack and the Old Man in private, "We need to get Bobby to take control and get organized in order to be effective. Until Bobby takes full command and control, we simply cannot get under way. It is like a car with only three wheels. We need Bobby now."

"Right," Joe said. "Let's get that done."

The second major problem, one that even the substantial political and financial resources of Joe Kennedy could not fix, was that Jack was viewed as young and Catholic. Jack said to Kenny and Joe in private that he was concerned that he was seen as unelectable and that that view would be reflected by most of the other candidates and the political elite. Jack believed that this opinion of his unelectability would combine with the left wing of the party, which remained extremely dubious of his position on labor, giving him in the end almost no solid base of support.

This concerned Jack deeply. He suspected, quite accurately as it turned out, that he would not be taken seriously. In fact, he would have to prove himself the hard way by going at it in the primaries, taking his case to the people. By doing so, Jack felt he would be able to pick up a great many delegates personally.

"Very early on," Kenny said, "the senator took the position that the leaders and professionals would follow their delegations. He believed that if he began to build a fire under these leaders by appealing directly to the voters and to the delegates, then the delegates would build a fire under the party leaders."

Jack and Kenny believed that to accomplish this he would have to "win, win, and win," meaning he would have to stay up in the polls, especially the Gallup Poll, which would help him win over as many delegates as possible. If necessary, he would personally talk to each delegate about why he would be the best Democratic candidate to beat Nixon, the presumed Republican nominee in 1960.

Jack knew full well that he could have an intellectual conversation with Philadelphia political strategist Bill Green or Pennsylvania governor David Lawrence or any of these other people and change their minds. But a strong showing in the polls would be the most persuasive argument in his favor.

In other words, Kenny indicated, "they all came to realize the only way he could make his case to the professionals was through the ballot box. Normally, even in state and local elections, a candidate would have to have strong party support and a number of delegates already lined up before entering the field. No question, it was an unusual approach for a national political candidate."

As they had discussed back in April in the meeting in Palm Beach, "The question then became exactly how to be in both the Ohio and Wisconsin primaries at once and how to best spend our energies. Despite the fact that he felt Ohio was a problem and Wisconsin presented an even worse problem, the senator seemed willing to take the gamble in Wisconsin."

Jack said to Kenny, "If we can wrap up Ohio, we may have to take that gamble and roll the dice with Wisconsin."

In the end, the decision as to which primary to participate in, Ohio or Wisconsin, or both, would be critical. Like any politician, Governor DiSalle of Ohio did not want to be embarrassed or lose. He wanted to back a winner. Jack's Irish Brotherhood had to convince him to take the risk, put aside his own ambitions and his concerns about the "Catholic issue," and go with Jack. They all agreed that if Jack had to go into Ohio against Governor DiSalle, and then go into Wisconsin, he would not have the resources to handle both campaigns. Kenny believed, as did O'Brien, that DiSalle could be dealt with and that a deal could be struck that would satisfy DiSalle and give him a way to resolve the dilemma.

"It became clear to me," Kenny said, "that Ohio would be a much better state for John Kennedy to run in than Wisconsin. I think he shared that view with me. I know Larry shared that view. However, that decision was not in our control. That decision was in the control of the Ohio party leaders."

The decision would be faced soon enough, but first the Kennedy team had to deal with the looming issue of the United Automobile Workers convention. The convention was in New Jersey in October 1959 and was in many ways the logical next step for the Kennedy organization. All the major candidates were expected to speak there, and this included Jack. It was decided that Kenny was the right man for the job of ameliorating any ruffled union feathers.

Everyone knew Jack had a great weakness on his left flank, largely due to Stevenson and Eleanor Roosevelt's suspicion of Jack's more conservative leanings. Bobby's work on the McClellan Committee had only inflamed that weakness.

Hubert Humphrey, the Minnesota senator, a potential candidate, assumed that he would easily pick off the support of the party's left wing. Additionally, Stevenson was a sleeper candidate who could take what little support on the left remained for Jack. This would leave the left wing of the party waiting to see what Stevenson would do at the convention and unwilling to commit to another candidate.

As Kenny saw it, "This was a potential source of real trouble to Senator Kennedy as we began the campaign. The senator had naturally moved to meet the challenge in any way that he could. By that, I mean he met directly with George Meany, the tough-minded head of the American Federation of Labor and one of the chief labor leaders in Washington, DC. The antagonism had diminished to some degree, which was in part due to Senator Kennedy's personal intervention with the leaders. I think despite themselves they had come to realize that Senator Kennedy had not been really harmful to them. Nevertheless, he still had to face a major drift and uncertainty on the left wing, which continued to be troublesome. This was, in part, due to the Walter Reuther–Eleanor Roosevelt–Stevenson troika and their ability to deal with the media."

"Our next trip," Jack told Kenny, "we should attend the UAW convention in Atlantic City and determine if we might be able to stop some of this drift." Kenny smiled. Kenny understood that stopping the "drift" would be his job. He didn't need any more direction than that.

The decision was made that Kenny would take Bobby with him to Atlantic City. "Maybe the UAW will be happy to see you," Kenny teased Bobby.

Over lunch, Bobby, Kenny, and Jack discussed the best approach to the convention. Kenny recalled, "With the UAW convention looming, Bobby pointed out to the senator that I had a good relationship with them, unlike himself. He said he felt that if anyone could do anything to repair the relationship with labor, I would be the one to do it."

So Kenny headed out in early October 1959, arriving at the convention three days ahead of Jack. "I arrived in the lobby of the hotel," Kenny recalled, "and immediately spotted Joe Rauh, who had preceded me in the check-in line. Joe was rigorously campaigning for Hubert Humphrey. After we had both checked in, we went into the bar and had a drink together. Joe and I had become quite friendly through the McClellan Committee hearings. However, we were friendly enemies at the moment.

"Jack Conway joined us in the bar for a couple drinks. Conway was a close personal friend of Joe Rauh's. He had become quite friendly with me as well. However, when he came into the bar and saw that Joe was sitting with me, it was an embarrassing and awkward situation for Conway. The UAW as a general rule had not made any final decision about whom to support."

Kenny stood and shook Conway's hand, inviting him to sit. "Look, we know you have not made a decision. I know you guys give every candidate a fair shake. That is all we are asking for—a fair shake."

Conway nodded and took his seat as Kenny ordered them all another round. It was a small but important step forward.

"He didn't," Kenny joked to Bobby, "run for the door, and that was good. Course, I didn't have you with me, so that may have been part of it."

Bobby laughed but admitted to Kenny ruefully that there was perhaps some truth to the comment.

The first day involved a major demonstration of political strength for Hubert Humphrey. Kenny was intrigued, since Humphrey represented the largest threat to Jack's candidacy.

This was particularly frustrating, Kenny said, "because we all knew that Humphrey had no chance to get the nomination, yet the road for us to the nomination led right through Hubert."

The UAW's love of demonstration was everywhere at the convention: There were pro-Humphrey signs and pictures, slogans, buttons, and pins. They were preparing to go all out for Humphrey's arrival.

Kenny watched the organization with great interest, looking for a way to break in. "In the process of walking around watching them get ready for this and having conversations with people, I ran into a few of my friends from Ohio who worked for the local union where Dick Gosser was vice president. They were quite friendly with me, and they were anti–Walter Reuther.

"Now within the UAW itself the Gosser forces were opposed to Reuther and vice versa. These fellows indicated to me that Walter Reuther was 100 percent for Hubert Humphrey. They told me Reuther, under the influence of Eleanor Roosevelt, had already made up his mind and that he was now trying to force the members to go along with his choice of Humphrey."

But what Kenny was finding was that the members themselves were not all in agreement with Reuther and resented being forced to back a candidate they believed would not and could not win the party's nomination at the Los Angeles convention. Kenny had suddenly found his way in, isolating UAW members whom he could pick off for Jack.

Within hours Kenny arranged a meeting with Dick Gosser. "We chatted for a while and then we went and had a few drinks. By the end of the evening we had maneuvered into a position where it became clear that Richard Gosser was totally for John Kennedy."

Gosser said to Kenny, "Don't worry, we will have a bigger demonstration for John Kennedy than Hubert Humphrey could have in his wildest dreams!"

This was progress.

A bonus for the Kennedy organization was the fact that Dick Gosser's district in the union was extremely large, including Ohio and parts of Indiana. He ran a powerful local that had strong connections in the key primary state of Pennsylvania as well.

"By now," Kenny explained, "the Gosser people had connected me to members, and I had begun to make inroads. I met all the Pennsylvania UAW and the New York UAW people. I then was able to track down the Massachusetts UAW people. So by the end of the first evening we had a large and powerful demonstration set up for John Kennedy. There was now an internal argument within the union forces about who would have a larger demonstration, the Kennedy or the Humphrey crowd. I left those internal arguments to the union and went to bed. I was pleased to know that at the end of the first day I was able to get those commitments and get the demonstration plans under way. When I had arrived, we had no idea that this was something Humphrey had planned, so had we not been able to get an equal or better demonstration set up for Senator Kennedy's arrival. It would have looked very bad in the press and to potential delegates."

When Kenny filled Jack in that evening before heading to bed, Jack was delighted. It was clear that Bobby's suggestion to get Kenny up to the convention with a three-day lead was already paying off.

Kenny remembered, "I spent the next day really walking around and talking to the fellows and introducing myself. I talked to them about their concerns and about Senator Kennedy, the usual stuff. I got along with them all very well. That night, Jack Conway, Joe Rauh, and a tough-minded UAW member by the name of Millie Jeffrey invited me to join them over at a tavern where they all hung out to have drinks and dinner. The tavern was an insiders' place where they talked business, and outsiders were not welcome. That I was invited was good news. I was very pleased to be included. When I first walked in, the room fell silent. I think many were surprised to see me there.

"It was an uncomfortable moment, but then Millie Jeffrey indicated I had been invited, and the atmosphere changed. I met most of the leadership, and we got along really well. We didn't talk campaign stuff too much. We just had a good time. We had dinner and drinks and the whole inner leadership of the UAW was there. It was a real coup to be invited and included in such an evening. Joe Rauh turned out to be a great dancer with all the pretty girls from the UAW. Joe danced better than I did! I actually got up and danced with some of the girls myself. Joe and I feigned this real competition about who was the better dancer and could get more pretty girls. It was great fun. For the first time, I think Senator Kennedy was making real inroads with these fellows, because they saw me as a regular guy, one of their own, and not an elitist snob. This was how they perceived the people around Kennedy. Of course, it was not true, but sometimes these perceptions can really be hard to overcome."

When Kenny returned home to tell Helen his story, Helen, who had been an aspiring actress and amateur dancer in her younger days in

Worcester, burst out laughing. "I can never get you to dance. The things you will do to get Jack Kennedy in the White House!"

Most of the union's contacts with John Kennedy had been through Sorensen and Bob Wallace, who was then in the Senate office.

"The problem," Kenny noted, "was that both Sorensen and Wallace are sort of eggheads, to say the least. They are not regular-type guys. The unions were convinced that Kennedy was sort of an elite type and an egghead guy since they rather felt that the fellows around Kennedy were sort of egghead types as well. My job was to change that perception. The issue to them was that Sorensen and Wallace were not their type of guys. The union guys to some degree felt Sorensen and Wallace talked down to them. Now here they have a guy like me, who is a regular guy and will go in and have a couple drinks with them and be able to talk to them. We had some drinks, dinner, lots of laughs. While I am not sure who won the dance contest, I bet it was me. But seriously, at the end of two days, I felt that I had made a pretty serious dent in Hubert's strength in the UAW. If not actually getting them to commit to John Kennedy, at least their attitude toward John Kennedy had begun to change."

While Kenny may not yet have switched any votes, he had undone much of the fear and damage created by the McClellan Committee hearings. In giving himself to the UAW as a middleman, he had opened their minds to the possibility of a Kennedy presidency.

Kenny had not yet met Walter Reuther, but by the second day he had met almost all the influential UAW people.

By the next day, reports had made their way back to Reuther about Jack Kennedy's new man in the campaign, a blue-collar, regular guy. And the impression he was making on the leadership was positive. They were beginning to talk about a second look at Kennedy. What bothered Reuther, though, was that Kenny's contacts were mainly through Dick Gosser.

Gosser and Reuther were engaged in a serious inside battle over power in the union. Gosser was old-school and Reuther was the new face of the

UAW. Reuther had been trying unsuccessfully to purge Gosser. But Gosser still had more power than Reuther. When news of Kenny's inroads and friendship with Gosser got back to Reuther, he was concerned enough to call Jack Conway and ask for a meeting with this O'Donnell.

Walter had of course known Kenny and seen him in action around the McClellan Committee, but this was different. This was presidential politics. In Reuther's mind, union insiders had already committed to Humphrey, and this O'Donnell fellow was stirring things up.

Kenny quickly called Jack Conway, asking him "to attend the meeting with me. Conway and I went up together to meet with Walter," Kenny recalled. "Walter was careful but cordial. We had met on several occasions before but had never carried on any great conversations.

"He was extremely friendly. We talked politics for about an hour. Walter told me how pleased he was with Jack and how wonderful things looked for the campaign. Then, in a rather direct fashion, he began indicating that Dick Gosser was really not such a wonderful fellow. Walter went on to say that he hoped I would stay with Jack Conway and that Conway would introduce me to the real leaders of the UAW.

"Reuther made no direct or implied threat, but it was clear that he felt that he was communicating that Gosser did not represent the best elements of the UAW. He went on to say that by sticking with Conway and the fellows Conway introduced me to I could probably do my candidate more good. After all, that is 'why you are here.' He then asked when the senator was coming to the convention. He asked for an advance copy of the speech and a chance to chat with the senator. He made no clear threats of any kind, but I got his point. It was an extremely pleasant conversation. He made no commitments to us but made clear that he was pleased with my presence and felt that it was a good sign for any potential future relationship between the UAW and the senator."

Kenny and Jack Conway left Reuther and headed to the bar for a drink. Kenny was careful. He was pleased with much of what he had heard from

Reuther, but Kenny was savvy enough to recognize that Gosser still could do them good in key primary states. And while Kenny did not want to make Reuther or Conway angry, he was also not going to give up Gosser.

The "cold hard political reality" was, as Kenny said to Jack later, that "they still had no commitment from Reuther, so it was worth going after Gosser. Risky, but worth it."

He said none of this to Jack Conway. They had drinks and were later joined by Joe Rauh for dinner in the UAW's favorite tavern. It was assumed that Kenny had gotten Walter's message. But nobody asked directly, and Kenny was relieved that he did not have to lie. But while Kenny may have been pleased with his success with the Reuther leadership, he still held tight to his relationship with Gosser, whom he secretly planned to introduce to Jack as soon as possible.

Conway no doubt believed that Kenny had gotten the message and, like so many others, would not dare go against Reuther's orders. But Jack Conway had a lot to learn about Kenny and the Irish Brotherhood. From Kenny's point of view, his job was to seek Jack's best interest; that was why he was here. Jack always came first. Always.

Jack was scheduled to arrive that night from Hartford. Kenny recalled, "That was the evening of a very funny conversation with Millie Jeffrey. Millie was a rather difficult person. She was not really my cup of tea, but I seemed to be making some real progress with her.

"Millie was important because she was on the UAW Executive Board. She was kind of inclined to be for John Kennedy but did not want to admit it. She was nominally for Hubert Humphrey but had switched from being anti-Kennedy. This was due to the efforts of Jack Conway. It was now clear to her that neither Jack Conway nor Walter Reuther looked with disfavor upon John Kennedy."

But Kenny had not totally convinced her. "We sat and we sipped our drinks. She was pumping me and being extremely friendly with me. As I say, we had had drinks the night before at the insiders' bar, actually both nights before, and had been up until three or four in the morning both nights that I had been there.

"We were on the best of terms by this point. She was truly shocked that a working-class guy from Boston had gone to Harvard, worked for John Kennedy, was reasonably intellectual, and could discuss the issues with her in as much depth as Ted Sorensen."

Millie made clear that she thought rather highly of Ted Sorensen and referred to him as "her kind of Kennedy man." She questioned Kenny at great length and was rather taken aback that he knew anything about labor laws. She couldn't believe that an Irish guy like Kenny knew anything more than how to buy votes in the wards of Boston.

Kenny explained that Jack Kennedy surrounded himself with people strong enough to do the hard work that has to be done but intellectual enough to discuss the issues. As Kenny recalled, "We were sitting in a hotel bar on the boardwalk, and the table we were sitting at was right in front of the window. I had a view across the boardwalk. At about that moment the door burst open, and in strolled Steve Smith and Dave Powers.

"They threw themselves in the chairs around us, completely uninvited, I might add. Steve was his usual smooth, charming self. Steve had met Millie before, so they had a wonderful chat. Steve ordered a drink, and Dave quickly ordered two fast drinks, to 'steady his hand,' as he put it.

"Those drinks were gone in minutes, and after a long day of campaigning, the alcohol hit him like a ton of bricks. As if on cue, Dave began to realize Millie's worst fears of an Irish ward politician. You would think you were in the middle of *The Last Hurrah*. He went on and on. It was unbelievable.

"Steve and I just could not contain ourselves. We were laughing hysterically. In minutes, all my hard work had been completely undone. Poor Millie was being entirely serious discussing the issues. Powers had never been so funny. The more serious she got, the worse he got. Steve and I agreed later that we were both laughing so hard we thought we'd wet our pants. At one point, Dave actually said to her, 'The minute I saw you, I knew you worked for the UAW.' Millie asked how, and Dave replied, 'I could tell by your bumpers!' She was shocked. Then he gave her a big hug and kiss. To avoid him, she literally fell out of her chair. She got right back up and sat down again, but she was just red-faced. I could tell she was sort of complimented though, as she was not the kind you would naturally compliment in the looks department.

"Then they got into an argument about Hubert Humphrey. Powers told her that he took a rather dim view of Humphrey, because he seemed to talk a lot and did not listen. Of course, he was just teasing her, but she got quite upset.

"She said to him, 'The problem with you people is in your damn polls!'

"Powers said, 'See, they are prejudiced, the Humphrey people are prejudiced, and here they are knocking the poor Poles. I am shocked, just shocked. After all, you have a lot of Poles in your union.'

"Poor Millie was reduced to trying to explain she did not mean *Poles* as in Polish; she meant *polls* as in pollsters, like Lou Harris. This went on and on for about an hour, maybe two hours. Steve and I finally felt we had to jump in and save her and our relationship. But Steve was so charming, and Millie was laughing so hard by the end of it, we knew it would be all right. Finally, we were able to pull Dave away. Steve and I went up to see the senator and catch up with him.

"As we went up, I told Steve that I was quite sure that all my efforts to prove to Millie and others that the Kennedy organization was not like their perception of the typical Boston Irish pol had all been undone. I said to Dave, 'Look, you have just undone a whole day's work.' I can't repeat what Dave said to me here, but he was not too concerned."

From there, Steve, Dave, and Kenny went into Jack's suite and met with him. "He wanted to know blow by blow what I had been doing, whom I had talked to, and what had happened," Kenny remembered. "I brought him completely up to date. Humphrey had spoken that day and gotten a tremendous reception, so we talked about that. We went over his speech, and he asked me to make some comments. I read it, made a few suggestions, but overall I thought it was a great speech for this audience."

Kenny told the others that he felt sure that not only would the speech go over well but also that Jack would be surprised by the reception he would receive. Jack listened, but based on what he knew, he remained skeptical. He assured them, however, that he very much wanted Kenny to be correct.

They ordered dinner in, and the meeting lasted well past midnight. As they turned to leave, Jack had one last question: "I hear you won the dance contest the other night, Kenny."

Kenny turned and smiled. "I did."

"The things you will do to get the UAW endorsement," Steve teased.

Jack gave Kenny a look. "Let me ask you something. Do you think your dancing helped or hurt us?"

They all started to laugh. "Well, Senator," Kenny replied, "when you get their support, you will know who was responsible." With that he demonstrated one of his better moves.

Jack laughed. "Get out of here. I am going to bed."

When they finally left Jack's room, Steve and Kenny went to the bar for one last drink. Tomorrow was crucial. While both men knew they would not be able at this early date to secure the UAW's support, slowing Humphrey's momentum was essential.

The next morning, Jack, Kenny, Steve, and Dave met for an early breakfast in the senator's suite. This is where Kenny made his move. "I told him before he left for the speech that despite what Reuther had said, it might be worth it for him to at least say hello to Dick Gosser. I pointed out this convention was not a UAW thing totally. I could not see Reuther being too upset if Jack just said hi to Gosser. My point was, even though we had not made a decision on the primaries yet, if we did go into Ohio, having Dick Gosser on our side was going to be a major benefit to us. It might be at least worth a handshake and hello."

While Jack agreed in theory, he was concerned about going behind Reuther's back and undoing all Kenny's hard work. Kenny had thought of that already, suggesting to Jack that after his speech "you could return to your suite for a bit and I would then sneak Gosser up, so as not to upset Walter Reuther and Jack Conway."

Jack smiled. "It might work."

The speech had been brilliantly written by Sorensen. "It got a tremendous reception," Kenny remembered. "In fact, it was a very different reception than Hubert Humphrey got. Though Humphrey's crowd was loud and enthusiastic, Senator Kennedy's reception was wild and almost frenzied," to Walter Reuther's surprise and suspicion.

Thanks to their newfound friend Dick Gosser, Steve Smith later noted, "a great deal of Jack's crowd came from the Indiana, Ohio, and especially New York regions. After the speech he went into a private room and chatted with Walter Reuther, Jack Conway, and other members of the Executive Board. He had a cup of coffee with them. They were so impressed with him. He was not what they had expected."

"All of them," Kenny said, "seemed shocked at what a good speech he had given. They were really impressed with his personal charisma. The speech was a real rabble-rousing speech, more in the Humphrey tradition than Jack Kennedy's style. But everyone was very excited. It was their opinion that Hubert's speech had been better, but they thought the senator's speech was right behind Hubert's." Given how far the Kennedy forces had to come to impress the UAW, such praise was not to be taken lightly.

It was evident that the groundwork had been laid by Kenny. Jack as usual made the most of the opportunity. As he left the meeting room to return to his clandestine meeting with Dick Gosser, he put his hand on Kenny's shoulder and whispered, "I hope we don't blow it all with this crazy idea of yours to meet this fellow Gosser."

Kenny smiled. "I will go get him. Reuther will never know."

With that, the men parted. Jack, Steve, and Dave headed to the suite while Kenny went to find Gosser and lead him up the back stairs.

As Dick Gosser and his men entered Jack's suite, Kenny saw Jack's eye widen a bit. He gave Kenny a quizzical look. "Never had to come up back stairs before," Dick Gosser was saying as they walked in, stopping once he saw Jack. He seemed surprised, almost awed to be in his presence.

"The first thing you must understand," Kenny explained later to Bobby, "Mr. Gosser is very much the old-school labor union type of fellow and not of the new breed. It was a significant contrast from having just left Walter Reuther. Mr. Gosser had a couple of his boys with him. They both looked like wrestlers, the kind that might break a few legs or heads when called upon."

Jack looked at them in astonishment as he shook Gosser's hand, then shot Kenny a dirty look as if to say, "What the hell have you got me into?"

Nevertheless, Jack realized that this meeting was necessary for gaining union support in Ohio. The two men quickly moved to a discussion of Ohio and Ohio politics, and their discussion focused largely on the upcoming primary and the circumstances surrounding Governor DiSalle. It was a critical discussion, as the Kennedy team had yet to make a final decision about the primaries.

According to Kenny, "Mr. Gosser told the senator that Governor DiSalle was not in very good shape politically. That if Senator Kennedy chose to enter the primary, DiSalle would instantly fold. Gosser told the senator quite frankly and directly that he was for Senator Kennedy for president. Gosser made clear he and his men did not agree with Walter Reuther and the 'intellectuals' who had taken over the UAW."

Despite appearances, as the two men talked, it was quickly evident that Dick Gosser not only had political power in Ohio but also was savvy politically. He made clear to Jack that while he liked Humphrey personally, and Stevenson for that matter, he was thinking about the general election. Gosser was sure that neither of these men could beat Nixon.

"Walter Reuther," Gosser told Jack, Kenny, and Steve, "has decided that Ohio and the Ohio union do not agree with him."

Kenny explained, "No matter what position Walter Reuther and Detroit took, Gosser was going to be for John Kennedy for president and support him in the primary should he enter Ohio. As far as Gosser was concerned, all the resources that he could bring to bear in Ohio would be put at Senator Kennedy's behest.

"As he was speaking, Gosser began to get more and more emotional, and much to Jack's horror, Gosser's false teeth kept popping out. In between sentences he would reach up and shove his false teeth back into his mouth. Jack was appalled and kept giving me this dirty look. At one point, Gosser pulled them out altogether and examined them before trying to hand them to Jack, saying with his teeth in his outstretched hand, 'These damn things keep slipping out all the time. They never fit right. Ever have that problem?'"

Jack quickly stepped back. Kenny, who was standing behind Gosser with Steve, was in hysterics watching Jack's reaction. Kenny said later, "With Jack's love of physical beauty and strength, it was hilarious to watch him try to handle the moment gracefully, but he did it beautifully. I do not think he appreciated Steve and I too much at that moment."

Humor aside, Dick Gosser surprised both Kenny and Jack. He was articulate, smart, and well versed in his state's and national politics. Despite appearances, he was very intelligent, which Jack had not expected. His policies and political station within the union made him different from Walter Reuther.

Gosser made clear that he felt Reuther did not take into consideration the feelings of the rank-and-file members, who were overwhelmingly for Jack Kennedy, not Hubert Humphrey or Stevenson, whom they saw as someone whose time had passed. As for Humphrey, most of the rank and file liked him all right, but they did not believe he could beat Nixon. For the most part, Gosser indicated, they went for Jack Kennedy. This was exactly what the Brotherhood believed, and they were delighted to have Gosser confirm their views.

As the meeting ended, the two men shook hands. Jack was leaving to do a television show. It was decided that Kenny would stay on for a few more days. If he had found Dick Gosser, perhaps another day might lead to another opening. As they began to depart, Jack pulled Kenny aside. With a nod to Dick Gosser's departing figure, he said, "Where do you come up with these guys, Kenny?" Kenny laughed and kept walking.

Once Gosser and his men were safely gone, Kenny returned to the suite. He, Jack, and Steve had a few more things to discuss before heading out.

"That went well," Jack said. "Reuther will be none the wiser."

Kenny nodded. "That was the plan." Then they got on the elevator and headed to the lobby. But, Kenny remembered, "As we walked off the elevator we ran right into Walter Reuther, Leonard Woodcock, and Jack Conway as they were stepping onto the elevator."

Bob Wallace, who worked with Sorensen and was traveling with Jack on what would turn out to be his last trip, was also on the elevator. He was, in Kenny's words, "an affable but none too bright guy," who immediately greeted Reuther, "Hi, Walter, how are you? Dick Gosser was just up in the suite with the senator. What a great guy."

Jack stared in disbelief at Wallace. Quickly, Jack grabbed Reuther's arm to pretend to ask him a question. Jack Conway glared at Kenny. But the damage was done. So much for the private meeting between Gosser and Kennedy.

"You know this was supposed to be under the table. Kenny's three days of hard work are now all in jeopardy!" Jack snapped at Wallace upon his return from a very upset Walter Reuther.

Kenny told Wallace to meet them at the car. Jack turned to Kenny, absolutely livid, saying, "I can't believe anyone would be so stupid. That was supposed to be a private meeting. He knew it was a private meeting. Why couldn't he just shut up? Where the hell did he come from? Get rid of him."

Kenny told Jack that Sorensen had hired him, but he would take care of it.

Needless to say, that was the end of Bob Wallace as far as the Kennedy campaign and Jack were concerned. Wallace took one last trip with Jack to Oklahoma, where Jack was putting in a preprimary appearance at a football game. From there, Wallace was "sent to home," as Kenny and Bobby liked to say.

It was through this rather uncomfortable situation that Kenny suddenly found he had another job assignment.

"Advance," Jack said.

Kenny looked at him as they stood at the car. "What?"

"Advance," Jack said. "You are now in charge."

Kenny shook his head. "Do we have an advance staff?" he asked Jack.

"That is your job and your problem," Jack snapped.

Kenny nodded. He knew better than to ask, recognizing that Jack was still fuming over Wallace's screwup. Kenny would just have to figure it out.

Just then a young woman came up and asked the senator to autograph a copy of his recently released book, *Profiles in Courage*. He smiled at her and took the book but glared at Kenny as he signed it.

"What?" Kenny asked after the woman had walked off.

"I am trying to figure out if you find these people on purpose just to drive me nuts," Jack said.

Kenny chuckled, shook his head, and turned to walk away, "Ye of little faith."

"What are you going to do, Kenny?" Jack called after him suspiciously.

Kenny turned and smiled, "Listen to Symington. He comes in tomorrow."

"Sure he does," Jack replied. "Well, work hard, Kenny."

Kenny laughed. "I always do."

Jack began to climb into the car but stopped one last time. "I am sure you will work very, very hard," he called after Kenny, a hint of irony in his voice.

Kenny stopped and turned. "You are just bitter because you don't like Oklahoma football."

Before Jack could reply, Kenny had disappeared back into the lobby to find Jack Conway and Walter Reuther. Kenny had some explaining to do to these men, and he prayed that he could repair the damage that had been done by Wallace's gaff. Timing in politics is everything.

CHAPTER 14

Ohio or Wisconsin?

T HE STORIES OF the Kennedy campaigns in the primaries have been told and retold, but Kenny felt there were several unacknowledged moments that were critical in putting the Irish Brotherhood in the White House. As Kenny recalled, the first crucial decision "was Bobby's and Bobby's alone." "You and Jack are going to Pittsburgh," Bobby had said.

"Why Pittsburgh?" Kenny asked, sitting on the desk, his feet on the other table, as Bobby sat across from him. This question, of course, was related to the Wisconsin or Ohio decision. At the moment this decision depended entirely on Pennsylvania governor Mike DiSalle. As Kenny had correctly predicted back at the meeting in Palm Beach, many of the next steps the campaign needed to take were not entirely in the Irish Brotherhood's control.

"Bobby's decision rather early in the campaign," Kenny said, "was that in these big states, despite the fact that we just did not have the professionals on our side and were correctly seen as outsiders, we had to break in with what we had."

This meant entering the critical primaries to demonstrate Jack's strength, just as they had in '58, but also to show that they had the ability to overcome the "Catholic thing." Without overcoming that issue, there would be no way for Jack to get nominated at the Democratic National Convention in Los Angeles.

"These were hard and perplexing decisions in the earlier chain of moves and deals that led Kennedy into a primary at Wisconsin and from there," Kenny made clear, "into the all-decisive religious confrontation in West Virginia, which neither Jack nor any of the rest of us relished at the time."

Kenny was also clear that "the most critical decision facing us was whether to enter the primary in Wisconsin or Ohio. It had to be one or the other. Jack did not have the resources to run in both of them."

Their first choice, as Kenny recalled later, was Ohio. "We had made a deal with Governor Pat Brown in California that, in return for a promise of Brown's support at the convention, Jack would come to Los Angeles as the leading candidate. However," Kenny said, "Jack was in no mood to make a similar tentative deal with former Toledo mayor and now Ohio governor Mike DiSalle, who was running as a favorite-son candidate in Ohio."

Mike DiSalle, an Italian-American and a Catholic, qualities that made him essential to Jack Kennedy's push for the nomination, was originally from New York City but had moved to Ohio when he was three years old. To complicate matters from the Kennedy campaign's point of view, DiSalle was a friend of President Harry Truman, who was also no supporter of Jack Kennedy. DiSalle's loyalty to Truman dated back to 1950, when in December of that year, President Truman had appointed Mike DiSalle to head up the Office of Price Stabilization, a Korean War–era agency designed to enforce price controls. When that ended, DiSalle had returned to Ohio to run for and win the office of mayor of Toledo, with Truman's support. So he owed Harry Truman, and he knew it.

In fact, Jack and Kenny were sure that unless forced in another direction, DiSalle "was fully expected to throw Ohio's sixty-four delegate votes to Stuart Symington, Truman's candidate, or to Lyndon Johnson, another old friend of Truman's."

"Don't forget," Jack reminded Kenny and Bobby, as if they needed reminding, "DiSalle was one of the Catholic leaders who opposed us in the 1956 vice presidential fight."

Running as a favorite son was a political tool that was most often used and fashionable during the nineteenth and twentieth century. Any candidate who was known statewide could run as a favorite-son candidate, as DiSalle planned to do in Ohio. Such a candidate would, if he won, control all the delegates from his state at a national party convention. The victorious favorite-son candidate would have power over the delegation in the nominating process. From this position of influence, he would in turn be able to deliver those delegates to the candidate of his choice.

In a meeting that Steve Smith arranged in Washington, he made clear to Jack, Bobby, Kenny, and Larry that "the campaign simply could not afford an all-out battle in both Ohio and Wisconsin." So, as had been discussed back in the Palm Beach meeting, they would have to decide between them. Kenny said, "The senator would have to enter one of the primaries; then the other primary would have to be wrapped up for us through the favorite-son avenue."

Jack was feeling that Ohio might be more easily wrapped up than Wisconsin, but Kenny argued that Ohio had its own problems. DiSalle was in an internal political battle with Ray Miller, who was, Kenny recalled, "the Democratic leader in Cleveland, Ohio. Miller was anxious to beat DiSalle with the Toledo organization in such a battle for party control of the state."

Dave Powers recalled that he and Jack had traveled alone to meet with Miller in Cleveland to see if something might be gained. "Miller, who went to Notre Dame and who was a staunch alumnus," Powers said, "was also the brother of one Don Miller, one of Knute Rockne's Four Horsemen."

In late October 1959, after Jack and Dave had returned to Hyannis Port for the weekend, they met up with Bobby, Kenny, and Steve Smith.

Dave told them, "They take their politics as seriously as Notre Dame plays football!"

Neither Kenny nor Jack was thrilled. They wanted to avoid a nasty internal political battle in Ohio, so that meant pressuring DiSalle to back Jack. That meant that if he ran and won as a favorite son, Jack, assuming he received the nomination, would be assured of Ohio's critical delegates. That delegation was essential to put Jack over the top at the Democratic Convention in Los Angeles. Kenny was pushing hard for the Ohio primary, believing, because of DiSalle's allegiance to Truman, that he could not be pushed.

Bobby disagreed. "In the end," he declared, "DiSalle is going to be a realist and vote with the politics of today, not yesterday."

Kenny, sipping his beer in Bobby's vast living room at the Cape, which was now turned into presidential campaign central, oceanside, argued hard that DiSalle's sense of loyalty to Truman should not be so easily dismissed.

"Remember," Kenny warned, "he is Italian-American, his parents are immigrants, he owes his career to Truman, and they tend to be very loyal and will not be easily convinced to break ranks."

Jack watched Kenny protest with amused silence, finally saying, as he rose for a lunch of milk, clam chowder, a sandwich, and chocolate cake at his mother's house across the driveway, "You and Larry just don't want to go to Wisconsin in the dead of winter!"

"You're damn right," Kenny snapped, as they all followed Jack over to join him for lunch at Rose and Joe's house. "I don't want to be chasing Hubert Humphrey's ass around the farmlands of Wisconsin, freeze to death, and be up to my neck in snow!"

"It is very, very cold," O'Brien agreed.

Jack turned and looked at them as they walked. He was slightly ahead, his hands stuffed in his pockets as they strolled. He walked as if he had not a care in the world, a stiff breeze off Nantucket Sound whipping across Joe's vast lawn and ruffling his hair, which he would occasionally try in vain to control. Jack, who always liked to be well coiffed, rarely looked so informal, in contrast to his brother Bobby, whose hair and clothes were often a mess—his sleeves rolled up and shirttails hanging out. He also often left a trail of discarded clothes behind him wherever he went; Ethel would often dispatch a housekeeper to Helen and Kenny's home in Bethesda to retrieve his forgotten articles.

Kenny noted, "Jack knew he had to enter as many primaries as possible, though money was not unlimited in this case because presidential campaigns were not the Massachusetts variety—even Joe Kennedy had financial limits on this one [or so Kenny believed at the time]. Jack was such an outsider, an underdog, and a Catholic, which was a category all by itself. Never mind that the decision whether to enter Ohio or Wisconsin first could decide the fate of his campaign and even his chances to win the Democratic nomination in Los Angeles."

As they climbed the front stairs to Joe and Rose's house, Larry O'Brien added the politically obvious, that Senate majority leader Lyndon Johnson, not Senator Hubert Humphrey, was Jack's real opponent. Kenny and Larry agreed that whatever decision Jack made, "Lyndon would be safe, warm, and comfortable in Washington, DC, campaigning in the cloakrooms of the Senate, convinced he and Sam Rayburn, Speaker of the House, could convince and round up enough delegate votes by exerting political pressure on the Democratic congressmen and senators in Washington, so he sought out like-minded local politicians to support his candidacy."

As the group arrived at Joe's house and Jack greeted his mother and father, Bobby remarked, "Yeah, but we know after '56 and the lessons of Senator McClellan, it does not always work that way!"

Jack turned and smiled evenly at Kenny. "You just don't want to go spend the cold winter in Wisconsin!"

Everyone laughed.

But Kenny's instinct, which was increasingly in tune with Jack, told him something else. As they sat down to lunch, Kenny thought to himself, *I better make sure that Helen gets me a warm winter coat.*

◆◆◆

WHILE JACK CONTINUED to review and weigh all the options, Bobby, later back in Washington, was eager to get a move on. Bobby was all about action, some action, any action at this stage! Bobby decided, as he had in Massachusetts, to send Kenny and Larry to break into the big states and drum up support before the primaries.

"You and Larry will now take the lead. We don't have the professionals. We won't until after Los Angeles. So we will have to do it ourselves," Bobby told Kenny.

Kenny noted, "Bobby was certainly taking a risk. From this point forward, I traveled with Jack constantly. Bobby decided to keep Steve Smith in Washington to work on campaign structure and the all-important financing for the national push. Steve and the senator also decided that Ted Sorensen should stay there full-time as well, working on policy and speeches. A decision I completely supported.

"Dave Powers would travel, as he always did, with the senator, but as we know, he performed a different function. Bobby made the critical decision that we were not going to get the professional pols on our side at this stage. Therefore, the only way to proceed was to have Larry and me, experienced only in Massachusetts, accompany the senator everywhere and set up operations in the big states. This was a turning point."

Hy Raskin agreed. "Bobby Kennedy stayed in Washington mostly, quarterbacking the entire operation, directing the strategy that the senator and the Irish Brotherhood, led by O'Donnell, as well as Joe Kennedy, had already agreed upon."

The resulting victories in the primaries, Kenny argued, demonstrated that Bobby had made the right call. Kenny and Larry both believed it had led to victories in the primaries and put them on the road to the nomination in Los Angeles.

Kenny's first dry run with Jack was in Pittsburgh, in December 1959. With the decision about which primary, Ohio or Wisconsin, still up in the air, Bobby had scheduled meetings with Governor Lawrence of Pennsylvania, as well as the mayor of Pittsburgh and groups like the steelworkers. Of all the groups they met with, Kenny said the steelworkers were the most positive. While the first primary was up in the air, there was no question that Pennsylvania, with its huge cache of delegates and a Catholic governor, was a must for Jack to lock up.

"To our surprise," Kenny noted, "the Pittsburgh trip was a huge success. They were very high on Senator Kennedy. He received a very enthusiastic welcome."

The meeting with Governor Lawrence was not as successful. He proved evasive and unwilling to commit, restating many of his usual reservations about Jack being young and inexperienced, which Kenny and Jack were increasingly beginning to understand as code words for "Irish and Catholic."

The meeting with Lawrence was a "tough" one, and while he and Jack never spoke of it outwardly, Kenny said they were both exasperated. As they left the meeting, Jack shot Kenny a frustrated look. Without giving his concerns voice, Kenny shared Jack's worry, the Catholic issue. Was it really going to be that much of an issue? Only time would tell.

Later Kenny complained to Bobby over the telephone from their hotel in Pittsburgh about "the damn Catholic thing. Nobody will say it out loud, but you can feel in the air."

There was also the darn elevator, which didn't work at their hotel, and, naturally, they were on the top floor. Kenny and Jack had to trudge up and down the stairs, which for Kenny, despite the shrapnel in his leg, was not really a problem. But for Jack it was agony.

"If you weren't so rich we'd have been on the first floor," Kenny joked to ease the tension as they climbed the stairs.

Jack was not amused.

The end result of the Pennsylvania meetings was that Jack would have to enter the primary, do an all-out push, and at least for now he could not be guaranteed that Governor Lawrence, a big-state, northern liberal Catholic, would endorse him. The only chance they had was to win and win big, thus forcing Lawrence's hand.

As the time to make the official announcement of Jack's candidacy approached, the decisions on which primary, Ohio versus Wisconsin, would need to be made.

JACK MADE HIS announcement to run for president of the United States on January 2, 1960, at the Senate Office Building. The Kennedy for President campaign, such as it was, was now official.

As Kenny remembered, "During the week prior to the announcement, the senator had to get Mike DiSalle's word that he would support the senator, or else the senator had to announce his entrance into the Ohio primary. We had all agreed, going back to the Palm Beach meeting, we could not enter both Ohio and Wisconsin. We needed an answer from DiSalle."

Jack and Kenny had many discussions during this period on the complicated issue of Ohio and getting DiSalle to publicly commit to Jack by announcing it early, almost simultaneously with the announcement to run for president.

"I said to him," Kenny remembered, "it seems to me you cannot take chances. You must have DiSalle's agreement and then he must announce it, so he cannot change his mind. Everybody agreed. Bobby felt very strongly about this as well. We all felt we had no alternative but to force Mike DiSalle to publicly announce his support for Kennedy and not allow him to give only a private assurance."

In a dissatisfying telephone conversation with Governor DiSalle, Jack listened as the governor said point-blank: "I am for you totally. You are the best candidate, but under the circumstances, as a Catholic governor, I don't think it would be politically wise for me to be the first to announce. Why don't you get another couple of guys, non-Catholics, to announce, and then I will follow suit."

Kenny, Bobby, and Larry felt that was not enough.

When Jack hung up, he looked over at Kenny.

The wolfhound shook his head. "It was too easy," he felt, "for DiSalle to slide off the hook after the fact. Look, he has his own political problems. His first priority, as with any politician, is going to be to take care of himself. We need to force it [a total commitment] before the announcement. Afterward he will be too scared and under pressure."

Bobby joined in. "Kenny is wrong most of the time," he teased, "but this time, he's completely correct."

"Which," Larry chimed in, "is unusual."

They all laughed. The tension broken, the issue remained: How do you get a powerful governor of a big state like DiSalle to cooperate publicly without telling him you don't trust him?

They felt they needed DiSalle to make his position clear publicly to ensure that Ohio was tied up, which then meant they could go into Wisconsin confident that they would not have to double back and fight in Ohio. A fight in Ohio, in Kenny and Bobby's view, would "doom their candidacy before they had gotten through the first primary." DiSalle's hand had to be forced. But how?

Jack and the Kennedy forces were anxious for a unified "Democratic port," as Kenny called it, behind them in Ohio. Before pushing DiSalle too hard, Jack decided to take John Bailey with him and try one last charm offensive.

"Then," Jack said, completely seriously, "we unleash Bobby."

"And you call me the wolfhound?" Kenny laughed.

DiSalle agreed to take a meeting with Jack and John Bailey at a motel in Pittsburgh, but it had to be kept secret or all bets were off.

Steve Smith, doing what Jack teased was "remarkably original," booked two rooms under the name Smith.

Jack and John Bailey arrived on the *Caroline*, Jack's private Convair campaign plane named for his beloved daughter.

Kenny laughed later when recalling the near disaster. "Because of headwinds, the Kennedy team was an hour late. On top of that, they had the name of the wrong motel! When they raced breathlessly into the lobby, the clerk told them he had no reservations for Smith.

"John and I guessed that maybe DiSalle had booked under another name; it was late. So Bailey and I ran around the crowded parking lot, getting down on our knees to search in the darkness for an Ohio license plate. The well-oiled Kennedy machine had collapsed again!"

Kenny and Dave would joke about this later. But when they returned to the lobby of the motel to tell Jack the bad news, he was furious. "Great," he groaned, "you two have ruined me in Ohio!"

Kenny recalled, "We decided to wait for DiSalle to make a late appearance and the desk clerk mentioned the airport had another motel . . . with a similar name." To reach it, Jack, Kenny, John Bailey, and Dave had to race through the airport. While riding up an airport escalator, Bailey spied Governor DiSalle, his administrative assistant Maurice Connell, and DiSalle's secretary Millie Cunningham.

"There they are!" John practically yelled.

Jack shot him a *be quiet* look.

DiSalle looked up, relieved, and waved to them.

"Later," Kenny said, "the entire episode was like a Marx Brothers comedy."

In the end, they finally all returned to the correct motel, where DiSalle had been waiting all along in a room reserved for "Mr. Smith." Jack and DiSalle met alone for two hours in the room; Kenny, Bailey, Powers, and DiSalle's staff waited in the motel's little diner for the meeting to end.

After such drama, Kenny hoped for good news. When he saw Jack's expression as the governor and senator joined them in the motel's diner for coffee and a sandwich before parting ways, Kenny could see it had all been for naught.

As they sat on the *Caroline* and headed back to Washington that night, Jack tiredly told Kenny, "DiSalle was at best evasive and stalled for time, using the potential primary fight in Ohio as a reason he could not come out publicly. Though he pledged his private support, he could not do so publicly. At least not yet," he had told Jack privately.

"That's not good enough," Kenny said.

Jack sat exhausted with his eyes closed as the plane headed back home. "I don't need you to tell me that. We may have to get Bobby involved," Jack said before drifting off to sleep.

The problem was, according to Kenny, "DiSalle had moved to a position which now made the senator's situation much more difficult."

DiSalle was all but forcing Jack, by demanding a public announcement, to say, "I don't trust you now." Not the best way to secure his support or build a long-term relationship as they faced the nomination battle in Los Angeles.

After extensive discussions in Washington involving Jack and the Brotherhood, however, "the decision was made by Jack to have Bobby go see Mike DiSalle." Bobby was not happy about it. He made clear he felt he was not the right choice, but Jack and Kenny disagreed. "This requires somebody to be tough, play hardball politics, and speak for Jack Kennedy in a way that cannot be put into doubt. Only another Kennedy can do that and that, Bobby, is you."

Bobby groaned.

"Bobby did not want to," Kenny said, "but we had a meeting, and Jack said to Bobby, 'Now, look, Bobby, you are mean and tough and can say more miserable things to DiSalle than I can say. And if you get too obnoxious, then I will disown and disavow what you said and just say to DiSalle, 'Look, he's a young kid who does not know any better.'"

Bobby stared from Kenny to Jack.

"Thanks a lot," was all Bobby said.

Jack had John Bailey go out with Bobby. Kenny felt Bailey would balance the situation and demonstrate to DiSalle from a political point of view that even the more experienced professionals on the Kennedy team felt that DiSalle had to go public with his support. John Bailey, a politician from Connecticut with solid credentials, a man who spoke DiSalle's language, would balance Bobby; and he could make clear to DiSalle that even the experienced political pros felt that Jack needed DiSalle's endorsement, publicly, before the announcement.

"This move to send Bailey was brilliant on Jack's part," Kenny noted. "It took away some of the sting of that 'We don't trust you, Mike DiSalle' issue. Of course, the way the meeting went," Kenny laughed later, "trust was the least of our problems. Bobby would get DiSalle's endorsement, but at what a price!"

Things did not exactly go according to plan, to put it kindly. Kenny said, "Mike DiSalle called me after the meeting and was furious. He said to me Bobby was the most obnoxious kid he had ever met. He said Bobby practically called him a liar, telling him, 'We can't trust you. You will do what you are told.'"

"In essence," Kenny recalled, "Bobby did exactly what Jack told him to do. Jack naturally disavowed it later when a livid Mike DiSalle called him. Jack explained, Bobby was young, inexperienced, and out of touch. However, that was not enough.

"John Bailey called me privately," Kenny said later, "and said he was simply horrified at the conversation. He said, 'Bobby was awfully tough, completely unreasonable, rude, and obnoxious and demanded that DiSalle come out immediately, threatening him if he did not.' Bailey claimed Bobby's demands sounded like a mob threat." The more experienced

Bailey had warned Kenny, "You guys sound like a bunch of mobsters! Not politicians! You cannot talk to people like that."

It was very early January 1960, but Kenny was concerned. Even for Bobby, this was too strong and brought back memories for Kenny of their early meetings with the UAW at the McClellan Committee.

When Bobby returned to Washington, Kenny pulled him aside. "I made clear to Bobby that he had gone too far. 'Look,' I said, 'While we know you can be rude, obnoxious, and pushy,'" Kenny teased, trying unsuccessfully to lighten the mood, "'you went too far, Bobby. This is politics, but not the mob! You can't threaten public officials like that, especially not a governor like DiSalle.'"

Bobby quickly protested and pointed out that his father and Jack had already called him. In fairness, he argued he was doing what he was asked to do. They had all been at the meeting at Christmas when they all agreed that DiSalle's private support was not enough. And once he heard Bobby's version of events, Kenny realized that Bobby was correct.

"DiSalle had been planning to play us," Kenny told Jack in defense of Bobby's actions. "Bailey is wrong; DiSalle would have walked had Bobby not forced his hand."

Jack nodded. "Fine. Let's hope we are not in that position again." Kenny agreed.

Bobby said to Kenny, "I was indeed very tough on DiSalle, but I felt DiSalle was evasive. He was refusing to give the commitment that we all deemed essential, and he was, in fact, even backing off what he had told Jack over the phone."

Bobby also pointed out that he had not wanted the job of talking to DiSalle in the first place, which was true.

"Bobby is not the most diplomatic fellow on the planet to begin with," Kenny said. "Bobby probably overstepped the bounds with DiSalle. John Bailey was used to the evasive language of dealing with the average politician, I think, and was shocked at Bobby's conversation and behavior."

Nevertheless, John Bailey called Kenny, saying, "If we have not blown the DiSalle thing now, it cannot be blown at all!"

Eventually, Bailey would claim that he personally "was able to patch up things with DiSalle and that the Kennedy forces almost lost DiSalle after this meeting." Kenny shrugged it off.

Later, Mike DiSalle told Kenny "that while he was furious at Bobby, he never wavered in his support of John Kennedy. He did not relate Bobby's bad behavior, in his view, to his brother," as Kenny recalled later.

Kenny understood. He never told DiSalle that Jack had in fact sent Bobby on a mission to put DiSalle up against the wall or that Bailey had already complained.

"Let us be clear: Jack had told Bobby to be as tough and as mean as necessary to get the job done. Bobby did what he was asked to do. He got the job done. Such was Bobby's role," Kenny said later.

While Kenny felt, as with the UAW meeting, that Bobby had perhaps gone too far, in the end you could not argue with the results. "Bobby came back, and he admitted that he had been perhaps tougher than he might have been, but we had all agreed he could not allow DiSalle to wiggle off and say he had not been asked in the proper terms. Bobby was speaking with authority. DiSalle knew that Bobby would not dare have this conversation without permission. He also realized that Jack was prepared to file petitions in Ohio to run himself, if he did not get what he wanted."

The plan was unorthodox but effective. It was a successful tactic that they would employ throughout the campaign.

Later, during one of Jack Kennedy's trips to Columbus, Ohio, DiSalle, who was still reeling from his meeting with Bobby, defensively explained to Kenny that he had always planned to come out for John Kennedy. "His only concern was a political one that he ought not to be the first one out of the gate since he was a Catholic governor.

"Of course, there was also pressure from Miller. Ray Miller was the head of the Democratic operation in Cleveland and long a thorn in Mike

DiSalle's political side. Miller's agenda was to get rid of DiSalle, and he was willing to use Jack Kennedy to help marginalize DiSalle if necessary."

The conflict between DiSalle and Miller had worked in the Kennedy campaign's favor even before Jack's official announcement. Prior to Bobby's meeting, Kenny explained, Steve Smith had done some advance work of his own in Ohio. "Steve talked to Miller, who indicated he was getting petitions to run ready. Whether Miller did that just to gig DiSalle, I really don't know. The reporters, seeing this as a beautiful fight, a brawl between Kennedy and DiSalle, were running with this story about the petitions. So there was a general storm growing, and the pressure on DiSalle was intense, which was fine with us, as long as it benefited us. That's politics."

DiSalle would later claim that he was just asking for time to think about the best candidate. He was not strong politically. He understood that he could not face John Kennedy in a primary.

"Without question," Kenny said, "it was a terrible spot to be in." In the end, Kenny noted, "DiSalle simply decided the best course for him was to enthusiastically join the Kennedy operation. He would announce it publicly. He would go over the announcement with Jack and would do everything that was asked of him by the campaign."

On January 5, 1960, Mike DiSalle endorsed John Kennedy for president. Jack had now secured Ohio, which meant he would enter the Wisconsin primary and Kenny would be unhappily wintering in Wisconsin.

"Don't worry," Bobby declared, "we will be roommates!"

Kenny stared evenly, remembering Chicago in '56, when the cost-conscious Bobby had turned down the penthouse at the Palmer House, a suite that actor Peter Lawford (Jack's brother-in-law) had secured for them and paid for but never used. Bobby, horrified at such waste, had moved them instead to a small room with twin beds.

"Gee," Kenny said, sarcasm evident, "I am can't wait!"

Bobby laughed.

◆◆◆

THAT OHIO AND Wisconsin were interlocked was in no small part due to the political moves of former president and would-be kingmaker Harry Truman as well as Missouri senator Stuart Symington.

In 1959, Symington was chairman of the National Security Resources Board in Washington, DC. At the urging of Truman, Symington was planning to make a move for the 1960 presidential nomination but not participate in the primary process.

Symington, like Johnson, was sitting it out, hoping the backroom bosses, led by Truman, would secure the nomination for him. The conventional thinking by Truman, Symington, Johnson, and others in the Democratic political power structure was that Humphrey, who was considered too far left to secure the nomination, would defeat Kennedy easily in places like Wisconsin and clobber him in West Virginia and elsewhere, which would damage the Kennedy candidacy.

They felt Humphrey could not secure the nomination for himself, but he could keep Jack Kennedy and his upstart political staff from getting the nomination. At that point, Symington would easily secure the nomination with Truman's backing. Humphrey would fall in line and no doubt support a Symington candidacy.

"Truman and Symington were shrewd political men," Kenny said. "They saw the Kennedy activity in Ohio; they saw the constant meetings, etc. Any reasonable professional would know that one of two things was in the works: One, that Kennedy was pressuring DiSalle for an announcement, thus they knew Kennedy's announcement was near. Two, that Kennedy was going to either get Ohio via DiSalle's endorsement or, if DiSalle did not endorse him, then Kennedy would enter the Ohio primary. Ohio was tailored for Kennedy's talent."

Most of the establishment would figure that DiSalle, as experienced a pol as he was, would tell Kennedy that he would be for him at the proper time, but not publicly, and hold Kennedy up as long as possible. Kennedy being young and new to the game would accept DiSalle at his word and not demand more.

Kenny remembered, "The Catholic issue being what it was and with Humphrey in a favorable position there, Kennedy could get beat in Wisconsin. DiSalle being a shrewd operator would lay that down for Kennedy, push Jack toward Ohio, and then hold out for as long as possible. And there would be a million openings between now and convention time to allow DiSalle as much room as possible. They would assume that DiSalle would play Kennedy and win."

Kenny and Jack both recognized that "the pros like Symington, Johnson, Truman, and their political operators would assume that Kennedy, being young and naive, would not know any better."

While flying to Wisconsin to kick off the Kennedy campaign there, Kenny and Jack discussed DiSalle and Bobby's move to get his capitulation and formal endorsement. Kenny said, "This is what Bobby sensed and why, in many ways, Bobby was as brutal as he was with DiSalle. But Bobby did that, acted in the manner he did, because you had recognized you were being played and wanted Bobby to shut the last avenue off. This was a shrewd political move, hardball politics, and shocking to DiSalle and many of these others. Your tough decision to push DiSalle to a wall, dispatch Bobby, and get the result you wanted shocked and stunned the traditional politicos. It changed the entire political situation. Changed the situation and was really a significant turning point on this first stage. I just think, Senator, they were shocked, because this meant that you could play hardball politics as well as the next guy; you were willing to do what had to be done to win."

"I agree," Jack said. "It has been a decisive turning point, but such a move is not without costs." He shrewdly recognized that such a tough blatant political move was bound to generate a response. This was, though, a decisive factor in the first stage of the campaign.

"It was a major breakthrough," Kenny noted, "on many levels, primary-wise, and more importantly a major breakthrough with the professional politicians. I think their entire attitude toward John Kennedy would change. Now the down side, very frankly, was that this maneuver hardened up the forces opposing Kennedy. They now saw him as a serious potential threat and recognized he was willing to be tough to succeed, so this hardened their determination to stop him. He became more than just the 'Catholic candidate' for the presidency but became a serious, tough candidate and, in all eventualities, must be dealt with at all times. I would think any other potential candidate is now frightened stiff that they have allowed Kennedy to get too much of a jump on them by not taking him seriously. Or that Jack would now certainly be in a position to dictate many terms in Los Angeles at the least."

Kenny said later to Bobby, with a smile, "This alone would make would-be candidates like Symington, Stevenson, Johnson, not to mention Harry Truman, panic totally."

"This was totally against [Stevenson's] understanding or acceptance of how you operate in politics. Adlai would look at John Kennedy and say, 'He is more like his father than I thought he was,' which, by the way, did not make these fellows like him any better, either. The whole attitude of the professionals took a total switch at this point. The second thing it did was that it solved our problem — well, that is not right. It did not solve our problem. It relieved [Jack] from having to make a decision about which primary, Ohio or Wisconsin."

With the DiSalle issue settled, Jack Kennedy would now go into Wisconsin and face this fight with Humphrey.

Kenny recalled, "The first trip we take into Wisconsin is via New Hampshire and then on to Wisconsin and is geared to set up a psychological situation, which, in fact, was true: that we should be the underdog in Wisconsin because of Hubert's proximity to Wisconsin. The reasons why we were not anxious to go into Wisconsin were evident: It was Hubert Humphrey's backyard and not a place particularly friendly to Catholics."

Now faced with having to enter Wisconsin, Kenny and Bobby embarked on a sort of political public relations and psychological campaign. They pushed the possibility of Jack entering the New Hampshire primary with glowing, laudatory statements about the people of New Hampshire he had met, their proximity to Massachusetts, and the local connections that existed from the many trips the Kennedy family had taken there.

During a meeting in Hyannis Port to map out a strategy for Wisconsin, Kenny and Bobby explained to Jack that this move would put them in a position where Jack was favored to win New Hampshire. Because it was next to Massachusetts, it was taken for granted that Jack would win New Hampshire. Then the Kennedy team would argue that it was a similar situation to Wisconsin and Minnesota, where Humphrey was expected to win Wisconsin since Minnesota was the neighboring state. Then Jack would go and make a big deal about having the courage to enter Wisconsin, despite Humphrey being so heavily favored. This would then make any victory by Jack in Wisconsin twice as impressive.

"We had two explanations ready for the press," Kenny explained. "One, if the deal with DiSalle did not jell, and two, if the deal with DiSalle did jell, and then we go into Wisconsin."

The plan was for Bobby to call a press conference, now that it was clear it would be Wisconsin, to explain that with Ohio secured for Kennedy, they planned to go into Wisconsin.

The political theory was that "if Humphrey could be beaten in his own backyard, then he was not a viable national candidate for the Democratic nomination. While you [Jack] will have then overruled me [Bobby], making clear that you have decided that rather than meet Humphrey on neutral ground, say a primary in California, Oregon, Maryland, or Ohio, we will challenge him in his own backyard."

"The theory being," Kenny followed up, "that it shows we are not afraid and that we have this presumed strength or we would not take on Humphrey in what people claim is his political stronghold."

Kenny and Bobby outlined their theory for Jack during an organizational meeting in Hyannis Port. "We would go through the organizational phase of it. Then Bobby would hold a press conference, and that would be the first question: 'Are you entering the Wisconsin primary?'"

Kenny recalled, "Then Bobby would set up the opposite of the situation of New Hampshire, outlining all the gloomy possible problems and prospects that Senator Kennedy would have in a state like Wisconsin, lovable and wonderful though the people were there." As a brother of the candidate and the campaign manager, Bobby recommended, based on everything that he knew, that the senator not enter the Wisconsin primary.

"The New Hampshire versus Wisconsin thing would really cancel each other out. We would tell the press that Hubert should have his next door states, we should have our next door states, and we should meet on a neutral battlefield such as Ohio, California, or Oregon, where neither one of them had any particular advantage. Or in Nebraska, Maryland, or Indiana, where none of these things like proximity to candidates' home states enter into the choice. In these states, Senator Kennedy and Senator Humphrey would in fact meet on neutral grounds.

"We explained this was an attempt to get our psychological picture across, but it also was when the senator would announce that he was going to go into Wisconsin. He would announce he was going in, cite all these problems, but then overrule his brother publicly and make clear that he makes those decisions and that he has decided that the primary route is the only way to go, that he thinks the people ought to have a voice through their vote, that he thinks the people, whether they are in Wisconsin, New Hampshire, or Massachusetts, wherever the people had a chance to express their views on the presidential candidate, that they should be given that option.

"He would indicate that he had long said the primary route was the only fair, equitable manner that the American people had to express themselves. So under those circumstances, no matter how unfortunate geography had made the problem, that he intended to enter each and every primary as a matter of principle."

Jack was quiet for moment, staring at Bobby and Kenny.

Finally, as if he were considering their elaborate explanation carefully, Jack said, "Look, call your press conference, say what you need to say to position the thing. The bottom line is, we just go into every primary and win, starting with Wisconsin." He then rose from the rocking chair, which Bobby's wife, Ethel, had strategically placed, and said, "It is simple enough. We need to just win each and every damn primary."

"We could do that as well," Kenny said with a laugh, "but a little political hardball can't hurt."

"Fine," Jack nodded, warming his hands and, Kenny suspected, his sore back at the fireplace.

"In fact," Kenny explained later, "the senator did all these things and they did occur exactly as we had planned them. Ohio did fall into position on time; it did force the senator into Wisconsin, Pennsylvania, West Virginia. We entered them all. It allowed him to speak at length about how no one should get the nomination who did not allow the American people to hear their views, work for their votes, and expose themselves to the voters. Jack, from the beginning, had felt that in any contest he could beat anybody if given the chance.

"It allowed him to make the point," Kenny continued, "if he could not beat [the other covert candidates] in the primaries, then he could not get the nomination and did not deserve it. He felt that if you could not win the primaries, then you could not win the general election, so you ought not to get the nomination. He had to face up to this and he had to throw the gauntlet down, and he was prepared to do it. This was the route he had chosen from then on in. He was in the primaries, and he spent from then to the end demanding to know why the other candidates were refusing to face the American people. In fact, it was a perfect position from his viewpoint, especially since he was such an effective campaigner on the road and in the area he was working on," Kenny explained. "This is how we laid the thing out to the public and the press; and it was also largely for consumption by other would-be candidates, especially those who would not enter the primaries.

"But," Kenny said, "we had one stop before that. Our next stop, before Wisconsin, was Governor David Lawrence and securing Pennsylvania. Lawrence would represent a different type, but as tough a challenge as DiSalle and Ohio."

"Can't wait for the cold and Wisconsin," Kenny joked to Bobby, who found it all less than amusing.

CHAPTER 15

Wisconsin, West Virginia, and the Catholic Issue

"So," KENNY DECLARED, "this is our situation as I head to the Hotel Wisconsin, much to my dismay. Ohio has fallen into shape. The senator announces. Ohio announces for him and there was the follow-up we earlier detailed. We then have to make an organizational decision. Bobby then called me one day and asked me to come over to his house; this was early January.

"Bobby said to me, 'If we do go into Wisconsin, you will have to go out there full-time and live.'"

Bobby then told Kenny, "We would have to run the same type campaign we ran in Massachusetts, so therefore we needed to have someone full-time from the Kennedy organization actually giving day-to-day direction to their operation in Wisconsin."

"In fact," Kenny recalled, "it is right after Jack's announcement that I moved full-time to Wisconsin." Kenny told Helen, somewhat sarcastically, "Having looked at the state and analyzed it, I am terribly excited about spending January, February, and March in Wisconsin at the Hotel Wisconsin, because there was not much snow on the ground and such a pleasant place to trudge around."

"At least you have a warm coat," she joked, trying not to add to his concern. By now, Helen was as enthusiastic as Kenny was about Jack's candidacy. Besides, she figured, win or lose, Kenny would be home, back to a regular job, as he had promised.

On January 21, in Milwaukee, Jack Kennedy with Jackie at his side announced his plans to enter the Wisconsin Democratic primary.

Wearing his new warm navy winter coat, Kenny kissed Helen and his children good-bye and headed for Wisconsin. Bobby picked him up for the ride to the airport. "Hey, roomie!" Bobby said with a laugh, waving to Helen and the kids.

"Don't," Kenny muttered, giving Bobby a cold stare. Bobby laughed. Kenny was admittedly none too happy to be spending the winter in Wisconsin. He was pleased that they had secured the endorsement of DiSalle in Ohio, but that did not mean he had to be happy about going to spend the coldest months of the year in Wisconsin.

"Figure out how to put the Christmas present together?" Bobby asked as they drove to the airport.

Kenny and Bobby had started a tradition. Each year they would find the most complicated Christmas present to send to each other's children. The plan was that each of them would be stuck putting the present together all night on Christmas Eve. This recent Christmas, Bobby had sent Kenny's children a full-size train set that they could ride in.

Kenny had glared at Bobby. "You just wait till next year."

Bobby laughed. "All night, huh?"

Kenny refused to answer out of pride.

Kenny would spend the next three months "of my lifetime trudging around Wisconsin in the freezing cold with Jerry Bruno and Ivan Nestingen. The real excitement would come," Kenny said sarcastically, "when Bobby came out full-time as we got closer. As promised, he moved into my little hotel room at the Hotel Wisconsin rather than spend the money for his own room."

"I will even pay for you to have your own room," Kenny had offered, as Bobby moved into the room and took over.

"You have no money, Kenny," Bobby reminded him with a chuckle.

"Oh, that's right," Kenny laughed. "I guess I'm stuck with you. Remember, you are the one moving in with me!"

They both shared a tired laugh as they headed downstairs to find someplace to eat.

The terms of entering the Wisconsin primary were certainly less complicated than anything they had faced in Ohio. Wisconsin's governor, Pat Lucey, had indicated in his every manner, direct and indirect, that he would welcome Kennedy's entry and support him. However, Lucey thought it best not to openly commit himself. He would come as close as he could to that and then make available to Kennedy's team his political operation without overtly supporting them. The understanding was, until he could publicly endorse the senator, he would come as close as he could. It would be obvious to anyone that he did support the senator and that the team could build on his operation. This was far different than Ohio, where the Kennedy team had to literally force DiSalle's support for Jack.

With the understanding with Lucey reached, one of the first steps was to secure political people in Wisconsin. One of the first on board, who would become a key player for both Jack and later Bobby, was Jerry Bruno. A tough-minded political type, former marine, and man made from the same mold as the Kennedys, Bruno had come highly recommended by both Senator William Proxmire and Governor Lucey. He would be their first Kennedy man on the ground in Wisconsin and would be able to provide them with a lay of the land. He and Kenny became close friends, and he would eventually be an essential member of Kennedy's advance team, which Kenny ran, both during the 1960 campaign and in the White House.

Bruno was tasked with securing the first Kennedy for President offices in Wisconsin. The offices that Bruno had originally set up were across from Marquette University. The next step was to successfully persuade Ivan Nestingen, then mayor of Madison, to join the team.

Kenny, having just arrived, told Bruno, "I have not met Ivan yet." Kenny recalled that Nestingen, "like Bruno, would prove vital."

Kenny and Ivan would also become the closest of friends, and Justine would quickly recruit Ivan's wife, Jerry, to join the Kennedy operation.

"In truth, being a Catholic," Kenny explained, "his open support would not be beneficial to us. Wisconsin attorney general John Reynolds and a few other political pros in the area were supportive, but since they were all Catholics, it was not the right time, so the search went on to find a non-Catholic. That is how we ended up with Ivan Nestingen."

Ivan was the Norwegian Lutheran mayor of what Kenny termed the "so-called intellectual capital of Wisconsin, and he also had been head of the 'Joe Must Go' club during the horrendous McCarthy days. So he carried impeccable credentials for Kennedy. Ivan was a good solid liberal who was not completely convinced that Senator Kennedy was a real liberal. Ivan met with the senator on several occasions. . . . He feared Jack was a 'convenient liberal,' but after our third meeting, the deal was sealed. Ivan was finally convinced that Jack was the best hope to beat Nixon. It was a very touch-and-go situation. Ivan was the ideal candidate to assume the campaign's leadership role in the state, at least on the surface, assuming that Lucey and Reynolds would run what would consist of the full Wisconsin operation, once we had enough non-Catholic support. Once Ivan acquiesced, Bruno, Ivan, and Lucey went to work. They would be prepared as best they could in case the senator ran in the primary."

As they began to get the lay of the land and set up shop, Kenny and Bobby began to see that Jack's tough approach was having the intended affect among the political professionals. It would make it a bit easier going forward. It had already helped in Wisconsin.

Kenny was convinced: "Watching the going-over that Jack had given DiSalle, other political professionals, such as Lucey, Proxmire, and Ivan

Nestingen, came aboard more easily and quickly. The political professional discovered that Jack Kennedy and his team were not to be taken
lightly."

"Suddenly," as Kenny put it, "the political elite were dealing with hard-
bitten, cold professionals, no matter our age. They realized that we were
tough, knew how to work the system, could organize the precincts, and
unlike Adlai Stevenson, we had a candidate willing to play hardball to get
what he wanted. They suddenly realized the victories in Massachusetts
were not accidents nor luck nor a result of Joe's money. They realized Jack's
rise to prominence was based much more on political shrewdness and skill
than looks or charm or money."

With Ohio secure, Jack's team moved into Wisconsin, West Virginia,
Indiana, and Maryland in a much stronger position.

With the help of Bruno, who laid out the political issues, pitfalls, and
possibilities across the state, both Larry and Kenny looked at the state and
analyzed it. Wisconsin was absolutely critical for Jack. That Kenny was
given sole direction and control of the state operation spoke volumes about
the amount of trust Jack, Bobby, and Joe placed in Kenny.

"Of course," Sandy Vanocur later said to Kenny, "if you lost, you would
have been dead."

Kenny laughed. Truer words were never spoken. "Clearly, they trusted
me," Kenny said. "They knew I could handle it. Quite clearly, if I lost
Wisconsin, it would have been the shortest presidential campaign experience I ever had."

But, Kenny said, Bobby had "more confidence in me than anybody
else for personal reasons. Secondly, it made reasonable sense after the '58
campaign for them to be convinced I could run a state campaign."

It was Kenny's view that Larry would have "done better dealing with the
politicians across the different states than I could."

Bobby wisely agreed with Kenny. As in Massachusetts, Larry was given
the task of working the political professionals.

"I felt Larry was quite good," Kenny explained, "and there was no one else who could handle the professional politicians with his competence and political savvy. He spoke their language."

Kenny explained, "Winning was the only option. If we beat Hubert in his backyard, that should be the end of Hubert. The others were not going to come into the primaries, not after Ohio. With Ohio and Wisconsin back to back, we felt sure that the senator would be on his way to the Los Angeles convention."

As Kenny listened to Bruno lay out the state, Kenny saw immediately why Bobby and Jack had placed Kenny there full-time. Fortunately, Wisconsin was structured in many ways like Massachusetts. With Kenny in charge and with guidance on the local level from Mayor Nestingen and Jerry Bruno, the operation was efficient enough.

Bruno had great political instincts and was, as Kenny said, "the kind of guy who could run with the ball on his own when needed."

In Kennedy campaign parlance, that meant that whatever was dropped in Jerry Bruno's lap, he could handle. The Kennedy team highly valued such skill and flexibility.

What they discovered fairly quickly was that, as they had expected, their experience at the grassroots level was not enough. They needed a two-tiered operation, so Larry O'Brien moved quickly on securing the establishment while the others worked on get-out-the-vote efforts. "Let's be honest," Kenny said later, "Larry did not have the sort of rough edges that Bobby and I had. That worked beautifully for us." As with Massachusetts, "the girls" were brought in, headed by the tough and capable Helen Keyes.

Larry would work the professionals, relying on Joe for the heavy hitters. While Kenny would continue to work with Jack on the day-to-day events around the state, Bobby, Kenny's new roommate, worked on overseeing all aspects. It was a complicated, intense operation.

Justine O'Donnell put it this way: "Bobby and Kenny realized quickly that even though the state looked politically similar to Massachusetts, it was larger, the issues more complicated, and you could not simply translate the Massachusetts model intact. In other words, as [Kenny] said, 'we needed to create a model that could adjust immediately for the political variables in the state.'"

Justine remembered being in the headquarters on one very cold morning when Kenny came in with Bobby after a telephone conference with Jack and Joe Kennedy.

"Put out the call," Bobby instructed. "All hands on deck." Justine hit the phones, from Kennedy family members, to Kennedy cousins, to Kennedy family friends such as Bobby's best pal from Milton, David Hackett, to Jack's friend Lem Billings and anyone and everyone else.

When Kenny heard that Lem was coming, he asked Bobby directly, "I can understand a sharp fellow like David Hackett, but what exactly does Lem Billings do, except to be annoying?" Bobby glared at Kenny. "If anyone annoys you, Kenny, all the better."

The two friends laughed. Such was their friendship, an opportunity to tease one another never lost.

"If you were thin-skinned," Helen Keyes had said, quite correctly, "the Kennedy team was not the place for you. They were a tough, take-no-prisoners but get-the-job-done crowd." Helen Keyes herself was unusual. She was and remained for years the only woman to truly take charge of and head up a Kennedy political campaign.

"It was mostly a man's operation," Justine said, "until Helen came along. She was tough, smart, and did not take guff from anyone. She knew her business and she could hold her own with Kenny and Bobby. They all came to respect her enormously."

Dave Powers teased Justine, "Jack said, 'If he has got a pulse and can walk upright, get 'em here!'"

She did, and her recruits would include both O'Donnell brothers, older brother Cleo and younger brother Warren O'Donnell, who had become best pals with Teddy Kennedy, Jack's youngest brother.

"Can't Kenny have picked a warmer place?" Warren griped with a laugh. Justine handed him his assignment and pointed to the door. "Just go!"

He did. So did everyone else. "I don't think," Cleo said, "we left a door unknocked upon, no matter how high the damn snowdrifts."

The Kennedy family was also enlisted to help, and pretty soon Wisconsin, like Massachusetts, was drowning in famed Kennedy teas. Jackie, for whom this would be a rare campaign experience, also showed up in Wisconsin. She was very pregnant with John Jr. and, following doctor's orders, would participate little beyond Wisconsin and West Virginia. But where she did campaign, she dazzled, even prompting Jack to complain that she was attracting larger crowds than he was.

The Kennedy forces even recruited Pat Kennedy and her husband, Peter Lawford, from Hollywood. "Everyone wanted to meet Pat and Peter," Justine O'Donnell recalled. "They could not be everywhere, so we would set up a tea, promise they'd be there, and then some other Kennedy family member would show up instead. We would claim that they got stuck in Hollywood, when in truth they might be a few doors down hosting another party. But whatever Kennedy family member showed up was exciting enough."

The heavy schedule and cold weather took their toll on everyone. Kenny dreaded the early morning calls, leaving Dave Powers with the dangerous job of waking Jack up at 5:00 a.m. to go shake hands at some plant in the bitter cold. Despite the weather, his bad back, swollen and frozen hands, and a myriad of other health issues, Jack made every meet-and-greet.

Kenny understood the seriousness of the health issues and marveled at Jack's stamina. On one particular trip, they were headed to a TV station for an interview Bruno had arranged. When they arrived, Bruno waited to pick them up and Jack complained about the weather.

"In Wisconsin, this is just a flurry," Bruno said with a chuckle.

"Anywhere else," Kenny complained, "it's called a blizzard."

They headed out anyway on terrible roads, Kenny recalled. "It was not too long before we were stuck. We were trying to make it up this hill. Hell, I could see the TV station tower off in the distance but could not imagine how we would get there."

As the wheel spun helplessly, Kenny jumped out, followed by Powers and then Jack. As Bruno tried to steer, the wind and snow whipping around them, Kenny, Jack, and Dave pushed, prompting Jack to quip, "Jack Kennedy, presidential candidate, lost in a snowdrift somewhere in Wisconsin. He had such potential."

They all burst out laughing just as the car broke loose. Jumping into the car, Kenny shoved Bruno aside and they took off.

"I think," Bruno said, "we broke every speed limit and went through every light there was. I think the wheels even left the ground a few times. It was the scariest ride I had ever been on."

They pulled up in front of the TV station moments before airtime, and Jack jumped out and walked ahead, limping slightly, clearly in pain. Kenny clipped along closely at his heels. Kenny turned just before disappearing after Jack. "Pretty impressive driving, huh?" Kenny asked.

Bruno, still shaken, could only nod.

Kenny smiled. "I know," he said, with that smile just at the edges of his mouth. "Especially when you realize I don't have a driver's license."

Bruno watched in awe as Jack walked quickly into the station, his right hand lightly tapping the wall as he walked. These Kennedy guys were maybe a little crazy, pretty tough, and maybe a little ruthless, but in the end, Bruno figured, "they were going to be a hell of a lot of fun to work with. Jack Kennedy was going to be my kind of president."

"This guy," Bruno said, "was a new kind of politician. I liked what I saw. I was sure most of the Wisconsin voters would as well."

Kenny recalled, "The family was in Wisconsin full-time after a while. In fact, the senator himself was there full-time. The fact is, Bobby spent about as much time in Wisconsin as I did. He would go back once in a while to Washington, but he was living with me at the Hotel Wisconsin.

"I knew Wisconsin was critical. Jack would ask me occasionally to go talk to some professional political fellow, who needed to be spoken to roughly, which I happily did. But I spent 100 percent of my time in Wisconsin, and at a certain point Bobby spent 98 percent of his time in Wisconsin."

While Joe Kennedy wisely stayed home and worked the phones, staying out of the public view, the Kennedy family was everywhere.

"Eunice, Pat, and Jean appeared at receptions and house parties and rang doorbells," Kenny noted. "Teddy even risked his neck making a much-publicized ski jump on his brother's behalf."

"Bobby," Kenny said, "worked twenty-four hours a day."

Hubert Humphrey even began to complain that beyond all the money being thrown into the Kennedy efforts, there were just too many Kennedys. In an often-repeated story, Hubert was quoted as saying, "Teddy or Eunice talks to a crowd, wearing a raccoon coat and a stocking cap, and people think they're listening to Jack. I get reports that Jack is appearing in three or four different places at the same time!"

On April 5, Jack would win the Wisconsin primary, Kenny recalled, with "more popular votes than any candidate in the history of the state's primary, carrying six of the ten congressional districts and getting two-thirds of the delegate votes. That pleased the Kennedy forces, but ultimately it was not enough to sew up the nomination."

Underlying the victory were some ominous signs that would lead them straight into West Virginia. Jack had lost what Kenny and Bobby called "the three so-called Protestant districts in the western part of the state, and he lost to Humphrey in the second district around Madison, an area they had expected to win."

It was a cold bucket of water thrown on what should have been a clear victory for the Kennedy forces.

"His victory," Kenny said, "was belittled because it came from strongly Catholic districts."

Despite losing a neighboring state that should have been an easy win for him, Humphrey felt entitled to claim some sort of moral victory, vowing to fight on to West Virginia.

This enraged the Kennedy forces. Now it was only a spoiler campaign or, as Kenny called it, "a Stop Kennedy campaign. If Hubert could not win Wisconsin, a neighboring state, he could not get the nomination. His decision to go into West Virginia could be construed as nothing more than Kennedy antagonism."

They would have to win a largely Protestant West Virginia and fight again. In Jack's hotel suite at the Milwaukee Hotel, the Kennedy forces watched the returns with no sense of victory.

"What does it mean, Johnny?" his sister Eunice asked.

"It means," Jack said, with exhaustion evident in his voice and without turning to look at her, "we've got to go to West Virginia in the morning. And then we've got to go to Maryland, Indiana, and Oregon and win them all."

The room was quiet.

Symbolically, the Kennedy win in Wisconsin had been a kind of failure. "Damned Catholic thing," was all Jack could say. After the two victories in New Hampshire the previous month and now Wisconsin, the Kennedy team headed to West Virginia aboard the *Caroline* for the next big battle.

The campaign was now swarming with political pros, family members, and friends recruited by various Kennedys. Ralph Dungan, now full-time with the campaign, remembered that the campaign quickly began to break into different operations or camps. "There were two kinds of Kennedy people," he recalled. "There were the pros directly working with the senator and Bobby, who, you know, didn't worry about the moral judgments of political decisions. Headed by O'Donnell, their job was to get the senator elected. That was especially true of Kenny. Kenny dealt with things in a fashion that the senator appreciated. In other words, if the job is to win this primary, let's win it. Then let's win all the primaries; let's win the nomination and get elected. Let's worry about how we dealt with any moral issues after the election.

"O'Donnell especially was tough on everyone, tough on the Kennedy family forces. Everyone knew he spoke for Jack, but he was especially tough on family friends who often were well-meaning but got in the way, screwed things up. People were scared of him. I was not. Even though I worked with Sorensen, because of my union ties I had earned Kenny's acceptance. Kenny could say and do things that Jack wanted done, without Jack having to handle it himself."

Hy Raskin agreed. "Kenny's job, as he saw it, was to get Jack elected, period." It was best not to get in the way.

This tough, no-holds-barred attitude permeated the upper echelons of the Kennedy operation, personified by Kenny, Bobby, Steve, and Joe, and there was little doubt to those who understood Jack Kennedy that this reflected Jack's approach to the campaign. Jack Kennedy had handpicked these men, and their selection in no small measure reflected his personality. It was this seasoned operation that took on Hubert Humphrey in West Virginia. Angry that Humphrey had forced this showdown on them, the Kennedy team members were determined to win, and in winning they would make sure Hubert paid a price.

The Kennedy effort in West Virginia was headed up by Bob McDonough, a tough, capable West Virginian who would prove critical to Kennedy's victory. Kenny and Bobby flew into a meeting McDonough had arranged at the Kanawha Hotel.

Lou Harris's poll, taken just four months prior, showed that Kennedy could beat Humphrey in West Virginia by a comfortable margin of seventy to thirty. Therefore, while Jack, Bobby, and Kenny were not happy about the upcoming battle in West Virginia, they entered it with some confidence.

As they took their seats at the front table in the overcrowded room at the hotel, Bobby was delighted by the turnout. "What are our problems?" Bobby asked pleasantly.

After a moment of awkward silence, a man in the back of the room stood and shouted, "There's only one problem. He's a Catholic. That's our goddamned problem!"

With that, Kenny gulped. He and Bobby exchanged worried glances as the room broke into an uproar. Jack was in Washington, DC, and as soon as the meeting ended, Bobby and Kenny ran to a telephone. Bobby called Jack to give him the bad news. The Catholic issue was back with a vengeance.

"In truth," Kenny told Larry later, "the Catholic issue never went away."

Now the polls were completely reversed, and they were in trouble. Jack was "taken aback by Bobby's discouragement," saying to Bobby and Kenny, "Come on, it can't be that bad. Don't forget the Lou Harris poll that showed us ahead."

"No, Jack," Bobby explained, his face ashen and his hands slightly shaking as he spoke on the phone. "The people in that poll just found out that you were a Catholic."

Jack was quiet. Stunned. "You guys come back to Washington for a few days," Jack said, "and we'll see what we can do with Hubert."

The first strategy turned out to be pointless. Humphrey had no way to get the nomination, so the Irish Brotherhood thought that perhaps he could be persuaded to withdraw. Everyone who could be enlisted was enlisted to call on Hubert. The effort understandably had the opposite effect.

"I am not sure how I would react to a lot of pressure telling me to quit, either," Jack said later. Indeed, Humphrey himself said that he had resented the pressure, though later he came to wish he had listened to them.

The Kennedy team was furious. Hubert had no chance to win. Why stay in other than to stop Jack? In the end, no amount of persuading could get Hubert to change his mind.

To make matters worse, he was being pushed by Lyndon Johnson, Senator Robert Byrd, Symington, and the Stevenson forces to stay in. They all wanted the nomination for themselves, but they were not willing to put their names on the primary ballot. Their collective goal in West Virginia was to use Hubert to stop Jack.

"We went into the campaign," Kenny said, "in a gloomy mood, figuring that the odds were stacked against us and praying that Jack might at least be able to keep Humphrey from winning more than 60 percent of the vote so that we could at least claim the moral victory that Hubert had claimed in Wisconsin."

But Jack, Kenny, and Bobby did not find out until later about the pressures that had been brought to bear on Hubert. "Labor lawyer Arthur Goldberg," Hubert said, "was the key man for the Kennedy forces, and he urged me not to go into West Virginia. I explained to him why I was going in. I told him, 'Look, no matter what happens in this election, you know that I will be out for the ticket.'"

"They said," Hubert remembered afterward, "'please try to conduct yourself so that if things don't go well for you, there can be some rapprochement after the election.' In terms of their promise of a Kennedy–Humphrey ticket, I never believed them."

As Kenny recalled, "Aside from the challenge of the religious issue, the primary in West Virginia became such a blatantly open effort on the part of all the other contenders to stop Kennedy that Jack's Irish temper made him eager to plunge into it."

Jack, however, "was cheerfully unperturbed. He seemed almost eager for the battle. I was thinking, Here we are, starting an entirely new kind of fight against emotional prejudice, with nothing working for us except the courage and personality of this fellow with the unruly hair sitting beside me in the back cabin of the *Caroline*."

When they arrived later that afternoon at the Kennedy headquarters in Charleston, West Virginia, Bob McDonough had already brought together a crowd. But the greeting was something Kenny and Jack had never experienced before. The crowd was polite but distant, standoffish. They seemed almost to pull back from Jack when he went to shake their hands, as if they might catch something. There were several Pinkerton agents there to protect Jack and the headquarters, something else Kenny had not yet experienced.

"Most of the crowd moved away from Jack as he approached," Kenny said. "They moved into the shadows across the street. Only two men approached him to shake his hand."

As they headed into the dreary Kennedy headquarters, Jack walked along quietly in front of Kenny, his hands stuffed in his coat pockets. Kenny sensed Jack's surprise at the outright hostility of the West Virginians.

Kenny said, "As we walked down the hallway toward the clerk's office and then on to the Kennedy offices, people in the office and in the hallways literally shrank back against the wall to let him pass."

Jack turned to Kenny with a wry smile. "Those two guys who approached you must have been a couple of visiting Catholics from Pennsylvania."

They laughed. "At least," Kenny joked, "we have not totally lost our sense of humor." Not yet anyway.

When they finally had some time alone in Jack's suite at the Kanawha Hotel, Jack turned to Kenny and shook his head. "Well, I guess you and Bobby weren't exaggerating."

Kenny smiled faintly. No, they had not been.

"Let's call everyone," Jack said. "If they want a fight, let's give them one."

They were in West Virginia now. As ugly as the fight was shaping up to be, Jack, Kenny, and Bobby put out the word to "summon all the troops."

"The first time Jack spoke out about the religious issue," Kenny recalled, "was before a big crowd at a noon rally on the main street in Morgantown."

The crowd was surprised. So were Kenny and Jack, who later said that he had simply gotten tired of it and had decided it was time to address the issue head-on.

"I was with him all day," Kenny said, "and I had no idea he was going to do it."

"Nobody," Jack declared during his speech, "asked me if I was a Catholic when I joined the United States Navy."

Kenny declared that the entire thing was "so unexpected, like having a bucket of water thrown in my face."

It was the first time anyone recalled Jack addressing the Catholic issue publicly, and especially in front of a Protestant audience. He went with what Dave and Kenny called "fire and dash," rhetorically demanding to know whether forty million Americans had given up their right to run for the presidency the day they were baptized Catholics.

From there, Jack made it even more personal, exclaiming, "That wasn't the country my brother died for in Europe, and nobody asked my brother if he was a Catholic or a Protestant before he climbed into an American bomber to fly his last mission."

If Jack had asked beforehand, Kenny, Bobby, and Dave would have advised against such a speech. Jack, as usual, went with his gut.

Jack believed that the people of West Virginia were straightforward fighters, no-nonsense people who, no matter how they viewed his religion, appreciated his candor. The victory to come would show that once again Jack's decision to go with his gut was the right one.

When they climbed back in the car to go to the next stop, Jack turned to Kenny, who was seated in the back, and asked, "How did it go?"

"Good," Kenny replied, though he admitted later that he was still in shock. "Keep it up."

Jack used a similar version of the same comments in every subsequent speech. And he gave so many speeches that he eventually lost his voice, forcing Ted Sorensen, a Protestant, to pinch-hit for him, an irony that was not lost on the Brotherhood.

Later, Jack laughed it off. He had Sorensen give the damned speech because Sorensen wrote it!

Jack felt, and Kenny later agreed, that they had finally broken the back of the religious issue with a combination punch: First, at Joe's behest, they brought in Franklin Roosevelt Jr., who raised his father's name at every occasion possible, putting up two fingers and saying, 'My daddy and Jack's daddy were like this.'"

For West Virginians, FDR remained a god, and this was a powerful endorsement. On several occasions Franklin Roosevelt Jr. questioned Hubert's patriotism in both subtle and not too subtle ways, asking why Humphrey had not served when Jack was, after all, a "war hero."

Humphrey, who was legitimately 4-F, resented this, but probably not as much as his wife, Muriel, did. Such slights are not easily overcome. This was, as Kenny called it, "one step too far."

Once again, the slight was blamed on Bobby, not because Bobby told Roosevelt to do it but because he did not tell him to stop saying it. Bobby was all about victory. He knew they were still running behind and would leave no weapon in their arsenal unused.

Kenny was not sure where the idea of a debate came from. He later said it was Hubert's idea, which was not exactly correct. Hubert said the idea came from the Kennedys. In Kenny and Larry's view, Jack had all the edge on the issues, but nothing of substance could be debated on television as long as Hubert kept pressing the Catholic issue.

Hubert was nonetheless sure that the idea for the debate had come from the Kennedy side. Hubert had first broached it in Wisconsin, but Kennedy, then ahead, had avoided it. Now that he was behind, Jack wanted the opportunity.

"I was in the middle of a meeting, a conference call with labor leaders, and I received a telephone call saying, 'Senator Kennedy has accepted your invitation to debate,'" Humphrey recalled. "I was surprised. I had never invited him to debate. I knew it was not my strength."

But once he accepted, Humphrey could not back out. It was a Kennedy ploy, and it worked.

The reason for Jack's wanting the debate, which took place on May 4, was that it played beautifully to his strengths. Jack had clearly mastered the new medium of television.

"The debate itself," Kenny said later, "was inconclusive because of the similarity of the liberal stands both candidates took on the campaign issues."

However, just as with the Nixon–Kennedy debates that would be broadcast shortly thereafter, Jack was poised and cool, witty, fast on his feet, and confident.

Bobby pushed Jack hard before the debate to accuse Hubert of being a stalking horse for the "ghost candidates." Ever the prosecutor, Bobby wanted to "have Jack handle himself like it was the McClellan Committee," as Kenny teased.

Jack knew better. He seemed completely at ease, in sharp contrast to Hubert, who, according to his own later admission, "was nervous and uncomfortable."

"Look," Jack explained to Bobby, "I could say to him, 'You're not a real candidate. You are just a stalking horse for Johnson or Stevenson.' And Hubert would say, 'That is wrong. I am a real candidate.' Where does that leave anybody? What good does that do? We still have to show we can defeat Hubert and the Catholic issue at the polls."

Jack's second major rebuttal to the religious issue came in a Sunday evening broadcast on May 8, before voting day. Jack appeared on television and delivered what Kenny called "a serious and moving plea for tolerance, explaining that a Catholic president who allowed his decisions to be influenced by his church would be breaking the oath of office and could be impeached."

Dick Donahue, another Boston Irishman and extended member of the Irish Brotherhood, was with Jack in the TV studio. Donahue noted, "The speech, beautifully done by Sorensen, was considered by many to be one of the greatest speaking performances of Jack's entire career."

Another main component of the campaign was money. Joe spent it with abandon in West Virginia, as he had in Wisconsin. Humphrey was not wrong to feel that the primary was being "inundated with money." Historian Robert Dallek noted that "where Humphrey's total expenditures on the campaign amounted to about $25,000, the Kennedys spent $34,000 on TV programming alone." But it was not Kennedy money alone. Rumors have long been whispered about a favor involving Joe and Frank Sinatra and some friends in Chicago, but it was not as unusual as it might sound.

The final element, which may or may not be true, was, as one friend described it, "a little help from our friends in Chicago." Apparently, Joe Kennedy did make a few well-placed calls to Kennedy admirer Frank Sinatra, asking for help. According to Tina Sinatra, Frank's daughter, "Joseph Kennedy asked the singer and actor to talk to the Mafia about securing the labor union vote in the crucial West Virginia primary."

Frank, for his part, was happy to make the call and help. Chicago mob boss Sam Giancana assured Frank that "the request would be met with a couple of phone calls" on his end. Believe it or not, Kenny noted, "they all planned to vote for Jack as well. A vote was a vote." And a call for a little help was just a call for a little help.

Frankly, Kenny said, "Jack did not involve himself in such matters," leaving it to Kenny, Bobby, and Joe.

Kenny said later, "The earthy and realistic people of West Virginia were accustomed to seeing the local candidate for sheriff carrying a little black bag that contained something other than a few bottles of bourbon whiskey. This is one of those stories where less is more."

On May 10, the day the votes were cast in West Virginia, despite the effort on all fronts, the Kennedy forces remained worried. While Jack had made great headway on the religious issue, it seemed to still lurk just underneath the surface.

"Bigotry," Jack said, "is hard to overcome. Maybe we did. I hope we did."

Kenny recalled, "On the morning of the primary voting, Jack flew to Washington to spend the day with Jackie and to appear with her at the Democratic women's luncheon. When Bobby and I drove back to Charleston after watching the *Caroline* take off, we felt our presidential campaign was over."

Jack had prevailed in primaries in Illinois, Massachusetts, and Indiana after his victory in Wisconsin. Despite these successes, however, a loss to Hubert in West Virginia would, as Kenny said, "be a barrier blocking Kennedy from the party's nomination."

A loss would be pinned squarely on the religious issue. "They would say, 'If he can't win there, he can't beat Nixon, because of the damned religious thing,'" Jack said to Kenny over a drink one night after a long, hard day of campaigning.

Kenny demurred. He remained convinced that there had to be a way. As Kenny and Bobby climbed out of the car after seeing Jack off, they trudged back toward the West Virginia headquarters.

Bobby moaned, "We might as well stay home and watch the convention on television. Damn that Hubert Humphrey."

"Don't be such an optimist, Bobby," Kenny teased, trying to lighten the mood.

But Bobby had spoken too soon. Hubert had told his aides in the closing weeks of the campaign that he felt the primary slipping away from him. His assumption had been correct.

"If only we'd had more time and money," Humphrey would later say. Thankfully for Jack, they did not. At nine o'clock that evening, as the first returns began to come in from a precinct in Hardy County, "Kennedy had ninety-six votes to Humphrey's thirty-six," Kenny said. It was an early sign that West Virginia was about to seal Jack Kennedy's ticket to Los Angeles.

In the end, Jack Kennedy won by a 35 percent margin, soundly defeating Hubert Humphrey in Protestant West Virginia and sealing the nomination.

Jack correctly feared, though, that reports of the Catholic issue having been put to bed were greatly exaggerated.

Kenny and Bobby called Jack at his home in Washington, DC, where he had had dinner and gone to a movie with his friends Ben and Toni Bradlee.

When they got back, Kenny said, "Jack found a note from Bobby left for him by his assistant, Provi Paredes, and he let out a whoop of joy, opened a bottle of champagne, and drank a quiet toast with Jackie and the Bradlees before flying aboard the *Caroline* to West Virginia to thank supporters and workers."

With Hubert's defeat in West Virginia, Jack had the nomination. No matter which other ghost candidates still envisioned opportunities for themselves, Jack and Kenny knew better.

So did Hubert. "We went into West Virginia, and I made some statements that I would have been better off if I had not made then, in retrospect—primarily about money—because I sensed I was being inundated. I never made them personally about President Kennedy as such."

Jack noted with pleasure that he had even won Sophia, hometown of West Virginia senator Robert Byrd, who was a major supporter of Lyndon Johnson's ghost candidacy.

Bobby studied the telegram from Hubert conceding defeat and congratulating Jack. "God, this must be awful for poor Hubert, ending up this way after working so very hard in two states." Bobby made his way in the cold, icy rain to Hubert's headquarters. Both sides remained somewhat bitter, but Bobby was determined to put everything behind them. Walking into the Humphrey headquarters, Bobby, who underneath the toughness could be an emotional man, as Kenny well knew, moved to Muriel Humphrey's side and gave her a hug.

Hubert recalled, "When Bobby arrived in our room, he moved quickly to Muriel and kissed her on the check. Muriel stiffened, stared, and turned in silent hostility, walking away from him, fighting tears and angry words."

While the anger remained that night, Jack, in his characteristic fashion, would ultimately work things out with Hubert.

"Sure," Hubert said, "I was angry. I gave John Bailey a good working-over a couple of times. But after the West Virginia primary, I went over that evening and complimented and congratulated Jack Kennedy. Afterward, I had a visit with him in Washington, in my office. He came down to see me, and we talked about the future and Los Angeles."

Later, Hubert would admit something he had up until then told only his beloved wife, Muriel. "I never said it publicly or to my staff, but I felt we were licked in the last week. I just felt it was over. There was nothing to be done at that point but see the damn thing through."

Kenny put it this way: "It was all over. Jack had won. He was now going to get the nomination. All we had now was the final cleanup work as we moved toward Los Angeles. There was now no question that the senator would get the nomination. The chips were beginning to fall into place. We proceeded from here to other primaries, now that the teeth had been pulled from the opposition behind Hubert."

Jack agreed and told Kenny that he firmly believed that "with this victory, the opposition would be placed in an extremely difficult position. If they were afraid to meet me in a state that was so disadvantageous to us as West Virginia, it seemed to me that they would not dare take us on in some of the other states."

From here forward, Kenny explained, "We made a basic mental assumption that the ball game was over, and unless we made some major mistake, John Kennedy would be nominated in Los Angeles on the first ballot."

Kenny would later recall that one evening while relaxing at the White House with the president after a busy day, Jack reflected on the critical events and decisions that had brought them to 1600 Pennsylvania Avenue. He also reflected on how often the most important events were ones over which they had no control. How they reacted to those events made all the difference.

"Just think," Jack said to Kenny, "if Wisconsin had turned out differently, we might not be sitting here right now."

As Kenny said later, "Like his fortunate defeat in the floor fight for the vice presidential nomination in 1956, Kennedy's less-than-decisive win over Hubert Humphrey in the 1960 Wisconsin primary was a disappointment that later turned into a blessing."

Jack's symbolic loss in Wisconsin gave Hubert just enough hope to "challenge Kennedy once more in the West Virginia primary, forcing Kennedy to run against a Protestant opponent in a Bible Belt state that was 95 percent Protestant, where Kennedy's Catholicism was the burning issue."

In West Virginia, Jack would carry forty-eight of fifty-five counties. Kennedy's victory was, as Kenny said, "much to the astonishment of most of the Democratic leaders around the country, who then made haste to climb aboard the Kennedy bandwagon."

Challenges still lay ahead if they were going to win the nomination, but they had truly come a long way since the first meeting in Palm Beach just a year before.

CHAPTER 16

Hardball Politics in Pennsylvania

Pennsylvania was the final piece of the puzzle in the Brotherhood's strategy. Pennsylvania governor David Lawrence was particularly difficult.

Kenny noted, "We ran into a Catholic governor of a big northern state who simply did not want to come out publicly for Kennedy. So we had to do some maneuvering." The difference, Kenny later explained, "was that a Pat Lucey of Wisconsin, who was in the same position, was able to make his network available and thus by circumstance supported us, then could come out publicly. Lucey did not face the same political dilemmas other governors faced. Governor Lawrence was in a reasonably untenable position. He was fighting very hard and being very unshakable about it. Senator Kennedy was very disturbed that he was unable to shake Lawrence. Pennsylvania was a key to his thinking for a certain first-ballot victory in Los Angeles. As with DiSalle, we needed to play hardball and force Lawrence, but he was a much tougher nut to crack. The senator was using every tool possible to shake Governor Lawrence and the Pennsylvania delegation. We rode up on the plane. It was going to be a closed meeting with Lawrence."

As they sat on the *Caroline*, discussing their approach to Lawrence, Kenny said to Jack, "Don't you think it is about time you either say to him or infer, 'The fact of the matter is you are going to go to Los Angeles with a pretty good block of delegates; that everybody must think it is about time that a Catholic candidate with your support, having won every primary, having beaten everyone who ran in the primary, and having won every contest possible goes to Los Angeles and wins on the first ballot'? We should make clear to him that the public will find it unacceptable that a candidate such as yourself, who has won every primary, is defeated by these backroom deals simply because he is a Catholic . . ."

"We kicked it back and forth," Kenny recalled. "[Jack] ran it in his own mind and went through three or four different phases, but finally he said, 'Kenny, I don't know. I would rather not go there. I think that is something we don't have to do or need to do just yet. My feeling is once you start threatening people, you've put yourself in a corner. To do this publicly at this luncheon gives Lawrence no maneuvering room. If we need to go there, I will let you know. Then you can take it and run with it, privately. I will disavow your actions. But not yet.'"

The *Caroline* landed, and Jerry Bruno, now fully on board, had arranged for a car to pick them up. They went directly to the luncheon. It was well attended and the governor got up to introduce Senator Kennedy.

As Kenny recalled, "The governor's introduction was not very warm. He inferred during his introduction that the primary victory should not be misunderstood, that there were many good candidates, who because of the circumstances had not been in the primary but should still be considered.

"The governor then went on to say that this should not be considered a political meeting or an endorsement of any kind, that this was simply a political meeting to give everyone a chance to meet the candidate, who in this case was John Kennedy. The governor was obviously trying to head off anything from happening at that meeting. We had learned later that prior to our coming there had been heated arguments and fights about why they simply don't endorse Senator Kennedy at this meeting! How can they have all the big states around them for Kennedy and not be for Kennedy? The

Pennsylvania delegation was very upset with the governor, but he would not be moved.

"However, when Jack rose to speak, he had no way of knowing that much of the delegation agreed with his position, and that position was that Governor Lawrence, as head of the delegation, should come out publicly and endorse Jack Kennedy; after all, he had won the primary. This would only strengthen Jack's position heading into the Democratic National Convention in Los Angeles, which was the next stop."

By the time they arrived, the governor was very upset and it was obvious, though Kenny made clear, "Neither he, Kenny, nor the Senator had any idea at that time why he was so upset."

"Governor Lawrence's introduction," Kenny said, "was close to being considered rude. The senator got up, and in much better English than I would have used," Kenny recalled sarcastically, "he laid it on the line for them."

As he watched Jack's face during the impolite introduction, Kenny later recalled, "It was evident that the senator was upset. I could tell as Governor Lawrence was speaking that the senator was very angry. He got up and laid out the facts, as the senator liked to say, 'cold and hard' to them, that these political leaders better think what was going to happen to the Democratic Party if the candidate who has won all the primaries and amassed all the delegates can be denied the nomination simply because he is an Irish Catholic. He told them in an ice-cold tone that they better think long and hard about what will be left of the Democratic Party should they follow this course. He then launched into a very tough ten-minute speech about why he should be the nominee and why he would win the presidency and why he would make a good president. He ended with a very tough—and I mean tough—political attack directly on Governor Lawrence. He kicked him good and hard where it hurts the most. I was not surprised to see this side of the senator. I knew he was angry, but I think Governor Lawrence was in shock. Because the senator was always so gracious with people, it sometimes shocked them to see this tough, very tough, side of him. Often these people, like Lawrence and others, underestimated the senator."

"As Jack spoke," Kenny said, "all the color drained from Governor Lawrence's face. He was stunned."

When Jack finished, he stood for a moment, waiting for the weight of his words to sink in. Then he moved to sit down, catching Kenny's eye and giving him a look.

Kenny nodded.

This was exactly what Kenny believed Lawrence needed. Kenny said, "There was a muttering in the room and nodding of heads in agreement and some cold looks directed at Lawrence. It was the toughest, coldest, and most direct speech I had ever heard John Kennedy give publicly to a politician. It was given in the coldest, toughest, most metallic tone that I have ever heard from John Kennedy. There was no question about exactly what Senator Kennedy meant. There was no question exactly what the threat was and exactly to whom he was speaking. He never took his eyes off Lawrence and it was cold as ice."

"By the time Jack was through," Kenny said, "Governor Lawrence looked flushed and got up suddenly, almost knocked his chair over, and rushed out the door, claiming to his startled aides and the entire room that he had a meeting to go to. Though it was interesting: his staff seemed to know nothing of this and were so busy falling over Senator Kennedy, they did not even care that he had left. Most of them were indeed delegates themselves. Lawrence did not even say good-bye to the senator, just fled the room. The rest of the people at the meeting suddenly spontaneously got up, cheered, and swarmed the senator!"

All Kenny could do was stand back and enjoy the moment; this sort of tough-guy politics is what Kenny felt had been needed. Even though Jack had won Pennsylvania and other later primaries such as Maryland and Oregon, still the political establishment had resisted him. It was time, especially with Lawrence, who should have been on their side, to kick in some political doors. Kenny felt that was exactly what Jack had done verbally, and nobody could do that better than he could.

Kenny moved around the room after the meeting to talk with a few people and get a feel for their true reaction to what clearly had been an unusual political moment.

"No politician I know," Kenny said, "would have had the guts to do what Jack Kennedy did that day. They would have been too afraid of offending someone, but the senator knew it was time to get tough. Get tough he did.

"I watched in amazement as the mavericks were falling all over Kennedy, which was annoying the regulars more than anything. But there were these big tough steelworkers and hardworking fellows and they were asking for him to sign his photograph and wanted to get his autograph.

"The political leaders were getting photos signed for their daughters and their sons; it went on and on. It was in the end a very successful meeting from our point of view. He shook Lawrence pretty good and shook up the regulars as well, which in my view is what needed to be done.

"[Jack] then talked to Bill Green, who was the Philadelphia leader, and Bill was enthusiastic. Bill felt he had scared and stunned the heck out of Lawrence. Green was pleased. Green felt the message had to be delivered to Lawrence: 'Enough of this crap. You are not a kingmaker and the days of political backroom deals with only the insiders involved, well, John Kennedy would not stand for it.' Those days were over, and about that the senator had left no room for doubt.

"As we left the meeting to return to the *Caroline* for our next stop, we rode in silence for a moment. Then he turned to me with that look."

Kenny recalled, "I smiled and said, 'Senator, if that's being nice and not tough, I would hate to see just what tough looked like.'

"He shook his head and said, 'Just as long as you don't think I was taking your advice.'

"'Never, Senator,' I said, 'never crossed my mind for a moment.'

"We laughed."

As Jack had at first predicted to Kenny, publicly threatening a political leader was not without unintended consequences, as they were to find out the next day.

"The next day," Kenny recalled, "there was a story written by Earl Mazzo that Kennedy himself had raised the Catholic issue and that he had literally threatened the Pittsburgh leaders that, in fact, if they did not support him, then Catholics would take their revenge at the polls in November.

"He wrote a really damaging a story out of this meeting, which obviously had been leaked by Lawrence. We were very upset. We felt it was petty and unprofessional, since it was supposed to be a closed meeting and Lawrence had obviously done this in retaliation."

Jack showed Kenny the paper during breakfast the next morning. "When we get to Los Angeles," Jack said angrily, "I may let you have a few well-placed words with Lawrence."

Kenny nodded. "Just tell me when."

While Jack had been incredibly and publicly tough on Lawrence, it was a closed meeting, as agreed upon, and there was a sort of unwritten rule that you did not leak to the press, at least not in these circumstances and on your own.

"In other words," as Bobby said, "it is the cheapest of politics to use the press as a club against Jack, when in truth Lawrence fled the room. He should have stayed and had it out with Jack then and there if he felt that strongly."

Kenny and Jack completely agreed.

To leak it was "rather cheap politics," as Jack said to Kenny.

Further disconcerting was that Earl Mazzo was known to be a friend of Kennedy press secretary Pierre Salinger, so Jack ordered Kenny to be sure that the story had not been leaked out by their camp.

"It had not," Kenny said after checking. "Jack was relieved. The second concern he had was perhaps that he had hit Lawrence too hard. Then the more he thought about it, the more he decided, no, he had done the right thing by hitting Lawrence right where it hurt. He could not understand Lawrence."

Finally Jack said to Kenny, "The hell with it. It is about time we laid all our cards on the table, because if they deny me the nomination by back-room deals, I will follow through on my threat. So they might as well know it. We don't have time to play games with them. Governor Lawrence needs to get on board."

Kenny completely agreed. He simply could not understand Governor Lawrence and what Lawrence thought he would get out of this at all. If Jack won the nomination without Lawrence, then went on to beat Nixon, then Lawrence would be out in the cold.

"Politically," Kenny said to Jack, "it makes no sense that I can see."

As the Kennedy forces battled with Governor Lawrence before the convention for the Pennsylvania delegates, Bill Green, a very critical and important political leader from Philadelphia, looked on in the background. Kenny and Bobby knew Bill Green nominally from the McClellan Committee days. He had been involved in peripheral fashion when Kenny came down to Washington to work with Bobby on the committee.

At that time Bill Green was under indictment for engaging in an alleged conspiracy having to do with a contract at the Pennsylvania Armory with a labor leader, which in some way is how he came to the attention of the committee.

"Bill had been very ill after the indictment and had gone into the hospital and had come close to dying. The case had to be postponed four or five times, as Bill was literally at death's door," Kenny recalled. "I thought to myself and said to Bobby later, 'If he comes out of the case clean, which by all reports I got he should, and if he lives, we've got an excellent connection here.' Bobby just stared at me in disbelief, I think," Kenny said with a laugh. Shaking his head, Bobby said to Kenny, "And they call me ruthless!"

In the end, to Kenny's relief and most certainly Bill Green's, the case was dismissed before Bill got out of the hospital. "The judge attacked the United States attorney for bringing the indictment in the first place and said it was clearly politically motivated," Kenny said.

"Now I had never actually met Bill Green as of this moment," Kenny remembered. "I don't know whether he was guilty or innocent. He was another chairman of a city committee. At that time, I didn't then understand the Philadelphia political complex or how strong they would be with a candidate such as Kennedy. But in 1959, I went up there to speak at a Harvard Club dinner at the request of a couple of classmates of mine.

"I had been to Pittsburgh, the western part of the state," Kenny continued, "and at that time I had sort of assumed Pennsylvania as a minor responsibility in the few times when I was not traveling with the senator, so I wanted to find out as much as I could about the situation in Philadelphia. Dick Dilworth was the mayor of Philadelphia at this time. He is for Kennedy in any possible way, but Dilworth took the position that he could not deliver one-tenth of one vote if Jim Clark, who was the finance chairman of the party, and in fact the power behind the throne at this time, and Bill Green were not for whatever position he took.

Kenny told Bobby and Jack later, "Dilworth made clear, he would come out for Kennedy, if Kennedy wanted him to, but he felt it was best from Kennedy's viewpoint that he did not take any action until the Pennsylvania delegation took some action or until Bill Green could be in place in some position where he would either not be angry or would himself come along and support Kennedy."

In particular, Kenny explained, "[Bill Green] felt the Kennedy brothers, especially Bobby, were in fact 'cops,' and he did not like them very much. They were not his kind of Democrats. He felt [Bobby], in particular, was a bully. Jack Kennedy was a left-wing liberal, and he said to me, 'The only thing worse than a cop and a liberal was, well, I can't put on the tape.'

"He explained that he was struggling about whom to support. Stevenson was unspeakable to him; he liked Lyndon Johnson but could not take much of him." Kenny recalled, "He later told me, and Lyndon told me the same story, that Lyndon, [and] Rayburn had had a long conversation with Bill Green, and they tried to pressure him to go with Lyndon. They had about the same conversation with Green that they had with Daley in Chicago, and as with Daley it backfired, just too heavy-handed."

But Bill Green, like Mayor Daley in Chicago, said to Johnson and Rayburn point-blank, "Look, we can't be for you in this city, Philadelphia; you can't win; you can't carry the state. You are a nice fellow; I like you; you are a good majority leader, but I could not possibly be for you in a state like Pennsylvania and survive politically."

Fortunately for Kenny, his road was made a bit easier about this time with the help of Congressman Eugene "Gene" Keogh. "He just happened to be Billy Green's best friend in the Congress, and they are very close," Kenny noted, "and they had lived together for years.

"Gene Keogh was, of course, a total Jack Kennedy supporter all the way. Keogh has been working on Bill Green through all of this, explaining that John Kennedy had nothing to do with the indictment and that he only served on the McClellan Committee because his brother asked him. He pushed and pushed. He worked Green relentlessly and used every tool at his disposal." Kenny said with a laugh, "He has many. Gene has great influence in [Green's] final decision. But at this time [Green] was for anybody but Kennedy, and Keogh is working on [Green]. Rayburn is working on [Green] in the other direction.

"Mr. Kennedy had some contact with Green and eventually went to see him. This meeting with Joe Kennedy," as Kenny recalled, "turned out to be critical. I came to understand and I got to know Bill Green very well. He is at heart a young Irish boy who fought his way up from nothing and was rather honored to have Joe Kennedy, who he admired as an Irishman, who had made it and become rich, [support him]. Kennedy was probably his father's age, and Green's father had died young. So Joe Kennedy worked this angle, and Green probably understood or admired Joe Kennedy much more than he did the boys who he saw as rich and spoiled. Joe Kennedy had come up the hard way and done it on his own and could speak Green's language. Keogh could speak Green's language, and all these tough Irishmen were for Kennedy. It was now becoming pretty untenable for Bill Green to not be for Jack Kennedy.

"I could see all this," Kenny said, "and finally we let Jack loose on him. I could see he was melting Green, especially by the last visit. So, after some period of time, Gene Keogh tells me, Bill Green went over to Senator Kennedy's office and the compact is sealed. Green is for Kennedy all the way.

"He now understands—thanks largely to Joe—that Green does not just become a politician for Kennedy; he becomes a Kennedy leader. There is no question that Green was under tremendous pressure from his own organization; they all wanted to be for Kennedy.

"So, at some point, Green made the decision, whether it was in contact with the father or Jack directly I am not sure; I know Keogh played a very important part. Later, just as a footnote after the convention, Keogh, Green, and I became fast friends and went out for dinner and drinks, and Keogh was relentless, prodding Green about how late he was to get on board. Course, Bill Green had been pretending to everyone that he was the most original Kennedy person of all time."

"Politics," Jack noted, "is interesting in how it really works and how often it comes down to these personal connections."

Kenny said, "The bottom line is I know these facts to be true and this is the background to how we got Bill Green on board. Our plan was to get Bill Green to get Governor Lawrence. Funny how it worked out. That is why politics is a fascinating process.

"The senator knew that Governor Lawrence could not go to the convention with 70 or 80 percent of his delegation going off the reservation for Kennedy. In fact, if Green went, Lawrence was cute enough to realize that he could not even hold the Allegheny County officials once the big Philadelphia complex went, and Philadelphia and those that they were allied with would represent forty or better of Pennsylvania's eighty delegates.

"The key was, mentally, to separate Jack Kennedy from Bob Kennedy. As he and I got to know each other, he began to separate Bob Kennedy from the McClellan Committee and John McClellan, and then he began to forget the whole thing.

"Then Bill began to say to me, well, you know it is awfully hard for me to be for someone who does not even have the guts to put their name on the ballot and run in the campaign. If they haven't got the guts to go in against Kennedy, I don't want to for them. It is awful tough to get these [delegates] who are in fights every day politically, fighting for their political lives, to support a candidate who cannot even be for himself."

From Kenny's perspective, all these things were indications that Bill had shifted his thinking and that as a good politician he was now laying the groundwork for his transition.

As Kenny remembered it, "This is where Pennsylvania was as we arrived in Los Angeles for the convention. The senator, Bobby, and I analyzed and deduced as politicians that Pennsylvania had no place else to go. We also realized there was nothing more we could do about it. The fact was, if Bill Green goes, Lawrence goes; if Bill Green stayed, Lawrence will stay and attempt to deny us the Pennsylvania delegation as a bargaining point. But there was probably nothing else [Bill Green and Dave Lawrence] can do at this stage. The delegation was all picked. Reporters would go talk to Green and he was very cute and said, 'Well, we have to wait till we caucus.' This is where Pennsylvania was left, and now the entire East is accounted for and we have to wait on Green, who was the key to Pennsylvania."

From here the Kennedy forces left Pennsylvania and began a swing west, going to the state conventions and meeting the leadership as a buildup toward their arrival for the convention in Los Angeles in July.

"We went to a big meeting in Minnesota at the hotel; Senator Humphrey was there, Governor [Orville] Freeman, Fritz Mondale, and many others. The Minnesota group was pressuring very hard to be for Kennedy. There was now no question that 20 or 30 percent were for Kennedy now. Freeman was strongly for Kennedy but trying to follow the leadership of Humphrey and trying to find where this leadership was taking them," Kenny remembered.

Bobby and Kenny were keenly aware that Senator Humphrey and Governor Freeman were fighting, and [they] were doing their best to exploit it. Having defeated Humphrey by now in West Virginia, they were eager to push everyone into the Kennedy camp as they headed toward Los Angeles.

"Senator Kennedy made an excellent speech and shook hands with them all, and it was an excellent meeting," Kenny recalled. "We then had a breakfast meeting with them the next day and spoke to each individually. But Senator Humphrey ran the meeting. He ran it very well."

Once again, Humphrey's people arranged with Kenny for Jack and Hubert to take a private meeting. This was in the wake of the West Virginia [primary], where Kennedy defeated Humphrey and afterward, unbe-knownst to all but a few, Jack and Hubert had several private meetings.

"The goal of which," Kenny said, "was to get Hubert to come out publicly and support Jack. The bottom line of the meetings was that Senator Kennedy came away with the impression that Humphrey would not be against him if Adlai were not in it. In other words, if you promise Stevenson, I will say yes. The senator knew that would be something he would never do. Hubert knew that as well, but part of politics is power, and Hubert wisely wanted to go into the convention controlling his delegates, so he would have some cards to play."

Much to Kenny and Jack's annoyance, news of the meetings was leaked, and there was some speculation building that Hubert was looking for the number-two spot. Kennedy had not offered it. As far as Kenny knew, Jack had not given candidates for the vice presidency any consideration.

"Jack Kennedy was a practical man," Kenny noted. "He was not one to offer the number two for a nomination he had yet to secure; nor would Hubert have taken such a thing seriously. Hubert is too savvy a politician and knows until you are actually the nominee, you aren't the nominee. There was no more than that to the meetings. There is nothing more. In fact, that was as close as you can get or we could get to pinning Hubert down; you know the way he is; he is for everything until he is against it. We left Minnesota with the feeling that when we got to the floor of the convention, that Freeman would be with us and at least half the delegation would like to be for Kennedy. That was the best we could do at this stage."

From there the Kennedy team went from Iowa to South Dakota. "All the candidates were speaking at an outdoor affair," Kenny recalled. "I remember Jimmy Symington was playing his guitar. Stu was unable to make it, but Jimmy was playing his guitar and replacing his father. All the candidates were there—that meant Symington and Kennedy. A meeting had been set up to meet with all the delegates. Kennedy went in and met with all the delegates, and this was a George McGovern operation totally." McGovern was going to run in the Senate against Bobby and Kenny's old friend from the McClellan days, Karl Mundt. Kenny remembered George McGovern saying, only half-jokingly, "It is going to look a little difficult in a state like South Dakota to have an all-green, Irish ticket. I am sure I cannot sell or convince anybody else that Kennedy, McGovern, and Fitzgerald is not the all-green ticket in South Dakota." Although he was for Kennedy, George was rather nervous about his own future. With very good cause. Quite frankly, both Senator Kennedy and I believed that George McGovern would have defeated Karl Mundt if Kennedy had not been on the ticket." As the senator said, "This is sometimes the price you pay in politics." But McGovern, who had much ahead of him politically, handled the defeat with "as much grace as one can, given it was the other guy who took you down," as Kenny described it.

They met with the South Dakota delegates, all of them downstairs in a hotel room. They were very friendly, with good questions. "The senator spent at least an hour with them. As usual in these states, 20 to 30 percent of them were behind-the-door Catholics and were for Kennedy. We found in the smaller states, they were much more willing to get on the record. The other 30 percent look liked those farmers from the Third District in Wisconsin, who were sort of weighing him and testing him; the other third were McGovern's people. They were a sharp, young crowd who wanted to be for Kennedy but wanted to wait.

"South Dakota was a Sarge Shriver operation. Shriver ran the meeting and he did a great job. He had taken general responsibility for this area now. It was Shriver's opinion that proved to be dead-on: We had at most four or five delegates in the delegation. He also was key in getting McGovern on board and also realized it would cost McGovern the race. So he did a good, tough political job. He's a disarming fellow, charming, suave, but can be very tough politically when needed, as we found out over the Martin Luther King issue, which is to his credit alone.

"We went from there to North Dakota and went through the same routine with the North Dakota delegation; they would later turn out to be reasonably key. The senator spent a great deal of time with them and it went well and they were handed over to Shriver."

With the convention in Los Angeles about three weeks away, the Irish Brotherhood had done everything they could possibly do to give Jack Kennedy the best possible chance of winning the Democratic nomination. There would still be some last-minute maneuvering, but they had no choice but to keep moving relentlessly forward.

CHAPTER 17

Los Angeles: The Democratic National Convention

T HE KENNEDY FORCES arrived in Los Angeles on Saturday July 9th. Kenny Powers recalled, "As the convention opened, the only big state that we wanted and had yet locked up was California, where Governor Pat Brown, who was still a hopeful favorite-son candidate himself, had said he would be for us, but he made no promises and was doing nothing for us." Kenny said that they arrived determined to nail him down, even if it took a little tough love from the Irish Brotherhood.

Joe had worked the telephones, leaving little to chance. Bobby's planning had been meticulous. Kenny said, "Bobby had learned every lesson there was from 1956. This time we would be ready."

Jack's arrival in Los Angeles was beautifully timed with a political shift, not just in California but across the country. Rosalind "Roz" Wyman, a California political powerhouse today but then a twenty-nine-year-old city councilwoman, remembered the buzz that Jack Kennedy brought with him to Los Angeles: "Power was shifting. John Kennedy had changed the atmosphere. Many people were entering politics in 1960 because of him. They were young, and it was the first time they had ever paid any attention to an election. They were saying 'What can we do?' Kennedy was lighting a new fire across America. He broke the cycle of older politicians. Bobby, his chief of staff, was only thirty-four. Pierre Salinger, his press secretary, was thirty-five. Kenny O'Donnell, his closest aide, was thirty-six. Larry O'Brien, the campaign manager, was an old man: He was forty-three. It was great."

When Jack arrived with Kenny and his team aboard the *Caroline*, he also had left little to chance. Dave had arrived four days earlier, as Kenny recalled, to find Jack a "hideaway apartment" in Los Angeles. The official residence for the Kennedy team was the grand Biltmore Hotel in downtown Los Angeles. Jack's suite was on the ninth floor, while Kenny, Bobby, and the Kennedy team set up operations in Suite 8315.

Jack wanted a private getaway, too. Jack's residence would be a penthouse apartment at 522 Rossmore Avenue in Los Angeles's tony Hancock Park district. "The building was ideal," Dave said. "It was a small, three-floor, brick and white stucco apartment house owned by Jack Haley, the comic actor, and his wife, Flo."

The hideaway was only a ten-minute drive from the Biltmore Hotel and the Los Angeles Memorial Sports Arena, where the convention was held. It had a "secluded drive," which allowed Jack to arrive directly at the door and take a private elevator to the penthouse. His neighbors, including, as Kenny remembered, "William Gargan, the actor who played Martin Kane, the private eye of early television fame," were all sworn to secrecy. Joe Kennedy and his wife, Rose, had chosen the estate of old family friends Marion Davies and William Randolph Hearst in Beverly Hills as their temporary residence. Finally, a model cottage Bobby had set up at the Sports Arena served as the public face of the Kennedy operation. The stage was set.

Bobby had covered every possible angle in terms of communication. There would be no repeat of the snafus that they had experienced in Chicago.

Hy Raskin remembered the cottage as an extension of the Biltmore Suite operations center. "The cottage was really where the Irish Brotherhood worked the floor."

Bobby had assembled a superb organization. They brought in all "the girls," and Justine O'Donnell recalled that "we had our card system with us. We had cards on every single delegate going back sixty years. We knew everything there was to know about them. Bobby assigned a Kennedy person for each delegation. They had to practically live with the delegation, eat, drink, listen, and not sleep. Sleep was not an option."

Their job from there was to report back to Bobby and the operations team on what was going on within the delegations. The convention opened on Monday, July 11, and Tuesday, July 12, was going to be Stevenson's day, and while Jack, Bobby, and Kenny knew there would be a demonstration for him, they were not overly worried. In the end, Jack and Kenny agreed that it was all about the delegates. All the enthusiastic demonstrations in the world would not change the math. Stevenson just didn't have the numbers.

Nevertheless, Stevenson's forces, led by Eugene McCarthy and Eleanor Roosevelt, planned a major demonstration. Roz Wyman, already for Jack Kennedy, was concerned, both for Jack's chances and for the convention itself.

She recalled, "We would say to Stevenson, 'Governor, you need to tell us what you want to do.' I was shocked because he was such an intellect— and that may have been the problem. Now he had come to Los Angeles, but he would not say whether he was a candidate. His people asked for credentials and for a parade on the convention floor. We're not sure to this day whether they dummied up more credentials than we gave them, but they packed the place."

But Jack believed that Lyndon Johnson was the other force behind the Stevenson effort. Jack told Kenny that Eugene McCarthy's speech nominating Stevenson was actually done at the behest of Lyndon, who despite it all still believed that he could get the nomination.

Jack was correct in foreseeing that Johnson, not Stevenson, posed the real problem.

Kenny remembered how it unfolded. "Jack Kennedy was at one of the outlying hotels, attending whatever caucus was then in session. Dave was with him. We were not able to reach him. Bobby and I were debating between ourselves about just what he ought to do. Again, it was the same old story as '56: We think we have the convention locked up, and we don't see anything to be gained by debating before the Texas delegation, from which we are not going to get any votes anyway. I had no question in my mind that John Kennedy could handle Lyndon Johnson, especially after the series of almost ridiculous performances put on by the Texas delegation the previous month. But I anticipated that the Texas delegation would attempt to embarrass Kennedy."

Bobby and Kenny's real fear was, as Bobby said, "that we will get into something on religion or race on a nationwide television show. It will not bother the convention, but it could hurt us with the nationwide audience in the general election." Bobby, Kenny, Larry, and Steve kicked it around. "In the end," Bobby noted, "we were all unanimous that he should not do it, that he should laugh at this offer and wonder where Lyndon had been for the last seven months during the primaries. We went through seven primaries, and they could have debated every day, all they wanted."

But Jack, always several steps ahead, had other ideas. Kenny recalled, "We heard that he was going to go to the debate. We were stunned. I don't remember how I heard. Bobby was upset enough that he insisted we try to reach the senator. I was strongly against it and wanted to give him my views on why he should not debate Lyndon. Of course, Jack paid no attention to me and seemed to relish a confrontation with Lyndon. He saw this as the last obstacle to removing Lyndon from consideration for the presidential nomination, and he was not going to turn down the debate. This also reflected the courageous aspect of his character."

Jack made clear to Bobby and Kenny that he planned to take care of Lyndon once and for all in this debate.

He was, as Bobby related to Kenny, "quite angry and dismissive of Johnson, which is why his eventual choice of Johnson for the number-two spot was both stunning and politically brilliant."

The debate, which also included the Massachusetts delegation, was on Tuesday, July 12, around two or two thirty in the afternoon. Jack, Kenny, and Dave, returning from a caucus at another hotel, slipped into the suite at the Biltmore. Senator Fritz Hollings of North Carolina, a Kennedy friend and ally, was there to meet with Jack.

Sandy Vanocur was also there, covering the convention for NBC News. He remembered, "Fritz came out, and the senator was ahead of him. I said to Fritz, 'What did you say to him?' Fritz said, 'I told him to do it; I said to him, if he did not do it, Lyndon would say he was backing down and was a coward, so how could he face Nixon?' Now everyone, I realize this now, is taking credit for telling him to do this, but why Fritz urged him to do it, I don't know. Frankly," Vanocur concluded, "I had the feeling that Fritz was with Johnson, but his heart was somewhere else. But it appeared to me from what I understood later, Jack had long made up his mind, even before talking to Fritz."

Vanocur's journalistic instincts were, as usual, dead on. Jack had indeed decided well before he talked to Fritz.

Bobby made that clear later. "I am sure he listened to Fritz, but he had already decided on his own; his mind was made up. Jack did not need Fritz Hollings to point out the obvious."

Kenny remembered that they could not reach Jack in the car to give their views. Jack had a phone in his car, which in 1960 was extremely rare. Charles "Chuck" Roach, Harvard football pal and fellow chum of Kenny and Bobby, was with Jack that afternoon. Kenny said later that when everyone began taking credit for Jack's performance in the debate, Chuck Roach had a different version.

Roach told Kenny, "I was with him. The senator would not take calls from anyone, especially you, because he had made the decision to debate and was not going to listen to any other views."

Why he did it would remain a mystery to many until his choice of vice president was revealed. At that moment, it seemed an unnecessary and perhaps even foolish risk. Johnson and Speaker Sam Rayburn had been behind many of the most vicious attacks on Jack, including rumors about his health, which of course were not rumors at all. While Kennedy forces had squashed them, the very questions made Jack, Bobby, Kenny, and Joe uneasy.

But while taking on Lyndon was potentially risky, Jack felt an avoidance of a direct confrontation would only give the Johnson forces more room to build on the health issues and cause further trouble. Jack, with his infallible political compass and sense of confidence, felt he could quickly dispatch Johnson. He was also quietly considering Johnson for the number-two spot. The sooner Johnson understood he could not win the nomination, the sooner the Kennedy campaign could move forward.

Kenny readily admitted later, "Nobody was privy to Jack's thinking about all this at that time. Later many would claim credit, but as often was the case when the president made an important decision, he reached the conclusion on his own. Once made, we all fell into line."

Vanocur agreed, telling Kenny later, "I don't know why he took the risk politically, but it was a great performance. Brilliant."

"None of us were particularly nervous about it," Kenny said. "We did not feel it was going to change one vote one way or the other. None of us had any question that Senator Kennedy would handle himself in the debate. Our larger concern was whether the Massachusetts delegation and the Texas delegation were going to have a brawl and embarrass the Democratic Party on national television. Jack was this young leader, and we worried that if something went wrong, the Democrats would look out of control, as if we could not manage our convention. 'How can they run the country?' That was our real concern. The Massachusetts delegation was very upset with the Texas delegation, and there were a few rough Irishmen in the Massachusetts delegation. Frankly, most of them were my guys, and they were Kennedy men who would not mind hitting a few Texans after some of the slurs they had made against Kennedy, Catholics, and the Irish. On the other hand, I am sure there were a few Texans that would not mind taking a poke at a few of our boys. Some calls came into our headquarters that the Texans were going to knock our blocks off and teach these Yankees a thing or two. The potential for the best ruckus of the year was there, and we knew, if it were to happen, the Republicans would play it over and over again, saying this fellow Kennedy and his people are young, inexperienced thugs; you can't have them run the country."

The press came out in droves for the event. "There were," Vanocur noted, "rumors that it was going to be a brawl on nationwide television— great press from our point of view."

But to the relief of Kenny, Bobby, and the Kennedy team, the press would come away impressed with Jack's debate performance rather than his ability to take a punch.

"Lyndon was desperate," Kenny said. "His conduct, or the conduct of his people, was deplorable. They attacked Kennedy for his medical issues. I had never heard that done anywhere, and to do this in a presidential campaign just did not make any sense at all, unless they were in total desperation or wanted to elect Richard Nixon. The Texans again betrayed total desperation and a total lack of political acumen, in my opinion," Kenny said.

As Kenny and Bobby watched on television, they saw Jack slip in while Lyndon was making his speech—a speech Bobby later deemed "pathetic."

Kenny agreed. "After missing seven primaries, sitting out the entire season, his position was he was entitled to the presidential nomination because he had answered more quorum calls than anyone. You know the average delegate did not know or care what the hell a quorum call was, nor did the average voter in America. Answering more quorum calls than anyone else was really not the reason you were nominating someone for president."

Jack stood in a gray tailored suit, looking tanned and handsome. Vanocur remembered, "Jack seemed almost above it all. He seemed like a man who knew the nomination was already his. He smiled that sort of quizzical, amused smile throughout. It was a deft performance by Kennedy, an untouchable performance. He did not need to get down there with Lyndon. He just dismissed him."

As Kenny recalled, "Lyndon opened himself up just like a man who had walked up to Joe Louis with both hands tied behind his back. When Lyndon did this quorum stuff, the senator could have knocked him out of the ballpark. Senator Kennedy's presence in that debate made one feel he was presidential. He just seemed above Lyndon. In politics, when a politician opens himself up in the manner Lyndon did, the temptation is to flatten him. And considering that Lyndon had been reasonably vicious to Jack Kennedy, Bobby and I had the temptation to flatten him. But the senator was savvier than we were. There was nobody in that room who would have guessed Jack Kennedy would have taken the route he took.

"Bobby and I left opened-mouth. The lesson here," Kenny remembered honestly, "is also that your political people, like myself, can give you their best advice, but in the end, the candidate has to make his own best judgment. Fortunately, Jack did not listen to me, because my advice was, as it turned out, incorrect."

Later that day, Roz Wyman remembered, "Eleanor Roosevelt spoke and told everybody to vote for Stevenson. To Democrats, she was a godly figure, and she made a moving speech. The convention just went wild. Kennedy's people were shaken. 'Is she going to stampede the delegates? Is she going to roll the convention?' Senator Eugene McCarthy placed Stevenson in nomination, and the Stevenson people went wild again. It was chaotic. The seats weren't linked; they were only set up, and it was dangerous."

Kenny made clear, "Despite the rumblings about Johnson and the fervent talk from liberals about a draft of Stevenson, John Kennedy went to Los Angeles knowing he had enough delegates to win on the first ballot."

It may have seemed to Roz Wyman and others that the Kennedys were worried about Stevenson, but Kenny said they were not. "Jack's real concern was Lyndon Johnson."

Jack told Kenny that they needed to handle Lyndon and that all Stevenson could do was make a lot of noise. As Jack made clear, the math was the math. The job was just keeping all the delegates, or "players" as Kenny called them, in place and on the same page. That would be Bobby and Kenny's job.

The Kennedy forces also had another backup plan, should Stevenson get caught up in the moment and decide to throw his name in: Mayor Richard Daley, the same man who had urged Jack to run in '56 and who was now squarely behind Jack again.

Stevenson, caught up in all the enthusiasm, approached Daley for help and support for his candidacy.

Daley was blunt. He said, "Well, Governor, you know I have always been for you. I supported you for the governorship. However, it is too late now. I think you are making a mistake. In answer to your question, Governor, in all candor, is none. You will not get one vote from the Illinois delegation."

The mayor made it brutally clear to Stevenson: He had no support in Chicago or Illinois. Without the votes to carry even his own home state, Stevenson's excitement quickly vanished, as did his support. If Jack was nervous about Stevenson, for whom he had great contempt after his refusal to support Jack in the primaries, he did not show it.

"The truth was," Kenny said, "all the noise from Stevenson and Johnson was just that—noise."

Press coverage of the convention played up intraparty conflicts, suggesting that the nomination remained up in the air as long as the party elite remained uncommitted to Kennedy. But the Kennedy team was sure it had the 761 delegates needed to win if Pennsylvania and Illinois were secure.

Hy Raskin remembered, "When we arrived in Los Angeles, we knew we had the votes. We knew that Bill Green and Governor Lawrence of Pennsylvania were gonna deliver Pennsylvania. We felt confident we had the votes. The two big states that I felt were critical were in our pocket."

Echoing Raskin, Kenny, too, believed the press coverage of the convention was way off. "In order to pass over Jack for the nomination, party leadership would have had to decide they had no interest in the election anymore; they could not go into a back room and take a candidate with 600 or 650 committed votes, and with every large delegation committed to him except California, then nominate a candidate who had no votes. They would not carry any of these big northern states. They had no choice but to nominate John Kennedy in that back room. By not doing so, they would be electing Richard Nixon."

Jack, Bobby, and Kenny counted and recounted and felt their only real potential problem was Lyndon Johnson. "The night when the Stevenson forces had the rally and everyone went wild," Kenny said, "we had expected it, but all that enthusiasm does not mean anything if you do not have the numbers. We had the numbers, and the leaders knew it. If they would have come to John Kennedy to ask him to take second place on a ticket with Stuart Symington or whoever they had, Jack was clear he would say no. He was here to win. Jack knew he had all the cards. Dick Daley and the rest of the big-city boys would have said, 'Let's quit kidding around, boys.' The minute he hit the six hundred mark in delegations earned just from the primaries, which caused those state leaders to throw in their lot with him, it was clear John Kennedy was going to be nominated."

Jack agreed with Kenny. "Anyone that had any political acumen at all would have known the party were flaying away at a dead horse at this time."

With Lyndon Johnson, at least from Kenny and Bobby's point of view, dispatched safely back to the majority leader's office in the Senate, the Kennedy forces began to prepare for Wednesday, July 13, when they would win the nomination.

As July 13 dawned, Jack rose at his penthouse rental at 522 Rossmore with the expectation that all his hard work was soon to pay off. Dave woke him early as usual, and Jack's first request was to speak with Bobby at the operations center. Bobby was up, never having gone to sleep at all.

Kenny recalled, "As the brothers talked about the day's schedule, Dave prepared the breakfast that never varied (except of course on Fridays, when, for a good Catholic, no meat was allowed): freshly squeezed orange juice, eggs, broiled bacon, toast, and coffee."

Jack was delighted after talking to Bobby and teased Dave about how good a cook he was. "Does your wife know you can cook like this?" Jack asked.

Dave, never one to miss an opportunity, replied quickly, "No, and don't tell her, either."

Before leaving, Dave could not resist saying to Jack, "Well, this is the day you've been waiting on for four years. This is the day you'll pick up all the marbles."

Jack smiled. Glancing at Dave, he quipped, "Let's just hope this breakfast tastes as good tomorrow."

They headed out to a series of meetings with various delegations, including a stop at the Roosevelt Hotel to meet with the South Dakota delegation and the Chancellor Hotel to meet with the Colorado caucus.

Jack happily picked up delegates along each stop. They left nothing to chance. Upon arriving at the operations suite at the Biltmore Hotel, Jack met with Kenny and Bobby. He wanted to see where they stood.

Kenny said, "We were confident. We had 739½ sure votes and were certain that day we would pick up the additional 21½ votes needed for the total of 761 that would give him the nomination on the first ballot."

Jack was pleased but told them to keep pushing.

He planned to return to the hideaway apartment to try to get some rest, then get his swimming trunks and head over for a swim and dinner with his father and mother at Marion Davies's home in Beverly Hills.

Bobby and Kenny planned to stay put at the operations cottage on the ground of the Sports Arena, should Jack need them.

As the moment approached, Jack and Dave headed back to the hideaway on Rossmore, which was distinctly less of a hideaway now, surrounded as it was by the press. Pierre Salinger, still on a learning curve, had slipped;

somehow the address had gotten out. Jack fought his way into the building, past the crush of media.

Jack munched on one of Dave's perfectly made chicken sandwiches with a glass of milk and tried to relax. Surrounded by family, Pat and Peter Lawford, and some other friends, they began to watch the process unfold on television.

While eating, Jack told Dave that they'd have to figure out how to get out of the place so that the press could not follow them to Beverly Hills. Dave ventured that a climb over the back fence might do the trick.

"Great," Jack said, "as long as they don't catch me just as I go over."

Suddenly the broadcast got interesting: "Alabama casts twenty votes for Johnson, three and a half for Kennedy, and—" with that, the fuse blew and the lights and TV went out.

Jack, tense and on edge, exploded. "God Almighty!" Jack barked. "I slave and I knock my brains out for four years to get this nomination, and now I can't even see it!" He ran down to William Gargan's apartment below, where he settled in to watch on their television.

Back at the Sports Arena, Kenny and Bobby were working every angle, pushing and prodding each delegation to keep their commitment. Vanocur remembered calling the Kennedy cottage, and Bobby picked up without a ring.

Bobby was livid, Vanocur recalled with a chuckle. "He said to me, 'How the hell did you get this number? Get your ass off this line! I will buy you a drink later. We have got to keep this line clear!'" Vanocur laughed. Bobby was focused on every count and was taking no chances.

Back at Rossmore, a private detective from Pinkerton had fixed the fuse box, and Jack was back in the penthouse, sitting tensely, watching the count as the numbers rose: 600, 650, and on the count went.

"When the roll call reached the Wyoming delegation, he knew he had it," Kenny said. "Regardless of how Wyoming divided its fifteen votes, he knew that he had enough supporters in the remaining delegations at the end of the list—the Virgin Islands, Puerto Rico, and the District of Columbia—to put him over the top.

"When he saw his youngest brother, Teddy, on TV, crouching in the middle of the Wyoming delegation with a wide grin on his face, Jack said, 'This may be it!' All of Wyoming's fifteen votes went to Kennedy, giving him the nomination."

Jack stood and grinned widely, relief spread across his face. He shook Dave's hand, his good friend Torby MacDonald's hand, and finally Dave's hand once again. He called Jackie at the Cape to tell her, then called his father. "We did it, Dad."

From there, Jack made his way through the media and to the Sports Arena to accept the nomination, stopping at the model cottage, where Jack and Bobby shared what Kenny called "an emotional, private moment."

Kenny remembered that he hadn't yet had a chance to call Helen. Jack walked over to him, squeezed his shoulder, and said little before he made his way up to speak to the convention, listening to the delegates sing the Irish melody "Tura Lura Lural" and the song "Happy Days Are Here Again."

"From there," Kenny said, "he stood on the platform with his mother and sisters, waving to the cheering delegates, and said a few words of thanks. Then he rode back to the apartment on North Rossmore."

While Kenny, Larry, Dave, and the Kennedy staff celebrated their victory, unbeknownst to them, Jack was already thinking about the number-two slot. His choice would leave them stunned and once again, Kenny noted, "demonstrate that Jack was always several steps ahead and his political acumen was absolute."

Kenny remembered it quite clearly: "All of us who were with Jack at the convention, including Dave Powers, who spent almost every waking minute of that week at Jack's side, were sure that Jack did not begin to give any serious thought or consideration to the selection of the vice presidential candidate until after his return to the apartment on North Rossmore the night of his nomination."

Kenny and Bobby were completely confident in their view that when Jack "arrived in Los Angeles on Saturday, July 9, just before the convention week began, he had made no promises or definite offers to anybody."

Kenny knew, for example, that Jack had a short, sort of tossed-together list but had given it no serious thought. Kenny recalled the list including Orville Freeman, governor of Minnesota; Missouri senator Stuart Symington; and Senator Henry Jackson, who was Bobby's personal favorite.

Kenny was well aware that Lyndon Johnson was on the list. He had been put there to just round out the list of possibilities. However, Kenny never considered Jack as being serious about Johnson. Kenny assumed that Jack viewed Johnson the way he and Bobby did, "as a conservative old guardsman opposed to the moderate liberalism of John Kennedy."

"None of us," Kenny made clear, "ever thought he would pick Johnson."

After getting back to North Rossmore, they drank a toast of champagne that Dave had hidden away for the occasion to the Democratic Party's new standard bearer. Jack worked his way through the telegrams but stopped at one that caught his eye.

It was from his old nemesis, Lyndon Baines Johnson, whose telegram said, "LBJ now means Let's Back Jack." Jack smiled and showed it to Dave.

"See if you can reach Lyndon," Jack asked Dave. Dave was startled. It was after 2:00 a.m. and, as Dave recalled, "a sleepy Johnson aide said he was in bed and could not be disturbed."

Jack then instructed Dave to call his secretary, Evelyn Lincoln, and get a note over to Johnson's suite that he wanted to meet with him at ten the next morning at the Biltmore. Dave, stunned, called Evelyn's suite and left the message with her sleepy husband.

Johnson? Dave thought. *My God, he's going to offer it to Lyndon Johnson. He can't be serious.*

The next day Jack returned to the Kennedy suite at the Biltmore Hotel early in the morning. He looked refreshed, rested, and ready, having had one of Dave's homemade breakfast specials. Upon arrival, Jack immediately instructed Evelyn to call Johnson's suite and see if he was up yet.

Lady Bird answered the phone and was asked, "Could the majority leader meet with Senator Kennedy around 10:00 a.m.?"

Lady Bird replied, "Yes, he could."

It was then that Dave understood that Jack was seriously taking this into consideration. Bobby arrived at about that time and the two brothers briefly conferred.

Dave heard Bobby say, "If you are sure that is what you want to do, then you should go ahead and see him."

It was only later, when Kenny laid out for Bobby the problems that the selection of Johnson would create with labor and the liberals led by Eleanor Roosevelt, that Bobby began to have second thoughts. At that early moment, Bobby was pretty much fine with whatever Jack wanted to do. He confessed later to Kenny, "he had not given it all that much thought."

Jack told Bobby first. Much has been reported of what happened next, but Kenny believed that Bobby played no role in the decision. Bobby, he believed, would have done whatever Jack told him to do at that point.

Jack told Bobby the news. Bobby then ordered someone to find Kenny. When Kenny arrived at Bobby's suite at the Biltmore, Pierre rather than Bobby greeted him. Bobby was soaking in the tub, still exhausted. Pierre looked ashen.

"What?" Kenny asked, still exhausted himself. He could not imagine what could have gone wrong this fast.

"He's just asked me to add up the electoral votes in the states we're sure of, and to add Texas."

Kenny froze. He stared hard at Pierre, who hated when Kenny got that look. "Don't get mad at me," Pierre pleaded. "I am just the messenger."

"You must be kidding!" Kenny growled, nearly spitting the words out.

Salinger shook his head, relieved that Kenny was too angry to belt anyone. "I wish I was."

Kenny pushed past Salinger and stormed into the bathroom, "Don't tell me it's Johnson!" Kenny growled at Bobby.

Bobby groaned and opened his eyes. "Nice to see you as well," Bobby replied sarcastically. "He is seeing Johnson now."

"Are you kidding?" Kenny was livid. All he could think of were the promises they had made to the liberals and the labor leaders, for whom Johnson was anathema.

"Do you realize this is a disaster?" Kenny snapped at Bobby. "Nixon will love this. Now Nixon can say, 'Kennedy is just another phony politician who will do anything to get elected.'"

Kenny paced the bathroom, punching a fist into his hand. "I want to talk to your brother myself on this one. This will destroy all we've worked for."

Kenny's anger stunned Bobby. Climbing out of the tub, he pulled a towel from the rack and wrapped it around his waist. "Okay," Bobby said. "As soon as I get dressed, we'll go see him."

"Make it fast," Kenny ordered.

Bobby shot him a look. He had never seen Kenny so angry.

They headed upstairs to Jack's suite on the ninth floor, which was filled to capacity with political leaders from across the country. Jack was speaking with the governor of Pennsylvania, foe-turned-friend Dave Lawrence, who was now acting, as Kenny said, "as if it was his idea."

Kenny moved forward menacingly. He wanted to belt Lawrence. Just then, he felt someone touch his arm. It was Sarge Shriver, who was, he assured Kenny, "feeling as terrible as you are." Sarge confided those feelings to Kenny, his hand fingering the ever-present rosary in his pocket. The moment diffused the tension and Kenny became distracted.

Bobby finally caught Jack's eye. Jack looked over at Kenny and understood at once. He beckoned Bobby, Kenny, and Sarge to follow him to the bedroom. The bedroom was also crowded with people, who upon seeing Jack crowded in on him.

As Kenny remembered it, "Jack, seeing I was about to explode, said to Bobby and Sarge, 'I better talk to Kenny alone in the bathroom.'"

Jack walked into the bathroom; Kenny followed behind and shut the door with a distinctive slam. Bobby and Sarge stayed by the door outside, to make sure they would not be interrupted.

"This is the worst mistake you've ever made," Kenny barked. "You came out here to this convention like a knight on a white charger, the clean-cut, young Ivy League college guy promising to get rid of the old hacks and machine politicians. And now, in your first move after you get the nomination, you go against all the people who supported you. Are we going to spend the campaign apologizing for Lyndon Johnson and trying to explain why he voted against everything you ever stood for? I thought you were different."

Jack was stunned. Even he had never seen Kenny this upset. Kenny recalled later, "He became pale with anger. It took him a few moments to collect himself. So we sat in cold, furious silence."

Finally, having gathered himself, his gaze meeting Kenny's, Jack said, "Wait a minute. I've offered it to him, but he hasn't accepted it yet, and maybe he won't. If he does accept it, let's get one thing clear."

His next words would haunt Kenny for the rest of his life: "I'm forty-three years old, and I'm the healthiest candidate for president of the United States. You've traveled with me enough to know that. I am not going to die in office. So the vice presidency doesn't mean anything. I'm thinking of something else: the leadership in the Senate. If we win, it will be by a small margin, right?"

"Yes," Kenny replied, not sure where Jack was going.

"I won't be able to live with Lyndon Johnson as the leader of a small majority in the Senate," Jack continued. "Did it occur to you that if Lyndon Johnson becomes vice president, then Mike Mansfield, somebody I can work with, trust, and depend upon, will be the majority leader in the Senate? If Johnson and Rayburn leave here mad at me, they'll ruin me in Congress, and I will be the laughingstock of the country. Nixon will say I haven't got any power in my own party. I'll lose the election before Labor Day. I've got to make peace with Johnson and Rayburn. Whether Johnson accepts my offer is irrelevant. It's just one way of keeping him friendly."

After Kenny heard Jack out, he began to see the fuller picture, though he was not thrilled. Labor and the liberals would be mad as hell in the short term, even if the wisdom of Jack's long game were evident. Kenny had done his best. He had made his point, and it was clear that Jack had made up his mind.

With that he opened the door and beckoned to Bobby, who squeezed into the room. "It was so quiet in here, I was worried," Bobby teased.

Jack nodded. "We survived it. Now you two go see Walter Reuther and George Meany and get to work on them, but," Jack warned, "don't tell them or anybody what I just told you about my reasons."

Bobby and Kenny made their way through the crowd in Jack's suite to find Walter Reuther and George Meany. As they stood at the door of the room filled with labor leaders who were ready to tear them to pieces, Bobby joked weakly, "Well, into the lion's den." Kenny turned to him and said, "Thanks, Bobby, just the image I needed right now." The two friends, who'd been through many battles up to this point, chuckled, opened the door, and faced the angry labor leaders led by one very angry Eleanor Roosevelt.

Kenny said later with a laugh that he felt Bobby only fully understood the predicament Jack's choice of Lyndon as vice president had put them all in when they entered the suite of the lawyer for the labor leaders, Arthur Goldberg. They were greeted not only by an angry group of men but especially by Jack Conway, who had become their warm good friend since the McClellan days and with whom they had had a warm and friendly dinner the evening before.

"Well, when Conway saw me," Kenny said laughing, "he came right at me with a fist ready to slug me!"

"You lying . . . SOB," he said as he headed for Kenny. Fortunately, others interfered and full-scale mayhem was avoided.

While in the end cooler heads prevailed, you could hardly blame them. Kenny later said, "Look, the night before we were eating their food, drinking their drinks, telling them the one thing we won't do is pick Lyndon. They woke up the next day to find out it was Lyndon!"

It took some doing, but Kenny was finally able to convince Conway, Reuther, and Meany that they had been as surprised as the labor leaders were to find out about Johnson. Still, those assurances and explanations did not prevent the labor groups from threatening a floor fight to oppose Johnson.

"We were shaken," Kenny admitted. "They chewed Bobby to pieces. It was very tough."

And it was not just the labor leaders who were angry. Kennedy's own ranks threatened revolt. Ralph Dungan recalled an angry conversation with Kenny. "Over my dead body," Dungan snapped when he heard about the offer to Johnson, later explaining, "It was a natural reaction. We had been working for months and months to gain labor's support and trust. I told Kenny, 'Lyndon Johnson has been the enemy for months, and now he is on the ticket!' When word came down from the central office it was Johnson, boy, we were shocked. I was really angry."

Shaken after Kenny and Bobby told them what was afoot, the rest of the Irish Brotherhood headed back to the Biltmore to speak their minds to Jack. By the time they arrived, Lyndon had already accepted.

"Should I tell him we may have a floor fight?" Bobby asked.

Jack agreed. "Tell him we may have a floor fight, but if he still wants it, it is his."

Nobody is exactly sure what happened next, but many stories and legends have since cropped up. Whatever occurred during that meeting, it permanently damaged the relationship between Bobby and Lyndon.

Bobby went to see Lyndon, starting with Sam Rayburn and John Connally. As Bobby later told Kenny, Bobby "went to explain to them that Lyndon might want to withdraw if he didn't want to get involved in a floor fight."

"Do you think he'd be interested in being chairman of the Democratic National Committee?" Bobby asked the incredulous Rayburn.

"Shit!" was all Rayburn could say before storming into the other room to talk to Lyndon.

Kenny said that later, "Bobby's errand was completely misinterpreted by Rayburn, who assumed Bobby was asking Johnson to withdraw."

Kenny said this was not Bobby's intention.

While Bobby waited in one room, Rayburn and Johnson panicked in the other room. A call was quickly put into Jack in his suite on the ninth floor. Jack was startled. How could such a simple errand have gone so wrong?

Employing a technique they had used since '52, Jack said clearly, "Bobby's been out of touch and doesn't know what's happening."

However, Dave Powers remembered it differently. Dave said that Jack told them, "I've announced that Lyndon will be the vice presidential candidate, and Dave Lawrence has agreed to nominate him. Can you put Lyndon on the phone?"

Jack then assured a shaken Johnson that if he was willing to engage in a floor fight threatened by labor leaders, the nomination was his. Johnson assured Jack that he still wanted the job and would take on such a fight.

Jack then asked to talk to Bobby. Bobby got on the phone, and Jack told him to forget the errand. It was done.

Bobby told Kenny later that he "was exhausted by the entire mix-up and felt as though he was banging his head against the wall."

As he told Kenny later over a drink, "This is going to come back at me, I just know."

"Nobody will remember this, Bobby," Kenny assured him, which turned out to be far from the truth.

After Bobby had hung up the telephone in Johnson's suite, he and Johnson stood face to face. Johnson said, "If the candidate will have me, I will join him in making a fight for it."

Bobby said to Kenny later, "I wanted to say, 'Why didn't you just say that in the first place?'"

Later, it would be reported by those less than kind to Johnson that he was near tears at the time, his lower lip trembling.

According to Kenny, "Bobby never said anything about that. He was just sorry he'd gotten into the whole episode. Bobby never mocked Johnson or anything like that. He was too exhausted by this point and just wanted it over with."

The drama unfolding over the selection of Lyndon Johnson never emerged. Around 7:30 p.m. Jack Conway called Kenny.

"Stop worrying," Conway told Kenny. There would be no floor fight and no candidate would be put in opposition to Johnson. Kenny found out later that Walter Reuther had worked out a peace pact with Johnson, directly avoiding any fight. Lyndon, a savvy, smart political operator, had quickly agreed to Reuther's request, part of which was easy enough: that Johnson put in writing his support for the party's civil rights platform. Johnson quickly agreed.

On Friday, July 15, at the Los Angeles Memorial Coliseum, in his acceptance speech John F. Kennedy would, for the first time, use a phrase that would come to symbolize his one thousand days in office. Kenny remembered it well: "He was tired after the grind of the convention, and the sun was shining in his eyes—but it was a speech that all of us remember because in it he made his first mention of the New Frontier. That phrase, which came to mean so much to our generation, was all his own."

Roz Wyman agreed with Kenny's assessment of the evening and Jack's speech. "It became known as his New Frontier speech, and the New Frontier became the keynote of his campaign and his presidency. I was later told that President Kennedy did not feel it was a great speech. But to me, and judging from the crowd's reaction, it was magnificent."

Facing west toward the setting sun, John Kennedy spoke to those fifty thousand people and to another thirty-five million watching on television.

"Today our concern must be with [the] future," he said. "For the world is changing. The old era is ending. The old ways will not do. . . . We stand today on the edge of a New Frontier."

Kenny called Helen and told her that night, "This was what we had believed in. This was our generation's moment." It was as much their New Frontier as it was Jack Kennedy's.

The battle with Nixon was about to begin.

CHAPTER 18

The National Campaign: Round One

THE LAUNCH OF Jack's national campaign would start with frustration. Jack was, as Kenny recalled, "stuck in Washington, DC, for quorum votes." A rarely scheduled August session of Congress, designed by Lyndon Johnson and Speaker Sam Rayburn months before in hopes of securing Johnson the presidential nomination, stuck a miserable Jack and Lyndon in the swelteringly hot DC summer of 1960. Vice President Richard Nixon, the Republican nominee, was free to hit the campaign trail and happily did so.

Kenny, Bobby, and Steve used the time to finalize the campaign schedule, raise money, and nail down any loose ends. Kenny tried unsuccessfully to convince Jack that August was a dead month politically anyway.

"Everybody's on vacation," Kenny said to Jack over breakfast at Jack's townhouse on N Street in Georgetown.

"Nixon's not," Jack growled as he glared at Kenny, who once again was caught stealing some bacon off Jack's plate.

When they could, Jack and Kenny would take the *Caroline* up to the Cape. Kenny would drive with Jack to Hyannis Port, where he would spend the weekend with Jackie and their family. Kenny would grab a car and snatch what time he could with Helen and their four children at the vacation resort of Popponesset, a twenty-minute drive from Hyannis Port.

Helen teased her husband that she had "almost forgotten who he was," since it had been so long since he had been home.

Kenny chuckled as he poured her a martini on the back patio of the house and lit her Pall Mall cigarette. He stopped and stared at the commanding views of the Atlantic. While his wife commented on the beauty, Kenny's mind was on delegate counts. He didn't hear a word she said to him.

He knew he would not have time off in the near future. Most of the time he was in Popponesset he was fielding calls from Jack, Bobby, or Larry in Washington, and there would be an occasional long conversation with Steve Smith, which would intrude on what were supposed to be Kenny's romantic date-night dinners with Helen at the Popponesett Inn.

It would not have mattered anyway, because once his presence was known to the neighbors—most of whom had been or were about to be pressed into service to volunteer their time for Jack's campaign—they would eagerly join in to talk politics, drink, eat good food, and dream about the White House.

To Helen's dismay, though not to her surprise, it was not much of a vacation and certainly not private.

Popponesset was a working-class Irish enclave. It was close enough for Kenny to be available to Jack when needed. Jack had gone as far as having a special line installed both at their beach house and in the bar at Kenny and Helen's beloved escape, the Poppenesett Inn. Jack, Bobby, and Joe were taking no chances with Kenny being out of touch. These phones would stay in place throughout the campaign and the White House years. Still, Popponesset was far enough away that Kenny was able to have a little independence and privacy.

As he said good-bye to Helen and headed to the Kennedy compound to connect with Jack, Helen joked that the next time she would see him would be the day of the election. Kenny smiled, kissed her, and told her that he would be back as often as possible in between.

Sure you will, Helen thought to herself. However well intentioned Kenny might have been, this was the big one for Jack: the run for the White House against Nixon. Personal life, such as it was at the moment, would have to wait. That stood true not just for Kenny but for all the campaign men, on both sides, Kennedy and Nixon. Politics called for toughness and sacrifice. Helen hoped that with a victory in the fall, with Jack headed to the White House, her sacrifice would have been worth it.

Jack was determined to bring as many adversaries to his side as he could during the first weeks of his national campaign. That included a fence-mending visit with Eleanor Roosevelt at her Hyde Park estate on August 14.

The visit, marred as it was by the death of her granddaughter a few days before, went ahead nevertheless. In her own way, Eleanor was critical. She represented the key liberal voting bloc that, despite Kennedy's win in Los Angeles, remained skeptical and uneasy about him. He knew well that he needed her blessing and support if he were to get the liberals to vote for him. He could not afford to have them stay home on Election Day.

However, while Jack would receive her blessing, he pointed out to Kenny that "vast differences remained." She still, Jack felt, did not entirely trust him, he told Kenny. Kenny agreed but pointed out that "politically she was probably the best politician on the planet, and no matter her personal views, she would not want Nixon to win."

So Kenny felt confident that they could completely rely on her support. "Thanks, I think," Jack joked.

While Eleanor and Jack may not have parted as best friends, the grande dame of the Democratic Party was now on his side, and this was crucial.

Kennedy aide Ralph Dungan, part of Kenny's political team and friend of Eleanor's, watched the transition in the relationship between Eleanor Roosevelt and Jack. Despite Jack's admirable performance during the primaries and on the campaign trail, the New Deal Democrats of the older generation remained suspicious of Jack's youthful Democratic insurgency, not to mention the involvement of Joe Kennedy in his son's campaign.

"They were never going to be close," Dungan said, "but Mrs. Roosevelt was, in the end, a political realist."

Next the campaign brought Hubert Humphrey on board. Humphrey, despite the bruising primaries, jumped in, ever the loyal Democrat.

"I made up my mind," Hubert recalled, "that I was going to be 100 percent in, and I tried to convince other people that we were going to carry Minnesota for Kennedy. I said, 'This is the only way we can really demonstrate, without a shadow of a doubt, that we're good sports and clean fighters and we're going to back him.' We went in and we pushed him. We gave him huge crowds. He worked them beautifully. He was very pleased."

Humphrey would meet them later in California, campaigning alongside Governor Brown and others to convince the critical California voters to vote for Jack, while they all knew it was an uphill battle.

All agreed that California was critical. Humphrey remembered the California swing. "I was surprised. I thought the campaign was not as organized as it could be. I thought they tried to do too much at times. But by the end, he was really a national campaigner. Running in all those primaries made John Kennedy. That's why he won."

Hubert remembered his relationship with Jack and Kenny during the 1960 campaign. "I got to know them both well. Jack would talk to me about civil rights. How far should he go? How fast? What was realistic with the Congress? He always looked to me, even afterward, you know, on those issues in that area. During that national campaign, our mutual respect grew."

The Hollywood crowd, led by Frank Sinatra and Peter Lawford, "brother-in-lawford" as Sinatra liked to call him, also chimed in with money and resources. Frank talked to everyone he knew, calling in every favor he could manage.

More importantly, Frank chimed in musically, with the help of composer pal Jimmy Van Heusen, a like-minded man about town. Jimmy, like Sinatra, came from New York and was a man of immense talent with lyrics, like another Sinatra chum, Sammy Cahn.

Van Heusen and Cahn rewrote the 1959 song from the Oscar-nominated film *A Hole in the Head* into a wildly popular theme song for the Kennedy campaign. Sung by Sinatra, who was then at the height of his power and popularity, the song would become a campaign staple of the Kennedy organization.

Frank had been watching Jack since their first chance meeting in 1956. He had been impressed at how gracefully Jack took a loss and turned it into a win. A man not unfamiliar with such experiences, Sinatra was instantly attracted to Kennedy.

It was because of Jack Kennedy that Frank repaired his tattered friendship with Peter Lawford, which had been torn asunder by one of Frank's famous temper tantrums in a little misunderstanding with Peter over Frank's gal Ava Gardner. Frank had wrongly assumed that Peter was making a move on Ava when he invited her for a little Italian dinner at Nicky Blair's Sunset Strip Italian joint. The truth was that they both had been on the set all day at MGM and wanted to get a bite to eat and a drink. It was an "all very innocent" Peter had assured a furious Frank.

But that was then; this was now. Friendships had been repaired thanks to Jack's sister Patricia Lawford's substantial efforts and, in no small part, because Frank wanted the friendship repaired now. He was all in for Jack, and in this case Peter was his way to Jack.

Frank was the son of Dolly Sinatra, who knew a thing or two about politics. Frank had learned from his mother how the game worked and was determined to help Jack win the critical state of California. In characteristic fashion, Frank threw himself heavily into the 1960 campaign. He not only contributed money, time, and his immense talent but also barnstormed the country for the campaign.

He would be rewarded, so to speak, in many ways, but especially when he was tapped to organize the inaugural gala for Jack. Frank and Kenny became friendly and Frank called Kenny often during this time, urging that they spend more time in California. Kenny admitted later that he resisted Frank's suggestions, opting in the waning days of the campaign for New York and the East Coast.

As Labor Day approached, Jack was chomping at the bit and driving everyone nuts, but the campaign was finally under way. Joe and Kenny knew that the Republicans had an enormous advantage over the Democrats in terms of fund-raising, and Jack needed all the help he could get. Joe began pushing all their connections, including their Hollywood friends, to fill the political war chest. As before, Joe was willing to spend whatever it took to get Jack elected.

Hy Raskin remembered being surprised to get a call from Joe Kennedy, inviting him to a strategy meeting in Hyannis Port. "I remember it was at the Cape. Bobby, Steve, Pierre, and some others were getting their assignments. Kenny was gone somewhere with Jack. He was always with Jack at this stage. Bobby announced that Teddy Kennedy was headed out to California for about ten days to meet with, among others, Roz Wyman, Sinatra, and other supporters to begin to set up the western state operations. I was told, not asked, to go with him and then head up to San Francisco, which was my home, of course, to direct the western states operation. This was the first I knew that Teddy and I would be working together. Bobby and Steve made clear that California was critical."

The schedule was relentless, and everyone on the campaign staff worked nonstop. Still, it would all come perilously close to the wire, as the campaign would continue to be dogged by an issue that haunted them from the beginning.

Jack's most ambitious attempt to dispatch the Catholic issue would come shortly thereafter in a now-famous speech delivered in Texas. The decision to give the speech was Jack's alone and showed once again how, at these pivotal moments, Jack made up his own mind about what course of action to take.

During the campaign's first trip to California, on September 8 and 9, Jack decided to take the Catholic issue head-on. The pressure had been building, and the inner circle knew that Jack was right when he noted, exhaustedly, "We will reach a point when we can't avoid it anymore."

The West was particularly tricky for the Kennedy camp. They were convinced they needed California to win, but they also had to shore up the states that polls showed to be a more natural fit for Jack. There was one funny incident during the Kennedy campaign's whistle-stop train tour through California with Governor Pat Brown, who would become infamous for the "brown suit speech." It was an embarrassing moment that the Kennedy team loved to tease Brown about for a long time afterward, much to the governor's chagrin.

Brown, a man Joe Kennedy had worked on for months before finally convincing him to jump into the campaign, was a reluctant warrior for Jack. Standing on the platform that jutted out from the rear car of the campaign's train, Brown gave a speech to a crowd assembled at the station. He got so carried away in the moment advocating for Jack's candidacy that he took off his brown suit coat and gave it to a man in the crowd to hold, not realizing his mistake until the train began to pull away. The poor man ran along the tracks trying to catch the train and return the governor's suit coat.

"Governor," Powers chortled, "why don't you just throw him the pants as well? Then he can have the entire suit at least!" Jack and Kenny roared with laughter. Minus one-half of a suit but with good spirits to spare, they eventually made their way to Sinatra's house in Palm Springs and then on to Los Angeles.

Kenny recalled that they ended their California swing in Bakersfield, then took the *Caroline* to Los Angeles. For weeks they had been mulling the invitation from a group of Houston ministers for Kennedy to speak, but as they climbed aboard the *Caroline* that night, Kenny told Jack that it was time for a decision.

Kenny had been against accepting the invitation from the start. He thought it could only do harm. He also agreed with Lyndon Johnson and Sam Rayburn's belief that "they're mostly Republicans, and they're out to get you."

On this point, all Kennedy's advisors, including Bobby, were in agreement. The one person Jack had not asked was Kenny. After they arrived at their hotel room, Kenny remembered, "the senator finally asked me, 'Ken, what you think?'"

Kenny shook his head as Jack got out of the bath and began to dress for his speech that night at the Shrine Auditorium. "You know what I think," Kenny said quietly but firmly. "I think it would be a mistake. If you have to meet the religious issue, Houston is not the place to do it."

Jack nodded, walking into the bathroom to finish shaving. He said little. Kenny did not offer more. With all his advisors against it, Kenny assumed Jack would agree with them.

Kenny was wrong.

He had just hung up a call from Bobby when Jack walked back into the room, having finished shaving. "Ken, tell them I'm going to do it. This is as good a time as any to get it over with. I've got to face it sooner or later."

Kenny nodded. By now he knew Jack well enough to know better than to argue when his mind was set. "I could see," Kenny said, "that his mind was made up, so there was no point in further arguments. When he came to a decision, there were no second thoughts, no more wavering questions in his mind, and he wanted no continued speculation about whether or not it was the right thing for him to do."

Kenny put it on the schedule, booking a suite at the Rice Hotel in Houston.

On September 12, the day of the speech, Jack was on edge. "He was," Kenny said, "as restless as a caged tiger." Kenny poured some bourbon for Congressman Rayburn, who had arrived to hear the speech.

"I hope he knows what he's doing," Rayburn said as Kenny handed him the drink.

Rayburn and Johnson also remained convinced that the speech was a mistake. As they told Kenny, it was a "dangerous move, and he would be exposing himself to humiliation that might cost him the election."

Jack knew all this. Nevertheless, he followed his gut. And his gut told him that some issues can only be handled directly. You hope you get your punches in and that the enemy gives you credit for at least having the balls to enter the ring.

As Kenny talked with Rayburn about the impending speech, they could hear Jack calling for Dave. "Dave? Where are you, Dave. Come here!"

Kenny excused himself to search for Powers, whose personal duties for Jack included his wardrobe, but could find him nowhere. Kenny reported the bad news to Jack.

Jack asked him, "Have you got a pair of black shoes that I could borrow?"

Kenny looked startled, looking down at his well-worn brown shoes. His only pair. Jack stood there in stocking feet, a dark navy blue suit, a blue shirt, and a blue-and-white-striped tie.

"I only have brown shoes," said Kenny, never known for his sartorial splendor. He was a man who, until Bobby bought him a belt, wore a rope around his waist. As they left the suite to go to the speech, with Jack in Kenny's brown shoes, Rayburn shot Kenny a look. Kenny shrugged. He didn't know much about shoes.

"I should send that damned Dave back to Charlestown for this one!" Jack snapped.

As luck would have it, when they arrived at the elevator bank and the doors opened, there stood Dave Powers, who graciously held the door open for them. Jack stared at Powers in quiet fury.

Kenny chuckled, "Dave tried to look every other direction, pretending nothing had happened."

"Dave, do you notice anything out of place in my attire?" snapped Jack.

Dave, trying to look innocent, cleared his throat and asked, "Are those brown shoes?"

"Yes," Jack growled, "those are brown shoes. Brown shoes with a dark navy blue suit. Thanks very much, Dave."

The elevator made what must have seemed to Powers the slowest descent in recorded history.

"Well, Senator," Dave said defensively, "they won't see your shoes on television. Besides, you know that most men in this country wear brown shoes." Dave pointed to the floor of the elevator. Everyone was, in truth, wearing brown shoes. "Do you realize that tonight, by wearing these shoes, you'll be sewing up the brown-shoe voters?"

Just then the elevator landed. Jack stared in silence at Dave for a moment and then burst into laughter. Kenny guffawed and shook his head. Kenny later said, "Jack left to face the Houston ministers in a much more relaxed frame of mind."

Jack's speech was hailed as a great success. Kenny said that in many ways it was "the best speech of the campaign and probably the best speech he ever delivered in his lifetime: intelligent, forceful, and sharply pointed, without a wasted word."

Watching from his New York apartment, Joe Kennedy was pleased, agreeing with Kenny. "It was the best speech Jack had given to date," Joe said.

"The real issues of the campaign," Jack forcefully told the ministers, "were not religious issues but more critical problems—the humiliation of Eisenhower and Nixon by those foreign nations that no longer respect the United States, the hungry children in West Virginia, the old people unable to pay their doctor's bills, too many slums, too few schools."

He went on to say, as clearly and as powerfully as Kenny had ever heard him speak, "I believe in an America where the separation of the church and the state is absolute—where no Catholic prelate would tell the president (should he be Catholic) how to act and no Protestant minister would tell his parishioners for whom to vote . . . where no man is denied public office merely because his religion differs from the president who might appoint him or the people who might elect him."

The Houston ministers seemed, Kenny said, "confused and awestruck." Jack was not what they were expecting.

Back in the suite at the Rice Hotel, Kenny and Dave were relieved. While Kenny made some quick calls to Bobby and Larry to get their read, Rayburn shouted, "By God, listen to him! He's eating 'em blood raw! This feller will be a great president!"

Kenny smiled. Here was Texas's beloved "Mr. Sam," the man who, along with Lyndon Johnson, had caused them the most problems at the convention by raising the dreaded health issues and damn near derailing Jack. Rayburn now saw what a tough SOB Jack was in action.

"I can't tell you exactly if all the Houston ministers came away convinced," Kenny said, "but I can tell you Mr. Sam was, and that was good enough for me."

The next day, as the Kennedy team headed out on campaign stops throughout Texas, Jack was loose and felt good. He had finally put the Catholic issue to bed. Sam Rayburn loved a fighter and told Jack that the people of Texas would love a fighter. Rayburn's speeches at every stop were fiery and challenged Texans to vote for Jack! The Kennedy team felt good. It was what Kenny called "a good, stimulating, psychological boost," which added confidence at a time when Jack was growing tired.

Suddenly, John Kennedy was an extremely popular politician. The Houston speech galvanized the electorate. Suddenly politicians were, as Kenny recalled, "not afraid to be seen with him. This was not true when he arrived in El Paso two days before the speech. There had been no wild scramble to be with the senator."

Jack noticed the change immediately, and it helped push him onward. He did, however, note something strange and mentioned it to Kenny. "It was quite clear that Lyndon Johnson was not a terribly popular politician in Texas," Kenny remembered. "At every stop, when the introductions were finished, Senator Kennedy would get by far the better reception. Sam Rayburn would get a warm hand, and, to our surprise, Lyndon would get a smattering of polite applause. Mr. Sam got happier as the trip went on; Lyndon got steadily unhappier and morose as we swung through Texas."

"It did not mean we'd won over all those bigots," Kenny noted, "but Jack had answered all their questions and shown that his religion was no reason to vote against him. In so doing, he had given them permission to vote for him."

As they returned to the road, Jack said to Kenny, "I think we've gotten a handle on this Catholic thing, once and for all."

Kenny agreed. "Look at the crowds since the speech. The evidence is in the crowds."

It was evident that taking on the Catholic issue directly had set Jack free emotionally, as it had in West Virginia. After the speech, poll results backed the positive reception that Kenny, Dave, and Rayburn had seen reflected in the crowds. They were convinced the Catholic issue was largely defeated.

Jack's Catholicism, though, was connected to what Kenny called "the Negro issue."

"Both," Kenny said later, "reflected an underlying bigotry that Jack knew had to be addressed together in those terms."

Coming off their post-Houston high, they faced the wider bigotry issue when the campaign came to Texarkana, Texas, on September 13.

"We were concerned the integration thing was such a red-hot issue at this time," Kenny explained to Vanocur. "Texarkana had arisen sort of out of the blue, a solution to our problems in Arkansas. We wanted to go to Arkansas. We thought we could carry Arkansas. But we did not want to have our picture taken with Arkansas governor Orval Faubus if we could possibly help it. The Republicans and Nixon were making a serious effort in 1960 with the Negroes. Nixon has a pretty good image with the Negroes. His campaign was using Kennedy's '57 votes with the Negroes very effectively, and

Lyndon obviously was no help here. They were murdering Johnson, which was my fear when the senator first chose Johnson to be nominated. Part of my argument and complaints with the senator about his choice of Johnson was that we would have real problems with the Negroes at this time—serious problems, and we were concerned that a picture with Governor Orval Faubus, transmitted throughout the Negro community, was going to be very harmful to us, and we were trying to avoid it. We were still dealing with columnist Drew Pearson running around talking about Alabama governor Patterson and about us having breakfast with Patterson, who was, of course, anathema to the Negroes.

"You could not be seen having breakfast with Patterson, who was, let us be blunt, a Ku Klux Klanner and friend of Mississippi senator Jim Eastland. Nixon had great access to the Negro press and made sure this was distributed as widely as possible."

Kenny explained their reasoning in Texas. "Texarkana is located on the border between four states: Texas, Arkansas, Louisiana, and Mississippi. There is a yearly state fair, and the invitation came for Jack to speak. I had talked at length about this to the senator. It seemed a real solution to our problem. We could hit Arkansas without hitting Arkansas, thereby avoiding Governor Faubus."

"But," Kenny asked Bobby, "how do you get Faubus to understand Jack can't be seen with him without losing his support?"

"In the end," Kenny said, "Faubus understood the problem and agreed to be a good soldier and a good Democrat. He avoided the fair. The crowd at the fair was huge. If Faubus had been there, it would have been a disaster. The last view I had that day was of Rayburn standing there by the car, shaking his head. He just could not figure out what had happened to the Texas he knew, which normally hated all Catholics and was not real fond of Negroes either. The crowd was huge, and Mr. Sam was wondering what this young man had that could draw such enthusiasm from these people."

"The senator," Kenny recalled, "felt he had a highly successful trip through Texas and that the campaign was finally off the ground. He had cut quite a swath through Texas. For the first time, Jack began to feel he was back in his old stride. His voice had come back totally, growing stronger and stronger. He had now become used to speaking outdoors to huge crowds. The campaign was operating at the level of a proper presidential campaign.

"Once again," Kenny and Dave agreed later, "in deciding to accept the invitation from the Houston ministers, Kennedy had instinctively done the right thing against the advice of all his advisors."

After the speech, Jack's energy renewed by what he knew had been probably the best speech he had given of the campaign, he told Kenny, "I didn't change any votes in that room, but I didn't lose any elsewhere."

"Such a successful speech had boosted his confidence," and, Kenny noted, "raised his political stock considerably with leaders such as Sam Rayburn and Price Daniel, the Texas governor. It also gave Jack himself a stimulating psychological boost and added confidence at a point in the early stages of the campaign, two weeks before the first debate against Nixon, when he needed it most."

From there, the Kennedy campaign surged forward, and, Kenny said, the "mysterious hoarseness that had bothered Jack in the California campaign disappeared."

"Next, we arrived in New York. The Liberal Party in New York was, of course, fighting among itself. Despite whatever problems we had had with the reform group and the Stevensonians in the past, they let us say we represented the left wing of the Democratic Party, particularly in California. In fact, the Liberal Party had not been a participant in any of these affairs. Both David Dubinsky and Alex Rose had been pro-Kennedy from the very beginning. They had been part of the Kennedy organization, once the primary was out of the way, particularly because of their association with Walter Reuther and the UAW. Despite their close relationship and affection for Mrs. Roosevelt, they did not always agree with her. They had not been part of this so-called defection of the left-wing liberals. The understanding was that the Roosevelt/Symington group was perhaps the most anti-Nixon wing of the Democratic Party. The reality was, once [Jack] had the nomination, they had no other choice than to be for Jack Kennedy.

"Their degree of enthusiasm remained to be seen; they did not unduly concern us. We felt that although they sometimes took the attitude of 'rule or ruin' in local politics, Nixon was such an ogre to them that they could not help but go along with us. The Liberal Party could not help but endorse Senator Kennedy, so his name went on the ballot under the Liberal Party ballot. The senator went to their luncheon and stopped by their convention. It was at this point he received the endorsement of the Liberal Party, which would give him a guaranteed four hundred thousand votes in the election. Obviously, these four hundred thousand were all Democrats. But because of the peculiar situation in New York, one had to go through their dog and pony show."

From there, Jack and Kenny headed to Joe's apartment at the Waldorf Astoria for some private meetings. There was a dinner for Adlai Stevenson that night and a senior citizens' rally the next day, among other meetings.

"The New York trip was really standard stuff," as Kenny told Vanocur. "The next day would prove an enlightening day to us. We drove across the bridge into New Jersey, going through the northern, heavily populated areas. There was a high concentration of Negroes in this area.

"We began in Patterson, but it was almost a continuous trip: Patterson, Newark, two or three other small communities along the way. This was a complicated route, and we were lucky to be able to make it through. The crowds were huge. These were by far the largest crowds that we had encountered on the campaign, nonstop all the way through and ten-deep, sometimes twenty-deep. It was obvious that whatever the merits or demerits of Senator Kennedy as a candidate in the South and the midwestern industrial areas of the United States, in the Northeast he was the greatest candidate that had come along since Franklin D. Roosevelt, if not better.

"I again was forced for safety reasons to jump from my car to the sena-tor's car to keep him from being pulled from his automobile. The schools were all out, and there was a heavy concentration of Negroes, which would indicate that our support from them would be rather high. This was a relief, because it told us that Nixon's propaganda and attacks were not succeeding. This was not a poll. This was living evidence for our own eyes.

"Of course," Kenny said, "we must look at the history of the Negroes in the North, particularly in this area. They were heavily Democratic, but there was no question that this was going to be a bastion of Kennedy sup-port. He finally spoke on the Newark City Hall steps. We had a fantastic crowd there in the square, and the police lines were again broken, and there were some wild moments. It was now becoming a pattern of the Kennedy campaign: motorcycles breaking down and burning, policemen being knocked over, and so forth.

"The senator's speeches were beginning to take on the content and the tone of 'getting the country moving again.' The senator was now deliberately sounding very New Dealish and pushing hard on the Roosevelt association, appealing to the rank and file and the working people in America. As a can-didate, he now interlaced the names of Kennedy, Roosevelt, and Truman. This is the first truth about the foundation and source of Kennedy's power: the working people of America.

"The senator reacted to the crowds and fed off it. His speeches were now all extemporaneous. After New Jersey, he threw away all the set speeches and almost exclusively, through to the end of the campaign, spoke off the cuff, certainly in all his outdoor appearances.

"We were running very late now. This was in the tradition of our cam-paign. Once the campaign picked up steam, we were habitually not just late but very late, mainly because the crowds became a factor and we were running longer motorcades. Previously, the appearances were set pieces controlled by the advance men. Now, when we had crowds of sometimes five hundred thousand people stretched for miles and miles along the route, with people darting out and trying to grab the candidate, running and jumping on the car, I cannot tell you how many times the motorcade would be stopped.

"In the northern industrial cities with the older, narrower streets, it was very easy for any large crowd to reach out to the senator to shake hands with him or grab him. They were constantly breaking police lines to touch him, and quite frankly it became rather hazardous. I had been riding in the bus or in the car behind the senator, and at this point I spent most of my time racing up to jump on the back of the senator's car to protect him or hold on to him to the point that often I would just ride on the back bumper.

"In my view, it was a safety issue for him, and he felt the same way. He was worried about his own safety and that of these people who would jump on the car and try to grab him. He was concerned about them falling under the wheels; often they had small children or even babies in their arms.

"The policemen were running their motorcycles in the crowd to protect the candidate, and the senator leaned over to me and told me to tell them to stop it. He was concerned they were going to hit somebody. I could not do anything about it because I could not chance leaving him and the motorcade, the crowds were so huge. He had never seen anything like it. While it was exciting, when they were out of control like that, it could be very disturbing for him.

"We ended up in Trenton with Governor Meyner. This was a more sparsely populated part of New Jersey in comparison to the northern part of the state. The governor was exuding so much happiness and cooperation, he never got around to discussing any problems we might have had in the past. We went to the mansion and had a lovely buffet lunch set up by Mrs. Meyner, who was a very politically active lady and very enthusiastic about Senator Kennedy. They had received word about the size of the crowds, and this was now the talk of the mansion and the political establishment. The governor was extremely pleased with the way the campaign was going. We could not have had a better, friendlier group than was there at that mansion.

"From there, the campaign went to Harrisburg, Pennsylvania. Harrisburg, where Adlai Stevenson had opened his campaign in 1956 at a fund-raising dinner broadcast on nationwide television. It had been a catastrophe for Adlai in '56, for the Democratic Party, for the dinner group at Harrisburg, and for anyone else who had hoped to see a Democrat in the White House. It was a mess for anyone else who happened to be watching television that night," Kenny recalled.

Sandy Vanocur agreed, having covered it in '56. "All you could do was sit there and cringe."

Kenny explained, "That event made a great impression on Senator Kennedy and also on Bobby. They were convinced that a fund-raising dinner was not the place to make a nationally televised speech. By the time Stevenson got on, half the crowd was stiff and really not interested in hearing the candidate. They talked through his speech and kept drinking and getting drunk. In order to speak to a Democratic fund-raising group, one must give the speech in private and then give a second speech for the American people."

To avoid Stevenson's mistake, Vanocur recalled, "The senator did do statewide television that night, but at a different event, and the Kennedy campaign paid for it."

Kenny agreed, saying, "We paid the exorbitant television costs, but he was not going to make the mistake of speaking at that dinner. The senator hated speaking at fund-raising dinners for the very reasons I mentioned. This television issue was a constant back-and-forth between us and the political chairs across the country. They all wanted to have a TV event with Senator Kennedy because he was so good on television, especially if they were running for office. We tried to avoid this. We didn't want it to appear as though he was endorsing anyone for fear of losing votes for ourselves.

"There did not happen to be an election going on in Pennsylvania statewide, since they run theirs on off years. Therefore, they were not terribly excited about putting it on, because the state Democratic organization had to spend money on a national campaign. They were on board now, though, and they wanted to elect Kennedy, so they requested and paid for a state-wide television appearance. Jack was aware that he was going to be on television and speaking to rank-and-file contributors to the party.

"There were many," Kenny said, explaining Jack's unusual approach, "who were not rich at this dinner, so he directed his speech accordingly, avoiding Stevenson's mistake of speaking lofty phrases to working people who are looking at their televisions and worrying about their jobs."

Jack decided to direct his speech to that audience, not the contributors, which caused some consternation. "Plus," Kenny said, "we insisted on an early speech to avoid having to talk over people who had had too much to drink. But our focus was the television audience. We knew the people in the room were with us, so we didn't worry about them. Jack directed his speech to the audience viewing from home." From Pennsylvania, the campaign had an active week prior to the first debate, with stops in Indiana, Maryland, North Carolina, and Tennessee. On September 22, they made their way through the stockyards at Sioux City, where Jack even rode a white horse around the ring, much to Kenny's astonishment and disbelief. Jack was generally allergic to both horses and silly political gimmicks, but he even allowed a cowboy hat to be placed on his head. He was sure to snatch it off before the cameras could snap his picture.

The next stop was an Indian reservation in South Dakota, where Chief Hollow Horn Bear "lifted the featured headdress and bonnet and gently placed it on his head." Kenny chuckled as he watched Jack's arms shoot up and remove the hat, again before any photos could be taken, revealing a mussed shock of thick reddish-brown hair. "Next time, Chief," Jack said, "when I am watching a western, I will be rooting for our side."

With Jack more confident in himself, his campaign style, and his message, they headed to Chicago and the first debate. On their flight, Kenny asked the senator how he felt. Jack smiled. "Happy," he remarked, rubbing his hand, which was swollen from endlessly shaking hands on the campaign trail. "Good progress."

Exhausted, he closed his eyes to get some rest. Kenny sipped his drink. Maybe the Catholic thing was done.

"Everyone knows," Kenny said later, "the real turning point in the campaign was the first debate with Nixon in Chicago. The contrast between Nixon's nervous anxiety and Kennedy's cool composure wiped out the Republicans' contention that Kennedy was too immature and inexperienced for the presidency and established him as a potential winner."

This was essential to the Irish Brotherhood's strategy; with this debate, they had to convince not only Republicans but also, importantly, those remaining establishment Democrats who had remained reluctant to fully support Jack's candidacy.

"The debate," Kenny said, "brought the remaining or at least most of them out of the shadows, off the fence, and they were finally willing to fully support the senator."

The first debate, Jack and Kenny felt, was critical, because as Bobby later commented, "while all the debates matter, the first one in Chicago was key for Jack's momentum going forward."

They entered the debate as underdogs; after all, Richard Nixon was vice president, senator, congressman, and a pro. In 1952, Nixon had been nominated for the number-two spot on the Eisenhower ticket but had gotten in trouble for accepting gifts.

The Nixons, who were, as Kenny dubbed them, "regular people, not people of means," had set up a fund for friends to donate money and gifts. The ethics of such a fund were called into question, thus endangering Nixon's spot on the ticket. Nixon decided to go home to California, where in Los Angeles, at the El Capitan Theatre, he gave the infamous and critical "Checkers Speech." In the speech, he said that while he intended no wrong, the only gift he would keep was a black-and-white dog named Checkers, whom the children had fallen in love with.

The speech saved his career, and Eisenhower went on to win in a victorious Republican sweep, save for the state of Massachusetts, where some upstart, outsider Irishman by the name of Jack Kennedy had won the 1952 Senate race.

While Nixon and Kennedy's relationship had been fairly warm, it had cooled considerably, as it was clear that they were both after the same address: 1600 Pennsylvania Avenue. In fact, Jack told Kenny that he had come to believe that Nixon was fundamentally ill-suited to the job of president.

Nothing about this first debate would change Jack's mind; indeed it would cement his belief that he had been correct. Jack and Kenny continued on what Kenny and Dave called a "backbreaking tour, arriving in Chicago," Kenny noted, at 4:15 Saturday afternoon.

Sunday morning brought no rest. Despite the looming debate with Nixon, Kenny had scheduled Jack to be in Cleveland, where he spent an exhausting day "with a crowd of well over a thousand at an outdoor steer roast, arranged by Ray Miller." Miller, who had for the moment anyway given up his battle with Governor DiSalle to support Jack in Ohio, was head of the Cleveland Democratic organization.

When Jack asked about the timing of such a schedule, which annoyed the hell out of him, Kenny pointed out that the Cleveland event had been scheduled long before the date of the debates had been agreed on. Miller and Ohio remained critical to Jack's winning strategy for November, so the commitment had to be kept.

That night, Jack headed back to his hotel in Chicago, where he tried to get some rest and recuperate for the next day. He confessed to Kenny that he was tired and that his back was killing him. As Dave helped lower him into a hot bath that evening, he asked Jack if he was worried about the debate. Jack leaned back in the steaming bath and closed his eyes. "Nixon," he said finally, "is someone who has been underestimated all his political life. He will be a tough debater. Nothing can be taken for granted."

While he agreed with Jack's assessment of Nixon, at the time Kenny still "felt and believed the senator would wipe the floor up with him, just as he had done with Henry Cabot Lodge in 1952. Lodge," Kenny noted, "had an equally impressive debating record." But Kenny felt that "Jack, always the outsider, seemed to relish the opportunity to take these fellows on and show them to be paper tigers."

In Kenny's view, no doubt, Jack was anything but a paper tiger. As Sam Rayburn had said watching him in Houston speaking to the ministers, "He's a tiger! He's gonna eat 'em raw." Kenny hoped for a similar outcome in the debate.

The next day, Monday, September 26, the day of the first debate, "Jack spent the afternoon at the Hotel Morrison," Kenny said, "giving a well-received rousing speech to the Carpenters Union."

That evening, as they headed to the debate, Kenny thought that Jack seemed remarkably cool and in control, in contrast to his nervousness before meeting the Houston ministers.

"He seemed not the least bit worried," Kenny realized, adding, "In part, this was because Jack had lost respect for Richard Nixon as a political adversary and thus paid little attention to anything he said. His disregard," Kenny came to believe, "came across strongly to television audiences during the debates, and his disregard, clearly visible to television viewers, was often more damaging than any verbal attack. While Nixon was sweating profusely with the pancake makeup slowly melting off [his] face, Jack seemed disinterested. Camera shots showed him watching Nixon's unraveling with a mixture of boredom and amusement, almost as if he was thinking Nixon was silly."

His dislike for Nixon was not because of his political views, Jack explained to Kenny. "There is something deeper there," Jack said. "He almost wants it too badly, and [it] makes me concerned about how he would use his power."

Kenny also believed that Jack saw Nixon as "a faker playing to audiences and willing to say what they wanted to hear to get elected. He was," Kenny declared, "simply too dull, coy, and disingenuous for Jack's taste."

As if to prove Jack's point, after the debate, Jack and Nixon shook hands. Just then, Nixon noticed that photographers had finally been allowed in and wanted to get a shot of the two men for the next morning's edition.

As Kenny watched, to his astonishment, Nixon began jabbing his finger into Jack's chest, as if telling him off. Kenny, too far away to hear what was said, was surprised and eager to find out what the hell had happened. As they headed out of the studio back to Jack's hotel for an early morning campaign call, Kenny asked, "What that was all about?"

Jack shook his head as he shoved his hands in pockets, wincing slightly. "I don't know," Jack said, "just the usual small talk. I wasn't really listening to him. We were talking about the weather, schedule, and how hard it is to get a good night's sleep on the campaign trail; he was watching the photographers out of the corner of his eye. When one of them was taking a picture of us, he would get this stern expression on his face and start jabbing his finger into my chest, so he would look like he was laying down the law to me, like I am some young kid, he is laying down the law about foreign policy or communism. Nice fellow!"

His irritation boiling over, Jack suddenly stopped and looked at Kenny for a moment just as the campaign car arrived to take them back to the hotel. "He's dangerous, Kenny," he said. "Something is very wrong. He is very unsure of himself. We have to win this election. He would be very dangerous as president. He would not be good for the country."

Later that night, when they were eating dinner in the hotel room, Kenny sensed again that Jack was still bothered by events of that evening. Suddenly, Jack looked across at Kenny, trying to make light of it, but Kenny felt "not too lightly."

Jack said, "I am telling you, Kenny, we owe it to this country to keep Richard Nixon out of the White House."

Kenny was startled by the cold vehemence with which Jack said it but did not pry. The debate now over, Kenny was already getting reports that Jack had cleaned Nixon's clock as he had with Lodge in '52. Kenny wanted to focus Jack on the positive news and the heavy campaign schedule ahead. Besides, Kenny thought to himself, *if we win in November—no, when we win in November—we will win again in '64 and Nixon will be a "done brother," politically. No chance of a political resurrection.*

Years later, after Nixon had become president, his paranoia had begun to build, and the country, Larry O'Brien, the Democrats, and Kenny found themselves on the wrong end of Nixon's so-called political hit list, Kenny would think, sadly, back to that Monday evening and Jack's words. Once again, Jack's political instincts and gut reaction had been way ahead, this time years ahead, of the rest of the country.

Senator Frank Lausche, among other Democrats across the country and voters of both parties, finally had come to recognize that John F. Kennedy had the "right stuff" for the White House, that Jack was, as he claimed, "a new voice for a new generation of Americans," Kenny recalled.

How did Jack know that he had done well in that first debate? That he had indeed won? The signal came early the next morning when top-flight advance man Jerry Bruno arrived at Jack's motel room in Painesville, Ohio, where the Kennedy campaign had spent the night, so they would be ready to hit the ground for a full day of campaigning in Ohio the next day.

"You're early," Kenny said. Jack looked up from his eggs, bacon, toast, coffee, and juice, surprised to see Bruno this early as well.

"The senator is waiting outside," a smiling Bruno explained. "He is in the car and would like to spend the day campaigning with you and Governor DiSalle."

"Senator who?" Jack asked, confused, looking to Kenny for an explanation. Kenny shrugged. This was all news to him. "Senator Frank Lausche,"

Bruno said. "He wants to join the party!" Interestingly, Senator Frank Lausche of Ohio had refused to appear with Jack just two days before.

Jack and Kenny exchanged smiles. "Guess we did all right last night, Senator," Kenny said.

"So it appears," Jack said, "so it would seem." With that he picked up his suit coat and headed to the car to greet his new convert.

The first televised debate between Jack Kennedy and Richard Nixon marked the beginning of the modern political era and had a direct and immediate impact on the electorate. There would be two more debates to follow in early October. They would be seen by millions whom he would not have otherwise been able to reach. They would change the odds for Jack Kennedy and make him a serious candidate for the White House in the eyes of the voters.

The voters could see Kennedy, with his cool demeanor, detached attitude, sharp and concise answers, and movie-star good looks, holding his own. In those debates Jack had been able to convince the voters that he was presidential timber; that the Democratic political fence dwellers came along as well was also an important benefit. "Television," Jack had predicted back in 1952, Kenny noted, "would and will change the very process of how we elect the president and candidate across the country. "A candidate who could not communicate on television, like the silent film stars who could not make the transition to talkies, would, in the end, Jack predicted, "be left behind."

CHAPTER 19

The Campaign

J ACK WAS CORRECT about the impact of television. He made sure in the debates that he mastered the facts, mastered the conversation with Nixon, and controlled the medium and the message. Political history was made and the presidential campaign process was changed forever and would never look back from that moment when the mics went hot in Chicago.

Barbara Gamarekian, who had come over from the Humphrey campaign to join the Kennedy campaign as an administrative assistant, described the debate a bit differently. "I did not know the senator well, but I think like many Democrats, the TV debates began to make me identify with him and feel that I knew him personally rather than as a Democratic candidate. And it felt great to get terribly excited about him."

While many in the Kennedy camp felt that Nixon had been beaten in the debates and many shared Barbara's opinion that Jack now seemed both presidential and yet one of them, Kenny, Bobby, and especially Jack were not so sure.

Richard Milhous Nixon was not a man to easily be dismissed. He was born on January 9, 1913, in Yorba Linda, California, and grew up in the working-class town of Whittier, California. His dad was a "gas jockey," as they called it, which meant simply that he owned a gas station and general store.

Nixon eventually obtained his law degree, secured a job in Washington, DC, and, when World War II arrived, served in the navy, rising eventually to the rank of lieutenant commander while serving in the Pacific. He was a vet like Kenny and Jack; he was years older than his actual age from that experience and had worked his way up the ranks in Congress from the House of Representatives in 1946, joining the same class Jack Kennedy did, which is where they first met. Nixon won his Senate seat in 1950 and ran as vice president with Eisenhower in the 1952 election.

Jack knew Nixon to be politically tough-minded and determined; while he may have gotten swamped in the first televised debate, he came back stronger in the second debate, but more importantly, as Jack told Kenny, "He knows it is the votes in November that count. He's not going to give an inch."

Kenny agreed, saying to Bobby, "He is not going to be scared off by a few tough debates."

While that may have been the inside view in the Kennedy camp, the crowds greeting Jack began to grow and grow wildly, so Kenny had to keep reminding himself that they were inside what Kenny liked to call "the campaign bubble." While they were seeing wild crowds, Nixon was barnstorming just as hard.

"How many of those people we saw today were registered Democrats?" Jack asked wearily as they flew on the *Caroline* one evening, headed to more campaign stops in Ohio.

Kenny had no idea. The discussion was dropped by the time they got back to Washington that night. Bobby, who was in Hyannis Port, had some news that would return them to earth rather quickly.

"You have problems," Bobby said.

"How come it is *you* when it is a problem," Kenny asked, "and *we* when it is going well?"

For once Bobby did not chuckle. "This is serious, Kenny," he said, dropping his voice.

Kenny knew that when Bobby did that, it was a matter to be taken very seriously.

"You see," Kenny explained, "what Bobby wanted us to see is that we were out of touch here to some degree. We saw the crowds, the wild enthusiasm, and we would call Bobby and tell him we might be able to crack this Oklahoma thing."

Bobby's reply was, as Kenny described it, "cold silence." His reply caught them off guard.

"We have a problem," Bobby said again. While Jack and Kenny were on the road, in the Kennedy campaign bubble, Bobby was in touch with the political leaders in various states outside of that bubble. "They were asking Bobby to pull us out of their state because of death threats and hate stuff," Kenny remembered.

Jack and Kenny were stunned. "We only react to what we can see with our eyes," Kenny explained.

"Look, Bobby," Jack said, "the crowds we see with our eyes are very enthusiastic, wildly so."

Bobby, however, back at headquarters, was getting phone calls and found that the religious thing had now come back very strongly.

"It's back, Jack," Bobby said. "The religious thing never went away. It just went underground, and now, quite frankly, it is threatening to derail the campaign. We are in real trouble."

Jack sat speechless.

Kenny remembered being sick to his stomach. There was no more time to address these issues.

Kenny said, "If it were anybody but Bobby telling us, we'd have doubted it. But Bobby couldn't be doubted. His tone was dire."

"The speech in Houston . . ." Jack began.

"Look," Bobby said, "the Houston thing dulled it for a time, but the religious thing is back. It is dangerous, and it could derail us. You've got to come back."

Nobody traveling with the candidate could have predicted the resurgence of the Catholic issue. As Kenny recalled, "Throughout the summer of 1960, we'd been to Philadelphia, Chicago, Oklahoma; we'd seen enormous crowds across California, Arizona, New Mexico, Texas. Wild crowds, uncontrollable crowds. Because we'd been coming on steadily, we thought, *This is over, we've won.*"

But Bobby's in-flight phone call to the campaign's mobile headquarters on the *Caroline* changed everything. "We've got to have an emergency meeting in Hyannis Port," Bobby insisted. "I think we're in serious trouble, and if we don't stop the bleeding, it could be over."

Senator Kennedy reluctantly agreed, and he and Kenny canceled their remaining schedule, rerouting their flight from DC to Massachusetts. They would have to figure out how to maintain campaign momentum, a campaign they had wrongly assumed was on a clear-cut path to victory.

Kenny and Jack made plans to meet with Bobby, Steve, and Joe in Hyannis Port to see just how bad the bleeding was.

Exhausted and still reeling from Bobby's call, Jack and Kenny headed to the Kennedy compound, where the early New England autumn chill had already set in.

"The plane ride there on the *Caroline* was marked by its silence," Kenny said. "We did not yet know what Bobby knew, so we could not begin to plan or even react. The only upshot was that in Hyannis Port Jack could see Jackie and Caroline, get some much-needed rest, and recoup for a couple of days."

Teddy White recalled that emergency trip to Hyannis Port. It was the first time he had not seen the candidate bound enthusiastically up the stairs. Instead, White noted, "He walked up the stairs slowly, a dark-blue mohair overcoat over his gray suit, bareheaded, slightly stooped. He was very tired."

As they took their seats in Bobby's living room, Kenny remembered, "Bobby's point to us was that we were not gaining momentum at all. For every vote we earned, anti-Catholic bigotry would cost us five. Given our success out west, Senator Kennedy and I had trouble taking this in."

But Bobby's bad news was backed up by polls and also by numerous calls from state leaders who, fearing anti-Catholic violence, had asked to have Jack's path through their states rerouted. Others wanted the Kennedy events in their states canceled altogether. Jack's eloquent speech in Houston on the separation of church and state had not vanquished the anti-Catholic sentiment after all. These forces of irrationality and paranoia had only gone underground and regrouped, and now they were back, more vicious than ever, and apparently more politically shrewd.

Bobby continued, "The polls indicate, and have indicated now for about a month, a 3 or 4 percent lead for Senator Kennedy on a national basis. This was the Gallup Poll. Harris was agreeing with Gallup pretty much all through this. The local polls turn out not to be too far off, and we are about where we expected."

But what they also showed was Jack losing support, and it was tied to the Catholic issue.

Jack rose and paced as Bobby ran the numbers. "How can this be?" he muttered quietly. "If you saw what we saw . . ."

"I am telling you," Bobby replied. "They aren't voting for you. We need to change strategy."

"How, at this late date?" Kenny wanted to know.

"That's your job," Bobby snapped. "I am just telling you, we've got to stop the bleeding or we will lose."

Jack looked over at Kenny, who was, as usual, back away from the crowd, arms folded, leaning against the wall. Jack did not say a word as he rose but touched Kenny's arm as he left.

Kenny understood.

Fix it was what Jack was saying.

The question of what to do at this late date in the campaign fell to O'Donnell and O'Brien. Jack figured, if anyone could determine how to quell this underground swell of anti-Catholic bigotry that threatened to swamp the Kennedy boat at the last minute, it would be those two. But the truth was, Kenny admitted later, they were unsure themselves. "This late into the campaign, schedules are largely set in stone and cannot be changed. Commitments have been made, and everything you can account for considered and covered, but we had not expected this and we had no real plan." Except maybe one. To call Richard Daley, the mayor of Chicago, the boss of bosses. If anyone could advise them, it would be Daley.

Kenny put in the call and laid out the facts for the mayor. The truth was, Kenny said to him, "this was just hardball, tough-assed politics, but we can't just let it go. We've got to fight back, but how?" The mayor was silent for a moment, and Kenny could almost hear the political gears turning in Daley's mind. But if Kenny had expected some magic bullet to solve it, he was about to be disappointed.

"There is nothing you can do at this late stage but swamp them at the polls. The key is to get your people to the polls. You leave that to me. A vote for our guy can stop a vote against a bigot any day of the week. Tell the senator," Daley said, "I've got his back."

That was it. End of conversation. When Kenny returned to Bobby's living room, campaign central, and relayed the news, there was only silence. Everyone knew instinctively that Daley was right: They would have to be sure to get their people to the polls. As Kenny placed a call to Washington and his sister Justine, who was now down at the Esso Building, he thought how it might all come down to this, "the damn Catholic issue" and registered voters. As he waited impatiently for Justine to come on the line, he wondered how many in the huge crowds they had seen were, in fact, registered voters.

Justine got the message, which Kenny delivered in his usual terse, no-explanation-given fashion: "Tell Maguire to get the damn people to the polls. Call anyone and everyone; it is going to be closer than we might think."

Justine was about to ask what had happened when the line went dead. Sitting at her desk, she stared at the telephone receiver and chuckled to herself. "Nice to chat with you as well," she said, replacing the receiver in the cradle. She went to talk to Maguire and then get the "vote girl" herself, the tough-minded Helen Keyes, who had been getting out votes for Jack since '52. They knew that Helen Keyes could shake every last vote out of every last tree there was.

◆

ANOTHER SIGNIFICANT SOURCE of concern for the campaign was Richard Nixon's strength with African American voters. But it was also an opportunity.

The endorsement of baseball great Jackie Robinson was bad enough, but Bobby heard that Nixon was courting Martin Luther King, and it had Bobby worried. King was, of course, a double-edged sword. Getting too close to him could cost them votes in the South, warned Mr. Sam wisely, yet Bobby also knew well that support from King on the right Sunday in black churches across the South could translate strongly into votes on November 7.

"The biggest problem," Bobby said to Kenny, "is that when it comes to Dr. King, Nixon has a relationship where we don't even have our foot in the door."

Kenny, campaigning with Jack nonstop in a whirlwind tour across the country, told Bobby, "You set it up; I will find a way to get him there."

In fact, Jack had just never sat down to think about the best strategy to secure the African American community's support. Certainly, it would take a tidal wave of confrontations between African Americans and white southerners across the South, instigated by Dr. King, to eventually get the Kennedy White House to act.

"It was not that they had not planned to act," Kenny later explained. "They did, but they planned to do it at the right time politically. Dr. King understood that all too well, and by then he felt they had waited long enough. It was at this time, as the civil rights movement came of age, that Martin Luther King was increasingly viewed as the man to deal with on the movement, whether you agreed with [Dr. King and the civil rights movement's] demands or not."

According to Kenny, Nixon grasped this importance much faster than Jack did and had a stronger relationship with the African American community.

"We need to find a way in," Kenny told Bobby. While Bobby no doubt agreed, the friends both knew it was late in the game to fit in such a strategy without looking like a faker or risking backfire. In fact, on June 13, 1957, Nixon and Martin Luther King had met, Dr. King responding to an invitation by Nixon for a "summit conference" to mark the nation's recognition of Dr. King's role with the civil rights movement.

King was initially wary; he had not been a huge supporter of Nixon, feeling Nixon was far too conservative and voted far too often with the far right of the Republican Party. Still, Dr. King went to the meeting, cautious but recognizing that freedom for his people could not afford party affiliations.

Bayard Rustin, a top King aide, indicated to colleagues that at the meeting Dr. King urged Nixon "to get the Republicans in Congress to pass a pending civil rights bill and to visit the South to express his and their [Republicans'] support for the civil rights movement."

Rustin recalled that Dr. King was, at the time, optimistic about Nixon's commitment to improving race relations in the United States. King told Nixon "how deeply grateful all people of goodwill are to you for your assiduous labor and dauntless courage in seeking to make the civil rights bill a reality."

Later, as they headed back home, Rustin inquired whether King really believed what Nixon had told him. Dr. King was thoughtful for a moment and finally said, "If Richard Nixon is not sincere, he is the most dangerous man in America!"

Ironically, Kenny noted later, "Had Dr. King and Jack Kennedy spoken about all this earlier, they likely would have shared the sentiment expressed by Dr. King."

However, it would take a series of events to catapult the Kennedy/King relationship into being and to provide a political opening for both candidates. However, Jack Kennedy had one major advantage over Nixon: He had Harris Wofford, Bobby Kennedy, and most important Sarge Shriver, an ardent Roman Catholic, often praying a rosary in his pocket as he moved through his day and "who was relentless," Kenny said later, "when it came to getting the senator to do what he viewed as the morally right thing, no matter the political cost."

The "King factor," as Kenny called it, would prove important in the latter stages of the political campaign.

As the days leading up to the election passed, the campaign pushed harder, looking for every break and opportunity; a critical one would present itself less than three weeks before the election when Dr. Martin Luther King was arrested in Atlanta on October 19. King, as the acknowledged leader of the civil rights movement, had continued to press hard for change and had pushed Nixon and Kennedy both. The Kennedy campaign had up until then appeared largely disinterested and distant. King, who had gotten a pledge from Nixon in 1957, had expected at this important time that Nixon would step up. At least put in a call.

Jack and Kenny were in a hotel room on a campaign swing through Ohio when they heard the news about King's arrest. As Kennedy rested in his suite, Harris Wofford among others began pushing hard for Jack to call Mrs. King, who was distraught that something might happen to her husband. Such mysterious "accidents" were not unheard of in these parts of the South.

Jack was hesitant, as Kenny recalls; he resisted what he saw as a campaign "gimmick." It looked like a cheap stunt to win the black vote, Jack thought. As they all considered this, Kenny, as usual, said little, standing aside and listening to everyone's advice.

Later, Jack pulled him into the bathroom. "What do you think?" he wanted to know.

Kenny said, "While I am sympathetic to what Mrs. King and her family must be going through, from a political point of view, all I can see is that it could backfire; we could lose key southern support that we worked hard to achieve. Furthermore," Kenny agreed with Jack, "it looks like a cheap stunt. I am afraid that is how it will appear to King and his supporters. You've never thought much about this, then suddenly you make this call. There are a million ways politically it could be a mess."

Jack agreed. Harris Wofford, who had been recruited to advise Kennedy on civil rights issues, was not deterred, he told Sargent Shriver.

Kenny remembered the moment well: "We had just had this big discussion about the thing. From my point of view and Jack's it was decided. While Harris Wofford pushed hard, he could only push so far, and I felt that the political considerations had won out in the end."

Jack was headed to take a hot bath and get some rest, so Kenny retreated downstairs for a drink and a moment to regroup.

That is when Sarge Shriver, fingering the ever-present rosary in his jacket pocket, caught Kenny in the hallway. "I want a few minutes," he said. "I want to reopen the King discussion."

Kenny said later, "I was not pleased. The issue had been decided and I did not want it reopened. We had a heavy schedule the next day and I wanted to move on, but Sarge would not budge."

The two men stood toe to toe in the hallway outside Jack's closed suite door.

"I never use my family connection or ask for a favor, but you are wrong, Kenny. This is too important. I want time alone with him," Sarge Shriver said.

Kenny said later, "For political reasons I wanted to tell him flat-out no, but the truth was he had never asked before and he was a family member. Unlike others, he never asked or abused that relationship, and, at some level, morally I suspected he might be right, though politically I still was against it."

"I haven't eaten yet," Kenny said quietly. "I'm going to get a hamburger and a beer."

Sarge nodded. They shook hands.

"You know I am right," he said to Kenny's departing figure.

"Maybe," Kenny said. "If it works, you'll get no credit for it; if it does not, you'll get all the blame."

They both laughed. They had both been there before.

When Kenny returned, Jack had made the decision. He would call Mrs. King. With that single call he changed the dynamics of the election. "If he'd listened to me instead of Sarge," Kenny said, "who knows?"

Unbeknownst to Jack, Kenny, or Sarge, Bobby Kennedy had been bothered by the events as well, despite agreeing with Jack, Kenny, and Steve that all should be left alone. Finding a pay phone during his travels on the campaign, Bobby on his own called the judge in charge and asked him to release Dr. King on humanitarian grounds. When the press called Kennedy headquarters at the Esso Building to confirm the story, they were incredulous, immediately issuing a denial.

When Bobby called in later, he sheepishly suggested to Kennedy aide John Seigenthaler that he might want to call the press back, because he had, after all, made the call. When Kenny and Jack heard about it later, they had to laugh. "You know politics did not motivate either Sarge or Bobby," Jack told Kenny.

While Kenny agreed and in the end it worked to Jack's benefit, the push and pull of politics versus the morally correct thing to do would always be a factor with the group around Jack.

"I felt my job was to always focus on the political factors and implications," Kenny explained. "I could do so confidently. The moral issues would be raised by Bobby, Sarge, Harris Wofford, or others; it was not my job nor, unless it was politically important, my role."

For his part, Martin Luther King, while deeply grateful to Kennedy, also expressed "disappointment that, despite his previous warm relationship with Nixon, when this moment came it was like he had never heard of me."

After Nixon's inaction after promising such strong support, King later told aides that he had come to believe that Nixon was instead "a moral coward and one who was really unwilling to take a courageous step and take a risk."

In the end, Jack Kennedy's reluctant phone call, with what they considered their "discreet publicity, so as not too upset too many southerners, in promoting Jack's role in releasing King from jail," helped tremendously in gaining black support and black votes for Jack in November. While Dr. King was pleased that Kennedy had acted, he remained cautious; he had been at this too long and seen how difficult it was to get political figures to do the right thing when political considerations came into view. He was hopeful that Kennedy could win in November with their support, but he was determined to stay focused on his own agenda no matter what party moved into 1600 Pennsylvania Avenue.

As the campaign continued in late October, Kenny remembered, "We arrived in St. Louis at the airport; it was dark. Senator Symington came on board the *Caroline* at the airport and chatted with the senator while he was getting dressed. There was a very large crowd in St. Louis. The advance man, a fellow named Bob O'Hare, was there with Congressman O'Neill." O'Hare went up to O'Neill and said to him, "This is terrible; the crowd is huge and surging. I hope the police can handle it. They seem not to know what to do with a crowd this size." Congressman O'Neill suggested that it was a bit late to worry about that now.

Kenny recalled, "About two minutes later the crowds broke the police line and surged forward, surrounding the plane, screaming and yelling Jack's name. Our advance man was able to get Congressman O'Neill to safety. Senator Symington started out of the plane first, and the crowd started screaming. Then Senator Kennedy came out behind him. The crowds just broke through the final barricades and surged forward. It was both exciting and a bit frightening. I grabbed Senator Kennedy and pulled him to safety.

"He was startled, and I was concerned. He returned quickly to the plane, followed by Symington. There were no police in sight now, and the crowd surrounded the plane and ran up the ramp. I slammed the door to protect the senator. They began pounding on the door and shaking the plane, screaming for Senator Kennedy.

"Senator Symington was stunned. He had never seen anything like it. We were less surprised. After Texas, we were beginning to see this happening; but honestly, for some minutes, there was a real fear of bodily harm to both senators and the congressman, as the crowd was totally out of control. I remember them shaking the airplane and it rocking back and forth and them screaming for him to come out. There is no question, had he come out, he would have been mobbed, as there were no policemen anywhere.

"It was decided that I should get help, so I went out the back hatch and almost lost control, with people trying to run over me to get in the door, but I had to find our advance man. We were afraid they were going to tip the plane over. The crowds were now so whipped into a frenzy, it was quickly escalating to a point of danger. I eventually found our advance man, who had been struggling through the crowd.

"Together, he and I struggled to find a policeman in charge. We eventually did, and the police after quite some time arrived and managed to get the crowd under control. This was the frenzy that we began to detect after Houston when we hit these northern cities. The Texas crowd had been huge, friendly, but reasonably orderly.

"This was new, I thought, a combination of a huge crowd, poor police work, and poor advance work that had not anticipated the size of the crowd. This frightened us to the point that we were tougher with our advance people in the future.

"They finally cleared a way through for the senator after about a half hour of the crowd hammering on the *Caroline*. The senator came down the stairs, and the crowd went wild again, but this time we had enough police. He gave a good speech, and then we took a motorcade to the Chase Hotel. There were crowds all along the way, chasing the car and so forth, trying to grab at him. I again got out of my car and jumped on the back of his car."

Vanocur remembered it well. "It was wild. Very frenzied and a bit frightening."

"I recall," Kenny noted, "we arrived at the Chase Hotel, and the senator was rather pleased with himself. He remarked rather wryly, 'God, there must be an awful lot of Catholics in St. Louis.' We all laughed.

"We discussed the situation at the hotel. Senator Symington was very impressed with the size, volume, and enthusiasm of the crowd. He thought Jack was doing well in St. Louis. But he was concerned about some potential problems: Missouri being divided almost into two states, with the big metropolitan areas, St. Louis and Kansas City, being one; and the rural central and southern regions another. The Catholic issue could rear its head again in the Missouri hinterlands.

"The senator got up the next morning to speak at the machinists' convention. This had been the most anti-Kennedy union in the past. It was a must from our point of view. It was very difficult to schedule, and it was not the proper time to go into St. Louis, but the machinists were very active in politics. They operated independently of the UAW unions, and they had their own funding and their own form of political action. They were an important union because of the location of their membership, which, generally speaking, followed the railroads through the South and the West. These were places where we would probably be the weakest.

"Jack made a good speech and got an enthusiastic reception. The labor unions were anti-Nixon enough that they were looking for a champion, and they felt they had found one in Senator Kennedy."

As the campaign headed into its final weeks, Kenny said, they continued to see wild crowds and it seemed that the Kennedy campaign was on a roll. "With all these factors working for us," Kenny said, "and the huge crowds, it was hard to envision that we could not defeat Nixon."

At the same time, they were still facing issues in the large and politically complicated state of California. Jack enlisted help on every front. His friendship with Sinatra brought in the Hollywood crowd and their money. On the political side they had Jesse Unruh. Unruh served as speaker in California's legislature. He was a tough-talking political genius whom Kenny respected a great deal.

Because of Nixon's obvious advantage in California as well as the complex nature of California politics, the Kennedy operation had to have two solid, big-city operations: one in Los Angeles and one in San Francisco.

Governor Brown, while helpful, did not know his state the way Unruh did. Kenny preferred to rely on Unruh. This particular trip out west had been designed to negate Nixon's strengths with the aerospace workers.

Kenny had no question that Douglas Aircraft had been a great recipient of pork-barrel funds from California's representatives in Washington. "I believe it was their Convair jet program," Kenny remembered. "Every time you drove by their San Diego operations, you could see they were still standing by. They were very sensitive about it."

Jack needed to make it clear in a speech in California that he would never have regional or sectional views about awarding defense contracts once he was president. In fact, he pointed out that he never had as a senator.

This was a reply to speeches, handbills, and leaflets that Nixon was distributing, particularly in southern California. These documents insinuated that Jack, as a candidate from the East, would remove most of the contracts from California and the western states, placing them in areas closer to his own home.

Kenny felt that "it was a clever and damaging ploy based upon a careless statement Jack had made in Buffalo, New York, at the Bell Aircraft

Corporation. Bell was in a dire position, having not done much since pro-
ducing the Aircobras in the war. During the statement at Bell Aircraft, Jack
felt that these contracts should be distributed in an equitable fashion and
not located predominately in one area of the country."

Nixon pounced on this and ran with the statement, distorting it. Nixon
began mentioning it in speeches out west and across California.

Kenny became concerned because "Nixon gave people the impression
that what Senator Kennedy really meant was that he would pull all the
contracts out of California. California at the time had about 20 percent
of all government work on space and aircraft productions. Accordingly,
Californians then must assume this would be reduced under a Kennedy
regime. Nixon then gave the impression: If you elect Kennedy, California
will take a hit right off the bat."

This spurred the campaign and Kenny, in particular, into action: "We
needed to win the state, so this was something that could not be left to
stand."

A good crowd greeted the Kennedy team. Jack spoke to them and,
as Kenny recalled, had a good reception. "There was no question these
charges were having some impact on the Democrats and Governor Brown.
Most of the California political leaders were concerned that this charge of
Nixon's was having some effect upon the senator's candidacy in California.
We attempted to put it to rest with this stop."

It was very late in the campaign. While Jack doubted one speech could
undo the damage, it was nonetheless "considered an essential stop by the
California people."

From there, they drove back to Beverly Hills and stayed at the Beverly
Hilton. This provided some much-needed downtime for Jack with his
brother-in-law Peter and allowed for a quick, fun-filled visit to Peter's house
in Santa Monica.

The next night, Jack spoke at East Los Angeles College and came back
to the Beverly Hilton to stay overnight. The next morning he gave a speech

at a Democratic women's breakfast at the Beverly Hilton. After that they went on to San Diego.

Jack spoke at the city hall plaza in San Diego, then the campaign moved on to San Jose. According to Kenny, "We had a very good crowd in downtown San Jose, close to the size we had back east, and that was good to see. We needed California.

"After San Jose, we drove back to San Francisco to attend a fund-raising dinner at the San Fran Sheraton, followed by a trip to the Cow Palace. Kennedy made a television broadcast from the Cow Palace, which was packed." Jack had been skeptical about the appearance, but Kenny had convinced him to do it.

Vanocur remembered the November 2 Cow Palace event being "jam-packed to the rafters." It was at the Cow Palace that Jack unveiled the Peace Corps.

"There will be quarrels," Kenny noted, "for years about the origins of the Peace Corps, but the Cow Palace was the scene of the idea's first reception by the public. Lots of people take credit. I personally give the credit to Ted Sorensen. For the first time, Sorensen really pushed it hard in a speech. It was their idea, the president and Sorensen.

"Both Senator Kennedy and Senator Humphrey had discussed it in prior years and Senator Humphrey deserves some credit here as well. But in San Francisco, for the first time, the senator put it out there as one of his platforms and campaign promises."

Later, after the votes were counted, Jack would lament losing California: "It was evident that we had such good operations in California and such support that, with more time, we could have taken the state."

Kenny reluctantly agreed, admitting that it was his decision to cut the last trip out to California, as he felt their time was better spent in New York.

"Kennedy would mention it to me, still, even when we were in the White House, almost in passing, that we had short-changed California, that we should have traded the New York days for the California days. He also felt strongly if we had spent more time in the Los Angeles suburbs, as we had done back east, that this, plus the extra days in the Valley, would have won us California.

"He was correct, but by now it was too late to change course. The decision was mine alone. We lost the state because we did not do as the senator had wanted."

From California, they headed to Phoenix, Arizona, where they had a brief reception at the airport and met with a hugely positive crowd. From there they headed to a hotel called the Westward Ho. Jack spoke there in the morning at an arranged breakfast.

Kenny remembered, "It was a very good crowd. We were confident now in general, although Arizona is not a state we were placing great confidence in. We felt Arizona was a Democratic state, and we hoped to carry it even though this was our only stop in the state."

From there, Jack headed to New Mexico to speak at the University of New Mexico in the stadium. Jack and Kenny were excited to be greeted by a huge, wildly enthusiastic crowd. It was the type of crowd, Jack noticed, that he was capturing again and again. It was this intermixing of college crowds, with which he had a terrific rapport, with, increasingly, young professionals, young families, and many returning veterans that represented Jack's unique new constituency. While in New Mexico, Jack also did a statewide television show, which went very well.

From New Mexico, they went on to Amarillo, Texas, and a rally at the airport there. This trip was followed by a stop in Wichita Falls on the campaign's way to Oklahoma. They arrived, exhausted, in Oklahoma that night and had a motorcade to a shopping center, where again wild crowds greeted them.

"Senator Kennedy and Oklahoma's Senator Kerr were in the back room. The crowd was enthusiastic, and Senator Kerr was surprised," Kenny said. "It was so loud that even in the back room they could barely hear each other. Senator Kerr was quite enthusiastic about this young fellow whom he was going to introduce. He could not have been friendlier."

While Kenny watched the huge crowd with great pleasure, he was startled when the young, recently elected Senator Fred Harris and "two or three fellows pulled the senator aside just before his speech."

They were all very concerned about the Irish Catholic issue, making clear that Kennedy would not carry Oklahoma because of it. As Kenny strained to listen over the roar of the crowd, he was puzzled. What were they saying? How was it possible that Jack was attracting such huge, enthusiastic crowds and yet here these guys were telling him that the Catholic issue was killing them?

Kenny couldn't reconcile the visuals of the crowds with this bucket of cold water being tossed in his face. It made no sense to him. Oklahoma was, after all, a Democratic state, so Jack should carry it.

"But they told us, no, Jack was a Catholic, and they were being told by everyone in the state that we would lose the state for that reason alone. Civil rights would have a nominal effect in a state like Oklahoma, certainly not enough to offset the anti-Catholic votes. Whatever effect Jack's support of civil rights did in some states, in these border and southern states, that did not help us.

"We were rather taken aback by the size of the crowd in some of these states, at the same time trying to understand the anti-Catholic issue, which we thought we had already dispatched. In retrospect, we realized our successful stump tour distorted the clearness of facts. Those who came to see you loved you and therefore were wildly enthusiastic. We always questioned afterward, 'Where is everyone else?' Well, we found out where they were on Election Day: voting for Nixon."

THIS PARTICULAR DAY was one of the wilder crowds. As they left the speech to go to the next event, the police lines broke down. People suddenly rushed Jack's motorcade, grabbing and pulling at him.

As Kenny remembered, "I had to hold on to him as tightly as I could while pushing people back. The Oklahoma people had never seen a candidate attract crowds like this. Like New Jersey, they were younger than the typical crowd at a political event. I had to jump out of our car, which was behind the senator's, get into his automobile, and literally hold on to him. People were climbing into the vehicle with him. There was a real danger he would be pulled out of the car. The police disappeared; they had been dispersed by the crowd."

Dave said later, "From my viewpoint in the back car, I thought again that the senator and Ken might well get crushed." At this time, there was no Secret Service. Kenny said, "I mean, you are running a campaign, trying to arrange police protection, while they think you are crazy because they have never heard of crowds like this. So they didn't believe it till they were being overrun.

"It was difficult, at times dangerous, but this was a campaign. We really were in a funny position. It got to the point that if we were not overrun with people jumping on the cars and trying to pull him out, if they were just running along the side or standing and just cheering, we were disappointed. Things get out of proportion at this level of support. But we were both very surprised and thrilled by the crowds all across these western states, including California."

That night they flew back to Washington. As they sat aboard the *Caroline*, Jack said, "Kenny, perhaps we might be able to crack this border state complex. I think we can win California with another trip."

Kenny understood, noting that Jack was beginning to sound like Sinatra, who continued to press hard for another trip to California; still Kenny resisted. He felt their time was better spent in the big, blue-collar, and industrial Northeast states. Kenny remembered the last weeks of the campaign as a whirlwind. He was haunted by Bobby's polls, but at this stage there was little they could do but tough it out politically and push everyone to do their utmost to get their people to the voting booth on November 7.

On their last campaign swing through Chicago and the Northeast, Kenny watched the crowds carefully. They remained wild, huge, and incredibly enthusiastic about Jack Kennedy. Kenny, for one, was relieved.

CHAPTER 20

Election Night

A
S KENNY REMEMBERED, "The polls had indicated for about a month that Senator Kennedy had about a 4 to 5 percent lead on a national basis. It was difficult to determine from our point of view, because we were seeing the crowds. Despite what Bobby had told us, we thought, *It has to be better than that. Look at these crowds.* The polls, both national and local, turned out to be for the most part not inaccurate, as I recall." The election would indeed come that close, as Kenny and Jack would find out that Election Day evening; Bobby's ominous warnings had been on target.

The crowds had been deceiving, and the anti-Catholic "thing," as Kenny called it, was eating away at their lead. The help brought in by the support of Dr. King and the black voters would prove much more important than Kenny could have imagined. For Sarge Shriver and Jack, supporting the African American community may have been a moral decision, but as it turned out, securing the black vote also helped secure Jack's win, so from Kenny's viewpoint, that was good politics as well.

"The only one that was really off was the Harris Poll saying that we were going to carry Ohio. Anyone who says that they thought we were not going to carry Ohio kept it very close up until election night. We all expected to carry Ohio and anyone who now says they thought we'd lose it simply is not telling the truth. I was there," Kenny declared, "and it came as a shock to all of us when we lost Ohio. I think at that point we were really depending on national polls. The local polls are usually those polls that are doing it for local candidates and then add the presidential election." While Kenny, Bobby, and Larry watched the polls, Jack was just pressing full steam ahead. Kenny recalled, "His speeches at that point were almost totally off the cuff, with the usual handout for the day's news. The senator is strictly on his own on the stump and he is getting better as the days go on."

It seemed to Kenny that "Vice President Nixon was holding steady in the polls." Kenny noted later, "This is what was deceiving. The polls did not show him picking up. In fact both Harris and Gallup showed a small but consistent Kennedy lead. Again, demonstrating the senator's point that polls really can't tell you much, you have to go out [and] just keep pressing ahead. In retrospect, the gap did not occur, which I would have looked for in mid-October, when we first took the lead. Nixon had been ahead and then in mid-October polls showed us gaining at first. Then we overtook him, and really, as it turned out, we never lost that lead, slim though it certainly turned out to be. In mid-October at first there was this rather dramatic switch to Kennedy. Then the gap tightened, but Kennedy remained in the lead. The switch began around the debate; really the switch to Kennedy technically began around late September and into October. Then to our horror, as Bobby had warned us, it had stopped completely."

The great breakthrough that the Kennedy team had been anticipating, "where we would really run away from Nixon, never occurred," Kenny concluded. "So at that point there are really only two questions on your mind. One question is, did we freeze at our current levels or in fact did Nixon now start to come on and we have lost the thing. Another way to look at it is this: You hear we have this momentary breakthrough and, as a staff, did we fail to exploit that breakthrough? Or was the breakthrough in fact never there in the first place? These are crucial questions, and it is a very disturbing element to have to ask these questions at that point in a campaign. The most frightening one of all is naturally, have you reached as far as you can go and have you frozen in a relative position, and if Nixon does continue to come on, what do you do? Can you do anything or are you simply frozen?" It was what Bobby called the "most frustrating and helpless feeling in politics."

Kenny explained, "It sounds odd, but at this late stage in the campaign, you really are almost too busy to think about polls. The senator also looked at it this way; you are frozen into a campaign strategy now. The candidate is doing everything that he can do. The staff is doing everything they can do—you are beyond committed in a campaign. I really do not think . . . we discussed it. We just felt that we just had to continue to press ahead, that there was little that we could do. You know we are in the last ten days of the campaign; in many ways the die is really cast."

Later, after Jack had won and the campaign analysis had begun, Kenny laughed and said that he and the president would "read of all these stories about peakings and strategy meetings and so forth, but our feeling was there was little you can change at this moment. There is nothing you can really do in the last ten days, unless you catch somebody red-handed in some way that breaks everything open. Even what Bobby told us on the Catholic issue, there was little we could do at this late hour. You just have to keep pressing relentlessly forward."

In the last ten days of the campaign, the Kennedy team knew they were in the final stretch and working on a system that had been in play since the early primaries. Kenny recalled, "At that point there was just nothing that they could change, even if you detect the problems that Bobby was detecting back at the headquarters. Nixon did not change his strategy much at all. Eisenhower came into play here, and that was expected at this point. I would have used him earlier, but Nixon waited." Kenny felt it was a mistake, allowing the Kennedy camp to keep that small but crucial advantage as Election Day closed in.

When Election Day arrived, everyone was exhausted. Kenny, for one, found it anticlimactic and frustrating. "There was nothing more we could do but wait." None of them—Kenny, Larry, or Bobby—was good at waiting. Jack, especially, detested waiting, yet on this day, Kenny sensed a certainty from Jack that he had not felt before. "He was either comfortable he had done all he could or his gut told him, as with the nail-biter in '52, we'd pull it out."

Kenny remembered later how exhausted Jack was when they finally arrived back in Boston. Not that Kenny wasn't, but he didn't have Jack's health problems. "We had to struggle through yet another noisy crowd from the Boston Garden to Faneuil Hall, the scene of important American Revolutionary protests. This is where Kennedy was filmed for the television program that closed his campaign."

Back inside the *Caroline*, Jack fell into his seat and admitted to himself and to Kenny that there was nothing left to do but wait. He looked out the window. Kenny said little. His mind was back on the night before, at Bobby's, when Jack had said, "Well, it's over. I wish I had spent forty-eight hours more in California."

Kenny's mind was racing. The decision to spend more time in New York rather than go back to California had been his alone. Everyone had weighed in; even Sinatra had pleaded for them to remain in California. Jesse Unruh and Governor Brown had said they needed more time in the Golden State. But Kenny had said no. He felt New York and the Northeast were more important. "Your call," an exhausted Bobby had told him. Kenny canceled the California trip. He could only hope he had been right.

Jack and Kenny parted at the airport. Jack headed to his Hyannis Port home for a few hours of rest and to spend some time with Jackie and family friend Bill Walton. Kenny stopped at the Yachtsman Motel to meet up with Helen. Larry's wife, Elva, was there, as was Dave's wife, Jo. After a few drinks, they all headed to Bobby and Ethel's home to watch the election returns. Joe and Rose watched from the big house on the compound. Jack and Jackie were in their own home, just behind Bobby's house.

Kenny had long before struggled to explain to Helen why he felt Jack had the special qualities required to win the presidency. "It was hard to explain. He was our generation, looking to the future, not the past. Eisenhower and Nixon were looking back at the 1950s. Jack was different. He wanted what we wanted for this country."

Helen shared Kenny's hopes. She too believed in Jack. Now they could only hope that the country had seen what they had seen, that they had transmitted Jack's message across many miles, endless handshakes, lousy motels, and the shifting political sands that distinguished the different regions of the country. Through it all, Kenny and Helen and the rest of the Irish Brotherhood hoped that America now believed in Jack Kennedy as they did, believed in this man's vision for leading his country into the 1960s. All they could do now was wait for the judgment of the American people.

Kenny recalled, "Eisenhower was now in Cleveland. Nixon was at a telethon, and the press was reporting huge crowds for both of them. Eisenhower, or whoever was writing his stuff, was tougher now than he had ever been, very partisan, much more so than he had been in the past. Nixon's people had convinced Eisenhower that Nixon's defeat would be a repudiation of Eisenhower. Gallup's last poll showed a fifty-fifty margin with a slight edge to Kennedy, though hedged by the Catholic problem. So we spent the day, this was Tuesday, hanging around in a very desultory fashion in the Yachtsman. All our families were down there. It was damned frustrating."

Once again, Ethel had given Bobby carte blanche to turn her living room and dining room into campaign central. Bobby had set up the telephone system to contact places around the country for returns.

The office staff, including Justine O'Donnell, was brought in from Washington. Each state was supposed to call in as they opened up and received returns. Each state also had certain bellwether counties they were monitoring.

"Helen and I went over at 8:00 p.m.," Kenny said, "and spent the night with Ethel and Bobby watching television and occasionally taking calls."

Jack, whose home was just behind Bobby's, strolled over a couple of times and was especially interested in the Connecticut returns.

"You know you are leaning on other people's advice to know what the returns mean," Kenny said, "and you just hope they are right. It really does not mean anything at this early stage to say that Senator Kennedy has 240,000 and Nixon has 195,000 in Ohio, unless you know where the figures are coming from and what they mean in a larger context. In truth, Bobby's telephone communications were more meaningful to us than anything we saw reported on television."

Connecticut was important to the Kennedy camp because by this point the polls had closed and reported.

"If we had lost Connecticut," Kenny recalled, "quite frankly, we would have known that the campaign was lost. But when it was reported for Kennedy, we at least hoped the trend would continue. Bobby, the senator, and I were all relieved and saw this as a sign of a positive trend. Winning Connecticut substantially was a good sign that we probably gauged things properly. Connecticut should run about the same as New Jersey, New York, and Massachusetts. We could then pick out nine or ten states based on Connecticut that we now knew we would win and could count on totally carrying. That would indicate to us, as Connecticut closed, not that it could be a bellwether for the whole country but a bellwether for certain groups of states."

There was not much chatter other than the rings of telephones as precincts and states reported in. They were all too tense to chat. It had all come down to this moment.

Jack tried to relieve the tension by returning home to have dinner with Jackie and Bill Walton. As she had from the beginning, Jackie created a cocoon effect for Jack. Despite the enormous pressures on him this evening, they had dinner as they would have done normally, as if there were no election.

The dinner was nothing out of the ordinary, which is perhaps what made it so very unusual. "Mrs. Kennedy," recalled Provi Paredes, Jackie's personal assistant, "always wanted to keep as much normalcy for him as possible. Given the circumstances, it was not easy. But she was very determined."

Kenny agreed. "Jack strolled in and out between his house and his father's house, trying to maintain equilibrium by avoiding Bobby's. He was very quiet and casual. Bobby's house was a bit chaotic. There were more people than jobs, and everyone was sort of in the way. As I always found whenever the Kennedy family was around, you get all these people and you don't know where they came from, and everyone wants to be delivering the news to them, good news, bad news, whether they are involved or not, whether they know what they are talking about or not. There are just all these hangers-on who want to flutter around the Kennedys.

"Frankly, it really annoyed me on an election evening of this importance. I have never been one of the guys that hung around at his elbow at such moments. I have never been one of those guys who believes at this stage the telephone does you much good. You have either won or lost.

"I really did not agree with Bobby's approach to hit the phones at this late stage. I felt that it could backfire. It turned out they called everyone in the world, and half of them were totally irritated. The state organizations were trying to get their people to the polls, and they keep getting calls from the 'Kennedy girls' in Hyannis Port asking for updates. One union guy said to me it took him twice as long to get his people to the polls for all the damn calls he took from Cape Cod."

Richard Daley called, livid, from Chicago, complaining to Kenny. "Daley got seven different calls from different people at the Kennedy operation, all asking the same question. At one point he yelled at Justine, who did not know that he had already fielded several calls with the same request. Daley barked at her, "Aren't you people all in the same house? Don't you communicate with each other?"

Kenny chuckled later, after victory was assured. "It was not one of the finer moments of the vaunted Kennedy organization."

Jack later said to Kenny, "Look, we are not doing this in '64. This is just foolish."

Kenny agreed. "One can be almost so organized that it can be chaotic. Richard Daley called me at the house and gave me hell. He said he was trying to get the votes out and was being interrupted by calls from Lem Billings asking for updates every five minutes. 'Get these people off my telephone lines!' Daley barked."

Needless to say, Kenny said, "I put a stop to that pretty quickly."

Perhaps the most unnerving moment for Jack, Bobby, and Kenny was the situation that arose in what Jack liked to call "our dear, old Ohio."

A few hours after the fire with Daley had been put out, Bobby came down from one of the children's rooms that had been converted to serve part of the operation. Bobby pulled Kenny aside. "Kenny, it looks like we are gone in Ohio."

Kenny said that the minute he saw the numbers, he knew Ohio was trouble. "Bobby and I were talking about Ohio when it started to come in. The returns were initially not good, but at first we didn't pay too much attention. Deciding to not even mention them to Jack, we assumed they would switch. It was early, scattered and so forth."

Kenny simply could not believe, based on what he knew of the state, the work they had done there, and the crowds Jack had drawn, that the Kennedy campaign could lose Ohio. "I said to Bobby, 'Let's calm down; where are the numbers coming from?'

"'Mostly rural,' Bobby replied. 'We need to tell Jack.'

"I said, 'Let's wait till Cleveland comes in. We'll make it up there.'

"Bobby gave me this wan smile and said, 'No, Kenny, you don't understand. These figures include Cleveland.'

"We just looked at each other for a moment. Then Bobby said, 'I think, Kenny, we've probably had it.'

"I didn't know what to say. I couldn't believe it could be over this quickly. We called Jack at his house, and he came over to see for himself. This time, unlike '52, we had no miracles to show him."

"We are obviously going to lose Ohio," was all Jack said. He looked at them both, perfectly calm. "There's nothing we can do now. If we win, we will find out why later. If we lose, it does not matter much."

Suddenly, he pulled Bobby and Kenny aside where they might not be overheard.

Calmly, Jack said, "Let's just wait. No reason to panic. We've got time to recover. You two are great optimists. You said we were going to carry Ohio. They are all working people. My people. You said we would win. What happened?"

Bobby and Kenny exchanged looks. At this stage they were as surprised as Jack. They had no ready answers.

Kenny said, "Senator, I don't know. I would have bet anything I own that we would win Ohio."

Jack nodded. "I feel the same way, but now everybody is saying they knew we would lose it. They never said that before. Nobody told us then the Catholic thing would hurt us there." Their minds all went back to the emergency meeting Bobby had called, warning of the dire undercurrent of bigotry that threatened to overwhelm the campaign. Kenny quietly wondered, *Was that what happened in Ohio?* It was just speculation.

"It does no good to second-guess," Jack said to him, almost reading this thoughts. Kenny nodded in agreement. But for the first time a big industrial state that Jack should have won, a state everyone said he would win, was clearly lost to Nixon.

"This is significant," Kenny said, "because we now have to assume we have troubles in Pennsylvania, Illinois, and Indiana we never counted on. In Michigan, the same problem was perhaps not as bad because the migration of workers from the South was less than we had hoped."

Quickly, Bobby and Kenny did a rapid check, and as they feared, there were a lot of southerners in the Wayne County area, which now translated into trouble there as well.

Again, Jack's cool demeanor in the face of what seemed like impending disaster would serve him well. Kenny and Bobby's fear that "as Ohio goes, so goes the nation" proved to be wrong.

Kenny explained, "We just could not figure it out. Perhaps that was what was the most frightening. Was it the Catholic thing again? And if it was, what does that mean for the rest of the industrial states?" Kenny and Bobby had no answers. "After Ohio, Bobby and I took nothing for granted."

Despite the Ohio loss, the Kennedy forces were still, at this early stage, substantially ahead. But the media, as it had in 1952, seemed to look at different numbers.

"On NBC, John Chancellor was driving Bobby and me crazy," Kenny said. "Bobby wanted to call him and tell him off. His figures were way off the mark. Chancellor was almost calling it for Nixon."

"I am going to call him," Bobby snapped.

This time it was Kenny's turn to keep Bobby calm. "Calling Chancellor and yelling at NBC won't help us. Let it go," Kenny urged.

"His figures are way off. Way off!" Bobby shouted.

Kenny could only repeat Jack's advice: "Don't panic."

"At any rate, we were now getting nothing from the West and obviously it was going to be very, very close, no question about it," Kenny recalled. "We were still leading substantially, but the projections were now falling off heavily. Bill Green called in reports from Pennsylvania that we had carried Philadelphia by 331,000.

"The victory in Pennsylvania was a turning point, a key break for us because, quite frankly, Ohio scared the devil out of us. We thought we might also lose Pennsylvania, and if we lost Pennsylvania, it was over. We had the same crowds in Pennsylvania as we did in Ohio, but now we were wondering, 'Did we misjudge these blue-collar voters?' Pennsylvania gave us a little bit of room to be optimistic."

From there, the states they were most concerned about were Georgia, Arkansas, Louisiana, and two or three others among the ex-Confederacy. Kenny's personal concern was with the Carolinas.

"Before the Ohio results came in, we expected to carry them," Kenny said, "because we had the organization down there, which makes the difference in a close contest. But after Ohio we questioned everything we had done.

"South Carolina, when it came in, was actually a pleasant report because by this time we had been murdered in Kentucky and Tennessee. We carried North Carolina by only thirty-five thousand, and that meant we had trouble in the border states. We were also getting murdered in Florida."

Again, they decided to call the senator over from his house.

"Bobby, the senator, and I discussed it after Florida came in," Kenny recalled. "The damned religious thing is really hurting us. It could have cost us the election."

Jack said little, but the frustration on his face was evident.

Illinois continued to go back and forth, but they had Daley's help, so they were sure they would win. "Our projections showed it as a breakeven," Kenny explained, "with us winning, and our projections matched up perfectly with the eventual results. Missouri was a problem, though. We conceded Missouri early, which the final results showed to be a mistake."

The night's shocks were not over. Wisconsin was soon lost. "That was the second shock and surprise to us. This meant Minnesota was in trouble," Kenny said. "Minnesota was a seesaw up until the very end."

Their focus now fell on Illinois, Texas, and California, which they felt to be key to their eventual success.

"We had no reports on California at all. Texas and Illinois were our immediate concerns. In addition to Texas, we couldn't win without Illinois. As a matter of fact, we probably counted on all three of them to win, but California less so.

"As we swung west, we were losing these states by substantial margins. The smaller Republican states we lost, though we never expected to carry them, and they didn't fit into our plan. But New Mexico was in a tighter fight than we thought. Nevada we won, but tighter than we thought. There was now no question that we had not done as well west of the Mississippi as we anticipated, which caused some concern over California. But politically California is very different from other states."

The mood in Bobby's house was topsy-turvy as they won states, then lost states.

Kenny said, "The evening went on in this fashion. Jack came over two or three more times. I remember he was really annoyed at John Chancellor and NBC."

Jack said, "I don't mind him closing the gap as much as I mind him smiling while he's doing it."

Jack berated Chancellor in colorful terms within earshot of his mother, Rose. Helen, who was seated next to Rose, told Kenny later, "It was beautiful; she never missed a beat. She just looked up as if Jack had told her what color shoes he was going to wear. 'Yes, dear. That's lovely,' Mrs. Kennedy said. 'But please do not use such sailor-like language.' Jack just stared at her for a moment and laughed."

With Ohio behind them, the one thing Kenny refused to think about was loss. "It is unthinkable, and you do not allow yourself to go there mentally. You cannot. Besides, by the time I left, I had talked to Mayor Daley extensively; he told me off the record we had it."

Kenny remembered the conversation with Daley. "Mayor Daley said they had 'robbed him blind downstate.' He told me about the district that included Peoria. There were areas with only five hundred voters, yet Nixon had beat Kennedy five hundred votes to fifty. Impossible numbers. Clearly there was major fraud downstate."

Mayor Daley said, "Kenny, they do it all the time. They lose their returns, and we have to slow down our returns until we see what they are doing down there and how they are going to come out. But as of right now, we are all right. As long as you tell your people to stop calling me. I will tell you, Kenny, and you can tell Jack, we are going to be okay. Jack can count on this."

Kenny found Jack and Bobby, relating to them what Daley had said and suggesting that Jack call Daley. They had a good conversation. Jack apologized for all the calls.

"I'd rather talk to you than Lem Billings and all those girls!" Daley said.

Jack and the mayor had a good laugh. Then Daley told Jack what he wanted to hear. "Listen, we've got Illinois."

Jack hung up and turned to Bobby, Kenny, and Larry, who had now joined them. "I'm going home, and you should do the same. We have a big day tomorrow."

Bobby's house had become even more chaotic and crowded. Jack joined Helen and Kenny by the front door. "Leaving?" he asked.

"I can't stand this stuff," Kenny said, nodding at the sudden influx of people who had never put in an appearance at one of the campaign's freezing-cold stops in Wisconsin.

"You are not going to throw up, are you?" Jack teased his brother, invoking a funny memory from '52. Kenny and Helen laughed. Bobby made a face at Jack and went back to monitoring the phones. Unlike Jack or Kenny, Bobby would stay until the bitter end, when he was certain victory was at hand.

"I agree," Jack said, looking around the room. "Who are these people? I have no idea who most of them are."

"The entire Kennedy family was there," Kenny said, "along with all these people none of us had ever seen."

As they parted ways just where the path behind Bobby's house cut through the hedges and opened to Jack's lawn, Jack turned to Kenny and Helen, smiling, and squeezed Kenny's shoulder. Nothing more was said.

"You two are a talkative pair," Helen teased as they climbed into one of the waiting cars for a ride back to their room at the Yachtsman Motel.

"Helen and I watched California from there," Kenny remembered. "It was a disappointing loss. But Texas was in; we had won Missouri, Michigan, Minnesota, and so forth. It was past 2:00 a.m. Helen and I knew Jack was in. There were finally enough delegates to elect John F. Kennedy president of the United States."

Just then the phone rang.

"Bobby," Helen predicted correctly.

They'd won.

Everything they had worked for since 1952 had now come to pass. Jack Kennedy was headed to the White House. What it meant for Kenny and the Irish Brotherhood who had helped send him there, nobody really knew. Kenny closed his eyes, finally drifting toward sleep. Suddenly, Kenny realized that he had worked himself out of a job.

CHAPTER 21

Taking Power

O N THE MORNING of Wednesday, November 8, 1960 Richard Nixon officially conceded, marking the first day of Jack's life as president-elect. It also marked the start of new lives for each member of the Irish Brotherhood.

After their parting the late night before on Bobby's back lawn, the next time Kenny saw Jack was later that same day, when he spoke to the gathered press and nation.

"This was the first time I had seen him as president-elect," Kenny remembered. "We were standing by the steps of the armory, Larry O'Brien, Elva, myself, and Helen. Jack came up the steps and stopped. He shook hands with me and Helen. Then he put his hand on my shoulder."

No words were spoken. It was, as Helen would later recall, "a very emotional moment."

Jack stopped in front of Helen, kissed her on the cheek, and held her hand for a moment before saying a simple "Thank you."

"It was done," Kenny said, "in the most charming fashion. Jack was very emotional, and so was Helen. I had been spending most of my time away for years now. Helen had sacrificed a lot for this moment. Jack was letting her know that he recognized and appreciated her sacrifice. Then he shook my hand, and we said very little. Frankly, I think we were both too emotional to speak," Kenny admitted later. "Remember, the president-elect, as he was now known, was the longest of long shots. It is hard to explain the rush of emotions one feels at such a moment. He only said, 'Thank you, Ken.'"

With their dreams realized, Jack expressed his personal gratitude to all those who had been with him for many years, and to their families, who had sacrificed so much.

Kenny said, "Everything was different. He was no longer Jack Kennedy, the candidate I had first met at the Bellevue Hotel in Boston with some skepticism. He was not the man who, filled with frustration, had walked down the hill from the Kennedy apartment at 122 Bowdoin Street to check our numbers for himself in 1952. He was no longer the candidate standing in the freezing cold at 5:00 a.m. in the frigid Wisconsin morning, bareheaded, and shaking everyone's hand until his was swollen and scratched nearly beyond recognition.

"Everything about him was different. He was humble and grateful, yes, but now wearing 'the hat,' as we called it, the heavy burden of the presidency. Jack was not the same man.

"After his speech, Jack took my arm and said, 'I will see you this afternoon. We have a lot to do.' I was surprised. I just said, 'Yes, sir, Mr. President.'"

Helen gave Kenny a look. It was not an unsupportive look; certainly this was her dream as much as his. But Kenny had promised some breathing room.

"We went back to the Yachtsman," Kenny said. "We had only just arrived and begun to relax when Bobby called again. 'Jack wants to see you at the house.'"

Kenny was surprised. "Now?"

"Now," Bobby said, "It's about the transition. We're sending a car."

Click. Kenny stared at the dead telephone receiver. "The next thing I remember," Kenny recalled, "was a series of meetings with the president and Bobby. They were back-to-back planning sessions and extremely high-pressured."

Kenny was still exhausted from the campaign but admittedly exhilarated as he headed out the door of the Yachtsman to the car Bobby had sent.

"Secret Service agents?" Helen had asked suspiciously when she saw the car as she walked him out of the motel. *What are you and Bobby up to?* was her immediate though unarticulated question.

As if reading her thoughts, Kenny said quickly, "Have no idea. Maybe Bobby thought I wouldn't show unless he sent armed escorts."

Her laugh broke the tension. Kenny waved at the two Secret Service agents, whom he immediately recognized, having met them the night before, actually early that morning. The moment that John F. Kennedy had become president-elect, they had moved into place in those early morning hours around the Kennedy compound at Hyannis Port. Kenny had handled their transition and arrival before he and Helen had returned to the Yatchsman, even before it was official that Jack had won; but he had done so simply because there had been nobody else to do the job. He assumed correctly that a similar team was in place around Nixon, had the election gone the other way.

As the car glided into the drive in front of Bobby's house, Kenny climbed out and stood momentarily, taking in the brisk November air rolling in off the ocean. His mind raced through the events from the football fields of Harvard, where he and Bobby had first met, to this moment. His mind was quickly brought back to the present when he realized that both agents remained at full attention and were now joined by others, whom Kenny immediately recognized by their attire and demeanor as FBI.

When he refocused on them, several saluted. Surprised, Kenny saluted back before sort of turning to see who was behind him. He thought somebody of some importance had come up while he was lost in thought. There was nobody there; he quickly turned back, trying to cover his confusion to the agents.

"They were asking for their orders." Kenny remembered first being confused, then simply stunned. "I said, 'Orders?'"

"They said, 'Yes, sir, the president-elect said you were in charge of Secret Service and the FBI on watch and we should report to you for the time being.'"

Kenny was speechless. He had expected, assumed, and hoped to be asked to transfer his entire operation from the campaign to the White House. He expected it would happen eventually, but they had never discussed it. Jack was not the type of man who made plans before all the votes were counted, and neither was Kenny. Kenny certainly hoped he would be rewarded with a White House post or, perhaps more realistically, the Democratic National Committee should the senator win, but it was never discussed.

The race had been down to the wire until the end; none of them, not Jack, Bobby, Kenny, Steve, or even Joe, dared to start measuring drapes for the White House just yet. So Kenny had not given any serious thought to his role going forward. He understood all too well the vagaries of politics and was too respectful of Nixon's political canniness to write the former vice president off—at least not until they had received the call that morning that told him and Jack that it was over. They had won.

Having absolutely no idea what to say to the agents, Kenny replied simply, "Keep doing what you are doing."

Kenny said later, "They hardly needed me to tell them what to do at that early stage, but I think it was just what was expected with the transition of power. The agents," Kenny said, "saluted back and moved into position. They were very good-natured about it all. These guys were all pros."

Hands stuffed in his pockets, Kenny headed inside Bobby's house to find out what was so damn urgent. He walked into the living room where the meeting was going on. The discussions centered around the plans going forward.

Bobby was sitting on the arm of the couch. He immediately got up and indicated that Kenny should follow him into the dining room, which still looked more like command central than a dining room.

Kenny stood with his back to the door, while Bobby stood across from him, hands on his hips, a wrinkled white shirt hanging out of his khakis.

Kenny looked him up and down and remarked, "I see winning has done nothing to improve your sense of style." Nodding toward the window where the Secret Service men could be seen getting into position, Kenny teased Bobby, "Afraid I wouldn't show, so you sent guys with guns?"

Bobby laughed. It was a good, hard laugh. Kenny had not heard him laugh like that for a while. Kenny thought it was perhaps the first time in months that he had seen Bobby actually get a moment to relax. But it was only a moment; he quickly snapped back to reality and the purpose for pulling Kenny aside.

"Jack wants you to go with him to the White House," Bobby said.

Kenny nodded, pleased. This is what he had hoped would happen. "Can I move the entire operation and team to the White House?" Kenny asked, assuming this was the political post he had sort of been occupying.

Bobby shook his head. "No, you don't understand," he said. "He wants you to serve as special assistant to the president. He wants you right there, outside his door. This is different." Bobby seemed slightly unsure of what the job was himself. "Don't ask me why," Bobby said with a slight smile, "he seems to like your company, which is more than I can say."

Kenny grinned that slight, at-the-corners-of-the-mouth, barely visible grin.

"What the hell does that mean? Special assistant?" Kenny asked.

"Whatever the hell he wants it to mean," Bobby replied.

"What about Sorensen?" Kenny asked.

Bobby laughed and nodded. "You will have equal power. Don't worry, he's as disappointed as you are."

Kenny chuckled, shrugging. "I see the president is already upholding the separate-but-equal-powers doctrine very carefully here."

Bobby, too tired to take the bait, nodded blankly.

Kenny recalled later, "Bobby then asked if I would go with Jack to Florida and stay with him there to help get everything set up. Before I could reply, the president-elect walked in, unannounced. I did not even know he was behind me. He said, 'You're coming to Florida with me.' It was not a question.

"I turned, saluted, and said, 'Yes, sir.'" He nodded, returning the salute. The relationship, Kenny said later, while always close until the end, had changed. He was no longer just Senator John F. Kennedy; he was the president-elect of the United States, the leader of the free world.

Kenny tried hard to explain this to Vanocur years later. "I saw it with Lyndon on Air Force One on November 22; I saw it that morning at the Cape Cod armory and again in Bobby's dining room that day. He had the weight and responsibility of the office of president—it changes a man immediately. It is not easy to describe, but the change in their persona, demeanor, and perception of themselves is immediate."

"Good," Bobby said tiredly.

"Then the president-elect said to me, 'You'd better make your plans. You will be there right through most of November and December and into January. You'd better tell Helen. Or do you want Bobby to call Helen and explain?'"

For a moment Kenny froze. Helen had sacrificed so much. It was not that he did not want to join Jack. He did. He also knew he had no choice. But he had no idea how to tell Helen.

"Mr. President," Kenny said, in his characteristic no-bullshit fashion. To Jack's great relief, not even the office of the president would change that. "If I go back to the motel and tell my wife what you just said, sir, I won't have a marriage to come back to in January, with all due respect."

Jack understood immediately; he looked past Kenny to Bobby. "Go call Helen and explain. Tell her how vital it is to me that Kenny come with me. Tell her I need him. Find out what she needs and work it out."

Bobby nodded and left.

"We leave for Palm Beach tomorrow," Jack continued.

Kenny saluted.

Jack nodded. Again he reached over and squeezed Kenny's shoulder. "We have a lot to do," Jack said. "Campaigning is one thing. Governing is something else," Kenny recalled him saying as he left.

"From there, the Kennedy forces took the next step," Kenny said. "The key for the president here was to keep that inner circle together as we planned the move to the White House and the setup of the White House itself. Everything would fall into place as expected."

Kenny briefly joined the others, greeted Steve and Joe, and gave Ethel a warm hug. He had some coffee before he noticed the president give him the high sign. He walked out with the president, who was returning to his own home at the compound, behind Bobby's, to have lunch with Jackie, Caroline, and some family members.

"Get ready to move," was all Jack said.

Kenny commandeered another ride from the Secret Service and returned to the Yachtsman to talk to Helen. "She was not terribly happy with me at that moment. I was worried, but Bobby had talked to her, and she was fine by the time I got there. She understood, but that did not mean she was happy."

Kenny and Dave prepared to head to Florida with Jack. Helen and Elva, Larry's wife, packed up to head back to Washington, DC.

Now all they had to do was form an administration.

"We packed up and left within a couple of hours. The only thing I remember, because I was still so tired, was one very funny story," Kenny recalled. "We got off the plane in Washington to transfer to the *Caroline*. Here, the girls would get off to go home. Helen got off the plane. She was very unhappy with me and with the president-elect, frankly, and let us both know it in no uncertain terms. President or not, he got an earful. I had not really been home for any stretch of time since 1955.

"We got off the plane. My son Mark was at the gate with Helen's mother, and this was 1960, so he would have been about four years old. The president-elect greeted everyone and was walking back, but he went over to say good-bye to Helen. He hated to leave with her still so upset. He was very nice and gracious in a fashion. He knew she was upset, and I think he was trying to comfort her a bit.

"Mark saw him and yelled to him, 'Hey, Mr. President.' The president-elect kept talking to Helen, then to other people, shaking hands, and Mark yelled again, 'Hey, Mr. President!' Nothing. 'Hey, Mr. President of the United States!' The president-elect kept talking.

"Finally, in frustration, Mark yelled, 'Hey, Jack, don't you know your own name?' The president turned and burst out laughing. He walked over to Mark and talked to him, and everybody was laughing. Mark shook his hand and told him some story, I have no idea what it was, but it was a very funny moment. It broke the tension beautifully.

"The president-elect said later to Helen and me as he and I turned to walk to the plane, 'I heard [Mark], but I completely forgot that was now my title.' In fact," Kenny laughed later, "I think the president-elect wanted to say, 'He's a fresh little bastard,' but to my relief he did not get to finish that thought. Helen had just joined us with Mark. Helen was mad enough. All I needed was the President knocking my kid's manners!"

Having survived, Jack, Kenny, and Dave climbed back on board the *Caroline* and headed to Palm Beach. The first night was wonderfully free of the burdens that would soon consume them. It was the first time Kenny had allowed himself to actually relax.

"We stayed at the house. Joe and Rose were there. We had drinks, dinner, and a lovely evening. We chatted casually. Jack reminisced about the journey to this point. He told funny stories, laughed, and relaxed. Mr. Kennedy pulled me aside at one point. We had a brief conversation. It was a very nice thing for him to do and a nice moment. We'd had a lot of tension from the beginning, but starting with the '58 win, he accepted that we knew what we were doing, had Jack's interest at heart, and I think had begun to recognize he could trust me. We had a nice conversation from which our relationship would always move forward in a positive manner."

That evening, the only business Jack raised was bringing on Clark Clifford. Clifford was a Washington, DC, lawyer and political fixer who had served in the navy from 1940 to '44. Then he had served as an aide to Harry Truman; he went on to become friends with Truman and was widely credited as the architect of Truman's stunning 1948 political upset.

Kenny did not know him personally at all but knew of him, since Kenny and Larry had studied Clifford's '48 political race for Truman and had designed Jack's '52 campaign along those lines.

Jack asked Kenny what he thought of him. "I know you don't know him, but what do you think of him?" When Kenny asked why, Jack explained, "I intend him to be the liaison man between the outgoing Eisenhower regime and the incoming Kennedy regime."

"I knew Clifford's name and obviously knew his background," Kenny said. "The president's father was there; I assumed he had suggested Clifford, but I had no objection. Frankly, I told the president quite bluntly, I saw [Clifford] as someone apart from us, part of the establishment in Washington with some continuous relationship with Truman, Eisenhower, and now the Kennedy regime. It appeared to me to be a good logical choice. Quite honestly, I said to the president, "Ike or not, I believed we did not really have the credentials, skills, or connections to do that job ourselves. First, we'd have to be introduced to people to be able to even know where to start or negotiate this sort of thing. The choice of Clifford as a liaison seemed like good judgment."

With that settled, Jack told Kenny and Dave to go out and enjoy themselves. "It might be a while before you get to do it again. At least four years! I want to spend some time with my parents," Jack explained.

Kenny sensed that Jack understood what they all did: The pace during the campaign had been constant and brutal, though Kenny loved it, thrived on it, and he felt Jack did as well. At the White House, Kenny rightly suspected, the problems were going to be bigger and the pace would not lessen in the least. So for the night at least, the Irish Brotherhood intended to celebrate!

The next day, Kenny remembered, "Kennedy family members started to arrive. While Dave was disappointed," Kenny said with a laugh, "I was uncomfortable. I felt it was inappropriate for us, any of the transition, soon-to-be White House staff, to stay at the house. He was now president-elect. Joe and Rose had invited us to stay, but to Dave's complete disappointment, I insisted we stay at a hotel. That included all staff members, who were not too happy with me that day. But it was time to enforce the line. He was president now. Everything had changed. Also, I felt he needed time with his family. Dave and I had a lot of work to do besides.

"Jack completely understood. Honestly, I think he was a bit relieved, saying to me, 'Thanks, Kenny.' Though he had not asked the staff to step back, he was relieved we had."

The next day proved to be their first introduction to the media's surveillance of the president of the United States, and it was jolting. Kenny and Dave returned to the Palm Beach house and joined the president-elect by the pool to go over names for the new administration.

"The picture would appear in *Life* magazine, much to Helen's annoyance when she saw it," as Kenny recalled. "The photo was of a sun-drenched Kennedy palm villa, by the pool with the ocean in the background, and there with sunglasses on was Dave, the president, and I having a meeting, and then we all decided take a swim and have a bottle of beer around noontime. Suddenly a plane appeared, flying so low over us that we could not hear. We could see them taking pictures. The noise was deafening, and suddenly there were tons of boats driving back and forth as close as they could along the beach compound. It was impossibly noisy."

The president-elect, trying to relax and enjoy the afternoon, stared in frustration at Kenny. He asked Kenny testily to talk to the Secret Service and get the press to back off.

"We can't live like this," he growled to Kenny.

Kenny quickly found agents Jerry Bain and Jim Riley and asked them to do something about the ruckus. They seemed a bit taken aback.

"I think they were used to the press," Kenny said, "They were old hats at this, real pros; but this was all new to us. I probably did not properly explain what we wanted. I was still just learning. But suddenly they tripled their manpower. Now we were at the pool surrounded by Secret Service in 'Indian fighting style.' They are up in the palm trees, on the roof, all in their black Brooks Brothers suits with sunglasses on. The president-elect thought it was rather humorous."

Jack looked over at Kenny in exasperation and said, 'Great, Ken, this is so much better. Thanks. Now we can all relax."

Jack then gave him his first order as president-elect. "Look, Ken, get them to back off a little bit, at least a few feet away, and tell them to take off their suits and put on sports shirts so they can at least be comfortable. And tell them to sit the hell down. They are making me uncomfortable. Nobody is going to shoot me, so tell them to relax a bit."

"I transmitted the president-elect's request," Kenny said. "So the Secret Service changed shirts, and suddenly they were dressed in identical sports shirts, loafers, and light pants. They were all so relieved.

"Then they moved the perimeter out. The coast guard arrived and backed the boats off, which meant relieved Kennedy family members could again use the beach without fearing their children would be frightened by photographers. Even for family members, Jack's ascendency to the presidency was taking some getting used to.

"As for the plane rented by *Life* magazine, unfortunately there was not much we could do about that. The president-elect told me he was sure there was a rule that planes could not fly that close. I checked with the Secret Service, and they were happy to have authority to their job. They knew what they were doing; they just needed to know what the new president wanted. Each president is different.

"The Secret Service could not order the planes backed off, as Jack was still just president-elect, but they could scare them a little bit and they were happy to do it. The coast guard, however, was much less original. They brought in several boats and began bobbing and weaving and doing these exercises.

"The president-elect said to me, 'What the hell are they doing? What do they think, Castro is going to land on my beach? If he does, I'll invite him to lunch. Get them under control before they hurt one of the residents.'

"I was still learning and did not realize I could order the coast guard to stop, but by now I understood that the Secret Service was my best ally. I approached them at the president's request. The Secret Service understood immediately and ordered them to back off the beach.

"For me, this was a learning curve. For Jack, it was the beginning of a new phase of life in which his every movement would be monitored. He would not allow it to slow him down or change his habits."

But it would prove to be an interesting experience for the Secret Service, Jack, and Kenny; and with the cooperation of the press corps at that time, Jack would try to live as much of his own life as he could, whether it was wise or not, and whether Kenny agreed or thought it a good idea or not. Kenny would often find himself walking a line between Jack's public and private life. Their new lives had begun and it was going to clearly be an adventure.

Clark Clifford came down the following week from Washington to meet with the president-elect, and the work on the transition went full-throttle. Kenny found Clifford impressive and "without any of our biases. This meant that the advice he was giving the president-elect was really at a different level than anything I think he could have received from his current advisors. We were too insular. Clifford had a much broader view of Washington."

Next on Jack's schedule was a meeting with his defeated rival, Richard Nixon. The meeting with the losing candidate was necessary, being part of an American political tradition, though Jack, embittered by some of Nixon's statements, was less than thrilled.

Kenny remembered that Joe insisted on it. "The meeting with Nixon happened because the president-elect's father convinced him to do it. It had been a very narrow election, and it would be important for the country to see him with Nixon."

Kenny felt that Joe was correct. So together with Dave Powers and Kenny, Jack chartered a helicopter to Key Biscayne, Florida, to bury the hatchet with Richard Nixon.

Kenny remembered that they did not have a very substantial talk. For his part, Kenny enjoyed meeting Herb Klein, Nixon's press secretary, more than he enjoyed meeting Nixon.

During the meeting, Jack, who had known Nixon for years, made clear his intention to ask some Republicans to join the Cabinet. Nixon thought it was a good idea, though the difficulty of such a close loss made the meeting "challenging" at best, as Kenny said.

Kenny remembered that Nixon had suggested Douglas Dillon. Dillon was a patrician Republican from New Jersey. He had gone to Groton and Harvard, taken over his father's firm in New York, and worked for John Foster Dulles in the losing campaign of Thomas E. Dewey, the Republican "dream candidate" bested by Harry Truman in 1948. He went on to work for Eisenhower in 1952, later becoming ambassador to France, undersecretary for economic affairs, and then undersecretary of state, all under Eisenhower. He was what Kenny would describe as "one of those Republican, well-connected Washington types."

"I don't remember exactly. Nixon thought it was a very good idea, but I don't think it was any meeting of minds," Kenny recalled.

"Losing an election," Jack said thoughtfully, as they headed back to Palm Beach, "is never easy. Especially the presidency."

Kenny nodded.

After they returned, Kenny said, "We came back to Palm Beach, and Jack wanted to take a swim. So we were at the pool having a beer. I could tell something was bothering him. He had been unusually quiet and reflective since the visit with Nixon." Finally, Kenny could stand it no longer and he asked, "What's up? You seem preoccupied."

After a long pause, Jack finally looked across at Kenny and said, "I cannot figure out why or how I only beat Nixon by one hundred thousand votes. You've seen the same lack of substance in the man that I have seen. You've seen how there seems to be something wrong. Off track. Yet how is this possible that the election could be this close?"

Kenny hated to say it, but here were the remnants of the Catholic issue. "Bigotry," Kenny said. "My own view is, though I can't prove it, that his people fed the bigotry, used certain code words and actions to keep the fire stoked. That meant a lot to haters and people who vote by fear who came to the polls."

"Maybe," Jack replied as he relaxed in the pool. "But I should have done much better. That seems almost too easy an answer and conveniently means we did not do anything wrong. We could have done better."

"My father," Kenny said, "would tell you that, in politics as in football, a win is a win."

"Perhaps," was all Jack said in return.

The other significant thing left unsaid in their meeting with Nixon was that plans had already been laid by the Eisenhower/Nixon administration for the Bay of Pigs invasion of Cuba.

Jack told Kenny later, "Nixon never mentioned it. You would think he would have."

Kenny affirmed this. "If Nixon had raised the Bay of Pigs, Jack would have told me. He had never heard of the Bay of Pigs until December. Dulles told him that December, but not before. I was with him constantly in all those meetings.

"Even then we did not know the whole story or receive specific plans until about a month before the invasion. From this point forward, we never did things this way. After the Bay of Pigs, I was kept informed about such things, as was Bobby. But this invasion was presented to the president as though it were inevitable. Dulles acted toward the president as if he had no right to ask questions. The president learned from the disaster. I remember he told me that they made light of the Bay of Pigs and really pushed him on Laos as being the more immediate and serious danger, because, in my view," Kenny told the president later, "they did not want you sticking your nose into the Bay of Pigs."

The Bay of Pigs and Laos would weigh heavily on the Irish Brotherhood as two quick stumbles out of the gate. But at the time, Kenny said, "it was clear there was more to the story, but one got the feeling you were being pushed back for even asking more questions." There would be plenty of time ahead for more questions and scrutiny on both issues.

In the meantime, staffing the White House remained the major focus. The next visitor to Palm Beach was Connecticut's governor, Abe Ribicoff.

"Jack," Kenny remembered, "felt a deep obligation to Ribicoff. "I think very frankly Abe Ribicoff could have had anything he wanted from John Kennedy. Jack had assumed Abe would want to be attorney general, so he offered it to him."

"The Democrats had a very strong plank on civil rights, and the president-elect intended to carry it out," the president told Ribicoff. Jack felt Ribicoff should lead the battle as attorney general.

Jack was shocked when Ribicoff immediately turned it down.

"The governor felt," remembered Kenny, who sat in on the meeting, as he would all these discussions, "that the Negro vote had been very decisive in the election. In addition, he felt [the president] had a moral obligation to carry out the platform."

The governor then explained, in what Kenny called "political terms," that he believed, as much as he might want to be attorney general, "that he felt the worst thing in the world, in his opinion, would be for a Jewish attorney general to be carrying out the orders of an Irish Catholic president, the first in history, to impose a solution on the white Anglo-Saxon Protestants of the South for the Negroes. That this would not be good politics, in his opinion, and could actually cause a host of problems that they might not anticipate."

Kenny said, "Jack agreed with Abe," and the president made clear that it bothered him to admit that politically the governor was correct. However, the president "nevertheless felt his obligation to Abe was substantial enough that he owed him the job if he wanted it."

"It is yours if you want it. I don't mind the fight if that is what we have to do, if you want the job," the president said.

In the end, Abe would go on to head up the Department of Health, Education, and Welfare, a position he was perfectly thrilled to receive.

"We found someone much less controversial for the attorney general job," Jack later teased his younger brother Bobby, who would reluctantly end up with the job.

"When Jack told Ribicoff pal and patron Hubert Humphrey of his choice, Humphrey was surprised. 'Ribicoff,' Hubert said, 'had been considered a rather conservative governor. He wasn't looked upon as one of the ADA [Americans for Democratic Action] types of fellows, the overly liberal types. He would have had a much easier time getting through the Senate.'

"I remember when the president told me of his decision, thinking to myself, *How wise. How very very shrewd.*"

About this time, Bobby came down to Palm Beach. So now it was Clifford, the president-elect, Bobby, Kenny, and Sorensen, who was the last to arrive. Clifford had a big black book with notes on all the jobs, the problems associated with each position as he saw them.

Kenny remembered, "The president-elect kept looking at me, and his reaction was the same after every conversation that he ever had with Clark. Afterward, the president-elect would say, 'I don't know what we talked about.'

"This is where Sorensen was really important. He could talk to Clifford; where the president-elect and I have little patience with those types.

"Then Dick Neustadt arrived, and the president was now really focused on who he would bring into his cabinet." Neustadt, historian, advisor to President Truman, and author, would go to work with Dillon and Clifford as an advisor on several important areas. Neustadt and Clifford began talking about the issues that Jack would face as they related to those people he should select.

Kenny could tell that the president was getting increasingly frustrated. "The president was an action-oriented, get-to-the-point kind of fellow," Kenny said. "These sort of well-meaning roundabout discussions did not work well with his approach. An accomplished writer, historian himself, he could hold his own with them, but for the purposes of staffing the White House, the president wanted much less talk and more of a direct approach. And, looking far beyond the filling of the positions, what were the problems in the long run that they had to face? Laos? Cuba? What were the problems that General Eisenhower is going to leave on his doorstep? What positions should he begin to fill, vis-à-vis those problems?" Kenny remembered that the president-elect wanted to move things along.

Frustrated, one late evening after dinner and endless discussion, Jack called Kenny back into his father's den, just as Kenny began to leave for the hotel. "We will get you a ride back later," Jack said. "I want to ask you something."

Kenny nodded. He poured them each a drink. Jack sat in a rocking chair, no doubt in pain. Kenny sat as usual on the edge of the couch, wound up, ready to spring.

The president-elect said to Kenny that "he was trying to look at Clifford and Neustadt and determine whether, like so many of these people we had met in the last seven or eight years, they had all been paper tigers.

"He asked my views," Kenny said. "They seem to talk tough. Then when you push them, they back right down."

"I told him I thought they were both paper tigers, because their judgment seemed to change instantly if the president-elect changed his mind or he challenged them.

"I said to him, 'You say one thing, and they immediately shift their views to parrot what you said. You would say or speak very clearly and forthrightly about how you felt about a certain thing they would have been arguing the opposite a minute before, but when you made your case, they would immediately agree with you as if it was their position in the first place.' I told him that made me uncomfortable and I did not think they were in sync with him or serving him as well as I hoped they would."

Jack sighed and agreed.

Kenny suspected that the president-elect was steps ahead; Kenny was simply articulating what Jack already knew.

"I told him," Kenny recalled, "'If you don't, with those two, we will be here the night before the inaugural going over their lists and reading memos about memos.'"

The president laughed. "I agree," he said, seeming to relax. "Call Bobby now."

Kenny reached for the telephone and did just that. While it was unorthodox at the time to rely on unseasoned political hands for the formation of an incoming administration, Jack told Kenny that he felt his team had worked all through the campaign, and they were the best ones to take the lead on staffing the government. "'Bobby and Sarge will get the job done, pick the right people, bring me the final choices I need to make, and we can get moving forward. I don't have time for discussions and meetings to discuss meetings," Kenny recalled him saying.

The choice of Bobby and Sargent Shriver may have been unorthodox, but knowing Jack as they did, it would turn out to be a brilliant decision.

"Given their family relationship to the president," Kenny explained, "his trust in them was absolute and this gave them freedom of action. It did not mean that Clifford or Neudstat would not continue to serve in an advisory capacity; they did just that, but it meant that now they went through Bobby and Sarge. "Watch out for the black books," Kenny teased Bobby on the telephone. It was not until later, when Clifford presented Bobby and Sarge with stacks and stacks of unread memos, overviews, and résumés in three-ring black binders, that Bobby truly understood why his brother had called him.

Kenny admitted to the president that he had not been terribly impressed with these Washington types. "They seem to meet to meet and nothing ever gets done; it is all theory. It is time for some reality and some action," Kenny believed.

That, of course, was Jack's view, which is why Bobby and Sarge took the reins. They were two men well versed in Jack's approach. Theory and discussion were important, but, in the end, they had to lead to action.

With their assignments laid out, they prepared to head back to Washington, DC, and get to work. Their goal was to utilize the machinery of the Democratic National Committee to attract high-level talent to the Kennedy administration.

The day they left the president, Dave and Kenny were by the pool having lunch and a beer, going over the afternoon's schedule. Who the president wanted to see next and so forth. Bobby looked over at Kenny as he prepared to depart for Washington and shook his head. "You've got the tough assignment," Bobby teased.

"It's a burden, that's true," Kenny responded, not missing a beat. Winning the White House had not changed their relationship at all.

Around this time, Jack also surprised Kenny with something else. He called Helen up in Washington and asked if she would like to come down and spend some time in Palm Beach. Helen was thrilled, and Kenny was relieved. He would be down in Palm Beach for much of November and December before the January inaugural.

Kenny said to Jack, "Maybe you saved my marriage."

Jack laughed. "I do what I can."

In the end, Kenny noted that it was a wise move. "There would be many more trips like this, and getting Helen on [Jack's] good side was going to make it that much easier for both him and me."

"After Helen," Jack teased, "the Soviets can't be too hard to mollify."

MEANWHILE, LARRY O'BRIEN, Dick Donahue, and Dick Maguire were assigned the task of rewarding the rest of the Kennedy campaign staff. Kenny's sister Justine would eventually go to work for Dick Maguire at the Democratic National Committee, playing a role as a vital party link to Kenny at the White House. Those they wanted to duck but not lose altogether were often happy to meet with Justine for lunch, dinner, or drinks. If they had vital information, Justine made sure it made its way to Kenny.

Another name that came up around this time was Arthur Goldberg. Kenny said, "The president-elect was anxious to have Goldberg as part of his administration. [Jack] thought very highly of [Goldberg]." Goldberg had served prominently as a labor attorney. Jack had enormous respect for this strong, well-connected Democrat from Chicago and wanted him for the administration. Goldberg would eventually go on to serve, much to Jack's delight, as secretary of labor, before later being appointed to the Supreme Court.

Another name that surfaced was Kenny's old pal Jack Conway, who was considered for a reasonably high-level position. "The president-elect was concerned that he was a UAW official and my close association with him could both distort my judgment and be misunderstood. I had to agree with him on that point, but he thought very highly of Conway and wanted to bring him in if possible."

Jack was a careful man, especially in his approach to major issues such as civil rights, the Soviets, and many of the other decisions he would soon face.

Kenny said later, "In making up his mind, he was extremely cautious. This would prove to be true with one exception, the Bay of Pigs, which led directly to his conviction that caution was the better approach."

At this early stage, Jack had not thought of the government or how to run the government. Kenny described Jack as "a very single-minded person. Politically, each battle he fought was fought only at that time. Then, when he won the battle, he would go on from there."

This was his approach to forming a government and to running the country. "When he ran for president of the United States, Jack ran on his own terms, his own program. After he had been elected, then he began planning the formation of his government."

In Jack's mind, only a few things were clear at the moment of his election. For one thing, Adlai Stevenson would not, under any circumstances, be appointed secretary of state.

Kenny recalled, "He did not feel Stevenson exhibited the qualities necessary for that position. He did not feel he owed it to him, either. But the main thing was that Stevenson would not be the type Jack could work with. He admired Stevenson's mind, and though Jack felt Stevenson should be involved in public service, the president-elect ended up making Stevenson ambassador to the United Nations.

"He was clear that neither Adlai nor Chester Bowles would be secretary of state, but he had to find a place for this rather difficult twosome in the government that would not lead to vexation for those who would eventually end up working with them."

Kenny was characteristically blunt about this decision. "I told him I thought the ambassadorship the best spot for Stevenson if he had to give him anything. Frankly, given Stevenson's performance, or lack of it, during the campaign, I told the president I thought he should be happy to be offered anything."

Jack laughed and admitted that he completely agreed, though he could not say it, which is why he had Kenny.

In addition to secretary of state, the other positions Jack had concerns about were those in Treasury and Defense. He wanted a Republican in Treasury; there was no question about this from the beginning.

Joe Kennedy was personally very high on Bob Lovett. He mentioned him many times and always with a degree of admiration and regard.

Kenny explained, "Jack did talk to Lovett, but his health would not allow him to take a post. Jack was unconcerned about Lovett's age but still wanted him, though ultimately the man could not be enticed into the cabinet."

These were all rather casual conversations. The minor departments would be a mechanical problem to a great degree. Jack hoped that Sarge and Bobby and the rest of the group would handle them.

Jack viewed the staffing of the State Department, however, as a great challenge. Still, he was confident in his ability to oversee it. "I suppose like any president your main concern would be the State Department," Kenny remembered. "In large measure, the Hill and the State Department had never been able to hit it off."

Sorensen was now getting ready with the presidential speeches and messaging and also overseeing different task forces on housing and energy issues.

"I had not thought much about the cabinet," Kenny recalled. "I did not expect to be consulted on the cabinet and did not see that as my role, but as it turned out, Jack very much wanted my views on these things. I realized now that the president-elect felt he could think out loud with me, and we could go back and forth on things. He knew my only agenda was what was best for him, so I became a good sounding board for him. We had a mutual confidence in each other, born out of many years campaigning together. I would not say that he officially consulted me on these things, but we discussed them. He would privately and casually ask my opinion of people or situations, and I would give him my unvarnished views. I think he had come to appreciate my candor."

Robert McNamara's name, Kenny recalled, came from Bob Lovett. "The president, I recall, at first recoiled, assuming from his last name he was an Irish Catholic. That would have gotten him stricken from the list," Kenny said.

But McNamara was neither Irish nor Catholic; he was a Protestant Republican who had actually voted for Kennedy. McNamara was then newly appointed president of the Ford Motor Company, and Bob Lovett had been impressed with him. While declining any position for himself, Lovett pushed hard on McNamara.

As Kenny remembered, "The president was intrigued by McNamara's background and sent Sarge Shriver to quietly meet with him to sound him out about accepting the Treasury position. Sarge was impressed but found McNamara not particularly interested. He made clear that he had no desire to leave his current position and to have to sell his company stock at current interest rates in order to take a position in Washington. He also made clear he had no interest in Treasury anyway, and Defense interested him, but not enough to leave his current position. Still, Sarge pushed hard.

"As a matter of courtesy, he agreed to meet with the new president in December. The meeting would take place at the president's home on N Street; Jack would succeed in persuading McNamara to come on board. Ultimately, the final cabinet would consist of Robert McNamara as head of Defense, C. Douglas Dillon at Treasury, and Dean Rusk would become secretary of state.

"But," Kenny pointed out, "in the meantime, cabinet and staff selections had to be interrupted by a trip to Lyndon Johnson's Texas ranch, in order to mend some political fences, damaged during the campaign."

"The trip to Texas, of course, came off in a rather peculiar fashion," Kenny recalled, "a total shock to me. We were having lunch by the pool, a beautiful day, going over staffing questions for the White House, and suddenly Jack told me he was going to the ranch and I just stared at him. I didn't know why at the time he felt he had to go to the ranch, but he, from the beginning, had accepted the fact that the vice president is a very sensitive fellow and that he, being younger and a junior in the Senate, wants to keep him happy. Therefore, he must show some deference and have him involved in the government in some fashion rather than have him around grousing as an unhappy vice president.

"Okay," Kenny said, listening to Jack's explanation but still not wanting to actually hear it, for fear he too might have to go to Texas. "But the president made clear to me," Kenny said, "especially when he saw my unhappy face, that he wanted to get Lyndon squarely on the team; this was why he agreed to go to the ranch. He and the vice president are talking every day now. We are at Palm Beach, the weather is beautiful, and we are lolling around the pool in a rather jolly fashion after a long strenuous four or five years; so I was not terribly excited about going to Texas. He was not very excited either, as I recall, but felt it was a duty, an obligation."

Kenny sent out an equally unhappy advance team, now with Secret Service agents: "For reasons that always have escaped me I ended up in charge of both Secret Service and FBI, so I am swamped at this moment, taking at least half my time.

"Anyway, they call back and their reports are horrendous. The reports are about all the problems, logistics are a nightmare, as well as the physical problems they are having. I had the director of the FBI, Hoover, screaming at me and the Secret Service screaming that it can't be done. I told them point-blank it has to be done. Make it work. This is what the president wants, I told Hoover. Make it work." Kenny hung up angry.

"Look," he explained later, "I agreed with Hoover. I did not want to them to go either, but this is what the president wanted, so you have to do it. We left lovely Palm Beach and headed to Texas. As were leaving, much to the president's and my annoyance, Powers ducks out of the trip. Turns out he is needed in Palm Beach to take care of the wives and take them all to dinner.

"We couldn't believe it; we found this out as we took off. Turned out poor Congressman Torby MacDonald and I ended up as the party of two to accompany the president to the ranch. Torby said to Jack, 'With friends like you . . .'" They all laughed.

"The night they arrived, I remember it was dark and raining and the vice president was nowhere to be seen; he was solving a soil problem of some kind. Dark and rainy, just miserable. We drove around and went to Poppy's grave, and the president didn't know who the hell Poppy was. I just remember driving around forever and there was nothing to see."

The Texas trip, designed to shore up the relationship with LBJ, would turn out to be a series of fiascos, though Johnson remained somewhat oblivious to it all.

"All I really can say," Kenny said with a laugh, "is that the president was furious with me for bagging a deer before he did, which meant I could go back to bed. He had to run around all morning, driving around in Lyndon's Cadillac trying to track down a deer for Torby. I mean, the president got his right away, but Torby could not shoot one if it was standing still waving a flag of surrender. The story was hysterical, though the president did not see it that way at the time."

Kenny told Bobby the entire tale later, even admitting that Jack refused to speak to Kenny for twenty-four hours. "It was your damn idea," Kenny said to Jack as they thankfully flew out of Texas and back to Palm Beach. Jack gave Kenny an ice-cold stare.

"I don't have to take you to the White House, you know," Jack said, still clearly annoyed.

Kenny laughed. "Yeah, but you'd miss me."

Jack ignored him. He may have been president, but little in their relationship had changed.

"You're just bitter because I got my deer first," Kenny teased, still unable to let it go.

Jack turned and stared at him. "Your deer was sickly and unwell and wanted to be put out of its misery. My deer, I actually had to make an effort to catch, as it tried to get away, and I nevertheless got it."

Kenny burst out laughing. "If you say so, Mr. President."

Kenny could not remember exactly when it happened, but seventeen days after the election, John F. Kennedy Jr. was born in Georgetown Hospital. John Kennedy had his second child, his first son, and somehow it seemed all to capture the spirit and glamour of the new administration. Newly chosen White House press secretary Pierre Salinger released a simple statement: "Mother and son are doing fine."

John's birth allowed for Kenny to make another return trip to Washington, DC, where he spent some much-needed time with Helen and his four children. Jack was ecstatic over the birth of John and told everyone who would listen about what a beautiful baby he was and how beautiful Jackie looked when he saw her at the hospital. Kenny remarked to Helen, "While he understands the responsibilities ahead, he is for the first time in a long time truly happy."

If Kenny thought that would translate into some downtime, he was wrong. The phone call came late one night. "Come over," the president-elect said, "I want to discuss Bobby." As he arrived at the president-elect's house on N Street, Kenny assumed that this would be more of the same, filling in those final slots for the new administration. Bobby, Kenny figured, could have pretty much what he wanted. But it frankly never occurred to Kenny that Bobby would become the next attorney general. Later, Kenny admitted, it would prove to be the best cabinet selection Jack Kennedy made—at least that was Kenny's view and, most important, a view Jack seemed to share wholeheartedly.

CHAPTER 22

That Jack Magic

K ENNY ADMITTED LATER that while he was not surprised that Bobby ended up with a top-flight job in the administration, he had never thought or even gotten the impression that "the president was considering Bobby for the job of attorney general." At first Kenny was unsure; a president had never before appointed someone in his family to such a powerful cabinet post. Kenny was also not sure of the political implications—it would be a controversial way to begin a new administration, especially after such a close election. He was sure it was Joe who had mentioned it to Jack one night after dinner. Kenny felt that Jack took it in passing, as if he were not seriously considering it but only humoring his dad. It would not be the first time, Kenny said later with a laugh, that he read Jack wrong.

Jack had never mentioned it again, so Kenny let it go—Kenny had enough on his plate, learning his new job as they planned the transition to the White House. He figured he did not need to worry about Bobby. As for the attorney general spot, once Governor Ribicoff had turned it down, Kenny had wondered what Jack would do, but they had not focused on it just yet. Kenny mentioned all this in passing to Helen. Fortunately for Kenny, Jack had several trips between Washington and Palm Beach while he worked on building his team and fully grasping the issues that he would face during his presidency. It was during one of these trips to Washington that Kenny mentioned Bobby and the AG spot to Helen.

"But it is Bobby," she said sharply, meaning that Kenny's support of his friend should be a given. "You should push the president. It would be wonderful for Bobby."

Kenny looked at her surprised.

"You are the one who is always saying how invaluable he is to the president," she insisted.

Kenny guessed so; he had not really given it that much thought. Helen looked at him annoyed. He shrugged. "He's now one of the most powerful people in Washington, just by being the president's brother," Kenny said defensively. "He can do anything he wants."

"Bobby," Helen said sharply, "helps everyone and never asks for anything in return. The president should at least give it some thought."

Kenny knew better than to argue with her when she got that look in her eyes. "Who knows if Bobby would even do it," Kenny said. His mind turned back to Massachusetts and Jack's soon-to-be-vacant Senate seat. Maybe, just maybe, Bobby could be persuaded to run for Jack's empty Senate seat, though he dared say none of this to Helen, who would have been none too happy to hear him mention the words *campaign* and *Kennedy* in the same breath.

Kenny was not exactly sure on the day Bobby called to talk to him; he was upset. About what? Kenny wanted to know.

"I don't have a job and I don't know what to do?" Bobby said.

Kenny was incredulous. "You can do anything you want," Kenny said laughing.

Bobby, hurt, said angrily, "Easy for you to say. You have a job!" With that he hung up the phone. Kenny couldn't believe it! When he told the story to Helen with great relish, she immediately took Bobby's side.

"He is the brother of the president; he can do anything he wants for Christ's sake!" Kenny said to her again, still not understanding what she and Bobby did not get about Washington politics and the game of power.

"Well, that's fine," Helen said. "As Bobby said, you have a job. You could at least help Bobby get one as well."

Kenny stared helplessly. Fortunately, the car had arrived to take him to N Street to join Jack for a trip back to Palm Beach. Wisely, he decided to let it go. "Bobby will be fine," he assured her, kissing her on the check as he left.

As it turned out, Jack was ahead of Kenny and much more in step with Helen. As for the Senate seat in Massachusetts, as it would turn out, Kenny would be on the right track, but had the wrong Kennedy in mind. As Jack mulled over and discussed the possibilities with Kenny as they planned the next step, Kenny continued to work on the White House move, seeing his role, as ever, as Jack's sounding board. One night as they flew back to Washington on the *Caroline*, the president asked him, "What do you think of Bobby as attorney general?" Kenny looked over at Jack startled, thinking of his conversation some weeks back with his wife. But this was not Helen; his role here was political.

Kenny immediately made the political and historic-precedent argument that had gotten him into such hot water at home. Jack listened thoughtfully, and when Kenny finished he asked, "What do you really think?"

Kenny was quiet for a moment. "Anything Bobby decides to do, he will do well. You could not have someone better at your back."

Jack nodded. "Dad agrees with you. I agree with you, but Bobby does not want to do it." Kenny laughed. Jack smiled a sly smile. "Yeah, that's what I said," Jack said. They both laughed.

The day Bobby's appointment was announced, they were all in Jack's home on N Street. It was an ice-cold day, with a bitter, biting wind; N street was awash in media, waiting for the news that had leaked and been rumored around Washington circles for weeks. As they prepared to go to the door to meet with the press, Jack looked at his brother Bobby, whose thick hair had a mind of its own, reminiscent of election morning 1952. "Brush your hair for Christ's sake, Bobby." They all laughed.

"Yes, sir, Mr. President," Bobby replied with a wry smile.

Later, Jack had teased that he wanted to wait until late at night when everyone was fast asleep and then open the front door, just a crack, and whisper, "It's Bobby!" Politics made that impossible, so the brothers went out to face the media, the tough questions, and the outrage in some political circles.

Helen asked Kenny, "Do you think Bobby will be all right?"

Kenny had laughed. "I am not worried about Bobby," Kenny told her, "but if I were a bad guy, named Hoffa or any of those mob guys from the committee, I'd be worried." Kenny and Helen chuckled. But Kenny was thoughtful for a moment. Bobby as attorney general could be a double-edged sword; still it was done now, and certainly Bobby was going to be too busy to reopen that can of worms from the McClellan Committee days.

The decision to appoint Bobby was Jack's first major controversy and would prove to be critical. In the end, Jack explained one night at the White House to Kenny, "I wanted somebody in the cabinet I could trust completely, whose opinion was always unvarnished and in whom I had complete confidence."

Kenny nodded, tossing a football over to the president. "Made perfect sense to me. Besides," Kenny joked, "Bobby needed the job."

Bobby's time as attorney general would be anything but smooth sailing, marked as it was in turbulence and difficult decisions, but he seemed in many ways perfectly suited for the job and this moment in history. Though he had at first resisted taking the position, telling Kenny, among others, that "he was tired of chasing bad guys," in the end, he knew he had to do it. It was the best way he could help and serve Jack as he had done since 1952, perhaps always reluctantly. But he was never afraid of the task, the hard work, or the challenge. In the three years ahead, Bobby's role would continue to grow, his skills would be put to the test, and his role as Jack's truth teller, speaking truth to power for Jack's best interest, would prove critical in the White House.

With Jack and his team busy with the business of creating and staffing what would be dubbed the New Frontier, campaign aide Hy Raskin, who had been drafted to help with the work surrounding the transition, remembered the excitement of those days: "I remember like it was yester-day. Everything seemed special. I had come to Washington to have dinner with Ted Kennedy, to talk about what he wanted to do next. He said to me, 'Let's go to the hospital to visit Jackie and John Jr.' I felt it was not my place, but he insisted. Everyone was there. The family was very excited. I saw the president-elect briefly. It was a heady moment. He was a different man than he was as a candidate. It was truly a new beginning."

With the birth of John F. Kennedy Jr., Kenny had never seen Jack both so excited and concerned: He was excited to have another child, delighted to have his firstborn son, but he was concerned as he got more and more information as the outgoing Eisenhower administration briefed him. From the planned Bay of Pigs invasion to Laos to Berlin to any number of other problems, Jack was increasingly seeing that Eisenhower was leaving him with several hot spots and all of them were looming imminently. There also existed domestic challenges around the tax bill, rising prices, and a debt owed to Martin Luther King, which, King had made clear to Bobby and Jack, he had every intention of collecting. He said "that [African Americans] had waited long enough [to be free]."

"This is what you signed up for," Jack said to Kenny one evening, "but there is no question, campaigning is much easier than governing, because when you are president, you have to make the tough calls; when you are the candidate, you have no authority; you do not have all the information, so you get to sit back and just question and criticize." Kenny felt that the president had worked hard for this moment. Jack had sacrificed so much, as had his family and those around him. Kenny said, "The president was ready and excited to take on the challenges and lead the country."

Justine said it was a "giddy time, really, before all the hard work [began]. There were parties and jobs and new opportunities; it felt as if the whole country was excited," she recalled.

As January 20, 1961, and the inauguration grew closer, everyone had been drafted, a list that included Pat Kennedy's husband, actor Peter

Lawford, as well as Frank Sinatra, who had again been tapped to lend his considerable resources and talent to raise money to cover the debt owed by the Democratic Committee. Frank threw himself into the task with his customary gusto. Jack famously attended every party that night before his official inaugural, going as long as possible. Jackie, still recovering from the birth of John, attended many of these functions as well but would return to the White House early.

With Frank Sinatra and Peter Lawford headlining the event, it would prove to be the first time Hollywood and the Washington political set would truly join forces on behalf of the presidency, and it marked a change. Journalist Todd Purdum, writing in *Vanity Fair* some fifty years later about the "Sinatra Inaugural Gala for John Kennedy," commented, "It may have marked the moment when popular entertainment became an indispensable part of modern politics."

But that frigid evening, in a city draped in eight inches of snow, nobody was thinking about history. Instead they were thinking of the remarkable journey that brought this band of outsiders, this Irish Brotherhood, to this moment. As Kenny helped Helen into the car, she could not resist asking, "Did you ever doubt it?"

Kenny smiled that tight, just-at-the-corners kind of smile. "No. Never," he claimed.

As their limo complete with escort fought its way from their home in Bethesda, Maryland, to 1600 Pennsylvania, Helen looked out at the beauty of a frozen snow-covered city. She smiled. "I almost believe you," she teased him.

Helen, Kenny told her, looked beautiful that night. She wore a pale pink satin dress with matching shoes and bag, her brown hair coiffed by Jackie's stylist and her makeup done by a professional. Helen and Kenny's daughter Kathleen remembered watching her get dressed. "She looked so beautiful. I remember the smell of her Estée Lauder perfume wafting in the air. It was amazing to watch her transformation."

Helen joked to Kenny's mother, Alice, that they had spent more on the dress than their monthly mortgage payment. "Once in a lifetime," Alice had wisely replied.

Kenny wore a handsome black tuxedo that Helen had purchased for him; he tried to get out of it by claiming he'd be working, but Jack had called the house unbeknownst to Kenny and assured her that Kenny would have the night off. "Great friend you make," Kenny had complained to him later.

Frank threw himself into the event, which was held at the armory in Washington, DC. He recruited everyone and anyone who could be wrangled into attending and shut down two Broadway shows to ensure attendance. The stars included some of the biggest names in the business, such as Sidney Poitier, Fredric March, Nat King Cole, Ella Fitzgerald, Gene Kelly, Milton Berle, Jimmy Durante, Tony Curtis and his wife, Janet Leigh, and others. The evening naturally enough included a performance by Frank himself, singing a version of the "That Old Black Magic," now rewritten and sung as "That Old Jack Magic," much to the delight of the crowd. The president-elect, who later rose and thanked both Frank and Peter profusely, pointed out that, despite the frigid cold and eight inches of unexpected snow, there was literally not an empty seat at the Washington National Guard Armory that evening and they also had nicely retired the debt.

Justine, who was there in part in her role working for Dick Maguire at the Democratic National Committee, remembered meeting Frank for the first time. "He was so nice, so handsome in person," she recalled years later. "I remember he had the most beautiful, sleek tuxedo on with, I think, red satin lining. I'd never seen anything like it," she exclaimed, and she had told him so.

"I'm a thing of beauty, aren't I?" Frank had good-naturedly teased. "Your brother," he told her, after a pause, "he is a good man, tough guy. I like him."

Justine quickly assured him, "Everybody pauses like that before talking about Kenny." Then she wished she had said something less clumsy; she'd sounded almost critical. She began explain, but Frank understood, kissed her cheek, and whispered, "It's good to make people pause when they think about you." With that, he was gone, and Justine was forever star-struck. Later, when she told Kenny and Helen, Kenny responded with a terse "that's nice," while Helen agreed with Justine about Frank, "He's a dream." Kenny just stared at them both, then walked away to find friends he could talk to and a bar. He just would never understand women. Just never.

The glamour of the evening set off the beginning of Jack Kennedy's New Frontier, as he would call it the following day, and what Jackie would later refer to as Camelot. Well-respected biographer Carl Anthony would describe Frank Sinatra's role that night as greater than just his songs: "Frank Sinatra's musical contribution to the campaign and infusion of it with big-name entertainment made him the man to marry Hollywood and Washington. As Kennedy remarked at the end of the Inaugural Gala, 'The happy relationship between the arts and politics which has characterized our long history I think reached culmination tonight.'"

The day of the inaugural was cold and freezing but nevertheless great stuff. "We were almost oblivious to the cold," as she and her friends piled into one car at the crack of dawn and headed to the festivities, Justine remembered. The newspapers were filled with accounts of the parties and their famous guests. The Kennedys had descended on Washington with all the glitz and glamour that they could produce. "It was," Justine O'Donnell recalled, "like a breath of fresh air in Washington. These very young, glamorous, handsome couples with all these young children. It was a very exciting way to begin the 1960s."

Kenny was at work that first day of the administration, going through the day's newspapers and planning the president's schedule in what would become a normal routine for him. Suddenly Kenny heard Jack call him from the Oval Office. Kenny headed in immediately, assuming it was a request of some importance. "Kenny," Jack said, standing behind his desk, looking over the newspapers that were spread out there. "I don't remember meeting your mother last night."

Kenny looked puzzled. "My mother? My mother wasn't there. She did not feel like going. She stayed home to babysit."

Jack gave Kenny an amused, quizzical smile. "You sure about that?" he asked.

Yes, Kenny was quite sure.

"Then explain this." Jack handed Kenny the paper from Worcester, Massachusetts, which included a detailed description from Alice O'Donnell, describing her gown to the last detail, the parties, and visiting with the president and Jackie.

Kenny guffawed. "I can't explain it, Mr. President. Can you explain your mother all the time?"

Jack laughed. "No," he said good-humoredly, "and I try not to do so."

Theirs had been a relationship that had developed and strengthened over the last fifteen years. As Bobby had wisely recognized in bringing them together, they could and inevitably did help each other. For two men for whom trust did not come easily, by 1961, Jack Kennedy and Kenny O'Donnell had come to trust each other completely.

Sander Vanocur, who was the White House reporter for NBC and had gotten to know Jack and Kenny well, understood their relationship more than most. He recalled, "I know Kenny hated such crap, that sort of talk-about-your-relationship-with-the-president kind of crap. Hated it, but the truth is, every reporter knew that when Kenny spoke, he spoke for the president. All the reporters knew that. They knew when Kenny gave them an answer, they did not have to go any further. When Kenny answered a question, he answered it from the president. That is why many reporters never asked to see the president but talked to Kenny instead, since it was easier to get to Kenny." And it was not just reporters; Mayor Richard Daley of Chicago, a key linchpin to the Kennedy victory, noted, "[If] I called and spoke to Kenny about something, he could speak for the president and answer for the president. That was a fact. It was an enormous amount of power, but Kenny never abused it."

Such power Jack Kennedy did not relinquish easily, as Vanocur said: "The president did not grant the right to speak for him very easily, and he did not give it to anybody else in that administration. He certainly did not give it to Sorensen or even to his brother Bobby. A lot of people assumed he had given Bobby that right, but he had not, and Bobby confirms that he had not." Such power, Kenny reflected later, had indeed, perhaps, "happened over a period of time." Kenny said, "I did not have that right early. Politically I had that right, and then it expanded as his ambitions expanded. During the campaign he began to increasingly trust my judgment both politically and personally. Starting January, as we took office, our daily contact with each other is five to one over anyone else in the government. The truth is, by now we are much more than just boss and political aide. We are friends. Then he began to import instructions through me and because of the rather peculiar role I had beyond appointment secretary. Therefore I ended up at the president's insistence with duties in the government far beyond what I ever imagined. I think when he could not transmit the message himself, he would give it to me to transmit."

The truth was, Bobby Kennedy explained later, "that my brother found over the years that Kenny always transmitted it accurately and never took on anything beyond exactly what my brother told me to say. He never went one step further. My brother knew that and trusted him completely."

Thus began an increasingly unusual and expanded role and duties for such a peculiar and uniquely powerful position. "But, this was all given to me by the senator, then president; this was neither sought or requested or taken. The day the president passed away, the relationship between us was one in a million," Kenny reflected. "It was a unique relationship and my position was uniquely powerful. It was an accumulative thing really; by the time we got to the 1962 elections, he had great confidence in me politically."

From 1952 forward, the press, the political reporters, the "dirty finger-nail" reporters that did the hard work had slowly learned of Kenny's unique relationship—he had become for many of them the gateway to information.

Vanocur noted, "He would let you know if you were on the right track, right or wrong, so you never got out there and looked stupid. Reporters appreciate that; he never used us and in return we trusted that if he said it, it came from the president." The press wrote often about Kenny, much to his complete dismay, calling him "tight-lipped, sardonic, and extremely taciturn." "He was the only guy," another colleague, *Life* reporter Warren Rogers recalled, "who, if you wrote about him, he'd give you hell. He hated publicity. Hated it, almost as much as he hated having his photo taken; most photos of the Kennedys, Kenny's the guy running out of the frame! Most guys aren't like that. They get to love the publicity, the attention, and the power. They forget, it is not about them. It is about the candidate, the politician, be it senator or president. Kenny never forgot that. He had no ego. I had never seen anything like it before or since. He was completely at ease in his own skin; I think that is why the Kennedys, the president, and Bobby trusted him so much. He is not trying to get his name in the paper. He is not trying to use the president to expand himself and get his picture taken; and, as someone who was privy to all his professional and personal secrets, it is a job, it was Kenny's job to keep his mouth shut and be seen as little as possible." Kenny fit the role beautifully.

The job, to be Jack's trusted right hand, came easily to Kenny, who loved the power of politics, the possibilities for the good that he saw that Jack could do for the nation and the world, but he never saw it as opportunity to promote himself. Kenny was in this totally for Jack Kennedy. Kenny admitted, "Early on, I remember when my position and the power became clear. A reporter from *The New York Times* wrote a front-page piece about me and how much power I had. The president was not happy; I came into the office that morning; my desk was right outside his office; I had just put my coffee down and was preparing to go see him when he called or rather yelled for me to come in. Holding up the newspaper article he said, 'So you're the fellow with the passion for anonymity?' He was not pleased nor was I." Kenny quickly tracked down the reporter and with some rough words and in his best intimidating style made clear he was not happy and that it better not happen again. It didn't.

In return Kenny admitted, he cultivated his relationship with reporters, something he had done since the end of the '52 campaign; he had seen with the narrow victory in '52 how not having that relationship and that trusted access with the press had put "the senator," Kenny said, "at a distinct disadvantage." From that point forward, Kenny worked hard to cultivate a relationship of trust with the press corps, which was not always easy, as the political press in particular, Warren Rogers noted, "are wary of being used," but Kenny proved he could be trusted. "I would go to lunch with them as often as I could," Kenny admitted, "frankly because I received as much information from them as they received from me. Most of them by that time, I had a personal very good relationship with them. The truth was," Kenny declared, "I liked them more than I liked most political people in Washington. Most of these lunches were a pleasure, keeping a pulse on the news and listening to what the buzz in Washington was. I was never directed by the president to do this, though he was always aware naturally of who I was having lunch with and where I was, and when I returned he would grill me on the conversation." During a presidential campaign, "really the senator and I, then candidate, ate and lived with these people. Naturally when he became president, he could no longer do that, but he was very pleased I had kept up these relationships. He was pleased that almost all of my relationships and friendships were with reporters. He loved reporters and he would ask about them all the time, who I was going to see and how they were and so forth. Frankly, he was also pleased that I was hanging out with the reporters on a social basis, rather than the embassy cocktail party crowd or the social climber parties in Washington, whom he detested, as did Bobby and I. He loved the profession and I often believe, had he not been in politics, he would have stayed in the news business."

Kenny noted, "The Kennedys are gossips, as we know well. He loved hearing who was sleeping with whom and who was screwing whom politically and so forth. Reporters know all that stuff first. He loved gossip. The Kennedys all love gossip. Being president you are really walled off, almost shut off from the world. You are really in a bubble all the time. As time goes on you become more and more in the bubble defined by these staff people around you. It is a very dangerous thing. The president fought hard to not let that happen and actively tried to get access and stay engaged."

The truth was that Kenny became in many ways his access point. Jack wanted to know what was going on. Kenny admitted with a laugh, "It was a constant with him. Certain members of the cabinet would call to see the president and he would pump them about all sorts of things. If they could not answer his questions or were boring, he would say to me, 'He's a bore, wasting my time.'" If that that happened, Kenny indicated, "I made sure they never got in again. The president would say to me, 'He's a bore.' That to me meant don't let him in again; they would complain at cabinet meetings and so forth. For example, Secretary of Commerce Luther Hodges complained to the president that he could never get in to see the president, but I had already talked to the president about it. The president said Hodges is a bore; keep him out. Hodges would always come over on very trivial matters and never had anything interesting to say, so I kept him out. President Kennedy hated to be bored. He had to be in constant movement mentally and physically in some ways, hated to have his time wasted. I think it related in no small measure to his health issues. Time was constantly on his mind. He almost considered it a sin to waste a moment."

Kenny's approach in the White House was a continuation of the campaign; there were certain issues that could and should be addressed at a staff level. If they rose to the importance that warranted Kennedy's attention, Kenny made sure the information and individual got to see Jack, whether he was senator or president. But even for cabinet members, with the exception of Bobby, "access was not guaranteed. Most of them would offer the reason up front; I always asked them to write me a memorandum requesting to see the president. I would give it to him and he would read it and say, I will see him, or no, I won't see him. Often the cabinet officers would ask me to read the memo first to determine if I thought it was worthy of a presidential meeting. I did that, but reluctantly, as quite frankly I felt at their level they should know the answer to that before they called me. But often they don't and they are just looking to see the president."

Jack and Kenny figured out who did that pretty quickly, and at Jack's instructions, Kenny would just keep them out. Bobby of course was the exception, not because of the Cabinet role but, Kenny indicated, because he was the president's brother: "I never felt it was my role, unless Bobby asked me to and often he did, but unless he asked me to, I never intervened or stepped in between them. Though often Bobby would insist on my presence. But what was always admirable about Bobby was he never went around me; he would always call me first and explain what he needed. It was unnecessary, he knew that, but Bobby was just that kind of fellow. We were friends, he had brought me on board, and he would never go around me."

There were other telltale signs of the growing and expanding relationship as they entered the White House on January 21, things everyone would come to know well over the coming three years. Vanocur remembered the famous Kennedy press conference: "I remember Kenny walking in during a press conference, and that always signaled to me and to the press corps the meeting was over," Vanocur said. "I never saw Kenny communicate directly with [the president], so we always wondered. Oftentimes Kenny was not even in the president's sight line; he would slip in quietly, lean against the wall, but tense, at attention, his arms folded. It was as if the president felt his presence; the minute we saw Kenny, everyone would run to ask the last question and then people would begin to pack up to rush and file."

Kenny's role was one that he and Jack had developed over time from the campaign to the White House. "I would go in the door and stand there for a minute, look at my watch," Kenny recalled. "He knew what my presence meant. If it is a press briefing, I am his way out. If he is meeting on

Cuba, I would stand there and he would say to me, 'I will be with you in a minute.' That was a signal to me that meeting was important. If it was someone I did not think we should really keep waiting and he was still in his meeting, I might go back a second time, look at my watch again; he knew this meant whatever I had for him could not wait." In fact, they had really developed nonverbal signals: "I would walk in quietly and could tell by his look whether he wanted the meeting broken up or not. Sometimes he did, and I would break it up. I would look at the watch again and shuffle my feet back and forth for a while. Then he would get up, which meant he wanted me to get these people out of here. He wanted it broken up. Sometimes he would look at me, meaning, 'I need more time'; if I felt that was not possible, I would give him a look; there were other times when I would go in and he would give me a nod in a certain way. That meant he wanted me to make up a little white lie about someone waiting urgently or an urgent phone call so that he could escape the meeting." After a while, Bobby confirmed, everyone understood, if Kenny made a certain movement, suddenly everyone would rush to make their points, realizing the president was about to leave. "It was always nonverbal, the president and I just knew, then often would go to the Oval Office. If the president had another meeting, that is what would happen. At other critical moments, we would then discuss what had just happened, just the three of us [Jack, Kenny, and Bobby]."

There were certain groups and people that would leave automatically when their time was up, but there were other people that would stay all night and talk to the president about nothing if they could have. For Jack, being a natural politician, at first he would, Kenny said, "be as polite as he could be. You know he hated to be rude, as he said, 'That is what I have you for!' But sometimes he would have had enough, especially after the second Cuba incident. He would just get up and walk out, often while the person was still talking. It was a matter of relationship with him."

Often, Kenny recalled, "He could look at me and I could tell when he wanted to go or when he wanted to stay. We just worked hand in glove; we just got to know each other. I knew, for instance, when he wanted me to stay for a meeting to hear everybody out, so that he could get my thoughts after everyone had left, so I would move in quietly and lean against the wall and listen; often he would just give me a look and I knew what it meant."

For Kenny, the key was to keep the line, as he called it, between political and personal. It was a fact that despite Bobby's closeness to his brother, he never visited with him or had dinner with him in the private quarters. Kenny explained, "[Jack] had a line; he tried to keep some semblance of a personal life, which is not easy in the bubble of the White House." There were social things that the president enjoyed, Kenny said, or tried to: "He tried very hard to the extent one can as president to maintain a social life. Ben Bradlee was a reporter but a friend, and often he would want to have dinner with him, just for social purposes. Just for the break. My relationship with him was in large measure based on his trust of me that I knew where that line was; if Jack wanted to have lunch with Dennis Brogen, Ben Bradlee, or Lem Billing, Torby MacDonald or George Smathers and friends over for a swim and some fun, whoever he might want over, it was none of Ken O'Donnell's business."

Kenny understood instinctively, "There was a fine line between the president and the personal; to recognize it I would bend over backward, because it was more important to me that he had confidence in my political judgment than in my attempting to be critical of his friends or some of his friends' behavior or even his behavior. He knew I was not pleased at certain things or people; but that was not my job. I was his political aide, not his personal aide. I tried to always keep that in mind." There were, however, certain things, Kenny said, "that I saw as frankly none of my business unless they impacted politics, and if they did, then I had no problem inserting myself. Sometimes he appreciated it. Often not, but he always respected that if I felt I had to insert myself, there was a reason."

Kenny explained, "There was a certain group that would call and want him to have lunch with the Dennis Brogens, or Lady Jackson, who came over about three times a week or more if she could. Arthur Schlesinger, for example, would have people that [Jack] must see and slip them by me; I knew it was happening; it just didn't impact the political side, so I didn't care. Let us be blunt here. I could not have interfered with some of these social people or friends if I wanted to. The president was a very strong-willed man; he would have told me to go to hell. I did not intend to be told to go to hell and so rather than get into places I felt uncomfortable, I did not involve myself in anything remotely social if or unless he insisted that I did."

This was not true of his brother Bobby. "Bobby would often insert himself here, and even though they were brothers, I would tell you and you could ask Bobby this and he will confirm it, the president would look at him and tell him to go to hell as well! I certainly wasn't going to get into it unless I had no choice. Bobby was his brother, [Bobby] could do or say things nobody else could, just as I could say things to my brothers that nobody else can say. I always tried to keep that line, though often [Jack] or his actions would pull me across it."

However, Kenny was clear, if there were "political consequences, I had no problem taking him on, but I would do it in private and explain to him why I did not think at this time this was such a good idea. He would then hear me out, and often these social friends had, in my view, another agenda. If he knew the agenda and felt he could handle it, he would let me know. If he did not, he would see them anyway, but at least he was armed with the information."

There were different levels of this, as one can imagine. Kenny recalled, "If some friend was coming in and made a suggestion or request that on the face was unethical, the president would call me in and have me stand there and either tell them to discuss it with me, which most of them would immediately recognize as his way of telling them to go to hell, or if he thought it might have some merit, he would say, 'Take them to White House legal counsel Mike Feldman.' He was very good at that, but frankly often my presence alone to these social friends was enough of a signal that they had crossed a line. It worked well for him; he could preserve the friendship."

Kenny was the bad guy, but he couldn't have cared less; this was after all his job. "[Jack] would do this with social friends and frankly Kennedy family members," Kenny said, "who would come in with crazy requests. He would call me in and say, what do you think, Kenny? Then I would tell him the ten reasons why the answer had to be no. He would shrug and look at them as if to say, 'You know Kenny.' They would walk away upset with me but thinking he was terrific. It worked well for them, but I think many of his social friends and family members were not particularly enamored of me or my role as time went on, but I did not care; that was my job. I worked for him."

"Many people," Kenny said, "felt the president was a great fellow and I was as son of a bitch, which I was. That was why they did not get what they wanted. I did not care. I saw that as my role. Bobby understood this, but he often employed the same tactic [of denying people], saying, 'You know I would, but Kenny said no.'"

Kenny said later, laughing, "One particular family member, one of his sisters, left very angry one day because the president called me in and related the situation. I said no, which I knew he wanted me to say. I could tell by the look he gave me. So I said no. After she had gone, the president said to me, 'It is a good thing you don't mind everyone thinking you are such a son of a bitch,' and we both laughed. But that was my role. The request she had made was one he simply did not want to do, but did not want to get into it and argue with her, so he used me, as he often did."

Kenny said to Jack with a chuckle, "'I don't mind a bit, Mr. President. Rather enjoy it.' He laughed. But we saw that as my role. He knew that and appreciated it and used it when necessary, which was often."

While much has been written about the Bay of Pigs, what Kenny remembered the most was Jack's sheer frustration as the disaster unfolded and no one from the Eisenhower administration was willing to take responsibility. In what would become a pattern repeated throughout his time in the White House, Jack took personal ownership of the problem, even though it had become too late to find an adequate solution.

Kenny recalled, "He directed the troops himself during the invasion of Cuba. At one point, he had the commander on the telephone. Nobody had any answers. I say 'invasion,' if we are to call it that.

"Just then the other line rings. Evelyn Lincoln answers it. She begins a very jolly chat. I was never in a tenser moment while in the White House; this includes the Cuban Missile. We had people on the beaches, and it was clear it was not going well. People were dying. But Evelyn was on the telephone, and she was laughing, joking, giggling on the phone.

"She hands the president the phone, and he asked, 'Who is it?' He is at this point waiting to hear from the incident commander, and she said, 'It's Red Fay. He'd like to talk to you for a minute.' I thought he was going to pick up the telephone and throw it through window, and her along with it."

It was shortly after this that Jack made Kenny his gatekeeper. "He could depend upon me to be rational in my decisions, act as a barrier, and be trustworthy and loyal. I had been doing this right along, but the White House made this role more urgent."

Kenny was thrust into a uniquely powerful position, Sandy Vanocur remembered. "John Kennedy did not give the right of way to anybody else in that administration. He certainly did not give it to Bobby or Sorensen. A lot of people assumed he had made Bobby his gatekeeper, but he had not. He gave that responsibility to Kenny."

As the pressures of the office built for Jack, he would come to appreciate Kenny's candor, just as he had in the campaign. "He is not always right, but his only interest is my well-being. His opinions are unvarnished," the president said.

The transition from candidate to president is always more complicated and jarring than the winner expects. "There are many issues," the president told Kenny on one particularly difficult evening, "that seem easy to tackle from the safety of the campaign trail, but once in the White House, you realize just how truly complicated and complex the issues can be." The next three years would be harder, the issues more complicated than any of the Irish Brotherhood had imagined, even causing Jack to remark once to Kenny, his frustration showing at the edges, "I thought there would be more good days." But from the crushing and humiliating fiasco at the Bay of Pigs, to civil rights, to Berlin, to the Steel Crisis, and eventually the Cuban Missile Crisis, what would remain constant, despite attempts to suggest otherwise, was the Irish Brotherhood.

"The president," Kenny noted, "kept intact what had worked from the beginning, the inner core group that he had come to trust and rely upon," which was not easy with the pressures of the presidency. Yet Jack Kennedy recognized that this core group was his strength. "You know," Kenny noted, "at first, for example, he had constructed things a bit different, or envisioned them that way, but then by the time of the Bay of Pigs or after Bobby became more and more prominent and I was pulled in as well, he recognized that while he did not always agree with us, our opinions were, for better or worse, unvarnished and in his best interest.

"In the aftermath of the Bay of Pigs, the president made sure Bobby played a key role; they were very close from that point forward. Bobby would never okay something that he had not cleared with the president. Ever. That was not Bobby. We operated much as we had from the beginning; in the end, it proved, as we found out in October 1962, to be critical."

"The bottom line," Jack said to Kenny, as he slid painfully into his rocking chair that evening, "is that, from the outside, it all looks much easier to solve. Once you are in the White House, everything is complicated. Nothing is simple."

Kenny nodded and sipped his drink. "Any regrets?"

Jack smiled. "Not a one. And who knows what tomorrow will bring? Whatever it is, I'm sure we can handle it."

◆◆◆

EARLY THE NEXT morning, the O'Donnell house awoke to its usual chaos: kids getting ready for school, the housekeeper trying to make breakfast, corral children and assorted dogs, and get everyone out the door. Kenny came down, saw everyone off, and grabbed a cup of coffee as he prepared to head out the door. His mother, Alice, was down visiting from Massachusetts, and his sister Justine had stayed over that night. Kenny, working late with Jack, had not returned home until everyone was in bed. Justine quickly asked if she could catch a ride.

"Sure," Kenny said, as he kissed Helen on the cheek.

"Nice to see you, and you are?" she teased.

Kenny laughed, took his coffee, and turned to Justine. "I can have them drive me to the White House and then take you over to the DNC."

Justine rushed to organize herself as she recognized that Kenny was headed out the door that moment. She grabbed a comb and ran it through her black hair, putting on some pink lipstick. It would be another long day, but she'd never been happier.

"Did you hear the news?" Kenny asked his sister.

She gave him a "how dumb do you think I am?" look and said, "Yes, I did. And I told Helen congratulations on the new baby due in December."

Helen gave him a look and said, "The president and Jackie called last night."

Kenny turned and looked puzzled. "I know; he asked if he could talk to you. I did not know about what."

The women exchanged looks. "For somebody who is so smart," Helen teased, "you are clueless; he called to say congratulations on the new baby."

Kenny looked confused and threw his head back and laughed. "Well, he did not give me congratulations; I had a little something to do with it."

Everyone laughed. Just then the red phone, newly installed, a direct line to Jack at the White House, rang. Everyone became immediately quiet as Kenny picked it up. "Yes, sir, good morning, Mr. President," Kenny said, still getting accustomed to all this.

"Good morning, Kenny," the president replied. That familiar voice was clear and yet somehow different today, Kenny felt. "I want you to come right upstairs when you get here. I want to talk to you about today." With that Jack fired off several directives, before saying to Kenny, "Did you see this crap they gave us on the Bay of Pigs?" Kenny froze.

"No, not yet."

"Well, get in here. I want to discuss that and Laos. It seems pretty straightforward."

Kenny was quiet and then said probably exactly what Jack expected him to say: "Mr. President, nothing in politics is ever straightforward."

Jack, recognizing that Kenny was quoting his own words back to him, laughed and said, "You know, Kenny, maybe there is hope for you yet."

With that the two friends, their relationship both strengthened and changed forever, hung up. Kenny, now intense, focused, and in work mode, headed for the door without another word to those in the kitchen. Justine scampered to catch up with him. He had completely forgotten his promise to give her a ride.

Alice O'Donnell called after her son. "Kenny," she said, bringing him to an immediate halt, "are you happy?"

Kenny turned at the doorway, suddenly brought back to the moment by his mother. He smiled at his beloved mother and his thoughts ran to his dad, who had first pushed him toward Bobby and then Jack. "You know," Kenny said, "Jack is going to make a big difference. He is going to be one of the greatest presidents this country has ever seen. Fifty years from now, people will still be talking about Jack Kennedy."

Helen smiled. She was delighted to see how happy he was. He had— they all had—worked and sacrificed hard for this day. Alice O'Donnell smiled at her son and asked, "You think so?"

"I know he will," Kenny said. "Jack Kennedy was meant to change the world and make history."

"I suppose you knew from the moment you shook his hand back at the Bellevue Hotel," Helen called after him.

Kenny paused at the door and smiled, that tight, just-around-the-edges sort of smile. "Of course I did!"

With that, he greeted his White House driver. Justine was already in the car. He climbed in and the car pulled out and glided out into the circle, headed toward the White House. "What's on the agenda?" Justine asked.

Kenny mentally ticked through the list Jack had given him over the phone: "Cuba, Laos, and a lot more, but we will get it done; we have four years to do it, then four after that."

Justine stared in disbelief. "You are not really already thinking about the '64 campaign?"

Kenny smiled that tight smile. "Already know what we will do differently."

She shook her head. "You bunch of Irishmen, you really are like a brotherhood."

"An Irish Brotherhood," Kenny replied.

EPILOGUE

M Y DAD COULD not know or prepare himself or Jack for the challenges or the tragedies that lay before them on that first heady day, as he and his sister Justine headed to the White House.

When my parents died, I had the great privilege of being taken under the wing of Senator Edward Kennedy, Jackie Kennedy Onassis, and Joe and Michael Kennedy, who saw it perhaps as their role to help me further understand this inheritance, this legacy. Jackie ensured that I was then allowed me to spend much time at Jack's beloved Hyannis Port, where my parents spent much of their lives, including their honeymoon. I could not help but walk along the beach to feel their presence.

When I began this first book, I started out not sure what I would really find. I wanted to discover more about my dad, but instead these recollections are largely or exclusively about Jack and Bobby. I had to dig out and call on my personal experiences to bring in more about my dad, mom, and Aunt Justine. My dad recorded these stories with Sandy Vanocur to tell us who the real Jack Kennedy was and why he was important, because my dad truly believed that had Jack lived longer, he could have changed the world. As it was, during his short life, he changed my parents' lives and everyone else's he touched along the way.

As I close this part of Jack's story, I must say, often I would sit with friends on the patio of Jack's house, enjoying a glass of white wine in the evening air, eating one of the meals delightfully and deliciously prepared by Jack and Jackie's longtime personal assistant Provi Paredes, just perhaps as she had years earlier for Jack and Jackie. Sitting at what was then the Kennedy compound, I could see and hear the waters crashing off Nantucket Sound, and I could almost, if I listened closely enough, hear the laughter and feel the tension and excitement of what life had been for my dad and mom, Jack and Jackie, Bobby and Ethel.

The last time I was there, some years ago now, as I walked to beach, I saw Ethel Kennedy standing alone under the portico of her home. I imagined my dad driving up that same driveway that surprising morning, after Jack's election, accompanied by the Secret Service. He was to discover that day that he would have the great honor of accompanying Jack Kennedy to the White House—news that would come to him in a rather unorthodox manner but one truly befitting the relationship between Jack, my dad, and Bobby.

When I stood next to Mrs. Kennedy that evening, not sure exactly what to say, I became aware that while this is history, fascinating and enthralling, it is, after all, her lived experience. She was there.

She turned to me and smiled, looking as if it all had happened yesterday, and said something I will never forget and that defined the approach I took with this story: "Don't forget all the good times," she said softly. "There may have been difficult days, there was tragedy, but never forget how much fun we all had along the way. Not often does one get to live your dreams, and we did, they did."

My dad died when I was young, but I was lucky enough to spend a lot of deeply personal time with him breathing in the air of Jack, Bobby, and the Irish Brotherhood, as well as the excitement that was the Kennedys.

That tradition was continued after my dad's death by Senator Edward Kennedy, and while that has now passed, the legacy and hope that infuses this book remains a living, breathing thing—things that can and do inspire, enthrall, and mystify all over again. In the wake of Jack's death, my dad would often play *Camelot*, a version of the original soundtrack recording that Jackie had given him. I will confess that it drove my mom crazy, for she was afraid that if you spent too much time thinking about the past, it became difficult to embrace the future. For him, my dad, it would prove impossible.

Still, in honor of my father's love of Jack and Jackie, of his friendship with them that continues to endure in time and memory, they will always be impossibly young, happy, and full of potential. So I leave you with their favorite lines from that record, and I will meet you again as the new administration comes to life.

> Don't let it be forgot
> That once there was a spot,
> for one brief, shining moment
> That was known as Camelot.

ACKNOWLEDGEMENTS

THE IRISH BROTHERHOOD would not have been possible without the help and assistance of a great many people.

Sander Vanocur, a gifted, tough minded, no nonsense journalist. He is a class act. It was Sandy who was determined doggedly insistent on getting my Dad on tape especially at a time in my Dad's life when he was ready to speak about his friendship with Jack and Bobby Kennedy. It would prove to be the only time my father spoke with such candor, honesty and with such detail and length. The tapes are a tribute to Sandy's gifts as a journalist, his ability to ask the right question and know when to be wise enough to step back and let my father talk. It is also a tribute to a friendship that Sandy shared with my Dad, Jack and Bobby Kennedy. Their trust in him, as these tapes show, was complete. Nobody is more a member of The Irish Brotherhood than Sander Vanocur, whose interviews made this book possible.

Kathleen and Chris Matthews like Sandy have in so many ways made this book possible. I had the deep honor and privilege of working with Chris on his marvelous book, JFK, Elusive Hero. In that role Chris had me transcribe and edit all of my Dad's taped recorded interviews with Sandy Vanocur. That work made this book possible. It is a tribute to Chris's willingness to help others move forward, that rather than keep the material for himself, he instead urged me to write this book. He is a tough minded journalist and political junkie, but he is one of the few people who completely understood my Dad, his role with Jack and Bobby, and the importance of that role in the Kennedy story. His support of me and my endeavors to tell this story has been boundless. He is very much a Kenny O'Donnell type of fellow and I can imagine that he, Jack and my Dad would have had some very long tough conversations and damn good arguments about politics were such an opportunity to exist. He, like Sandy, belongs inside the Irish Brotherhood as well.

A special thank you to Tina Urbanski, Chris's producer at "Hardball." She never turned away a request or phone call from me for help, advice or assistance. Without her help on many occasions, things would have been difficult indeed. She is owed a debt of gratitude.

A special thank you to a dear friend, Gary B. LaForest and his family. While Gary editorial assistance, historical knowledge of the Kennedy clan and willingness to do the tough job that had to be done was critical, most important was his friendship, which can always be counted on through the good times and the bad. He will always have your back no matter the political weather, good or bad. He is the kind of fellow that my Dad would have loved to call a friend. I am honored to do so. A special thank you also to his sister Susan, his brother Jamie and Miss Nala for their support and faith in getting this story told.

Included in this thank you list is my sister Kathleen O'Donnell Schlichenmaier, along with her terrific husband Tom, son Jason & his wife Allison, as well as, Kathy & Tom's son Erin, brother-in-law John and his wife Cindy. I include in this list for special thanks and encouragement for many years, Christine Anderson O'Donnell & Kenneth O'Donnell, Jr. and their children, Molly and Jamie. Special appreciation for allowing unfettered access to the taped recordings. Thanks for all their support which made this story possible. A special note of thanks for Yvonne and Jack Schlichenmaier and Fran and Al Anderson, all of whom, loved my Dad and Mother, who invited me into their home with unquestioned love and support.

They all shared a love for my Dad, my mother, Jack and Bobby—and shared my belief that in the end this story is about my Dad, Jack, Bobby and their journey and that we will always be privileged to have had such fantastic parents whose belief in John Kennedy knew know bounds. They understood how lucky and blessed they were to have experienced extraordinary history unfolding in their lifetimes. They encouraged my love of history, reading and writing, which made me understand what a true gift one has been given as a writer.

The list of friends who each helped in their own way is far too long to list here, but among those who helped us in this journey with great honor must be included, Bob and Barb Benenson whose early support was a life saver and Bob especially is a man of deep honor, whom I will always respect. Joan & Jerry Boylan, Joanne & Greg Lagueux, Kathy, Tim and the extended Boylan Clan, too numerous to name! Dianne & Chuck Davis, Deborah Baeder and her terrific boys, they are a remarkable family.

The inspiringly elegant, smart & savvy ladies at 4101 Cathedral, a great place to live, each of whom inspired in their own way, they include, Jessie Hackes, Eleanor Blank, Evelyn Woolston-May, my dear Elia, wonderful Marguerite and dear Monica. Also, special thanks to the Carla and Don Seifman.

Kelly Paisley, Kirk and Amy Eklund for their support and encouragement, to Betsy Magee (wherever in the world you are tonight. . ., Sheila Murphy, Jim Martin and the good folks at Mount Ida College, who encouraged my love of writing and history. And, of course the Irish contingent over in Ireland and the UK, dear Martin McBride, Patrick & Daniel Silke, David Harvey of Circle Films, producer Martin Dwan and Mairead from Irish TV. A special acknowledgment to the Irish Film Board, who we plan to be bothering very shortly!

Special thank you to the late, but magnificent Angie Novello, Bobby's right arm who is no doubt in Heaven still keeping an eye on him! To Roseann Fitzgerald, my Aunt Justine's dear friend, who was there whenever she was needed. For Theresa Fitzpatrick for her support and help, Rob Swan who was a dear friend of the late Senator Edward Kennedy. Rob showed no hesitation in sharing his memories, photos and was terribly help-ful. The remarkable and elegant Provi Paredes, Jackie's personal assistant, who played so critical a role in the life of Jack, Jackie and John Kennedy, Jr. She is remarkable for her story and for her insistence on staying in faith and true to their memory. Her son Gustavo, who was John's dear friend.

A special thank you to the late Jacqueline Kennedy Onassis, Senator Edward Kennedy, Joe Kennedy and dear Michael, who always encouraged my writing and specifically this book though it took longer than we imag-ined, they all endorsed and encouraged my love of history and this era, and encouraged my dream to get the story told.

Special acknowledgement to the late, truly divine Washington Post edi-tor Ben Bradlee, who inspired me always. To the late but always helpful and inspiring Washington Post Reporters, Mary McGrory and David Broder, all of whom my Dad adored. Mary especially held a special place in his heart. The terrific Bob Ajamien of Time Magazine, Bob Merry of Congressional Quarterly who I had the honor to work for, the terrificly talented Warren Rogers and Jim Bellows. Thank you's to Aimee Bell at Vanity Fair Magazine who was always encouraging and inspiring, Liz McNeil at People Magazine for going the extra mile when needed.

A special thought on Ben in particular in my last conversation with him, before beginning this book, he sat with me and helped to outline the story, the scope and to educate me on the true importance of my Dad. This book is especially for him. Ben encouraged me to let me Dad tell the story, to help facilitate, but not get in the way. I hope I have done that and that Ben would be pleased.

My terrific agent Peter Beren is owed a special thank you and debt of gratitude for helping hone the book's direction and for bringing us to Charlie Winton and Counterpoint Press. Peter is an excellent agent and a good friend.

Finally, a sincere thank you and deep debt of gratitude to Charlie Winton. He is not only a top flight editor with a great sense of story, he has a wonderful way of guiding and encouraging you as a writer, which only serves to get the best out of you. He also showed how committed he was to the story and this book and how willing he was to go above and beyond the call of duty! His help was at times quite critical. He never hesitated to step up and is very much a KPOD kind of fellow.

Both he and Peter subscribe to the "no writer left behind theory"—they were always their when needed most, through the good and the bad times. For Charlie's help in bringing The Irish Brotherhood to life, I am deeply grateful.

Both Charlie and Peter have restored my faith in the publishing business; their help in guidance not only was important for this story, but for getting me and my writing career back on track.

Special hug and thanks to Kelly Winton, Megan Fishmann and the hard working, terrific staff at Counterpoint Press.

None of this could have been possible without Laurie Austin, MaryRose at the John F. Kennedy Library. As always, they were helpful, professional and fabulous. I cannot look at the photos that graces the cover of this book without thinking how blessed I am to have their help. They were indispensable in my first book as they are with this new book.

And, finally to two places that made the writing of this book possible, the terrific staff, who made me feel so at home, Michael, Lisa, Danielle, Maria and Mary at La Quinta in La Palma, California, which became my home base while researching the West Coast side of the story.

Finally, a special thank you to Ann Terry, Managing Director of the Hotel Harrington in Washington, D.C. The hotel is the oldest family owned hotel in Washington, D.C., while large, has the feel of a bed and breakfast with a terrific staff, most of whom have been here for 10, to 20 to 30 years or more. It is a blessed place and has been a Godsend for me. Ann Terry and her staff, Gail, Yolanda, Sergio, Jorge, Charneece, Deborah and to the terrific staff at Harriet's restaurant who kept me fed and full.

Specials thanks to the folks that make the Hotel Harrington work so well, my dear friends Lucy, her little darling daughter Angie, her sister

Lolita, fabulous Alice and Sabrina quite literally stepped in to at times, offer encouragement, a good meal, a well-timed hug that kept you going. Ann, herself is very much a Kenny O'Donnell kind of person and I am better for having known her. I am honored to call her a friend and her hotel my home base in Washington while finishing the book. It is a delightful old Washington, D.C. kind of hotel, blocks from the White House where I could stroll and be inspired while writing, it is full of charm and a warm welcome. A special thank you to one and all, and a special thank you from Eunice and Tiger Baby Man!

Finally, my own personal thank you to my Dad, Mother Helen and my Aunt Justine. Justine especially pushed hard for this book, which I wrote despite some substantial challenges. In writing this story, I have come to a deeper understanding of my Dad, my Mother Helen, Jack and Jackie. This book help bring my mother to life, and since I lost my parents when I was young, that was so special and helped me bring clarity to my life. My parents and Justine were remarkable, wonderful people and I hope they would be pleased and proud of this book and me. I have tried to do their memory honor. I only hope I have succeeded.

A special thank you to my dear, beloved Ron Joy, my dear RJ who always encouraged me to this new beginning in the belief that I could and would succeed in my dreams. He was right. It was just hard work! A special thank you to Mr. Sinatra and MM, who have inspired this and more stories to come.

Finally, I thank God for seeing me through the tough times and I know with this book we feel we have completed an important step in this new beginning.

SOURCES

THE MOST SIGNIFICANT source for this book is The Kenneth P. O'Donnell/Sander Vanocur Oral History Audio Tapes. These tapes were recorded in multiple sessions in 1965 and 1966 and are archived in the O'Donnell Collection at the John F. Kennedy Presidential Library in Boston, Massachusetts.

I also had access to The Robert F. Kennedy Oral History Interviews at the John F. Kennedy Library as well as their interviews of Ralph Dungan, Hubert Humphrey and Hy Raskin.

In addition, I utilized The United States Senate Oral History Archives; The Edward M. Kennedy Photo Archives (courtesy of Rob Swan) as well as the Select Committee on Improper Activities in Labor and Management, 1957 interviews with Ruth Watts, Angie Novello, and Walter Sheridan.

I conducted personal interviews with Alice Justine O'Donnell, Cleo O'Donnell, Jr., and other members of the O'Donnell family as well as Senator Edward M. Kennedy, Sander Vanocur, Ben Bradlee, Warren Rogers, Ron Joy.

BIBLIOGRAPHY

Arnold, Shayna R. "JFK: Gone But Not Forgotten." *Los Angeles Magazine* 22 Nov. 2013.

O'Donnell, Kenneth P., and David F. Powers. *Johnny, We Hardly Knew Ye; Memories of John Fitzgerald Kennedy*. Boston: Little, Brown, 1972.

Dallek, Robert. *An Unfinished Life: John F. Kennedy, 1917-1963*. Boston: Little, Brown, 2003.

White, Theodore H. *The Making of the President: 1972*. New York: Bantam, 1973.

Matthews, Christopher. *Jack Kennedy: Elusive Hero*. New York: Simon & Schuster, 2011.

Schlesinger, Arthur M. *A Thousand Days: John F. Kennedy in the White House*. Boston: Houghton Mifflin, 1965.

Sinatra, Nancy. *Frank Sinatra: An American Legend*. Santa Monica, CA: General Pub. Group, 1995.

Zehme, Bill. *The Way You Wear Your Hat: Frank Sinatra and the Lost Art of Livin'* New York: Harper Collins Publishers, 1997.

"Tina Sinatra" *60 Minutes*. CBS. New York, New York, 31 Dec. 2000. Television.

Wofford, Harris. *Of Kennedys and Kings: Making Sense of the Sixties*. New York: Farrar, Straus, Giroux, 1980.

O'Donnell, Helen. *A Common Good: The Friendship of Robert F. Kennedy and Kenneth P. O'Donnell*. New York: William Morrow, 1998.

INDEX

Printed in the United States
by Baker & Taylor Publisher Services